AUTO RACING COMES OF AGE

ALSO BY ROBERT DICK

Mercedes and Auto Racing
in the Belle Epoque, 1895–1915 (2005)

AUTO RACING COMES OF AGE

A Transatlantic View of the Cars, Drivers and Speedways, 1900–1925

ROBERT DICK

McFarland & Company, Inc., Publishers
Jefferson, North Carolina, and London

ISBN 978-0-7864-6670-2
illustrated case : acid free paper ∞

LIBRARY OF CONGRESS CATALOGUING DATA ARE AVAILABLE

BRITISH LIBRARY CATALOGUING DATA ARE AVAILABLE

On the cover: December 1906, New York City, Paul Sartori at the wheel
of Alfred Vanderbilt's "250-hp record breaker" powered by two
10.5-liter F.I.A.T. engines in a row (Library of Congress);
cover design by David K. Landis (Shake It Loose Graphics)

Manufactured in the United States of America

*McFarland & Company, Inc., Publishers
Box 611, Jefferson, North Carolina 28640
www.mcfarlandpub.com*

Contents

Preface 1

1. Bennett 3
2. Vanderbilt 14
3. Hippodrome Sprints 31
4. Auto Import 41
5. French Scenery 55
6. Specials 69
7. Mercer 82
8. Stutz 97
9. Mason-Duesenberg 109
10. Camshaft Handlers 121
11. Indy Expedition 138
12. Peugeot Career 149
13. Aero-Engines 161
14. New Wave Racers 174
15. Sheepshead Bay 186
16. Farewell Performance 196
17. Fiat School 215
18. Bugatti's Way Up 232
19. New Generation 251

Appendix A: Biographical Data 269
Appendix B: Technical Data 274
Appendix C: Riding Mechanics 277
Notes 283
Bibliography 295
Index 297

Preface

This book describes important and not so important individuals, events and mechanical developments in the early history of auto racing, in Europe and America, between 1900 and 1925. It is an attempt to capture the background of the transition from (in today's parlance) veteran to vintage, to revive the atmosphere of the era between Belle Époque and Roaring Twenties. The book does not attempt to bring together as many race results as possible. The narrative naturally pivots around transatlantic influences, around gentlemen drivers who engaged in the sport for the fun of the thing, around publicized professionals, and around the mutation of stone age titans into supercharged Grand Prix racers. The book relates how road racing came to America. It clarifies the beginnings of the first speedway specials and the genesis of the twin-cam engine and the straight-eight. It describes how the European and American development trends finally drifted apart.

The first chapters are centered on three legendary figures: James Gordon Bennett, Willie Vanderbilt and Barney Oldfield. While the 1904 and 1905 Bennett races are well-documented as direct forerunners of the Grand Prix, the first race of the series was essentially a failure and had more than a century to slide into obscurity. Moreover, the escapades of its promoter, the dazzling newsman Bennett, were always good for a scandal. Vanderbilt was just as wealthy as Bennett, but he came from the younger generation. He was a sportsman and a gentleman driver. His cousins, friends and rivals brought a whole range of French, Italian and German racing cars to the New York area and introduced road racing to Long Island. Barney Oldfield was the son of a farmer. He simply lifted dirt track racing into an art form and became the first speed king.

The next two chapters dip into the New York auto import community and the activities of the French Bennett and Grand Prix drivers in Paris. The New York auto importers not only brought the latest European cars to America but created their very own world. On the other side of the ocean, in Paris, it was the leading gentlemen drivers who arranged a network of auto dealers. The majority of the French drivers grew up as bicycle riders and many of them pursued careers as agency managers.

The central part of the book has a focus on the evolution of the racing cars on both sides of the Atlantic. The speedways in Atlanta and Indianapolis stood for a mixture of road racing and dirt track sprints. The first speedway special turned up in 1910, built by Marmon and devised by Ray Harroun who promptly took its wheel to win the first Indianapolis 500. Other specials followed, from National, Mercer and Stutz. Most of them were initially powered by engines from the production line, carefully modified for high speed work. It was up to the Duesenberg brothers to take a different path. They relied on a genuine racing car which was inspired by French Coupe de l'Auto trends.

Yet Peugeot and Delage won the 1913 and 1914 Indianapolis 500 races with obsolete Grand Prix cars of the previous year. Obviously, the local shops had to rethink their approach. It came as no surprise that Ray Harroun was the first to take over French long-stroke technology when he designed a racer for Maxwell. Stutz followed suit. The feature of the years 1915 and 1916 was a balance between European and American cars, between Peugeot, Delage, Sunbeam and Mercedes on the one hand, and Stutz, Maxwell, Duesenberg and a handful of new specials on the other. Road races became quite rare while board tracks were shooting up like mushrooms. The Sheepshead Bay speedway was one of the most impressive.

The straight-eight engine gained acceptance just after the Great War, coupled with a well-known name, Ernest Henry, and with a newcomer, Ernest Ballot. The road races at Elgin, the Vanderbilt and the Grand Prize disappeared after 1920. America went her own way, favoring speedway racing and pencil-thin single-seaters. In Europe, a group of young engineers working for the Fiat racing car department at Turin introduced progressive high-power-per-liter ideas and took over the leading role. A couple of these engineers did not feel at ease with Fiat. They were welcomed with open arms at Sunbeam and Alfa Romeo. The closing chapters focus on the origins of the Bugatti straight-eight, the Delage revival, and the work of the Maserati brothers for Diatto.

* * *

Until the 1920s, until the advent of the straight-eights, most of the successful racing cars were powered by four-cylinder engines. Contemporary press reports of races typically specified a car's bore and the stroke but mentioned the number of cylinders only when it was not a four-cylinder. This practice has been adopted for the book. Bore and stroke dimensions and tire sizes are given in millimeters for European cars and in inches for American cars, in fractional or decimal form according to the notation in the contemporary press. Tire sizes specify outer diameter and width; the inner diameter or rim diameter did not appear before the end of the 1920s. Tire sizes are also given in millimeters or inches in accordance with the manufacturer's practice in each case.

* * *

Photographs and illustrations come from the George Grantham Bain Collection of the Library of Congress, Washington, D.C.; the factory archives of Mercedes-Benz Classic, Peugeot and Renault; and from contemporary magazines, notably the *Allgemeine Automobil-Zeitung*, Vienna, Austria, and *La Vie Automobile*, Paris.

I am grateful to the many friends and colleagues who supported the research for this book, in particular to Silvie Kiefer of Mercedes-Benz Classic, to Hans Etzrodt, Alessandro Silva, Jean-Maurice Gigleux, Marc Ceulemans, Reinhard Windeler, John Humphries, Richard Jenkins, and the members of the Nostalgia Forum in the autosport.com Bulletin Board.

1

Bennett

The race for the Gordon Bennett Cup was run between 1900 and 1905. It turned into the first Grand Prix in 1906, the Grand Prix de l'Automobile Club de France. James Gordon Bennett, or JGB as he was often known, was a newspaper man, the son of the founder of the *New York Herald*, and a towering figure whose escapades were reported in the gossip columns. His newspapers published gossip columns. He invented them. JGB often quoted his father's axiom: "Make the people talk about *The Herald* and they'll have to buy it."[1] To give his readers news, Bennett handed over the Coupe Internationale d'Automobile to the Automobile Club de France. Bennett's strategy was not new. A Paris newspaper, Pierre Giffard's *Petit Journal*, had organized the great bicycle race between Paris and Brest in 1891 and the first serious automobile event in 1894, the legendary concours from Paris to Rouen. *Le Figaro* and *Le Journal des Sports* organized the race from Paris to Dieppe in 1897. *Le Matin* set up the Tour de France for automobiles and the race from Paris to Trouville in 1899. Bicycle and automobile races were a big factor in the development of the press, and vice versa.

"To the day of his death," James Gordon Bennett, Sr., the father, "spoke French like a Parisian and English with the broad brogue of the Highlands."[2] JGB Sr. came from Scotland. He was born at Newmill, Keith, Banffshire County, on 1 September 1795. For some time he went to the Catholic Seminary at Aberdeen to be educated as a priest, but left Scotland for the New World in May 1819. He landed in Halifax where he gave lessons in bookkeeping. After a few weeks he advanced to Boston and entered Wells & Lilly's book store as a proofreader. In the spring of 1823 he moved to Charleston, South Carolina, and made translations from French and Spanish for a newspaper, *The Courier*. The editor used a fast schooner to meet vessels many miles from the harbor to get their files of newspapers. This was Bennett's work. In 1824 he moved to New York, to *The National Advocate*, a Democratic paper for which he was active as reporter, paragraphist and editor. One year later he became the Washington correspondent of *The New York Inquirer*. He described not only the Senators, but the wives and daughters of the Senators, a novelty then. Between 1832 and 1835 Bennett tried to start his own paper. It was on 6 May 1835 that, with the aid of two young printers, he published the first number of the *Herald*, at the price of one cent. Bennett did everything himself. Working in a small office on Wall Street, he wrote the editorials and the news, did the reporting, and even carried the paper to the few subscribers. He included stock lists and money articles so that the *Herald* quickly won favor with the brokers and the bankers. No other journal had thought of telling them just what they wanted to know. After three months the *Herald* was turning a profit. When, on 16 and 17 December 1835, the Great Fire destroyed Wall Street, Bennett described it in such language that his report was a grand success and the *Herald* took its place in the journalism of the country. In 1837 the office of the *Herald* moved to Ann Street, between Broadway and Nassau Street.

Bennett was described as "tall, erect, neat in dress, quiet and dignified in manner."[3] In 1840 he married Henrietta Agnes Crean, and as a result, James Gordon Bennett, Jr., was born on 10 May 1841 in New York, on Chambers Street, "then a fashionable residence district."[4] Of course Bennett the second was educated as the future owner of the *Herald*, meaning private tutors in America and France and a thorough training in all departments of the newspaper. Bennett Jr. became in 1866 managing editor of the *Herald* and, when it was started in 1867, of *The Evening Telegram*. He became the owner when his father died on 1 June 1872, aged 76, at his residence at 425 Fifth Avenue, corner of Thirty-eighth Street.

James Gordon Bennett "holding walking stick:" Bennett introduced American sporting spirit in the ACF's mentality. His Cup accidentally replaced the inter-town races and served as a baseline for the ACF's Grand Prix (*Vanity Fair Album*, 1884, Library of Congress).

That the *Herald* was going to continue to be an eccentric and good newspaper was evident. It was the first New York newspaper to print weather reports. In the autumn of 1869, in Paris, JGB asked Henry Morton Stanley to find David Livingstone. Stanley was a newspaper correspondent who had just shown considerable aptitude and energy when engaged by the *Herald* to follow the British army in the Abyssinian campaign. Livingstone was a Scottish missionary and explorer who had set out to find the sources of the Nile and the Congo, and had disappeared somewhere in the middle of Africa. From time to time, rumors reached the coast that Livingstone was still alive, a mystery which captivated the world. Leading an expedition of two hundred men, Stanley found Livingstone in November 1871 on the shore of Lake Tanganyika, a brilliant feat to the benefit of the *Herald*.

On Monday morning, 9 November 1874, the entire front page of the *Herald* was occupied by a detailed story of the escape of all the wild animals from New York's Central Park Zoo. Some fifty persons, the story said, had been killed and the animals were still at large in the city streets, despite the efforts of hundreds of soldiers. Many hysterical New Yorkers barricaded their doors, while others armed themselves and went out looking for some big-game hunting. Only the very few who went on down to the last paragraph at the bottom of the last column were relieved when they found the statement that the story was pure fabrication and that not one word was true.

In 1879 Bennett sent the *Jeannette*, a former British gunboat strengthened for ice navigation, to the Arctic regions in search of the North Pole. The *Jeannette*, with a crew of thirty-three, sailed from San Francisco on 8 July 1879. The expedition discovered the Jeannette, Henrietta and Bennett islands. In June 1881 the *Jeannette* was caught and crushed by the ice and sank. The crew escaped with most of their provisions and three small whaleboats. Just one of the boats reached the Lena Delta; the other two were lost.

Meanwhile, during 1876, JGB became engaged to Miss Edith May, daughter of Dr. Frederick May, a prominent Washington physician. The marriage date was set for 26 December 1876, and Miss May's trousseau arrived from Paris. Then, something occurred. Wild escapades on the part of Bennett? Was the marriage date postponed to 3 January 1877? According to circulating rumors, JGB became so drunk at the 1877 New Year's party held at the home of his fiancée that he relieved himself in the grand piano and in the fireplace. In any case, on 3 January, Frederick May, the 24-year-old brother of the fiancée, waited for Bennett in front of the Union Club at 21st Street and Fifth Avenue: "Mr. May raised a large rawhide, which he had kept concealed on his person, and struck Mr. Bennett full in the face, blood following the stroke. A second and third blow followed, and before Mr. Bennett had time to recover his surprise at the suddenness of the attack, he had received two severe cuts on the face — one on the nose, and one over the left eye. On regaining his self-possession Mr. Bennett struck at Mr. May, and the two men clinched and fell. In the struggle which followed, Mr. May, who is a powerful man, being six feet one inch in height, and some 40 pounds heavier than Mr. Bennett, had the advantage and threw the latter twice, both men rolling in the snow together." Bennett insisted "on challenging Mr. May to mortal combat."[5] On 9 January 1877, Bennett and May met on the state line between Maryland and Delaware, "at a point on the farm of Mr. Nathaniel McGinnie, between Marydel and Dover. The pistols were discharged almost simultaneously, and neither man received a scratch." Bennett said he was "satisfied."[6] On 14 January he sailed for Europe on board the Inman Line steamer *City of Richmond*. He arrived in Paris on 22 April. It was there that four years later, in May 1881, he announced his engagement to Mademoiselle Jeanne Bonaparte, daughter of Pierre Bonaparte, a nephew of the great Napoleon I. The marriage was never celebrated.

The *Herald* had to pay 50 cents per word for telegrams on the transatlantic route, reason enough for Bennett to form the Commercial Cable Company in September 1883, together with John W. Mackay of the Bonanza Mines and the Nevada Bank. A first cable was landed in July 1884, a second in October, both running from Waterville, Ireland, to Canso, Nova Scotia, and then via Rockport, Maine, to Manhattan Beach just outside New York City. From Waterville the cables were extended to Le Havre and Paris. The owned cable backed the launch of the European edition of the *Herald*. The Paris *Herald* appeared on 4 October 1887, in a large *imprimerie* at 5 Rue Coq-Héron in the first Parisian arrondissement. The Paris *Herald* was to be the first European newspaper to use Linotype machines, doing away with the need to compose pages by hand. In 1899 the *Herald*'s circulation passed half a million because its Spanish-American War reporting was far superior to the competing papers of Hearst and Pulitzer. In 1902 an envious Hearst wired Bennett: "Is *The Herald* for sale?" JGB cabled back: "Price for *Herald* three cents daily. Five cents Sunday."[7]

Bennett had a residence at Newport, Rhode Island, on Bellevue Avenue, an Italian style mansion called Stone Villa. In October 1879 he bought the lot across from his house and, in December, commissioned the "Casino," his own exclusive club, from the architects

Bennett's steam yacht *Namouna*, launched in 1882 (Library of Congress).

McKim, Mead & White. From 1890 on, Bennett spent most of his time in France and on his yachts. In Paris, Monsieur Gordon Bennett had residences on the Avenue d'Iéna, in the Avenue des Champs-Élysées, and as "*locataire de la chasse du parc de Versailles*" was allowed to go hunting in the palace grounds around Versailles. In 1892 he bought a house on the French Riviera, between Nice and Monte Carlo, the Villa Namouna in the Petite Afrique quarter of Beaulieu-sur-Mer.

Between 1871 and 1874, and later in 1884 and 1885, Bennett was Commodore of the New York Yacht Club. *Namouna* was the name of his favorite steam yacht. It was designed by St. Clair Byrne and launched in May 1882 from Ward, Stanton & Co.'s shipyard at Newburgh, New York: 234 feet in length, schooner rigged and three-masted. The *Namouna* often crossed the Atlantic, mostly via Bermuda and the Azores, and even reached Penang and Singapore in 1887. In the spring of 1901 the *Namouna* was sold for $10,000 to the Colombian Navy, transformed into a cruiser and "fitted up with a battery of eight guns."[8] The *Namouna* was succeeded by the *Lysistrata*, named after "a Greek lady reputed to be very beautiful and very fast,"[9] designed by George Watson of Glasgow and launched in August 1900 by W. Denny & Brothers at Dumbarton, Scotland. The *Lysistrata* was built of steel, 285 feet in length, and cost $625,000. It carried a crew of one hundred men, and two of the finest Jersey dairy cows.

When the first horseless carriages gave proof of their reliability by running from Paris to Rouen in July 1894, Bennett sent out a reporter on bicycle. Bennett was involved in the organization committee of the 1895 race to Bordeaux and hence was a founding member of the ACF, the Automobile Club de France.[10] On 22 June 1899 the French club accepted to work out the regulation for "an international trophy to be competed for by the motor vehicle clubs of the world at an annual race, the scene of which is to be in France.... Name to be given to the race and distance to be decided at a future meeting."[11] In French circles, the race became known as "la Coupe Bennett," the "Gordon Bennett International Racing Cup." Bennett wanted a contest of sportsmanship and not a competition between rival makers seeking to gain a reputation. On 13 October 1899 the ACF's Commission Sportive published a first concept. In November the regulation was completed: The Gordon Bennett Cup was in the hands of the ACF. Every "*automobile club reconnu*," every foreign club recognized by the ACF, was free to compete for the Cup. Originally the ACF recognized the clubs from America, Great Britain, Austria, Germany, Belgium, Switzerland and Turin. The American Automobile Club, AAC, had been incorporated on 15 August 1899.

> Each club may be represented at the contest by one, two, or three vehicles.
> The competing vehicles must come within the following racing definitions laid down by the Automobile Club of France in 1899: The vehicle must weigh over 400 kilos, and must carry, seated side by side, at least two passengers, each of a minimum weight of 70 kilos, or should the passengers' weight fall short of the above figures, the deficit must be made up by ballast. The car weight of 400 kilos is taken to mean weight unladen, that is, without passengers or fuel, water and accumulators, without tools or spare parts, bags, clothing, or provisions.
> The vehicles must be constructed wholly and in every detail in the country of the clubs they represent.
> The vehicles must be driven by members of the competing clubs, and the two seats must be occupied during the whole of the course.
> The race shall be run on a road in a single stretch over a distance of not less than 550 kilometers and not more than 650 kilometers.
> The course may be made from town to town or divided into several courses, out and return, the distance of each course, however, not being less than 150 kilometers.
> The Cup shall be contested for at some date between the 15th of May and the 15th of August in each year.
> The race shall be run in the country of the club holding the Cup. This club shall, however, be empowered to run the race in France.
> After the homologation of the race, the Cup shall pass into the hands of the winning club within fifteen days. It is understood that no club shall actually win the Cup. The club merely holds the Cup.[12]

In view of the first Bennett Cup to be run in June 1900, the Automobile Club de France selected three drivers by ballot, the three Panhard drivers René de Knyff, Fernand Charron and Léonce Girardot, with Gilles Hourgières, Gaston de Chasseloup-Laubat, "Levegh" and Albert Lemaître as replacements. Levegh and Lemaître in particular did not agree, while another prominent driver, "Antony," was surprised that he was not on the list at all. In December 1899, *La Presse, Le Gaulois, Le Journal des Sports,* and *L'Écho de Paris* took an active part in the discussions and put into play the idea of an elimination race. But Étienne de Zuylen, the ACF president, was not impressed and replied that the selection was based on the long-distance races of 1898 and 1899, and that the shorter events of 1899 had not been taken into account. Hourgières, Levegh and Antony were *noms de course* of the Mors drivers, Georges Huillier, Alfred Velghe and Henry Debray. Huillier was the son of a well-known Parisian notary. Debray had obtained the first French driving license for "vehicles powered by a mechanical engine," delivered in 1888.

The Belgian club was represented by a Snoeck-Bolide driven by Camille Jenatzy. The original Bolide was French and of unusual design. It was assembled in the shops of Léon Lefebvre in Paris, 10 Rue Émile Allez, and was powered by a big horizontal 11-liter 4-cylinder with bore and stroke dimensions of 153 × 153 mm. The Belgian Bolides were built under license by Albert Snoeck's textile machine factory at Ensival-lez-Verviers, 15 kilometers to the east of Liège. The Snoeck-Bolides of de Caters and Lefebvre were delayed at the Belgian customs and did not appear in time. America sent out Alexander Winton's Winton, powered by a single-cylinder engine with bore and stroke of 6½ × 6¾ inches, 224 cubic inches. The other clubs had declined.

The first Bennett Cup was run on 14 June 1900, a Thursday, between Paris and Lyon, with cars starting at 2-minute intervals beginning at 3:14 A.M. from the entrance to the Parc de Saint-Cloud on the Versailles road, near the railway crossing of Montretout, then proceeding through Châteaudun (125 km), Orléans (173 km), Gien (236 km), Nevers (322 km), Moulins (376 km) and Roanne (476 km) to Lyon, a total distance of 566 km. "Despite the early hour quite 30 *chauffeurs* and 100 *cyclistes* were present."[13] Girardot, at the wheel of a brand new, untested 5.25-liter Panhard (110 × 138 mm), led at first: "The engine is governed on the hit-and-miss principle, and when the vehicle stands still and the engine is running, an explosion, occurring every three or four seconds, will set every sheet of partinium of the body vibrating, thus producing a strong metallic ring, which gradually dies out only to be reinforced by another explosion."[14] Second place was held successively by de Knyff, Jenatzy and Charron, with Winton last but following closely. At Châteaudun, Charron was in the lead ahead of Girardot and Jenatzy. Winton withdrew near Orléans with a bent front wheel and a rear tire badly split. De Knyff arrived at Orléans at a walking pace, his fourth speed having broken shortly after leaving Chartres. Charron bent his rear axle in crossing a gutter. He was able to go on. Girardot broke a rear wheel against a curbstone while trying to avoid a frightened horse. The damage was hastily repaired at a neighboring blacksmith's, but he lost over an hour. Charron reached Nevers at 8:42, and stopped for supplies. At Roanne, Charron passed at 11:03 and Girardot at 11:41. Jenatzy burst his two front tires at Chevreuse and was out of the running. The finish of the race was at the *Restaurant des Délices de la Demi-Lune*, a hostelry some six miles out of Lyon. Charron, with Henry Fournier as riding mechanic, arrived shortly after noon, very much exhausted. Charron won in 9 h 9 min 49 sec, averaging 65.85 km/h, better than the express train running between Paris and Lyon. Girardot took second in 10 h 30 min 28 sec.

Jenatzy claimed to have five dogs on his conscience. If the other contestants killed each as many, this was certainly an unlucky day for the dogs of France. It was not surprising that the populace did not like the races. Didn't a new breed of sportsmen and their stinking carriages break the dull silence of the country? Sportsmen not only moved and killed dogs. Sportsmen skidded and chickens died. Sportsmen made dust, they made smell, and they made noise. Sportsmen were goggled and unashamed. They were furred, stop-watched and horse-powerful. Plutocrats had money, sportsmen had motors. Sportsmen blew their horn and people scattered. Sportsmen stood still and everything trembled. Sportsmen broke roads and the rules of the road. Fortunately sportsmen broke down from time to time.

Fernand Charron was born on 30 May 1866 at Angers. His father was a butcher. The young Charron began his career as professional bicycle rider. In 1891, he won the *championnat de demi-fond*, the French middle-range championship, ahead of Henry Fournier and Henri Béconnais. He was "slightly built, small, dapper, and as quick as lightning when occasion calls for quickness."[15] In October 1897, Charron, Léonce Girardot and the third partner Émile Voigt launched the Agence Générale des Automobiles CGV with shops in the west of Paris not far from the Arc de Triomphe, at 2 Rue Brunel, at the corner of the Avenue de la Grande Armée. Léonce Girardot was born on 30 April 1864 in Paris. By the turn of the century he was also known as "*le Docteur de l'Automobile.*" Émile Victor Voigt was born on

They stood for CGV: Fernand Charron, Léonce Girardot and Émile Voigt (*L'Automobile*, 1905).

8 December 1871 in Lille. Until the turn of the century, CGV also maintained a larger show room at 45 Avenue de la Grande Armée. In 1902 the trio, with Étienne Giraud as *metteur au point*, as development engineer, began to produce own cars in an ultra-modern factory in the western suburb Puteaux, Rue Ampère. James Gordon Bennett was one of the first owners of a CGV car. Henry Fournier, Charron's riding mechanic between Paris and Lyon, was born on 13 April 1871 in Le Mans. Charron took him to Paris and placed him with Clément.

Jenatzy's Bolide was owned by the Belgian sportsman Champrobert. The Bolide was not slow. A few days after the Bennett Cup, on Sunday 17 June 1900, Jenatzy and the Bolide started in a short sprint in Belgium, and covered a flying kilometer between Diegem and Melsbroek in 38⅕ sec, 94 km/h. On 1 July, Jenatzy and the Bolide won the Critérium de Provence on the straightaway between Arles and Salon, covering 100 km in three heats of 33 km in a total time of 1 h 20 min 15 sec.

The driver and the car of the year 1900 were Alfred Velghe alias Levegh and his 7.35-liter Mors (119 × 165 mm), a combination which won the 1348-km race between Paris and Toulouse in the last week of July 1900. Velghe, another former bicycle rider, "had not the excitable character which is usually associated with the French nationality. Levegh was cool to the degree of coldness. He never appeared to hurry over anything, and never allowed anything to perturb him; and yet when driving he was a veritable whirlwind. His knowledge of his car was perfect, and much of his success was due to the high rate of perfection in which he kept it."[16] Levegh's father, Albert Velghe, had married a daughter of Édouard Lévy, the owner of the well-established antique tapestry house "Aux Vieux Gobelins" at 27 Rue Laffitte in the Ninth Parisian arrondissement. In March 1888 Albert Velghe took over the Gobelin business from his father-in-law.[17] Alfred Velghe's pseudonym Levegh was an anagram of Velghe that echoed the sound of his mother's family name, Lévy. In June 1897 Alfred Velghe was registered as *associé*, and an additional shop was opened at 48 Rue de Châteaudun. Levegh's sister was married to Gustave Ström, one of the Ström brothers of 16 Rue de la Chaussée-d'Antin, the famous *"tailleurs de l'automobile,"* tailors to the Automobile Club de France, makers of specialty motoring garments of rubber, silk and fabrics.

Levegh with a Mors and Charron and Girardot with Panhards were the French drivers for the next Cup race. The second Bennett Cup was held on 29 May 1901, concurrently with the 527-km race from Paris to Bordeaux, via Chartres (79 km), Châteaudun (124 km), Vendôme (163 km), Tours (220 km), Châtellerault (289 km), Poitiers (321 km), and Ruffec (388 km). Charron withdrew at Vendôme. The gearbox of Levegh's Mors broke near Gandé. Girardot finished ninth overall and won the Bennett Cup, 2 h 40 min behind Henry Fournier in a Mors. Fournier averaged 85 km/h, with top speeds of 115 km/h. Between 27 and 29 June 1901 Fournier also won the 1105-km race from Paris to Berlin in 16 h 5 min, while Girardot finished second 1 h 2 min behind. Levegh did not start because of a respiratory illness. With his brother Robert Velghe he moved to the Mediterranean, to Hyères. By the end of August 1902 he drove a Mors in the kilometer sprint at Deauville. Levegh died on 1 March 1904 at Pau.

The third Bennett Cup was embedded into the 991-km race from Paris to Vienna, which began on 26 June 1902. The Cup route was composed of two legs, Paris to Belfort and Bregenz to Innsbruck, the passage through Switzerland being neutralized (i.e., not timed as part of the race). There were six entries, Fournier's Mors, de Knyff's Panhard and Girardot's CGV for the French club, and three 45-hp Wolseleys to be driven by Grahame White, Herbert Austin and Arthur Callahan for the British club. None of the Wolseleys appeared, however, and at the last moment Selwyn Edge with a Napier took their place. According to the rules the French machines were painted blue and the Napier red. After Fournier, Girardot and de Knyff had broken down, Edge and the Napier won for the British club. Marcel Renault was first at Vienna. He did not drive one of the new 1000-kg racers but a Renault of the light car class, a 650-kg *voiture légère*. The components of the Renault engine were supplied by De Dion: "We made all the parts, cylinders, pistons, etc., but the Renault brothers assembled them. We are making all the parts for their two cylinder motors as well. We do not assemble them simply because we have not started yet to manufacture two and four cylinder motors."[18] Henry Farman in a Panhard Seventy was second at Vienna, and Edmond in a 650-kg Darracq third. The best Mors finished 18th with de Caters and 26th with Augières, a deep disappointment. Augières was the nom de course of Georges Auger. With his brother Émile, he was the owner of the Maison Auger, an elegant jeweler's shop at Place de la Victoire founded by their father in 1858. In November 1902, on the straightaway near Dourdan, Augières and his Mors took the world speed record, covering the flying kilometer in 29 sec or 124.137 km/h, and the flying mile in 46 sec. The best 400-kg voiturette at Vienna was not a Renault but a Darracq driven by Guillaume. The Renault voiturettes driven by Grus and Cormier took second and third, while Victor Oury, who had a 4-minute lead after the first leg at Belfort, withdrew after he came down the Arlberg pass with a bad cold. His Garage Oury, Schrader & Cie., at 64 Avenue de la Grande Armée, offered Renault, Mors, Clément and Panhard cars. Oury grew seriously ill and died on 8 July 1903, aged 36.

As a consequence of the British victory, the next Bennett race was moved to the other side of the Channel, to Ireland. The course went through Kildare County in parts through narrow roads with numerous bends, starting and finishing at Ballyshannon, about 50 kilometers southwest of Dublin. On 2 July 1903, Camille Jenatzy and a Mercedes won for the German club, ahead of the complete French team. Jenatzy was christened the "Red Devil" for his red beard and his devilish driving. When racing, Jenatzy was reckless, daring and excitable to the utmost degree. When away from his car, he was a meek and mild individual. The winning Mercedes, a 9.25-liter Sixty (140 × 150 mm), was owned by Clarence Gray Dinsmore. In March 1900 Dinsmore had been named official representative of the Automobile Club of America at the Bennett races. Dinsmore was born on 12 August 1847 in New York City. His father, William B. Dinsmore, was one of the founders and the president of the Adams Express Company and director of several railroad companies. Clarence Dinsmore's wife was "Miss Kate Jerome, a daughter of Thomas Jerome, and a cousin of Mrs. Cornwallis West who was Lady Randolph Churchill."[19] Between 1901 and 1905 Dinsmore bought a whole fleet of Mercedes racers. The cars were driven by Wilhelm Werner and Camille Jenatzy. Dinsmore spent most of his time in Europe, in the Rue Marceau in Paris, on the Riviera, in London, or in Houlgate. He was often seen in company of Robert Katzenstein, a Frankfurt banker and sportsman who made headlines in 1901, at the finish of the race from Paris to Berlin: "There was considerable amusement when Robert Katzenstein of Frankfort-on-Main came in with his auto-car running backward, having made thirty kilometers from Potsdam in that manner, owing to his vehicle's machinery being out of order."[20] Dinsmore's health was impaired for years, and he died of pneumonia on 8 November 1905, in New York at the Waldorf-Astoria.

After the victory of the German Mercedes and the end of the great town-to-town races caused by a series of accidents in the race from Paris to Madrid in May 1903, all the French manufacturers wanted to start in the Bennett Cup. In 1904 and 1905 the ACF had to hold elimination races, which were at least on the same level as the Cup itself. In these years the

Under Bennett's eyes are (*top*) the 1905 winning car, the no. 1 Brasier, with de Knyff, Pérignon, Le Roy, Michelin, Brasier, Caillois, Théry with mechanic Muller, and Duray; and the no. 17 Austrian Mercedes with Alexander Burton at the wheel, C.L. Charley, Jenatzy and Emil Jellinek (*Allgemeine Automobil-Zeitung*).

Bennett Cup was the most important event. Léon Théry and his Brasier won the French elimination and the Cup in 1904 and 1905. On 14 October 1904, Théry and his teammate Gustave Caillois, who finished fifth in the elimination run on the Circuit de l'Argonne, arrived in New York on the French liner *La Lorraine*. On 18 October they were guests of the Automobile Club of America. Théry gave a brief talk on his experiences in road racing, in French translated by Caillois. The Gordon Bennett cars, two 9.9-liter Brasiers (150 × 140 mm), followed on 23 October on the White Star steamer *Celtic*, and were exhibited at the Brasier agency of Edward B. Gallaher. Théry planned to drive his Bennett winning Brasier on the Empire City track on 29 October, in a series of 10-mile match races against Barney Oldfield in the Peerless "Green Dragon," Maurice Bernin in William Gould Brokaw's 60-hp Renault, and Paul Sartori in Alfred Vanderbilt's 90-hp F.I.A.T. "Théry's appearance on the track with his famous car was hailed with loud cheers, for the crowd was anxious to see the famous French racer." But Théry started in just one heat against Sartori, and withdrew: "I did the best I could, but it was my first effort in a track race."[21]

James Gordon Bennett's idea of a pure sportsmen's race did not match the requirements of the new industry. The great town-to-town races, from Paris to Berlin in 1901, to Vienna in 1902, and to Madrid in 1903, had degenerated into marketing events for the benefits of a few French manufacturers. The element of legitimate sport was lost. The French manufacturers did not accept the three-car rule of the Bennett races which "limit France, the greatest automobile manufacturing country of the world, to the same numerical represen-

Last Bennett winners: The 1905 Brasier with Henri Brasier standing just beyond the cockpit; seated in the car are Léon Théry at the wheel and mechanic Muller (Mercedes-Benz Classic).

tation as the latest arrived and least important automobile nation. The presence of six Mercedes cars, three German and three Austrian, is pointed out as an injustice and a danger to the French industry."[22] On 28 June 1905, a few days after the Bennett race in the Auvergne, the ACF decided that in 1906 it would not compete for the Bennett Cup. A new race with revised rules emerged and was called Grand Prix de l'Automobile Club de France, GP de l'ACF. It was a race "in which all builders, to whatever nation they belonged, should have an equal chance."[23] Overnight, the sportsman's version of a race was history. In the future the Bennett Cup stood for the transition between the inter-town races and the early Grand Prix era.

Bennett gave up sponsoring automobile races. Instead he supplied new trophies for aeronautical competitions, for balloons in 1906, and for aeroplanes in 1908. On 10 September 1914 Bennett married the Baroness Maud de Reuter, a

Bennett depicted in the garden of Villa Namouna, Beaulieu-sur-Mer (Library of Congress).

daughter of John Potter of Philadelphia. Her first husband, George Julius de Reuter, a close friend of Bennett and a younger brother of Herbert de Reuter, the head of the London news service, had died in November 1909 leaving two adult children. Bennett's marriage took place at the American Church in Paris: "The Baroness de Reuter is about 50 years old, and, while not of marked physical beauty, is of great intellectual charm and attractiveness."[24] Between 1914 and 1918, the Bennetts spent most of their time at Beaulieu-sur-Mer. In 1916 Bennett sold the *Lysistrata* to the Russian Red Cross. James Gordon Bennett died on 14 May 1918 at Beaulieu. His Villa Namouna was sold in 1925 to the perfumer François Coty.

2

Vanderbilt

The American counterpart of the Gordon Bennett race was the Vanderbilt Cup, launched in 1904 by William Kissam Vanderbilt II. Willie K. was born on 26 October 1878 in New York City, a great-grandson of Cornelius Vanderbilt, the Commodore, and a grandson of William Henry Vanderbilt, the famous railroad magnate. Willie stood five feet six inches tall. On 4 April 1899 he married Virginia Graham "Birdie" Fair at the New York residence of Hermann Oelrichs, the bride's brother-in-law. Birdie was "short, plump and spirited, with black eyes and a mass of curly hair worn parted in the middle."[1] The Oelrichses' interests ranged from shipping Virginia tobacco to importing guano from Peru and organizing the American business of the North German Lloyd, the renowned shipping company. In 1900 Willie Vanderbilt bought a German Daimler, a 26-hp 5.5-liter short-chassis Phoenix (106 × 156 mm). The car was quickly known as the "White Ghost" since it was painted white when it was imported: "With it came an instructor, who is teaching Mr. Vanderbilt the mysteries of its propulsion. The locomobile is said to have cost $8,000." The Daimler "kept up a speed of fifty-five miles for an hour's run."[2] In June 1900 Vanderbilt had it painted crimson and black. He regularly drove it to Newport, Rhode Island, where the Mayor "threatened him with arrest if he persisted in racing his locomobile through the streets."[3] On 6 September 1900, in the track races on the Aquidneck Trotting Park at Newport, Vanderbilt won the final. His White Ghost was described as a "French gasoline machine."[4]

A few days later, on 18 September 1900, a series of sprints were run on the old 1-mile Guttenberg track, New Jersey. Albert C. Bostwick won a 5-miler in 7 min 43⅗ sec, and the 10-mile final in 15 min 9⅕ sec, ahead of David Wolfe Bishop. Bostwick was the chairman of the racing committee of the Automobile Club of America. His car was qualified as a "flier."[5] It was the 16-hp Panhard (96 × 138 mm) in which René de Knyff had won the 1899 Tour de France and the Riviera race from Nice to Marseille in the last week of March 1900. Bostwick had sailed for Europe on 25 April and, one week later, purchased de Knyff's car for $12,000. The Panhard was a pure racer: "Mors and especially Panhard have worked so as to bring down the weight to the minimum. The motors built by these two firms are much lighter than those of similar types built in England and Germany. The bodies of the cars are, so to speak, suppressed entirely, and the driver sits on the oil tank surrounded by a sort of aluminum gallery. As for the second person who has to be carried, he also sits on the floor of the car, and his legs are hanging in a sort of cul-de-sac."[6] On 3 and 4 June Bostwick appeared as "de Bostwick" in the French press and finished third in the 318-km race between Bordeaux and Périgueux: "This was the American's maiden race in Europe and it speaks volumes for his pluck and skill to have secured such an excellent

Willie Vanderbilt (right) trackside (Library of Congress).

place."[7] Bishop's car was a smaller Panhard, a 3.6-liter (94 × 132 mm) bought from Fernand Charron.

On 17 February 1901 William K. Thorn, whose mother was one of the thirteen children of Commodore Cornelius Vanderbilt, started with his 5.5-liter Daimler in the 330-km "*Circuit du Sud-Ouest*," the southwestern road race at the French town of Pau in the shadow of the Pyrenees. Thorn had taken up his residence at Pau since the death of his mother in 1896. Although aged 52, he was an enthusiastic automobilist and president of the local automobile club, the Automobile Club Béarnais. Just two kilometers after the start a cart and horse crossed Thorn's way. The big Daimler left the road, turned a somersault, and came to stop against a tree. It was in this race at Pau that the "Daimler Mercédès" appeared for the first time. Claude Loraine Barrow was at the wheel, but only for a few hundred meters until the gearbox broke, a consequence of an accident at Versailles a few days before.

On 7 April 1901, in Paris, Willie Vanderbilt took delivery of his new Daimler Mercédès, a 35-hp 6-liter (116 × 140 mm), chassis no. 2081, for 20,000 Mark. He sold his White Ghost to Edward Russel "E.R." Thomas, a New York banker and broker. During the summer the 6-liter Mercedes was shipped to New York. On 30 August 1901, on the Aquidneck track, Vanderbilt drove it in a 5-mile match race against Foxhall Keene in a Mors. The Mercedes won in 7 min 3⅕ sec. The *Automobile Magazine* reported: "It is rather amusing to notice the feeling of the majority of the onlookers, they showing unmistakably whom they hoped would win. Each time Mr. Vanderbilt rushed past the stands there were any quantity of opinions expressed concerning his superiority as a chauffeur over Mr. Keene. This popularity is presumably due to Mr. Vanderbilt's conspicuous life in Newport."[8]

Foxhall Parker "Foxie" Keene was born on 18 December 1867 in San Francisco, the son of San Francisco and Wall Street stock broker James R. Keene, "the greatest Stock Exchange strategist that the world had yet seen."[9] Foxie Keene was a sportsman, an avid golfer and one of the world's best polo players. Keene's Mors was a 55-hp 10-liter (130 × 190 mm), similar to the car in which Henry Fournier had just won the races from Paris to Bordeaux and to Berlin. Vanderbilt, too, was the owner of a 10-liter Mors. On 16 November 1901 he sat on the floor of it while the great Fournier was at the wheel, on the Coney Island Boulevard, Brooklyn, between King's Highway and Bishop's Hotel. The Mors covered a mile in 51⅘ sec. Keene and his Mors achieved 54⅖ sec, Albert Bostwick and his 40-hp Winton 56⅖ sec. "It is the first time since Charley Murphy made his nerve-breaking bicycle run on a planked road behind a Long Island Railroad locomotive at Maywood, L.I., on June 30, 1898, doing the mile by that novel manner in 57⅘ seconds, that any machine off of rails has made a mile under any conditions whatsoever in less than 60 seconds."[10]

In view of the 1902 season, Vanderbilt bought the latest Mercedes, a 6.5-liter "Simplex Forty" (118 × 150 mm), chassis no. 2418, taking delivery on 2 February 1902 at his Riviera residence at Nice, 2 Rue du Jardin Public. In April, he drove it from Monte Carlo to Paris in 17 hours. In May, in the southwest of Paris, on "an excellent piece of level, straight road" between Chartres and Ablis, he covered the flying kilometer in 32⅖ sec, "establishing a kilometer record for automobiles weighing under 1000 kilograms."[11] For everyday use in Paris, Vanderbilt bought three light Renaults. In the first week of June, it was reported that "William K. Vanderbilt, Jr., and his wife are still at the Ritz. He is frequently to be seen

Foxhall Keene on horseback (Library of Congress).

driving his famous blue Daimler and is waiting until Mors finishes for him a 40–70 motor, which he will drive himself in the forthcoming race from Paris to Vienna."[12] The Mors was a 9.2-liter (140 × 150 mm). Keene bought a similar racer. "Foxhall Keene started at 3:45 A.M. He wore an ordinary lounging suit, instead of being muffled in a mackintosh, as were the other competitors. W.K. Vanderbilt, Jr., started at 5:43 A.M. His skillful maneuvering was much admired."[13] Just a few kilometers after the start, at Ferrières, Keene ran into a gate at a nasty railway crossing. Vanderbilt was 55th at Belfort: "I never had such hard luck; my tires burst twice, my radiator then got out of order, and next I ran over a dog. My automobile arrived at Belfort so damaged it could only go fifteen kilometers. That is why I gave up the contest."[14] In July, the Mors ran better and Vanderbilt finished third in the 512-km Circuit des Ardennes, behind Charles Jarrott in a Panhard and Fernand Gabriel in a similar Mors, ahead of Elliott Zborowski in a Mercedes Forty.

Zborowski was a wealthy sportsman who bought his racing cars and raced absolutely for the fun of it. He had no trade interest to sustain, no commercial banner to uphold, and no monetary gain to wish for. He took his car, made his own personal arrangements, and went through a race, enjoying every moment of it, and yet as keen on winning as if his very life depended on it. "Elliott Zborowski, known to his friends in this country and in Europe as Count Zborowski, was a picturesque figure in New York and Newport, where his youth and early manhood were spent, and in foreign capitals, where he lived after the death of his father, Martin Zabriskie, which occurred in 1878."[15] Martin Zabriskie had changed his name to the original Polish, Zborowski. He had been by profession a lawyer, but had devoted his time to real estate investments. On 7 March 1892, in Sioux Falls, Elliott Zborowski married a granddaughter of William B. Astor, Margaret Laura de Stuers, née Carey, just a few hours after Baroness de Stuers had been divorced, "bringing the whole trial to a climax which was a surprise to the New York friends of each."[16] After moving to England, the Zborowskis built a house at Melton Mowbray. On 13 April 1899, Zborowski ordered a 5.5-liter Daimler Phoenix which was delivered on 15 January 1900 via the Motor Carriage Supply Co., London. In April 1902 he drove the 5.5-liter Phoenix to victory in the 4-seat touring car class of the hillclimb from Nice to La Turbie. On 30 May 1901 he ordered a 35/38-hp Mercedes racer (118 × 140 mm). It was delivered on 10 June 1902 as a Forty (118 × 150 mm), just in time to start in the race from Paris to Vienna where he finished fourth. Zborowski was always immaculately dressed, even when racing. "While other competitors, at the controls between the stages, stopped their cars in the full heat of the noonday sun and in other undesirable positions, Zborowski seemed to have a gift to find a tree or another little oasis of shade. Lighting a cigarette he would imperturbably await the signal of the control marshal when his time was up, and then dash off at top speed over the next stage."[17]

Other Mercedes Forty racers were delivered on 20 March 1902 to the painter William Turner Dannat, on 1 May to Harry Harkness, the only son of Lamon V. Harkness, one of the biggest stockholders in the Standard Oil Company, and on 15 May to Clarence Gray Dinsmore. Zborowski ordered the latest 9-liter 60-hp Mercedes on 18 June 1902. The Sixty was delivered on 19 March 1903, and registered "37-MM." Zborowski drove it in the hillclimb up to La Turbie on 1 April: "The witnesses of the start of the race say that Zborowski showed considerable nervousness while awaiting his turn, he being the fifth starter. Imprudently he wore white kid gloves, which prevented him from having a firm grasp of the brake."[18] In the same corner where Wilhelm Bauer had a fatal accident in 1900, the Mercedes struck a rock, causing a sudden swerve, which precipitated Zborowski and mechanic Pallandt against a wall. Zborowski was killed instantly; Pallandt escaped with severe bruises.[19] Margaret Zborowski was awaiting her husband at La Turbie, expecting that they would lunch together at the conclusion of the race. "She was chatting gayly with friends, without displaying any anxiety regarding her husband's delay in arriving. Baron de Caters broke the sad news to her, saying at first that a serious accident had occurred and then gently revealing the terrible truth."[20]

The last town-to-town race from Paris to Madrid was started at Versailles on 24 May 1903, at 3:30 A.M.:

> No such great motoring event has happened so far in the history of Paris as this great 1,307 kilometer race. Toward midnight Versailles presented a scene of extreme activity, the gayly illuminated cafés being packed with people waiting for the start. It was estimated that 5,000 automobiles were crowded in the thoroughfares, many of them decorated with Chinese lanterns. Many of the contestants arrived during the evening, their huge machines trembling and groaning. The cars are denuded of all ornamentation, most of them reeking with oil and giving off foul vapors. The drivers wore rubber coats, drawn high and tight around the throat, and had their faces and heads completely enveloped in a mask. They did not wear goggles, but heavy plate glass was fixed in the mask, forming a miniature window, which afforded protection to the eyes without interfering with the sight. The contestants sat very low to minimize the resistance to the wind. Each competing machine is allowed to carry one mechanic.[21]

Willie Vanderbilt started in his no. 60 Mors, a brand-new 11.5-liter (145 × 175 mm) with four steel cylinders. It was a "*Dauphin Paris-Madrid*," a Paris-Madrid "dolphin" which had just been delivered by Henry Fournier's Paris-Automobile agency, Rue d'Anjou. Vanderbilt's no. 39 Mercedes, a 12.7-liter Ninety (170 × 140 mm), was driven by Koehler. Foxhall Keene appeared at the *pesage*, the scrutineering, with his no. 114 Mercedes Sixty, but did not start. No. 29 was Madame Camille du Gast's white De Dietrich: "Her machine was decked with flowers and her departure was the signal for a great ovation. She made a splendid run, passing five of her competitors before reaching Chartres."[22] Marie Marthe Camille Desinge du Gast, born on 30 May 1868 in Paris, was married to Jules Crespin, a director at the Grands Magasins Crespin-Dufayel in the Barbès quarter. Vanderbilt and the Mors were out before reaching Chartres, because of a "breakdown."[23]

Vanderbilt sold his Mors to C.L. "Charley" Lehmann, Jellinek's star salesman. The Mors was shipped to the Daimler factory at Cannstatt where it was dismantled and scrutinized. The Mors survived the devastating factory fire on 10 June 1903, and Otto Hieronimus used it in 1904 for practice on the Bennett course. Vanderbilt's Mercedes Ninety was exhibited at the Paris Salon in the autumn of 1903 and then shipped to America. On 27 January 1904, on the "wind-swept" Ormond Beach, Florida, Vanderbilt and the Mercedes covered the flying mile in 39 seconds, a new world record: "Two miles he took to start on his mile run, and he then ran on for two miles more. In the entire five miles he swerved from the edge of the foam-crested water but once, when an unusually high comber came upward. Several times little inequalities in the beach caused the machine to leap long and dangerously, but even this did not affect the young driver, for he was perfectly calm and not at all nervous as he dismounted."[24] After winning two 10-milers and a 50-miler, Vanderbilt "carried Mrs. Vanderbilt for a fast record ride up and down the beach, but no time was taken. Mrs. Vanderbilt seemingly enjoyed the experience, dismounting from the car coolly at the finish, but with exclamations of delight over the experience."[25] On 30 January, in front of the Hotel Poinciana at Palm Beach, Vanderbilt gave a bicycle exhibition "with the quickness, deftness, and grace of a professional trick rider. The automobile crack vaulted over the handlebars, rode backward, jumped and bucked the machine as if it were a broncho, stood on one pedal, on the saddle, and rode forward and backward."[26] In November 1904 Vanderbilt sold the Mercedes Ninety to Bernard M. Shanley, whose family owned the Shanley restaurants. In March 1905 Shanley decided "to abandon automobile racing"[27] and the big Mercedes racer ended up in the hands of W.L. Andrus of Yonkers.

Vanderbilt drivers: Victor Hémery, George Heath, Emanuele Cedrino, Felice Nazzaro, Paul Sartori, Arthur Duray, Joe Tracy, Walter Christie, Camille Jenatzy, Al Campbell, Bert Dingley, Vincenzo Lancia, Foxhall Keene, and Ferenc Szisz (*Allgemeine Automobil-Zeitung*).

A second Mercedes Ninety was imported to New York, for William Gould Brokaw. It was the racer initially owned by Clarence Gray Dinsmore and driven by Wilhelm Werner in the Paris-Madrid race. In addition, Brokaw owned a 30-hp Renault which was driven by Maurice Bernin and Joe Tracy during the 1904 season. Albert Bostwick received a 12.7-liter Mercedes engine in April 1904. It was mounted into a power boat. A Mercedes racer of the 1904 Bennett type was delivered to Willie Vanderbilt in July 1904, a 95-hp 12-liter (165 × 140 mm) with two low-mounted camshafts instead of one in the older Ninety. In September 1902 Willie's cousin, Alfred Gwynne Vanderbilt, had imported a Paris-Vienna Renault: "The racing car which Alfred G. Vanderbilt bought from Louis Renault, one of the competitors in the recent race from Paris to Vienna, is now stored in an automobile station on East Fifty-eighth Street, near Madison Avenue. It is a handsome vehicle of the French racing pattern with a red body containing two seats upholstered in black leather. The engine has four vertical cylinders and is rated at thirty-two horse power. Mr. Vanderbilt has driven the machine 625 miles in 12 hours 15 minutes over French roads."[28] In the autumn of 1903 Alfred bought a 9-liter Mercedes Sixty for $12,000. Other Sixty owners were Edward R. Thomas, Samuel B. Stevens, Bernard Shanley, George Arents Jr., Isidore Wormser Jr., and Herbert Bowden of Boston. On 18 July 1904, Paul Sartori drove Alfred Vanderbilt's Mercedes Sixty to victory in the main event on the Empire City track at Yonkers, a 15-mile free-for-all. The Arents Sixty was driven by Carl Mensel and finished second. Later in the meeting, the Vanderbilt Sixty overheated, breaking two cylinders and the crankcase.

On 7 June 1904, the Racing Board of the American Automobile Association announced that the "William K. Vanderbilt Jr. Cup" was to be held on 8 October: "It is practically the Gordon Bennett race transported to this country."[29] It was a challenge cup to be contested annually between 15 August and 15 October over a course of 250 to 300 miles, "open to teams from any automobile club recognized by either the American Automobile Association or the Touring Club of France, which practically opens the race to the world." Each club could be represented by up to ten cars: "Each car must weigh between 881 and 2204 pounds and carry two passengers weighing not less than 132 pounds each."[30] The 1904 and 1905 races had to be held in America.

Among the entries for the 1904 race were seven American cars: a 70-hp Smith & Mabley Simplex for Frank Croker; two White steamers for Webb Jay and Rollin T. White; two 60-hp Pope-Toledos for Albert C. Webb and Herbert Lyttle; the Packard "Gray Wolf" for Charles Schmidt; and a 40-hp Royal Tourist entered by C.A. Duerr for Joe Tracy. Alfred Vanderbilt entered a 14-liter Bennett Cup F.I.A.T. (165 × 165 mm) for Paul Sartori, William Wallace of Boston a similar F.I.A.T. for himself. The F.I.A.T.s were serviced by Hollander & Tangeman, the New York agency which had just been opened at 5 West 45th Street. Three 15.5-liter factory Panhards (170 × 170 mm) were driven by George Heath, who had won the third Circuit des Ardennes on 25 July, Georges Teste, who had finished second, and Henry Tart. Twenty-one-year-old Albert Clément took the wheel of his Clément-Bayard. R.E. Jarrige entered a De Dietrich (155 × 170 mm), "a big white torpedo-appearing machine,"[31] for the great Fernand Gabriel. Two De Dietrichs arrived on 30 September on the French Line steamer *Savoie*, one for Gabriel, the other bought by Edward C. Ellis, who died two weeks before he could take delivery. William Gould Brokaw entered a brand-new 90-hp Renault driven by Maurice Bernin. There were five Mercedes, the single 95-hp 12-liter owned by Clarence Gray Dinsmore and driven by Wilhelm Werner, and four Sixties entered by Samuel Stevens for Albert Campbell, by George Arents for himself, by Edward Thomas for Ed Hawley, and by Isidore Wormser for Willy Lüttgen.

Caricatures of Willie Vanderbilt (left) and the Panhard drivers Henry Tart and Georges Teste (*Allgemeine Automobil-Zeitung*).

"The course is 32.40 miles in length, including a 1.40-mile control at Hempstead and a .40-mile control at Hicksville. So the actual distance is 30.24 miles, and it will be covered ten times, start at the pump near Westbury. The longest straightaway stretch is about sixteen miles along the Jericho turnpike from Queens to Jericho."[32] The start was at six o'clock on Saturday morning, 8 October 1904, with cars leaving at two-minute intervals. Gabriel "was not at all favorably impressed by the course, which he declared to be unsuited for racing at high speed on account of the narrowness of the roads and the frequent turns."[33] In July 1905, Joe Tracy put it another way when describing the Bennett course through the Auvergne: "The Vanderbilt's course was child's play compared to it. In the Vanderbilt course turns were the exception, but in the Auvergne the turns were the rule, and one would wonder what was the matter when he came across a straight stretch."[34] Heath won the first Vanderbilt Cup in 5 h 26 min 45 sec, with Clément second 1 min 28 sec back, the only two cars to finish ten laps.

After the race, the De Dietrich driven by Gabriel was sold to Orlando F. Thomas, Edward's brother. Both were members of the brokerage firm of Thomas, Maclay & Co., 71 Broadway, and directors of several banks. Edward Thomas was also the owner of the famous power boat *Dixie* which, in December 1905, was sold to Edward Schroeder of Jersey City, the same Schroeder who was to be the owner of Ralph DePalma's "Grey Ghost" Mercedes in 1911. Edward Thomas was married to Linda Lee of Louisville, Kentucky, "one of the most celebrated beauties in New York and Newport ... a tall, stately blonde, with regular features, wonderful pink and white coloring, with golden hair and large, deep blue eyes."[35]

Two 12-liter and two older 12.7-liter Mercedes racers appeared on the beach at Ormond, Florida, in January 1905. Willie Vanderbilt brought his 12-liter 95-hp (165 × 140 mm), and Edward Thomas a similar racer just purchased from Dinsmore. The older ex–Vanderbilt Ninety (170 × 140 mm) was still owned by Bernard Shanley, and entered in several races for Shanley, E.H. Fredericks and A. Le Blanc. Samuel Stevens arrived in the Ninety bought from Brokaw. Herbert Bowden of Boston, or more precisely of Waltham, Massachusetts, came with a 120-hp special, his "Flying Dutchman" twin-engined Mercedes: a stretched chain-drive frame powered by two 60-hp engines in tandem. The special, assembled by his mechanics Charlie Basle and Charles Meyer, had been finished just one week before the meeting. One of the 9.25-liter engines came from Bowden's Mercedes Sixty, the other from his powerboat. The Flying Dutchman weighed 2,780 pounds (1260 kg) so that it could not start in the 1000-kg class. But it broke all records for overweight cars, covering a flying kilometer in 24⅗ sec and a flying mile in 34⅕ sec. A few weeks later, Bowden had his 12-meter power boat *Flying Dutchman III* built by the Williams-Whittelesey Co., using the same Sixty engines "installed in the boat on the steel side frames of the car."[36] The De Dietrich owned by Orlando Thomas was driven by Harry W. Fletcher, a former chief machinist on the *New Hampshire*. During the spring of 1905, Fletcher was involved in the design of Edward Thomas's power boat *Dixie*. The fastest racer on Ormond Beach was a Stanley steamer in which Louis B. Ross covered a mile in 38 seconds. It was described as "a double pointed tin cigar cut horizontally in half, and set low on four wheels, with the rounded side up, the driver's head just showing from the cockpit and a big protruding exhaust pipe raking aft from out the top. It looks like a duck hunter's sneak box, fitted for land navigation."[37] After the race, Ross sold the steamer to Charley Heineman of New York: "Joe Nelson will drive the car, which will be entered in all the important track events."[38] In May 1905, on the Brighton Beach track, Nelson crashed the steamer through the fence: "Nelson, to the relief of the spectators, was seen to leap from his seat, and a mighty volume of smoke at once went up from the smokestack."[39]

A third Thomas brother, Dr. Harold E. Thomas, a banker and lawyer, lived in Chicago. He was also an automobile enthusiast, of course. In the autumn of 1904, he ordered a Loco-mobile racer which was described as 80-, 90- and even 120-hp, and entered it in the 1905 Bennett and Vanderbilt races for Joe Tracy and mechanic Al Poole. The Locomobile was built at Bridgeport, Connecticut, and was designed under the direction of Andrew Riker. "Following the usual Locomobile model, the car has four vertical cylinders, each 7 inches by 7 inches, the largest with possibly a single exception that have ever been put in an auto-mobile."[40] The T-head followed early Mercedes or Panhard fashion. The exhaust camshaft was on the left-hand side. The ignition was of the make-and-break type with a Remy low tension magneto. The crankshaft ran in three plain bearings within a crankcase made of "special alloy."[41] Power was transmitted via cone clutch, three-speed gearbox, and chains to the rear wheels. The tank was made of riveted copper. Wheelbase was 109 inches; track 54 inches; shock absorbers were from Truffault; regular clincher tires from Diamond, 34 × 3½ front and 34 × 4½ rear, were mounted on "specially built wheels of hickory wood ordinarily used for making bows and arrows."[42] The clutch was operated by the right foot pedal, and the outside band brake on the countershaft by the left foot pedal. The engine control was by throttle and spark levers on the steering post, not on top of the steering wheel. Designer Andrew Lawrence Riker was born on 22 October 1868 in New York City, and was vice-president and technical director at Locomobile.

In the second Vanderbilt Cup which was run on 14 October 1905 on Long Island, Joe Tracy and the Locomobile finished third behind Hémery's Darracq and Heath's Panhard, ahead of Lancia's F.I.A.T. In January 1906, the Locomobile was exhibited on the main floor of the Sixth Annual Madison Square Garden Show: "The car looks very much as it did when it went bounding over the Long Island roads last October, the big numbers remaining as they were originally painted for the race."[43]

On 22 September 1906, "Dare Devil" Tracy and the Locomobile won the Vanderbilt elimination, "after a brilliant and thrilling struggle with Le Blon, the French driver of one of the three Thomas cars entered.... Tracy's fiancée, Miss Millicent Taylor, was in the grand stand, and here were the most earnest of the cheers that sped the driver on to victory. Friends of the couple said that they had agreed to get married without delay if Tracy won the race.... Tracy's mechanician, who has been with him in all his big races, is Alfred Poole, who has had much automobile experience abroad. Tracy has made a special study of automobiles, motors, and mechanical construction, and is acknowledged to be one of the most expert technical advisers on those subjects in the automobile world."[44]

14 October 1905 — Second Vanderbilt Cup, Mineola Circuit, Long Island. Joe Tracy and the no. 7 Locomobile are finishing third, with Vincenzo Lancia and no. 4 F.I.A.T. standing in the background: "Lancia had a lead of twenty minutes at one time. Through tire trouble he lost time. While repairing, Christie collided with him. His machine was partially disabled. But for this he would surely have won the race" (Library of Congress).

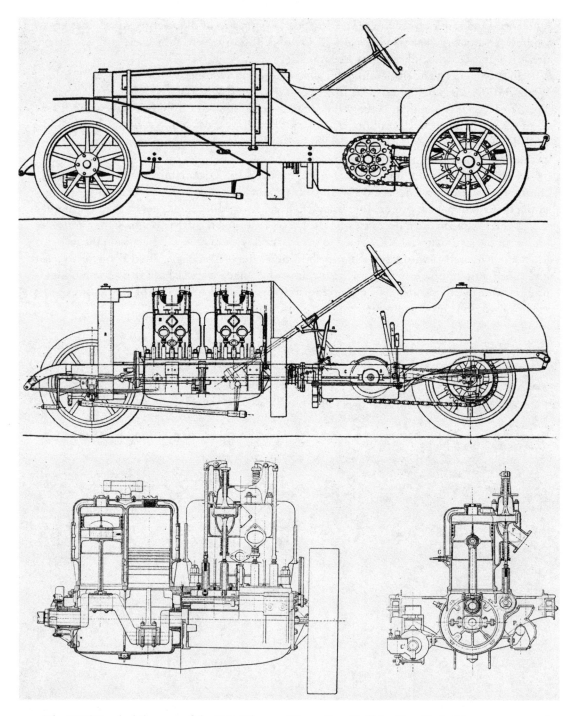

The 1906 Vanderbilt racer of the E.R. Thomas Motor Co., Buffalo, New York. Three cars started in the elimination. Hubert Le Blon finished second, Gustave Caillois sixth, and Montague Roberts ninth. The French drivers were involved in the design, so the Thomas was a mixture of French influences: Hotchkiss and Buchet for the engine, Panhard for the gearbox, and Brasier for the frame. The Thomas displaced 12.7 liters with dimensions of 170 × 140 mm (*La Vie Automobile*, 1906).

The Locomobile which won the 1908 Vanderbilt with George Robertson at the wheel was another car. The cylinder dimensions were 7¼ × 6 inches, and only one low mounted camshaft was used to operate intake valves in the head and exhaust valves in side ports. Wheelbase was 110 inches. In 1907 and 1908 this racer was offered in the Locomobile sales catalogue as "Cup Racer, 90 hp" for $15,000.

After the 1905 Vanderbilt race Hollander & Tangeman sold the 16-liter F.I.A.T. (180 × 160 mm) driven by Lancia to George W. Young, a prominent Wall Street banker, president of the George W. Young & Co. at 59 Cedar Street, and director of the Windsor Trust Co. In January 1906 three 16-liter F.I.A.T.s appeared on Ormond Beach. Young's racer was driven by Harry Fletcher and two Hol-Tan Co. cars by Lancia and Emanuele Cedrino. During the autumn of 1905 Alfred Vanderbilt spent $19,000 for a "250-horse power automobile, the highest-powered car in the world."[45] The special was built in Vanderbilt's garage at 335 West 39th Street by Paul Sartori and the French engineer François Richard. It followed the lines of Bowden's Flying Dutchman. A stretched chain-drive frame was powered by two F.I.A.T. engines in tandem, two 10.5-liter T-heads (150 × 150 mm). Sartori and Richard earned a salary and made heavy commissions on all the material purchased for the racer. The "long gray racing machine was ready for action just before Christmas,"[46] and rushed on a special train to Ormond-Daytona. Vanderbilt sent out invitations to his friends to accompany him to Florida to witness the racing machine traveling at two miles a minute.

December 1906 — New York City. Paul Sartori at the wheel of Alfred Vanderbilt's "250-hp record breaker," powered by two 10.5-liter F.I.A.T. engines in a row (Library of Congress).

"There were some preliminary spurts on the beach, and it was found that four of the eight cylinders refused to act. There was too much condensation in the aluminium pipes connecting the four sets of double cylinders, it was said, and the spring on the clutch was not strong enough to enable it to act just right."[47] Vanderbilt became disgusted and withdrew his entry. The racer was shipped back to the 39th Street garage, dismantled and left for the scrap heap.

Willie Vanderbilt took no active part in racing after the Florida meeting of January 1905. In September 1906, a few weeks before the third Vanderbilt Cup, Robert E. Fulton, the manager of the Mercedes Import Co., proposed a trial in a 16-liter 125-hp Mercedes (185 × 150 mm), one of the French Grand Prix cars. The racer was prepared by Willy Lüttgen in Vanderbilt's garage at Lakeville, adjoining the Cup course on Long Island. Vanderbilt took the wheel for a few laps and commented: "The new car is so much faster than my old Mercedes that there is no comparison when it comes to a question of speed."[48] The Mercedes was bought by George McKesson Brown, who entered it for Lüttgen. McKesson Brown, born in 1878, was involved in a leading wholesale drug business, McKesson & Robbins, and was a half-brother of David Bruce-Brown. During practice for the Vanderbilt Cup in the last week of September 1906, McKesson Brown "contributed the spice of variety to the racing arrangements yesterday by securing quarters in Garden City and sending down the entire crew of his schooner yacht, *Monimia*, to act as a bodyguard in various capacities to

6 October 1906 — third Vanderbilt Cup, Mineola Circuit, Long Island. Camille Jenatzy in a Mercedes leads Arthur Duray's Lorraine-Dietrich (Library of Congress).

Luttgen and his mechanics. The arrival of a yacht crew as an auxiliary to automobile preparations did not attract so much attention among the different motor camps as did the presence of the yacht's Japanese cook. 'That's a fine international combination,' remarked one of the visitors to the quarters, 'a Japanese cook catering to the wants of a German driver, a French mechanic and American assistants.'"[49] Willy "William" Lüttgen had acted as Foxhall Keene's mechanic during the 1903 Bennett Cup in Ireland, and then followed him to New York: "Luttgen has been called by a number of motorists in this city the most skillful driver of Mercedes cars in America. He gained his first automobile experience in the Cannstatt factory in Germany, where the Mercedes cars are made, and just before coming to America in 1903 he was selected to drive a Mercedes car to Russia to be used in the Russian army manoeuvres in Russian Poland, and he drove the car in all the tests to which it was put by the Russian army officers."[50] The German club was represented by two additional 125-hp Mercedes, the racer entered by Robert Graves for Camille Jenatzy, and the racer entered by Foxhall Keene for himself. Graves was "Treasurer of the Robert Graves Company" and "inventor of several electrical devices."[51] Keene's Mercedes was the same that he drove in the 1905 Vanderbilt Cup and which crashed into a telegraph pole near the Albertson turn in the fifth lap. During the winter the car had been thoroughly rebuilt in the Untertürkheim factory. On Sunday, 30 September 1906, Keene did some practicing with his racer at Belmont Park and arrived at his garage at Cedarhurst late in the evening. One cylinder was cracked so that Keene could not start. Louis Wagner in a Darracq led the 1906 Cup all the way:

24 October 1908 — fourth Vanderbilt Cup, Mineola Circuit, Long Island. George Robertson and mechanic Glenn Ethridge looking after the winning Locomobile. Because of a leaky radiator they had to stop at the end of the fifth lap for more water (Library of Congress).

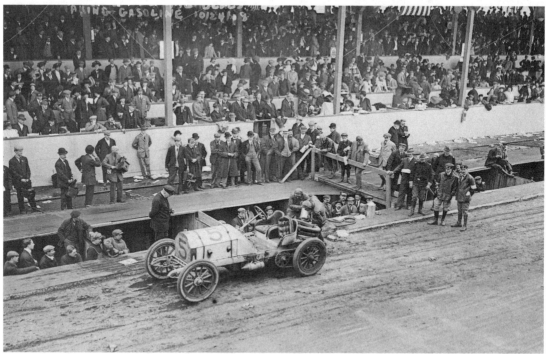

24 October 1908 — fourth Vanderbilt Cup, Mineola Circuit, Long Island. *Top*: Willy Lüttgen and mechanic William Pfeiffer started in Willie Vanderbilt's old 12-liter Mercedes which had been delivered in 1904. *Bottom*: Lüttgen and Pfeiffer refueling the Mercedes. They finished fourth, 30 minutes behind Robertson (Library of Congress).

"He is one of the quietest and most mild-mannered members of the foreign delegation. In this respect Wagner is in marked contrast to the irascible Hémery, who piloted the Darracq car last year."[52] Jenatzy finished fifth, Tracy in the Locomobile took tenth, and Lüttgen eleventh, both of them two laps back. The winning Darracq was sold to Lord Hale of Pembroke. In October 1907 Hale was touring in Western Quebec when the Darracq suddenly burst into flames and was destroyed.

On 26 and 27 June 1906, Elliott Fitch Shepard, a cousin of Willie Vanderbilt, drove a Hotchkiss in the first Grand Prix de l'ACF at Le Mans: "He and his car furnished one of the surprises by finishing fourth the first day, but the wire wheels, breaking on the second day, put the machine out of the race."[53] Shepard was born on 13 October 1876 in New York City, but spent most of his time in Paris. On the early morning of 8 September 1906 he arrived in New York on the French Line steamer *La Lorraine*, in company of his "very rosy-faced"[54] mechanic Charles "Baby" Lehman. Shepard was the only American driver in the French Vanderbilt Cup team: "The fact that he has been selected by the Hotchkiss car manufacturers is a high tribute to his ability and judgment as a driver of a racing car."[55] Two 16-liter Hotchkiss racers (180 × 160 mm), Shepard's bright yellow Le Mans car and a spare, were shipped on *La Bretagne*. Shepard did not finish the Vanderbilt Cup, and sold the Hotchkiss to Edward Thomas: "The big black numeral '6' painted on the yellow hood, designating its order of start in the race, is still there, but even without this mark the merest novice would not mistake that the car was built for racing.... Mr. Thomas, it was understood, intends to use the car as a runabout, and he will take it South with him this season."[56] Two

24 October 1908 — fourth Vanderbilt Cup, Mineola Circuit, Long Island. A misty early morning start for Foxhall Keene, mechanic R. Ahrweiler and the 14-liter Mercedes (Library of Congress).

years later, in the evening of 14 August 1908, Thomas drove his Hotchkiss "into one of the horses attached to a carriage on Ocean Avenue,"[57] Long Branch, New Jersey, and had his right knee fractured. The Grand Prix Hotchkiss reappeared in March 1909 on Ormond Beach with H. Judson Kilpatrick at the wheel: "Kilpatrick has spent some time in repairing the car and thoroughly testing it out, and prior to leaving for Daytona he stated that he was certain the car would make a good showing."[58]

Willie Vanderbilt separated from Virginia in 1909, and divorced in June 1927. A few months later he married Rose Lancanster Warburton. With his steamer *Alva* they traveled around the world to collect rare specimens for Willie's marine museum on Long Island. Willie Vanderbilt died of a heart ailment on 8 January 1944 in New York. "The first race for the Vanderbilt cup was a complete realization of the aims of its distinguished patron, William K. Vanderbilt, who, filled with enthusiasm over a new sport in which he had gained prominence by driving a mile in 39 seconds on Daytona beach, offered a trophy for an international struggle, that motor car road racing, which had met with much favor in France, might be popularized in the United States."[59]

3

Hippodrome Sprints

In October 1904, while the first Vanderbilt Cup was run on Long Island and focused on road racing, the Brighton Beach Automobile Club was incorporated with the objective of promoting track racing, "whereby the Brighton Beach racing track will become the head-quarters of automobile racing in the locality of New York.... An automobile club organized purely for the promotion and improvement of track racing is momething of a novelty, but the existence of such a club simply demonstrates the growing popularity of fast automobiles as sporting attractions."[1] Hippodrome racing stood for specials, for the Ford 999, the Winton Bullet, the Peerless Green Dragon, the Packard Gray Wolf and the F.I.A.T. Cyclone. It stood for engineers and manufacturers who were also drivers, for Henry Ford, Alexander Winton, Windsor White and Percy Owen.

The most famous hippodrome artist was good-natured, cigar-chewing Barney Oldfield, the game's Peter Pan. "I was born near Wauseon, Ohio, on a farm, being christened Berny E. Oldfield. Old records show that the date was June 3, 1878. The house was of logs and the roof sagged under the weight of a husky mortgage. Father was a farmer, and mother was a farmer's daughter and, of course, a farmer's wife. I was a farmer's son."[2] Concerning the cigar he always carried in the southwest corner of his mouth:

> That cigar was always a great advertisement for me; but that wasn't the real reason I carried it there, at least it wasn't the primary reason. Of course, when I found that the newspapers began to take it up and comment on it, explaining all about it, I did all I could to make it more prominent by being sure that whenever I appeared in public, there the cigar was also. But that wasn't the real reason. But I'll let the readers in on the real reason. It is so simple that you'll know it is the real one. Early in the racing business I found that I had a tendency to set my teeth firmly during the excitement of making fast miles, so that when I tried to relax at night my jaws felt as though they had been in a clamp all day. My teeth were as sore as they would have been with a bad toothache. Another thing: with one's teeth set like that, the least little jar is apt to loosen them. But with a soft object between them this jar was much lessened. If I happened to hit the fence or click a hub cap of the driver next to me, instead of my teeth taking an awful jolt the shock was absorbed by the cigar. This isn't hard to understand. The boxers do the same with the rubber buffer in the mouth.[3]

Oldfield's first experience, his entrance to auto racing, dated back to 1902 with the original Ford 999, at a time when "an old rutty horse track was considered plenty good enough."[4] Before, Oldfield was a bicycle rider. In 1894 he borrowed a Royal Flush racing bicycle, started in an 18-mile amateur road race and finished second. In the spring of 1895 the Dauntless Bicycle Co. of Toledo, Ohio, lent him a bike with which he won two silver medals and a gold watch. In 1896 the Stearns factory invited him to race as paid amateur.

Barney Oldfield (Library of Congress).

"Up until 1902 I spent most of my time selling bicycles and racing, and managed to make my income just about equal my expenses, but little more than that."[5] In the spring of 1902 his old bicycle pal Tom Cooper loaned him an old motorcycle racing tandem for an exhibition at Salt Lake City. It was at Salt Lake City that Cooper formed "a sort of partnership with an electrician and mechanic in Detroit — Henry Ford by name — for the purpose of building two racing cars."[6] Cooper wrote Oldfield that he was building two racers "of enormous power"[7] and on their completion expected to tour the country and give exhibition races: "He offered me steady work and a chance to make a chunk of money. The last word was what attracted my attention."[8]

In the late summer of 1902 Oldfield went to Detroit as mechanic and helper for Cooper and Ford: "The cars were in the last stages of completion when I got on the job. One was painted yellow and had the legend 'Tom Cooper' painted on the side of the seat. The other was painted red and had the name 'Henry Ford' painted on the side of its seat.... Our cars were four-cylinder, with a seven-inch bore and a seven-inch stroke, which Ford said made them eighty horse power."[9] The 1080-cubic-inch engine was designed by Harold Wills, a young draughtsman who began to work with Ford in the summer of 1902. The intake valves were automatic, standard at the time. Not mechanically operated, they sucked in their mixture, opening all alone during the intake stroke with the help of the atmospheric pressure, and closing with the help of a light spring. There was no crankcase, the crankshaft revolving in the open, ready to catch any dust or mud: "We had a sight-feed oiler on each of the cylinders. We oiled the motor by squirting oil on it with a long-snouted oil can."[10] There was no transmission, just a clutch, and no worm steering gear, or steering wheel. The steering gear was connected directly to a vertical steering column which was turned by means of handle bars. The cars had no differential and 34 × 4½-inch tires. The radiator was about the biggest thing on the car, as it extended from within three inches off the ground to somewhat above the engine. "The cars had a wooden-block clutch inside the flywheel, thus locking the main drive shaft to the crankshaft. We didn't have any reverse gear in the car, of course, since we had no selective transmission. We had only one forward gear, for the same reason. Further, the cars were innocent of any springs in the rear."[11]

The red Henry Ford special was finished first and taken out to the old Grosse Pointe 1-mile track which had been built in 1895 for horse racing, about 15 miles to the east of Detroit. The big four spit a few times. But this was about all. Was Henry Ford disgusted now? He offered to sell Cooper the whole affair for $800, including the two cars, a drill press, lathe and emery wheel, and the outstanding indebtedness. Cooper and Oldfield hurried around and managed to borrow the money. Oldfield tried to fix the machines up, assisted by Edward "Spider" Huff, an electrician whom Ford had met during his work for the Edison Illuminating Co. In the meantime Cooper got word from two old bicycle-racing friends, Carl Fisher, down at Indianapolis, and Earl Kiser, of Dayton, Ohio, that they were putting on a racing exhibition at Dayton and that Cooper and Huff could get in on 25 percent of the receipts if they would come down. Fisher had begun his dirt track career in 1898 on the second De Dion tricycle imported into America: "Its gears were open and exposed and at the conclusion of each race, Fisher had a polka-dot makeup."[12] The two Ford specials were shipped to Dayton. Huff was to drive and Cooper was going to ride with him to help operate the spark controls and other controls. It was at the Dayton meet that the red Henry Ford car got its famous name: 999. For publicity purposes Carl Fisher had announced it as faster than anything on wheels. He got the name from the world's most beautiful steam locomotive, the *Empire State Express No. 999*. When the yellow Tom Cooper car was rolled out onto the track and cranked, it refused to start. The promoter of the meet began to get nervous and came around to Cooper: "Tom, I don't want to give these people their money back, but I am going to if we can't give them an exhibition. Maybe if this car won't run, the red car will."[13] And really, the red 999 was good for a few laps. The meet wasn't a howling success, but Ford's racing special ran more than it ever had run before.

From Dayton the two specials were shipped to Oldfield's home town, Toledo: "I wasn't a bit proud, and I borrowed a vacant storeroom from a friend of mine and we went to work. With the help of a coppersmith, we redesigned an old intake manifold and the mixing pot which was the ancestor of the present carburetor."[14] The 999 was finished in time for a start in the Grosse Pointe meet on 24 and 25 October 1902. After a test one morning at three o'clock proved that it actually ran, it was shipped to Detroit. The boat arrived there on the early morning of the race. Cooper was tired and went to bed. Oldfield and Huff borrowed a horse:

> Huff and I got the racer off the boat and then looked up Hot-Dog John's lunch wagon. We had known John for quite a while; in fact, we had borrowed a great many sandwiches from John in the days we spent at Detroit. We ate a couple of sandwiches while we were telling him we needed his horse to tow our car out of the congested district. John drove his wagon home and brought his horse back. It was about daylight when we got to the wharf and hitched the nag to 999. We used the horse because we were afraid to run the car in the downtown district. We didn't have any exhaust pipe leading back to the tail of the car. Instead, the exhausts came out on the side of the motor and sounded like the battle of Vimy Ridge when we cranked up. We used John's horse until we got out East Jefferson Avenue a little way. Then we turned the horse loose and cranked up. We arrived at the race track without any further adventure.[15]

Up to this time Oldfield never had driven a car and had ridden in a motor car only twice. On arrival at the Grosse Pointe track, he asked Huff: "Why don't you let me drive the car? I believe I can drive it. I've been round it enough to know how to do it."

"All right," Huff replied. "I don't know what Cooper will say, but he's asleep."[16]

The 999 was entered in the 5-mile Manufacturer's Challenge Cup race, against Alexander Winton in his Winton, Charles Shanks in the Winton Pup, and W.C. Bucknam in a steamer. Oldfield won, driving the first mile in 1 min 7 sec, one of the intermediate miles in 1 min $4\frac{1}{5}$ sec, and 5 miles in 5 min 28 sec:

> The most exciting event at the Grosse Pointe Automobile races was the five-mile contest for the Manufacturers' Challenge Cup, which was run in 5 minutes 28 seconds. Barney Oldfield of Detroit, riding in Tom Cooper's place, beat Charles B. Shanks of Cleveland by a good mile, and was carried from his machine to the judges' stand on the shoulders of admirers, who rushed out on the track by hundreds when he drew up in front of the grand stand. W.C. Bucknam of Geneva, Ohio, with his black steam machine, which looks like a small locomotive, pushed Shanks hard for second place.[17]

On 1 December 1902, still at Grosse Pointe, Oldfield and the 999 "lowered the world's one mile automobile record for a circular track to 1:$01\frac{1}{5}$ sec, and the five-mile record to 5:20."[18]

24 October 1902 — Grosse Pointe track, Detroit, Michigan. Harry Harkness and his 6.5-liter Mercedes won a 5-miler in 6 min $1\frac{3}{5}$ sec. In August 1902, in a 10-miler on the Brighton Beach track, Harkness covered 5 miles in 6 min $2\frac{2}{5}$ sec and 10 miles in 11 min $54\frac{4}{5}$ sec (Library of Congress).

Alexander Winton at the wheel of his 8-cylinder Winton (*Allgemeine Automobil-Zeitung*).

In the spring of 1903, with the help of Billy Hurlburt, an engineer from Detroit, Oldfield designed a new carburetor for the 999, copied from the one-cylinder Cadillac. In addition the intake valves were given a mechanical operation by an overhead camshaft driven via a vertical shaft and bevel gears at the front of the engine: "The bevel gears were of the cheapest kind, being of cast iron. The brackets to hold the gears and the shafting also were made of cast iron. We governed the speed of the engine by moving the camshaft back and forth, the cams being cut on a bevel."[19] The carburetor had a fixed opening; there was no throttle valve. Cooper's yellow car was repainted red and fixed up in just the same way, and from then on it raced under the name "Red Devil." On Memorial Day, 30 May 1903, Oldfield drove the 999 in a match race at the Empire City track at Yonkers, New York, against Charles Wridgeway in a Peerless. The Peerless was one of two cars made for the 1903 Bennett Cup. The match race was to be in three heats. In the presence of 6000 spectators, Oldfield won the first two, which were of five miles, so that the third was not run. In the second mile of the second heat, Oldfield circled the track in 1 min 1⅗ sec. His best time for five miles was 5 min 31 sec.

On 19 and 20 June 1903, Oldfield and the 999 started at the Indianapolis fairgrounds in a meet promoted by Carl Fisher: "Barney Oldfield, of Dayton, Ohio, broke the world's records for automobiles on an elliptical mile track, from one to five miles, today, by driving his machine a mile in 0:59⅗. He clipped 23⅗ seconds off the five-mile record, held by Winton, by going the distance in 5:04⅗. He drove his 'Red Devil,' which was designed by himself."[20] On 4 July nearly 10,000 people gathered at the Driving Park, Columbus, Ohio, "the fastest driving course in the world,"[21] to see Oldfield in the 999. Barney, in a flaming red leather coat, bare-headed and with a partly smoked cigar in his mouth, "swung onto the track at the north gate, rounded the turn, and tore diagonally up the homestretch toward the outside fence, with a rush like a giant skyrocket. A mighty cheer arose from the crowd as he dashed by, just grazing the fence and rounded the first turn, throwing a cloud of dust to the outside of the course and into the faces of the spectators leaning over the fence. He flew down the backstretch at an appalling pace. There was a sudden but smooth drop into the homestretch, and the machine was going at its best speed when it passed under the wire."[22] Oldfield circled the course in 56⅔ sec, did the second mile in 59 seconds flat, equaled the records for three and five miles, and achieved ten miles in 9 min 54⅘ sec. Winton's last feather had been snatched from his cap. Two weeks later, on the half-mile dirt track at Jackson, Michigan, 2000 spectators "were alarmed at the terrific pace attained by the two Ford-Cooper racing machines, one driven by Barney Oldfield, and the other, Tom Cooper's, driven by Harley Cunningham, Mr. Cooper being dangerously ill in a Detroit hospital."[23] Oldfield won two 5-mile match races against his teammate whose performance was very creditable, "he having never before handled a big machine in a race."[24] In addition Oldfield drove a mile in 1 min 16 sec flat, breaking his own half-mile track record made at Marion, Indiana. On Saturday, 25 July 1903, Oldfield and the 999 were back on the 1-mile Empire City track at Yonkers and cut the 1-mile record to 55⅗ sec. The official announcer, through his megaphone, said: "I am requested by Oldfield to announce that he does not use Russian gasoline and would be pleased to meet any driver in the world."[25] In a 5-mile match race Oldfield beat F.A. La Roche in a 40-hp Darracq.

In the late summer of 1903 Oldfield accepted an offer to drive for Alexander Winton. On 9 September 1903, on the Grosse Pointe track, Oldfield and the Winton won a 5-miler and a 10-miler. In another 5-miler Jules Sincholle in a Darracq defeated Oldfield in the Winton Baby by an eighth of a mile. In the 5-mile Manufacturers' Challenge Cup, Oldfield finished third behind a recovered Tom Cooper in his Red Devil and Harry Cunningham in the Packard Grey Wolf. "According to my contract, I was to receive a salary of $2,500 a year, the Winton company was to furnish me with the car and a mechanic to keep the car in repair. The factory also was to pay all transportation expenses. I was to pay my personal expenses and keep all the money I made in race-meet participation. It was a good contract for me. I couldn't see any reason on earth why I couldn't make as much money as the President of the United States. I hated to part company with Tom Cooper, but I did it. He took my 999 and the Red Devil and went back to Henry Ford."[26]

A few days later, on 12 September 1903, the original yellow car, Cooper's Red Devil, ended its career at Milwaukee when it went through the fence and killed its driver, Frank Day. The car, completely wrecked, was shipped to the Ford factory and thrown on the junk pile. Its mate, the 999, was purchased by Lou Hausman in the spring of 1904. Hausman raced it in several match races through the south and then sold it to Bill Pickens, Oldfield's new manager:

> In the fall of 1904, while I was driving at Salt Lake, I met Bill Pickens, who owned the 999 at that time. Bill and I made a deal whereby he was to manage me. He shipped the old car to Los Angeles ahead of us. When we arrived we went down to the freight house to get the car out and found that the charges were $165. We decided that perhaps it would be a good idea to let the railroad company keep the car. So we did it. Later, when it was sold to pay charges, the mayor of Venice, whose name was Dana Burke, bought it and hired Bruno Seibel, a well-known coast race driver, to repair it. One of the cylinders was broken. Seibel repaired it and took it to Pismo Beach to make some records, but failed. He

campaigned it for a while, but it never did run satisfactorily. Bert Fuller drove a while too. But the old car wasn't working any better for Bert, and finally it found its way back into Mayor Burke's barn.[27]

After three years, when little more than the frame with the front and rear axles were left, William Hughson bought it. In the summer of 1903, Hughson, a bicycle-parts salesman of San Francisco, had purchased $5000 worth of Ford Model A's for West Coast distribution and thus had become the world's first Ford dealer.

There were three Winton Bullets which were driven at various times by Alexander Winton, Charles Shanks, Barney Oldfield and Earl Kiser. On 10 October 1901, "six thousand people at the Grosse Pointe track ... saw Alexander Winton of Cleveland drive his heavy racing automobile a mile in 1:12²⁄₅ sec, lowering the previous world's track record for that distance nearly four-fifths of a second."[28] The first Bullet was powered by a 4-cylinder of 6 × 6 inches, 680 cubic inches. It had a wheelbase of 100 inches, and weighed 2000 pounds. The Bullet No. 2 relied on a horizontal straight-eight of 5⅜ × 6 inches, 1090 cubic inches. Wheelbase was 112 inches, weight 2160 pounds. In order to save weight the Winton had no gearbox, just a clutch. Winton started in the 1903 Bennett Cup in Ireland, but the eight-cylinder Bullet was not really suited to the road course and broke down. The Bullet No. 3 or Baby Bullet used a horizontal four with the same dimensions as the eight, 5⅜ × 6 inches. The cylinders were cast iron with aluminum water jackets. The flywheel weighed 125 pounds. The gearbox had two speeds, with direct drive on high, and a reverse. There were no cross braces on the frame, the side bars being connected and held together by the radiator, engine and gearbox. The front axle was dropped and the springs mounted on top, while the rear springs were hung below the axle. The frame was of wood with ⅛-inch steel sheathing; wheelbase was 100 inches; weight was 1450 pounds, tires from Goodrich measured 34 × 4

Louis Mooers at the wheel of his Gordon Bennett Peerless (*Allgemeine Automobil-Zeitung*).

inches. Alexander Winton in his Bullet No. 2, Percy Owen in the Baby Bullet, and Louis Mooers in a Peerless were the American selection, the entries of the Automobile Club of America for the 1903 Bennett Cup in Ireland. At daybreak of 28 August 1903 Charles Shanks, Winton's friend and advertising manager, found Winston's wife drowned in Lake Erie. Winton did not take the wheel of his racers anymore after her death.

On Saturday, 3 October 1903, there were 5000 spectators in the stands of the Empire City track to see Oldfield in the Bullet No. 2, the star of the meet. In a 15-miler Barney started against Laurent Grosso in O.W. Bright's Mercedes Sixty, Harry Cunningham in the Packard Gray Wolf, John Beyer in Norris Mason's 24-hp Renault and Henri Page in a Paris-Madrid Decauville. Page immediately took the lead, but after the first mile Oldfield was in front. A great cloud of yellow dust hung over the track. Page and the Decauville were fast enough to keep second. Grosso dropped out in his fifth mile, coming to a stop just below the judge's stand, on the outside of the track. Oldfield, swooping down the homestretch, found Grosso's Mercedes standing just where he wished to take the outside preparatory to making his usual cross to the inside at the turn. Barney did not hesitate to shake his fist at Grosso as he flew past. Before he came around again, Grosso had ducked for cover. Oldfield finished his seventh mile in 6 min 54⅕ sec, and his eighth in 7 min 52 sec, making new world's records. He drove wide in the stretches, as was his custom, and "skidded dangerously on the turns, with a cigar clenched between his teeth."[29] Oldfield covered the 15-mile distance in 14 min 35 sec, while Page finished a comfortable second in 15 min 7⅕ sec and set a new record for 1800-pound cars. Two days later Oldfield was disqualified because his entry had been made too late. On 20 November 1903, Oldfield made his Los Angeles debut, covering the mile in 55 seconds: "Thousands cheer Barney and Bullet! Barney Oldfield's attempt to commit suicide at Agricultural Park only resulted in a compound fracture of the world's automobile record."[30]

After Earl Kiser, the Toledo agent for the Winton, had an accident when driving the Bullet No. 2 at Cleveland on 15 August 1905, the Winton Co. retired from racing. Barney Oldfield recalled: "Earl Kiser was competing with us at Cleveland, driving my old Winton Bullet. The Bullet wasn't wrongly named, for it was so fast Earl couldn't hold it on the turns, and he was a real driver too. Going around the turn, Earl was a little slow in straightening out, and his car headed for the inside fence. When we got to him he had one leg smashed to a pulp and was otherwise badly injured. He recovered and we staged a couple of benefit races for him, one of which, at Dayton, I remember, netted him something more than $2000."[31]

In the late spring of 1904 Winton and Oldfield had a disagreement. Oldfield jumped to another Cleveland factory, going with Peerless. Louis Mooers, technical director at Peerless since August 1902, remodeled for him the Green Dragon, Mooers's 1903 Bennett racer, painted green with a black front: "I decided to do all of my driving in a suit of green leather to match the color of my car."[32] For track work the engine was mounted lower into the frame, the flywheel clearing the ground by only three inches. It had four separate cylinders, 6 by 6 inches, made of steel ⅗-inch thick with cast iron water jackets, and a T-head, following French Panhard or Clément-Bayard fashion. The Dragon rolled on wooden-spoke wheels covered with disks of tin. On Sunday, 28 August 1904, Oldfield started in St. Louis, in the Louisiana Purchase Exposition Trophy, part of a special World's Fair program. In the dust of Alonzo Webb's Pope-Toledo, Oldfield couldn't see where he was going. The Dragon shot through the fence, went right into the crowd, and hit a tree. Two men were killed and several were injured. Oldfield had three broken ribs. The crash made scrap iron out of the Dragon.

Mooers built a second Green Dragon, this time a real hippodrome special with an underslung frame, a pointed radiator and a seat directly over the rear axle. The engine was cast in one block, 5¾ × 5¾ inches. There was no gearbox, just a clutch. On 22 October 1904, at Brighton Beach, Oldfield finished a poor third in the final heat against Maurice Bernin in Brokaw's Renault and Paul Sartori in Alfred Vanderbilt's big black 90-hp F.I.A.T. The revenge followed a week later, on Saturday, 29 October, on the Empire City track. Sartori won his 10-mile heat in front of Théry in the Brasier. Oldfield beat Bernin's Renault in the second heat and Sartori's F.I.A.T. in the final: "Barney Oldfield regained the position of America's premier automobile driver at the Empire City track which he lost temporarily a week ago in the races at the Brighton Beach track. He more than repaid the confidence of his friends, for not only did he entirely outclass Léon Thery, the last Gordon-Bennett Cup victor, in track racing, but he established a new world's record for ten miles at 9:12⅗."[33]

Whistling Billy was the name of the steamer built by a branch of the White Sewing Machine Co. of Cleveland, Ohio, whose production also included kerosene street lamps, roller skates, phonographs, bicycles, and precision tools. In 1905 Whistling Billy was usually driven by Webb Jay. On 4 July 1905, Jay and the White created a 1-mile record on the Morris Park track, New York, in 48⅘ sec and won the Thomas Cup against Louis Chevrolet driving Major Miller's big 90-hp F.I.A.T. and Walter Christie in his Christie. On 18 August 1905, the racing careers of the White Co., Whistling Billy and Webb Jay ended simultane-

During the summer and the autumn of 1911, Ralph DePalma and his 600-cubic inch Simplex (5¾ × 5¾ inches, T-head) were star performers on many dirt tracks, and broke records at Brighton Beach, Point Breeze and Guttenberg (Library of Congress).

ously when the car went over the bank at Kenilworth track, Buffalo, New York, almost killing Jay. Oldfield recalled: "Jay hit the turn in a cloud of dust, plunged through the fence and came to a stop in a pond. He had nine broken ribs, a badly crushed leg and concussions of the brain. He got well, stayed out of the racing game for a while."[34] Later, Jay confined his racing to speed boats, down at Miami.

The Christie was a front-drive oddity, with a V-4 placed crosswise at front axle level. The Packard Gray Wolf was designed and built by Charles Schmidt in 1902, and driven by him in 1903 and 1904. Schmidt, born in France in 1869, was a graduate of the Arts et Métiers school of Angers and patented the first bevel gear drive in France in 1898. He came to America in 1901 and joined Packard in April 1902. In 1905 he moved to Peerless as chief engineer. The Packard's exterior appearance was quite suggestive of its name. It was a very light car powered by a four-cylinder of $4\frac{3}{16} \times 5$ inches, using the Packard two-unit construction, with the engine and clutch under the hood and the gearset on the rear axle. In 1903 and 1904 Carl Fisher campaigned a Premier, a big air-cooled four, 7×6 inches, with a single overhead camshaft, whereby the whole mechanism worked in the open air. There were no springs at the rear, and a cross spring at the front; wheelbase was 112 inches and track $56\frac{1}{2}$ inches. With the money he made as a bicycle and motorcar agent and his rake-off from dirt track campaigns, Fisher got control of an "instant flame" illuminating system using acetylene and started the Prest-O-Lite Co. at Indianapolis, manufacturing carbide gas headlights.

The hippodrome sprints proved to be a good school for the drivers. Every horse track had its peculiarities, its own straights and turns. To win the race, the drivers were forced to find the perfect line and speed. When similar configurations reappeared as parts of a road race course, the hippodrome drivers just had to remember the right horse track. All early American racing cars were built for hippodrome sprints, for short distance events and one-sided track configurations. They were built to lap horse tracks at constant speeds and they went on strike when driven over hilly and winding roads. Lap times were improved by increasing the output of the engines and optimizing the balance of the car, the weight distribution. Better balance enabled Oldfield and the Peerless to compete with the European Bennett cars on the Empire City track, despite a power deficit. But in order to be successful in road races it was necessary to widen the power band, to add a real gearbox, to refine the chassis, and to produce resistant tires.

4

Auto Import

One of the first New York auto importers was Smith & Mabley, a company formed in 1899 by A.D. Proctor Smith, Carlton Ray Mabley and Lewis MacNamara. In 1901 S & M began importing Daimler Mercedes, within shops located at 513 Seventh Avenue. Then Panhard, for a few months CGV (Charron, Girardot & Voigt), and Isotta-Fraschini were added. The shops moved to East 84th Street. MacNamara was also the agent of the French body builders Audineau & Cie. In 1903 S & M engaged Gustave Edward Franquist to design a range of T-head engines and suitable frames. These S & M cars were advertised as "the American automobile that combines the merits of the Panhard and Mercedes cars."[1] They were assembled by the Smith & Mabley Manufacturing Co. in a factory at 614 East 83rd Street, and were offered under the name Simplex. Production amounted to 73 in 1904, 78 in 1905, and 75 in 1906. The 50/70-hp chassis (5½ × 5½ inches, wheelbase 124 inches) was offered for $6,400, the smaller 30/35-hp (4½ × 5½ inches, wheelbase 106, 111 or 114 inches) for $5,600.

A 50/70-hp engine was prepared for racing, designated "75-hp" and mounted into a shorter frame. The racer was completed by October 1904 so that its owner, Frank Croker, could start in the first Vanderbilt Cup. Frank Croker was aged 26 and was the second son of Richard Croker, the man who stood for Tammany Hall. The 75-hp Simplex (5½ × 5½ inches) was described as "a big formidable looking car,"[2] and had to be lightened by removing the emergency brake to get within the prescribed weight of 2,204 pounds. Croker completed the first two laps at 62 mph but had trouble with his tires during the succeeding three laps and withdrew in lap six. On 9 November 1904, on the Empire City track, Croker and the Simplex established new amateur world's records from 1 up to 12 miles, his fastest mile being a fraction over 57 seconds, and his time for 12 miles 11 min 32⅕ sec. Croker also owned one of the most successful power boats, the *X.P.D.N.C.*, which was launched in August 1904 and combined a Herreshoff hull with a 75-hp S & M Simplex engine. On 21 January 1905, on Ormond Beach, Croker "was driving his racing automobile at the rate of ninety miles per hour when the machine struck a motor cycle ridden by H.F. Stanley and plunged into the sea, turning over two or three times."[3] Mechanic Alexander Raoul died on the spot; Croker died the following day.

Smith was Commodore of the Motor Boat Club of America, which was founded in 1905. In 1904 Smith & Mabley built the power boat *Vingt-et-Un* for Willis S. Kilmer. It was designed by Clinton H. Crane, assembled in the S & M shops, and powered by the 5½× 5½-inch Simplex engine. The *Challenger* for William Gould Brokaw and the *Dixie* for Edward R. Thomas followed in 1905. *Dixie* was powered by a 150-hp Simplex engine in the dimensions of 6¾ × 6½ inches. In December 1905 E.R. Thomas sold *Dixie* to Edward

J. Schroeder. Schroeder's *Dixie II* was the combination of a hull by B.F. Wood of City Island with a V-8 with bore and stroke of 7¼ × 7¼ inches, rated at 200 hp at 800 rpm. The 200-hp engine was built by Clinton Crane's brother, Harry, at the Crane & Whitman Co. in Bayonne, New Jersey. In 1909 the Crane & Whitman engine was mounted into a hull by George Lawley & Sons of South Boston, and it was this hull and engine which, under the name of *Dixie II*, passed to F.K. Burnham in March 1910.

In 1904 the sole agents of the Società Anonima Fabbrica Italiana di Automobili Torino, or F.I.A.T., were Hollander & Tangeman, the company of Elmer Rand "E.R." Hollander and Cornelius Hoagland "C.H." Tangeman. Shops were located at 3–5 West 45th Street. Hollander was born in Boston, Massachusetts, on 16 August 1870. Tangeman was born in Hamilton, Ohio, on 21 August 1878, the son of George P. Tangeman and Cora, née Hoagland. Cora was the eldest daughter of Cornelius Hoagland, a founder of the Royal Baking Powder Co. In 1895, the baking powder's trademark alone was valued at $10 million. Initially, George Tangeman, the father, was also involved in the auto import business. In November 1899 Cornelius Tangeman started in the first run of the ACA, riding a De Dion tricycle. Hollander & Tangeman was renamed Hol-Tan Co. in December 1905, with Harry Fosdick as vice-president and J.B. Hines as head of the repair and supply department, at 244 West 49th Street.

The new company offered its own Hol-Tan cars, which were rebadged Moon Models C and D (4½ × 5 inches, wheelbase 110 and 121 inches). The Moon and the Hol-Tan were designed by the former Peerless engineer Louis Mooers. The first Hol-Tan arrived in New York in the last week of June 1908: "The new Hol-Tan car, which has been delayed for some time beyond the expected date of its appearance in New York, has arrived, and aroused considerable interest. The car is a racy looking gentleman's roadster, painted white and trimmed with black hand buffed leather. It is equipped with a disappearing rumble seat."[4] In 1909 the Hol-Tan Co. was reorganized as Hollander & Josephs, with Joseph S. Josephs as partner. Josephs was the former treasurer of the Auto Import Co., and was also a director of the Fiat Automobile Co. which, in 1909, began to produce a range of Fiat models in a factory on State Boulevard, Poughkeepsie, New York. The Auto Import Co., the New York agent of Rochet-Schneider, had been founded in 1903 at 1786 Broadway, with Benjamin Eichberg as president.

Hollander & Tangeman were very active in power boat racing with the *Fiat I* and *Fiat II*. The boats were designed by Henry R. Sutphen and built by the Electric Launch Co. in Bayonne, New Jersey. In addition to regular starts in the Vanderbilt Cup, Hol-Tan focused on track racing. During the spring of 1905 Hollander and Tangeman had a hippodrome special built in Turin, the Fiat "Junior." The Junior was a special for the "Middleweight Championship, open to cars weighing from 851 to 1,432 pounds."[5] It was described in Turin as "vettura da corsa su pista con motore 24 hp."[6] A pepped-up 7.3-liter stock engine (125 × 150 mm, T-head) as used in the 1907 Targa Florio was mounted without gearbox in a 273-cm frame with track of 135 cm; tires were 870 × 90 mm or 34 × 3½ inches front and rear. The Junior appeared at Morris Park, New Jersey, on 3 and 4 July 1905. E. Parker won a 4.17-mile sprint in 4 min 10⅖ sec, 6 seconds ahead of Guy Vaughn in a 40-hp Decauville: "The veteran Decauville, so long an easy winner among the middleweights, went down to defeat before Hollander & Tangeman's new 24 horse power Fiat track racer. E. Parker, who piloted it, gained 40 yards a lap on Vaughn and won by half a furlong."[7] Emanuele Cedrino drove the Junior on 25 August 1905 on the Cape May seashore track in New Jersey: "The tide was well out and the beach track was in splendid condition. Fully 20,000 persons

Emanuele Cedrino at the wheel of the Fiat Cyclone (Library of Congress).

thronged the Board Walk to watch the racing cars.... The event for middleweight cars from a moving start was won by Hollander and Tangeman's twenty-four-horse-power Fiat Junior, driven by E. Cedrino, in 0:39⅕. C.W. Kelsey was second in an eight-horse-power Maxwell."[8]

Cedrino was a former bicycle rider born in Italy, who came to New York in the autumn of 1904 in company of the Fiat Vanderbilt team. On 24 November 1904, he drove Hollander & Tangeman's 60-hp Fiat. in the Eagle Rock hillclimb, West Orange, New Jersey, taking third in the class for stock cars over $5,000 and fifth in the class for cars weighing from 1,432 to 2,204 pounds. After spending the spring and early summer 1905 in Italy, Cedrino was back on 9 September 1905, on the Readville track, Boston. He took second in the 5-mile final for the "National Championship," behind Barney Oldfield in the Green Dragon. The Junior was competitive until 1907, when on 30 May, on the Empire City track Cedrino established "new records for middleweight cars with his 24 horse power Fiat Junior. The track was not in the best of condition, but Cedrino circled the course in good time for 15 miles and succeeded in making new times for all distances from 10 to 15 miles inclusive. He made 10 miles in 9:47⅕ sec, beating the old time of 10:01 held by Bernin with the light Renault. His time for 15 miles was 14:45."[9] In the same meeting, a young David Bruce-Brown won a "hare-and-hound" race for Oldsmobile roadsters.

The Fiat "Cyclone" was a former 1904 Bennett racer (165 × 165 mm, T-head), with the wheelbase shortened to 265 cm. It was not entered by the Hol-Tan Co. anymore but by the Fiat Automobile Co. The Cyclone turned up on 3 March 1908 when Cedrino took the 100-mile Minneapolis Cup on the Ormond Beach, Florida, in 1 h 50 min 20 sec. He was the only finisher and won after running 60 miles on three tires and a rim, and after spending around 25 minutes in repairs. Three days later, Cedrino and riding mechanic David Bruce-Brown won a 256-miler in 3 h 21 min 27⅖ sec and continued to the 300-

24 October 1908 — fourth Vanderbilt Cup, Mineola Circuit, Long Island. The Renault driven by Lewis Strang and mechanic Lee Anderson was entered by Paul Lacroix (Library of Congress).

mile point, "completing the distance in 3 hours, 53 minutes, 44 seconds, making the phenomenally high average of 77 miles an hour, the fastest speed ever made in a long distance automobile race."[10] The young Brown took the wheel of a 60-hp Fiat and established a new 1-mile record for amateur drivers in 35⅗ sec: "Brown is only 18 years of age, and it is said he left school to come here and compete."[11] On 29 May 1908, Cedrino was killed at the wheel of the Cyclone when practicing on the Pimlico race track at Baltimore, Maryland: "The right front wheel collapsed. The spectators saw the car skid and turn over, three wheels were smashed, and Cedrino was thrown violently against the fence. His death, apparently, was instantaneous. Cedrino's brother, his mechanician was in the car with him, but was little hurt."[12] In the autumn of 1909, Hollander and Tangeman imported the 18-liter Fiat in which Nazzaro had made a 121.64-mph record at Brooklands in June 1908. The Fiat was sold to E.W.C. Arnold, a New York sportsman, and driven by Lewis Strang in the opening meeting of the Atlanta Speedway.

The Darracq importer in 1903 was the F.A. La Roche Co. at 147 West 38th Street and 652–654 Hudson Street. In 1904, the business was renamed American Darracq Company. La Roche started in endurance runs and, in 1903, in several track events and hillclimbs with a 40-hp Paris-Madrid Darracq. His friends quickly found the matching bon mot, the "Empty Gasolene Tancq": "A fellow who drove a Darracq / Went into a race on the tracq. / When he ran out of juice / He exclaimed, 'Oh, the duice; / My chances look horribly blacq!'"[13]

In June 1903, the F.A. La Roche Co. took over the agency for the transmission gears manufactured by R.W. Coffe & Sons, Richmond, Virginia. La Roche also built his own car, the 12-hp La Roche, and in the early months of 1904, mounted a 20-hp La Roche 4-cylinder in a 32-foot power boat designed by Charles Herreshoff. F.A. La Roche died on 4 March 1905, aged 43, after being ill for six weeks. "He was the largest importer of foreign cars during the past year.... His advice on automobile matters was frequently sought, and he was one of the leaders in the movement that led to making the Florida races open to all."[14] The Darracq Motor Car Co. followed the La Roche business and was incorporated on 12 January 1906. It was located at 1989 Broadway, with G.M. MacWilliam as general manager, and went into bankruptcy on 6 March 1908.

The 1905 Vanderbilt winning Darracq was sold to Samuel Stevens, and driven by Guy Vaughan in the 1906 Atlantic City meeting. Louis Wagner used it in the autumn of 1906 for practice on the Mineola Circuit on Long Island. Wagner's 1906 Vanderbilt winning Darracq and other racers were exhibited in January 1907 in the Madison Square Garden Automobile Show. But on 19 January, "early morning visitors were surprised to see the space on the main floor formerly occupied by the Darracq, De Dietrich, Fiat, and Hotchkiss Vanderbilt Cup cars filled with two closed foreign machines, a new Darracq, and a De Dietrich. On the opposite side of the floor the three American racing cars, the Locomobile, the Haynes, and the Thomas, were in their accustomed places."[15] European racers were brought into America under a racing or touring bond which entitled the owner of the car to use it for three months without paying a duty, but only for racing or touring, not for exhibition. Two or three years earlier, any foreign car could be brought in under a three months' bond without the payment of duty. The leading foreign agents found that small dealers were adopting this method to drum up business, bringing in one or two cars for exhibition, securing orders, and sending the cars back after the three months were up. This plan was stopped, so that in 1907 the regular duty had to be paid for any car brought in for exhibition purposes. A 40 percent duty was levied on completed machines. Alco, the American Locomotive Automobile Co. in Providence, Rhode Island, purchased the right to use the original designs of the French Berliet, imported the materials in the rough and had it finished by American machinery.

Sidney B. Bowman entered the auto business in 1900 by handling electric cars and securing the Clément and later, in 1902, the Clément-Bayard agency. In the 1890s Bowman was a bicycle dealer, and he had a cycling school. In 1896 the main store of the Bowman Cycle Co. was at the corner of 8th Avenue and 56th Street. On 27 January 1896, a new store was added in Harlem, on 125 West 125th Street. Bowman had a great head for figures. In February 1896 one of his employees, who was dealing with a customer, turned to the bookkeeper to ask the number of a particular Cleveland cycle. Bowman, who also was busy at the time, called out to the bookkeeper: "Never mind; it's 46,925."[16] Not five minutes later, when a customer came in to ask about his wheel left for repairs, Bowman turned to a boy, and told him to go downstairs and bring up Wheel No. 37,476. In October 1904 Albert Clément's Bayard took second in the Vanderbilt Cup: "The long, rakish, blue car driven by young Clément then rolled slowly up to the tape. Clément's ears and the tip of his nose only were visible from the thick folds of his automobile hood, and the car was emitting a tremendous amount of smoke and gasoline odor, showing that the motor was working to do its best out on the course. It was a typical racing car in appearance. Unlike most of the other cars, which carried two extra tires strapped on behind, Clément only carried one tire."[17] In 1908 Bowman also offered Clément airships, and in 1910 he added a

Marmon and Apperson agency. On 24 November 1911, "a fire last night in the basement of the four-story brick building at 231 West Forty-ninth Street, just off Broadway, occupied by the Sidney B. Bowman Auto Company, destroyed or badly damaged twenty-five automobiles stored there. The loss may amount close to $40,000."[18]

The "Renault Frères Selling Branch for the United States and Cuba" was established in November 1906 at 1,776 Broadway, New York, with Paul Lacroix as general manager. The repair shop and garage was at 214–216 West 65th Street. There were agencies at 1549 Michigan Avenue, Chicago, and at 316–322 Van Ness Avenue, San Francisco. Paul Louis Lacroix was born in Paris on 7 February 1880. In New York, he lived at 275 Central Park West. The Renaults coming from France were fitted with special reinforced axles and springs, with a clearance of more than eight inches. On 7 September 1907 Lacroix and Maurice Bernin won the 24-hour race at Morris Park in a 7.5-liter, 35/45-hp Renault (130 × 140 mm), covering 1079 miles. Bernin was the Renault agent in New Orleans, at 939 Perdido Street. In December 1911 Lacroix formed the Paul Lacroix Automobile Co., with offices at Broadway and 57th Street, and took over the New York agencies of Renault, Peugeot and Mercedes. In 1908, Lacroix was also vice president of Leon Rubay at 1697 Broadway, the importers of Lacoste magnetos, Blériot lamps and Malicet et Blin bearings. Moreover, Lacroix and Bernin were involved in Émile Lamberjack's Franco-American Auto and Supply Co., the Michelin importers.

The De Dietrich agency of R.E. Jarrige, Louis Frankel and Albert Le Maître was located at 4 West 44th Street. In addition the agency had an office and depot in Paris, on the Champs-Élysées, so that New York customers could take delivery in France. The New York Panhard Co. had shops at 1881–1885 Broadway, and was directed by André Massenat and A. de Magnin. Massenat was born on 18 August 1875 in Paris. Mors were imported by the Henry C. Cryder Co. at the corner of 63rd Street and Park Avenue. Julien Bloch was the director of the Motobloc agency at 244 West 69th Street. Bloch was born on 12 June 1870 in Paris. In the autumn of 1906, Edward Gallaher, the Brasier agent and a chairman of the technical committee of the AAA, sold the Grand Prix racer which had finished fourth in the Grand Prix at Le Mans to Harry Payne Whitney, Gertrude Vanderbilt's husband. The Brasier attracted a "great amount of attention"[19] during the New York automobile show. Edward Beach Gallaher was born on 28 April 1873 in Paris. The Gallaher agency was located at 228 West 58th Street. In January 1906, Gallaher also opened an additional office in Paris, 11 Rue d'Alger. Customers touring in Europe could have their mail sent to this Paris office.

Delaunay-Belleville was represented in New York by the Palais de l'Automobile directed by Henry and Albert Neubauer. In Paris, the Neubauer brothers owned the Palais de l'Automobile et du Cycle at 218 Boulevard Pereire. Percy Owen, Inc., at the corner of 62nd Street and Broadway, was the Bianchi importer. Owen was born on 19 January 1875 in Oswego, New York. In 1899 he began to work for Winton, and had opened the first gasoline car salesroom in New York City. Itala was represented by J.M. Lillie at 41 West 65th Street; Züst by Walter F. Sykes. The Westinghouse, which appeared at the 1905 Paris Salon and was built in Le Havre, was imported by Sidney Breese and A.M. Thackara. Breese was the son of James L. Breese, who entered a Christie in the 1905 Vanderbilt. In 1906, Sidney Breese and his friends Frank Lawrence and George Moulton founded the B.L.M. Motor Car & Equipment Co. at 31 Delevan Street, Brooklyn. B.L.M. entered a racer in the 1906 Vanderbilt elimination but the car did not start. In 1907 it was offered as a "Racing Runabout, 85 hp," for $12,000. It was powered by an L-head of 6 × 6 inches on a wheelbase of 106 inches and track of 52 inches; tires were 34 × 3½ inches front and, 34 × 4½ rear. In addition, BLM offered a 24-hp "Gentleman's Roadster."

In 1903, the German Mercedes was imported by the Allen, Halle & Co. at 69 Wall Street. The company was a branch of C.L. Charley's Mercedes Palace in Paris, 70 Champs-Élysées, which had secured the exclusive distribution rights for France and America. In 1906 the Mercedes Import Co. was launched with showrooms at 590 Fifth Avenue and offices at the corner of 42nd Street and Broadway. Robert Fulton was president and Walter Allen one of the directors. The Mercedes Import Co. had a fifteen-year contract with the German factory. On the other hand, Smith & Mabley continued to be Mercedes agents. In May 1906, Edward R. Thomas received from Europe his new 120-hp Mercedes which was ordered through Smith & Mabley and delivered by the Mercedes Import Co. The most expensive foreign car at the New York show in December 1906 was a 6-cylinder Mercedes for $14,500. In January 1907, Mercedes kept the Fifth Avenue show rooms open every night "for visitors at the Garden to come up here later in the evening and inspect the Mercedes 1907 models.... The new seventy-five horse power six-cylinder Mercedes is the latest thing from the German factory on exhibition, and orders for early deliveries have been taken from Commodore Frederick G. Bourne of the New York Yacht Club and John C. King. In addition there are several thirty-five and forty-five horse power four-cylinder cars that have lately come in. Among the visitors during the week who have purchased cars of the open touring type or with limousine bodies are Kinddon Gould, Stephen H. Brown, Dr. Allan Merwin, Cord Meyer, and E.V.W. Rossiter."[20] In the autumn of 1908 Fulton announced two Mercedes racers for the first Grand Prize race at Savannah, to be driven by Salzer and Poege. But the Mercedes racers were not shipped.

Benz exhibited four cars during the last days of December 1907, at the Importers' Automobile Salon at Madison Square Garden: an 18-hp chassis (80 × 120 mm, wheelbase 124 inches, price $7,500); a 40-hp touring car (120 × 135 mm, wheelbase 126 inches); a 50-hp touring car (130 × 140 mm, wheelbase 126 inches); and a 60/70-hp runabout (145 × 140 mm, wheelbase 124 inches). Two months later, on 4 March 1908, Louis Bergdoll drove his 8-liter Benz (140 × 130 mm, wheelbase 300 cm), a former 1907 Kaiserpreis car, in two races on Ormond Beach. The Benz weighed 2,700 pounds, or 300 over the limit, causing discussions before it was allowed to start. Bergdoll won a 150-miler for stock chassis in 2 h 40 min 33 sec, and a 125-miler for amateur drivers in 1 h 53 min 30⅔ sec. In the 125-miler, Bergdoll was the only finisher. Samuel Stevens drove the Fiat Cyclone and was in the lead by nearly five minutes but was forced to withdraw because of a broken rocker arm. The third starter, a small Christie entered by William Gould Brokaw and driven by R.G. Kelsey, went out after 50 miles. Bergdoll was up to start in the 180-mile Savannah stock car race by the end of March 1908, but the Benz was damaged during the shipment from Ormond to Savannah and could not be repaired in time. In April 1908, Bergdoll bought a Grand Prix Benz: "Louis J. Bergdoll of Philadelphia has purchased the Benz entry in the Grand Prix, and expects to bring the car to this country soon after the big race in France and enter it in the Vanderbilt Cup race. He will also try to drive it 100 miles within an hour at Ormond Beach next January."[21] On 24 April 1908 Bergdoll and his 8-liter Kaiserpreis Benz started in the Briarcliff stock car race. They completed seven of eight laps and were flagged.

The Bergdolls were a prominent Philadelphia family who operated the Louis Bergdoll & Sons Brewing Co., which had been founded in 1849 by Ludwig Bergdoll, a German immigrant. The brewery was located in a magnificent plant at 29th and Parrish streets, designed by Otto Wolf. In 1910 Louis Bergdoll founded the Louis J. Bergdoll Motor Co.

24 October 1908 — fourth Vanderbilt Cup, Mineola Circuit, Long Island. The Isotta-Fraschini driven by Herb Lytle and mechanic William Fehr was entered by Clifford V. Brokaw. The Isotta finished second behind Robertson's Locomobile (Library of Congress).

with a factory in downtown Philadelphia at 16th and Callowhill streets, a seven-story reinforced concrete and steel building with over 100,000 square feet of floor space. The Bergdoll 30 was offered as "Louis J." runabout or Toy Tonneau at $1600, or as a limousine at $2500, powered by a monobloc F-head four of 4 × 4½ inches, its crankshaft in two ball bearings, with a wheelbase of 115 inches. It was an assembled car: "Westinghouse-made motor, Driggs-Seaburg frame, Schwarz artillery wheels, William and Harvey Rowland springs, Standard Roller Bearing Co. axles, Livingston radiator, Warner Gear Co. transmission, Atwater Kent ignition system, Bosch magneto, R.I.V. bearings, Continental demountable rims and tires."[22] In December 1909, Louis Bergdoll "entered the aeroplane world in a manner that promises to make him one of the most conspicuous figures in the country in the new field of sport. He has purchased a Blériot XI monoplane, which is the exact duplicate of the air craft with which the famous inventor whose name it bears set the ears of the world ringing with his succesful flight across the English Channel.... Mr. Bergdoll purchased the monoplane from Rodman Wanamaker last week and it was delivered to him and set up in his private garage."[23] Louis' two younger brothers were Erwin, born in 1881, and Grover, born in 1883. There was also a sister, Elizabeth, who created a scandal in May 1909 when she married the family chauffeur, Albert Hall, who had been "engaged by the Bergdoll family about a year ago. A few weeks ago it was noticed that a fondness seemed to exist between the two young persons and the girl's brother had Hall discharged. The young woman took the chauffeur's dismissal calmly, but today's events showed that she had a plan of her own."[24]

Louis Bergdoll and his Blériot XI monoplane (Library of Congress).

On 26 November 1908, a team of three Benzes managed by Carl Neumaier started in the Grand Prize of the Automobile Club of America at Savannah, driven by Hémery, Hanriot and Erle. Hémery took second behind Wagner in a Fiat, with Nazzaro in another Fiat third, and Hanriot fourth, while Erle left the road and was pinned beneath his Benz when it over-turned. On 13 December 1908, *The New York Times* announced that "a Benz agency will be opened in this city shortly. It will be in charge of Jesse Froelich, Managing Director and Treasurer of the Times Square Automobile Co. The Benz car, in which Hemery drove second in the recent Grand Prize race at Savannah, will be placed on exhibition at 1599 Broadway and retained here until the Palace Motor Show, when it will be a feature of the Benz exhibit."[25] Later, shops were added at 244, 246, and 248 West 54th Street. In December 1909, Froehlich also secured the American agency for Gaggenau trucks. Froehlich's older business, the Times Square Automobile Co., was opened in 1904 with Morris Froehlich as president, Jesse Froehlich as treasurer and secretary, and Oscar Weingarten as vice president. In 1912, the Times Square Automobile Co. was one of the largest dealers of new and used cars. It was located at 1597–1599–1601 Broadway and 215–217 West 48th Street. In November 1910 the company moved to 731–733 7th Avenue, in a building formerly occupied by Studebaker Brothers, and later to 1708–1718 Broadway and 54th Street, with a showroom of 50 cars.

The Benz Auto Import Co. was quickly out of stock, and in February 1909 "Jesse Froehlich of the Times Square Automobile Company and Managing Director of the Benz Auto Import Company of America sailed for Europe on Wednesday to visit the Benz Motor Works at Mannheim, Germany, and to arrange for an immediate shipment of a second delivery of Benz cars."[26] Meanwhile a Grand Prix Benz was breaking records at Ormond-Daytona, a 12-liter (155 × 160 mm, OHV-head): "Robertson is going to drive the big Benz racer which Hemery drove to second place in the Grand Prize race last Thanksgiving Day. The car is one of the most powerful which will be seen on the Florida beach and Robertson is confident that he will smash some records with it. In certain events, however, the winner of the Vanderbilt will not hold the wheel of the big racer. In his place will be David Bruce-Brown, the wealthy young amateur of this city, who agreed to drive the car as soon as it was purchased last week by Hugh McIntosh, the Australian sportsman, now on a visit here."[27] On 23 March 1909, Brown covered a flying mile in 33 seconds flat. Next day he won a 10-mile free-for-all in 5 min $14\frac{2}{5}$ sec, 15 seconds ahead of Ralph DePalma in the Fiat Cyclone. On the same day, George Robertson, who drove his first race at the Empire City track in 1903, took the wheel of the 12-liter Benz in the 5-mile invitation race and won in "the phenomenal time of 2:$45\frac{1}{5}$, breaking the world's record for gasoline cars, hitherto held by Lancia with a 100 horse power Fiat, of 2:$54\frac{3}{5}$, made in 1906."[28] Just one month later Robertson was engaged by the Harry S. Houpt Company "to take charge of a newly organized racing department."[29]

On 26 April 1909 "New York's second annual automobile carnival was opened ... with a hill-climbing contest up the steep ascent to old Fort George. There were fully 15,000 persons present at the opening of the carnival, and hundreds of motor cars were parked on the plateau atop the big knoll."[30] Froehlich entered the 12-liter Benz for David Bruce-Brown who promptly won the free-for-all: "The big Benz car, with a rattle as of musketry coming from its exhausts, sped up the incline like a huge skyrocket in the fast time of 0:$28\frac{4}{5}$. H. Walter Webb, in a 120 horse power Panhard, made the next best time, negotiating the hill in 0:$31\frac{3}{5}$."[31] The next day, on Hillside Avenue, Jamaica, Long Island, Brown and the Benz took the honors of the day by spinning off a flying mile in $35\frac{2}{5}$ sec, equaling 101.4 miles an hour, and 2 miles in 1 min $16\frac{2}{5}$ sec. The 1908 records had been held by Kilpatrick in the 1906 Grand Prix Hotchkiss owned by Harry Levy in 38 sec and 1 min $19\frac{2}{5}$ sec. On 27 May 1909 Brown and the Benz won the Shingle Hill climb, held near New Haven by the Yale Auto Club, in $51\frac{1}{5}$ sec, and on 31 May the Wilkes-Barre hill-climb in 1 min $31\frac{3}{5}$ sec. On 11 June, in a trial on the Dead Horse hill near Worcester, Massachusetts, Brown smashed the Benz and could not start.

On 8 August 1909 it was announced that "the famous Benz racer, which Hemery drove so nearly to victory at Savannah last fall and with which David Bruce-Brown has been shattering hillclimb records all over the country, became the property last week of Barney Oldfield, who has raced more miles on circular tracks than possibly any other driver in the world. Oldfield will use the Benz to supplement his stable of National racing cars."[32] Oldfield had driven the Benz for the first time on 6 August on the Fort Erie track at Buffalo, New York, where he was defeated by Walter Christie. The "new Indianapolis motor speedway"[33] was opened on 19 August 1909. Oldfield broke the circular track record for a mile in $43\frac{1}{5}$ sec. In the same meeting Bob Burman in a Buick won the 250-miler for the Prest-o-Lite trophy for 301 to 450-inch stock cars. Two days later, in a 25-mile free-for-all, Oldfield shattered the world's track records for 5, 10, 15, 20 and 25 miles: "Oldfield shot the car around the track like a rocket, and the spectators rose to their feet as the machine flashed by the grand and field stands in world's record time."[34] On 7 September, a series of mile straightaway speed trials were held over a section of the Merrimack Valley circuit at Lowell, Massachusetts, as a filler between the stock car races. Oldfield covered the flying mile in $39\frac{9}{10}$ sec, and the standing mile in $51\frac{1}{5}$ sec. At the same time, Froehlich in "a big Benz machine"[35] made a short trip through the New England states.

On 5 October 1909 William H. "Bill" Pickens resigned his position as manager of the Buick racing team and switched over to Froehlich's Benz Auto Import Co. Lewis Strang left Buick at the same time, to drive for the Isotta Import Company. Pickens and Froehlich sailed for Europe in November to visit the Olympia Show in London and the Mannheim factory and "to look after several racing cars now in the course of construction in the big German factory for use in America. One of the cars is the 200-horse power machine, to be used by Barney Oldfield."[36] Froehlich was accompanied by his wife Alma. Cornelius Tangeman was on the same ship and made a trip to Turin to conclude arrangements with Vincenzo Lancia. On 8 November 1909, at Brooklands, Victor Hémery and the 200-hp Benz covered the flying half mile in 14.082 sec, the kilometer in 17.761 sec, the standing half mile in 25.566 sec, the kilometer in 31.326 sec and the mile in 41.268 sec. On 21 November, at New Orleans, "Barney Oldfield, in a 200-horse-power Benz, broke the local track record for one mile at the Fair Ground course, when he made the distance in 0:54."[37] Was it promotion à la Pickens? Oldfield was still at the wheel of his 12-liter Benz. Oldfield and Pickens had buried the hatchet: In September 1907, when he was manager for Walter Christie, Pickens got into a fistfight with Oldfield. He was put out of Pittsburgh's fashionable Fort Pitt Hotel, and would have been arrested had it not been for influential friends who were with him. Next day, both Oldfield and Pickens were carrying around bruised faces. On 8 December 1909, at Dallas, Oldfield, "with his face wrapped in woolen bandages and wearing heavy fur gloves and fur overcoat,"[38] and the 12-liter Benz broke the 50-mile circular track record in 47 min 18 sec. "Oldfield's drive was spectacular. The track was frozen in places, and the radiator of his car was filled with alcohol as the only preventive against freezing. At the finish of the drive Oldfield's hands had to be pulled loose from the steering wheel by his assistant, having been affected by the intense cold at so high a speed."[39] On 25 December, Oldfield drove a match race against "Dutchman" Ben Kerscher in a 1906 Grand Prix Darracq, on the Ascot Park track, Los Angeles. Oldfield lowered the track record for a mile to 52⅗ sec. On 9 January 1910, still at Ascot Park, Oldfield took records for 2, 3, 4 and 5 miles, the 5-mile time being 4 min 24⅕ sec. In November 1909, the press had reported that Hémery's 21-liter record car was imported on the *Majestic*. By the end of January 1910, Oldfield gave back his 12-liter Benz to Froehlich and added $6,000 for the 21-liter 200-hp record racer which became the *Lightning* and later the *Blitzen*.[40]

On Monday, 4 July 1910, at Reno, Nevada, the former heavyweight champion Jim Jeffries came out of retirement to meet Jack Johnson. It soon became apparent that a six-year layoff had robbed 35-year-old Jeffries of his world class ability. In round 14 Johnson sent Jeffries to the canvas three times, becoming "the undisputed heavyweight champion of the world."[41] Johnson loved fast horses, fast cars, and fast women, not necessarily in that order. In any case he bought a fast and expensive French Renault and promptly announced that he was just as invincible on the track as he was in the rosined ring. He sent Oldfield a challenge. Barney accepted. But Johnson's license had been withdrawn and the match lacked AAA sanction. On 11 October 1910 the AAA issued a caution against Oldfield. Of course Barney did not care a straw about it. Four days later he took the wheel of his 21-liter Benz at Readville, Massachusetts, against the orders of the referee. The consequence followed on 19 October. Oldfield was disqualified as an entrant, driver and owner. Even Bill Pickens was brought into the deal by the accusation that he had issued statements "injurious to the well-fare of the sport."[42]

In spite of everything Oldfield kept his word. The match against Johnson, a series of three 5-mile races, was to be run on the old Sheepshead Bay track, on 20 October, at 2:30

in the afternoon. On 16 October Johnson arrived in town. Because of rainy weather the match was postponed to 25 October. Only two heats were run, Oldfield in a Knox Six and Johnson in a 90-hp Thomas Flyer. Oldfield left Johnson far behind and won easily. A few days later Oldfield tried to enforce his entry for the upcoming Atlanta races in court. He lost. The Los Angeles meet in November was held up until he left the paddock. He was suspended until 30 April 1912. Starter Fred Wagner explained:

> Barney Oldfield's confidence is another variety of egotism. He is the most supremely confident driver I ever have known. He has absolute faith in his ability to win. I don't mean that he is swell-headed. He is anything but that. If Oldfield wrote the books on the races in which he is entered, he would make himself an odds-on favorite although his car might not be as fast or as dependable as those of his competitors. Back in the golden days when Barney was making a reputation for himself he ran away from challengers who apparently were just as expert and experienced as he and had the advantage in cars. I remember when the Renault makers imported a foreign star to clean Barney up and arranged for a series of match races at the Empire City track. Barney swept the card. He was unbeatable and I believe his confidence was a potent factor in his success.[43]

Fred Wagner, the sahib of all starters, was born on 13 June 1869 in Covington, Kentucky, and was the former Eastern reporter of *Motor Age*.

In the spring of 1911, Oldfield sold his 21-liter Benz to Ernie Moross, Bob Burman's manager, for $13,500. The Moross Amusement Co. also took Oldfield's Darracq, Prince Henry Benz and Knox, after paying the fine of $1,000 inflicted upon Oldfield's cars by the

2 and 4 September 1911 — Labor Day meeting, Brighton Beach, Brooklyn, New York. From left to right: Bob Burman, Louis Disbrow, Jack Tower and Arthur Greiner, in front of Burman's 15-liter Grand Prix Benz (Library of Congress).

AAA. Oldfield said a few years later, "There was a wild story circulated at the time that the A.A.A. had bought the cars for $50,000 to get me to quit my racing activities. This was bunk."[44] By the end of March Burman took the wheel of the Blitzen for the first time, in the 1-mile record trials during the speed week at Pablo Beach, Jacksonville, Florida. Burman's best time was 30.27 seconds, good for a $1000 cash prize, but no new record although the 21-liter powerplant (185 × 200 mm) had been tuned up during the 1910 season and delivered 225 hp at 1575 rpm now. In April, at Daytona, Burman and the Blitzen traveled "with the most spectacular burst of speed that has ever been witnessed on historic Daytona Beach,"[45] covering the flying kilometer in 15.88 seconds meaning 141.42 miles per hour, the mile in 25.40 or 141.73 miles per hour, and 2 miles in 51.28. Moross commented: "I intend to take my string of racing cars abroad, and expect to enter Burman at the Brooklands track in England and show the foreigners some real speed. I will pit Burman against the world's greatest drivers and prove his supremacy."[46] Fred Wagner recalled Burman's record attempt:

> Beyond all doubt, Bob Burman is the most fearless. He'll take more chances than any other driver I ever knew, not excepting the foreign wild men. Some people stamp the stories of Burman's daring as press agent buncombe, but I am not one of these skeptics for I saw Bob drive a mile at a speed of 141.73 miles an hour on the Ormond beach. In that record-breaking trial the wind pressure was so great that the glass lenses of his goggles were pushed out of the steel rims and the hitting of the tiniest pebble drove Burman through the cushion of the seat. After traveling at such a rate of speed without losing his life or suffering serious injuries, any other driver except Burman would have been satisfied. He was not. He begged me to allow him to make an attempt on the 2-mile record 5 minutes

April 1911 — Daytona Beach, Florida. Bob Burman and the Blitzen Benz covered the flying mile in 25.40 sec, meaning 141.73 miles per hour (Library of Congress).

after finishing the 1-mile drive. He had lost more than a foot of the tread off one of his rear tires. When I told him it would be certain suicide if he made a trial with such a tire he laughed at me. He cursed me when I ordered him off the course.[47]

On 27 April 1912 Jesse Froehlich left the Benz Auto Import Co., which had been sold to Benz & Cie., Mannheim: "Mr. Froehlich has decided to sever his connection with the Benz Auto Import Company of America after representing that company in this city for more than three years. Mr. Froehlich will be connected with an automobile company devoted to buying bankrupt stocks, surplus materials, and second-hand automobiles. He will also represent a Western tire company."[48] During the twenties, Jesse Froehlich was president of the Times Square Auto Supply Co. at 303 4th Avenue. He died on 13 May 1939. Bill Pickens managed to bring the French tennis star Suzanne Lenglen to America in 1926. In June 1934, Pickens suffered the loss of his left leg from blood poisoning after stepping on a nail at the Mines Field stock car race. Pickens died on 20 July 1934 in Los Angeles. Barney Oldfield continued to take the wheel of all possible racing cars until 1917. In February 1918, with his partners R.R. Colby and Frank Chance, he purchased the Forsythe Tire Service Co. in Los Angeles. The business was renamed Oldfield Tire Co., and it made a specialty of selling Firestone tires. Oldfield was married four times: in 1905 to Beatrice Oatis, in January 1907 to Rebecca "Bess" Gooby Holland, in December 1925 to Hulda Braden, and to Bess again in December 1945. Barney and Hulda adopted a daughter, Elizabeth. Barney Oldfield died of a heart attack on 4 October 1946, at his home, 523 N. Rexford Drive, Beverly Hills: "The death of Barney Oldfield brings to an end one of the truly colorful careers interwoven with the revolution in living which came to this country with the automobile age."[49]

5

French Scenery

The winner of the first Bennett Cup, Fernand Charron, intended to drive an 8-liter straight-eight CGV in the 1903 Paris-Madrid race. The cylinders (100 × 130 mm) were made of steel with copper jackets. The engine was claimed to develop 52 hp at 800 rpm. Power was transmitted by a two-speed planetary gear. But the car was not ready. Charron was forced to start in his last great race at the wheel of a 15-hp production car. Henceforth Charron centered his efforts on the production of his CGV company, "Automobiles Charron, Girardot et Voigt," which was incorporated in 1902, at 7 Rue Ampère, Puteaux. CGV produced luxury cars, some of them with magnificent double phaeton bodies made by the great

Caricatures of Fernand Charron with Leopold of Belgium (left); Fernand Gabriel (top); and Henri Brasier, René de Knyff, C.L. Charley, Henry Fournier, Jeanne Clément with her father Adolphe Clément, and Alexandre Darracq (*Allgemeine Automobil-Zeitung*).

carrossiers Georges Kellner or Albert and Louis Gustave Mühlbacher. Some CGVs had the lamps connected to the steering gear so that they turned in the direction of the front wheels. On 20 April 1907, at Neuilly-sur-Seine, Fernand Charron married Jeanne Clément, Adolphe Clément's only daughter, "la fille du grand industriel."[1] Adolphe Clément, who had a big interest in the original CGV company, presented the bridegroom with his entire CGV holding. Madame Camille du Gast, the famous *valkyrie de la mécanique* and ubiquitous *chauffeuse militante*, was in the limelight during the 1905 Monaco boat meeting with her *Turquoise*, the hull being supplied by Pitre & Cie. and the engine by CGV.

Charron's partner Léonce Girardot started in every Bennett race. Girardot and Étienne Giraud were announced on CGV racers for the 1905 French Bennett elimination through the Auvergne. Giraud did not appear but Girardot started. It was to be his last race. He drove a 12.8-liter CGV racer, a T-head with separated steel cylinders in the dimensions of 160 × 160 mm. The wheelbase was short in comparison to the competitors, 250 cm, track 135 cm, tires 820 × 120 front, 880 × 120 rear. During the third lap Girardot's CGV turned over after the two front tires burst on the winding descent towards Clermont-Ferrand. Girardot was carried off to the hospital with his legs badly injured. A few weeks later, at the Circuit des Ardennes, Girardot hobbled up to the starting point on crutches to see his CGV driven by Behr rolling out after a few yards because of a broken transmission. After CGV had been transformed into Charron Ltd., Girardot secured the sole selling right in France for the British Daimler "Sans Soupapes" engine, the Silent Knight sleeve valve engine, with immediate success. In May 1911, Charron Ltd. bought the patents of the valveless Henriod engine, and in May 1912, Girardot & Cie. took over the Paris agency of the Henriod engined Darracq.

In 1896, Henry Fournier took a De Dion tricycle to America, giving a number of exhibitions around New York and later in California. A San Francisco sportsman offered to buy the tricycle for $2,000. Instead of paying in notes, he handed over the $2,000 in coin of the realm, mostly 10-dollar pieces. Unable to place such a quantity of metal in his pockets, Fournier was obliged to walk with it in his hat. The next day the new owner of the tricycle became so afraid of his acquisition that he had the engine dismounted and placed in a boat. In May 1903, Fournier drove a Mors in the race towards Madrid:

> I had a fair start in spite of the immense crowd of spectators that lined up the Avenue de Saint Cyr at Versailles. The few battalions of soldiers that were posted along the road partially succeeded in clearing a passage, but ten kilometers from Versailles the danger from silly spectators, who pushed each other forward from the roadside, became greater. I continued under great difficulties for 25 kilometers further when a sudden jolt occasioned by blocks of pavement into which I ran in trying to avoid killing a group of spectators, knocked my oil box into pieces. In spite of this I continued, expecting to replace it at the first stop. However, I had another accident before arriving at Chartres. My magneto broke and the car came to a standstill. To repair it on the road was impossible and I was obliged to surrender all hopes of continuing the race. Considering the frightful number of accidents, I don't regret that my race came to a quick conclusion.[2]

The ACF claimed that nothing had been left undone to assure the security of the public. Fernand Gabriel, the winner of the race as far as Bordeaux, did not think so and

Opposite: Belle Époque beauty Camille du Gast drove a Panhard in the 1901 Paris-Berlin, a De Dietrich in the 1903 Paris-Madrid, and her CGV powered *Turquoise* in the 1905 Monaco boat meeting (Library of Congress).

"vigorously condemned the reckless imprudence of the spectators along the route, and the lack of official precautions to restrain them.... When they were warned by experienced persons that the approaching machines were speeding like express trains they laughed incredulously and only dashed aside in terror as the vehicles rushed past."[3]

Just after the 1901 race towards Berlin, the alarming behavior of some sportsmen was described in the "Reflections of a Motor Racer"[4]:

> Two A.M.! Time to get up, if I' m to be ready for the great Paris-Berlin race at 3.30. Feel very cold and sleepy. Pitch dark morning, of course. Moon been down hours. Must get into clothes, I suppose. Oilskins feel very clammy and heavy at this hour in the morning. Button up tunic and tuck trousers into top boots. Put on peaked cap and fasten veil tightly over face, after covering eyes with iron goggles and protecting mouth with respirator. Wind woollen muffler round neck and case hands in thick dogskin gloves with gauntlets. Look like Nansen going to discover North Pole. Or Tweedledum about to join battle with Tweedledee. Effect on the whole unpleasing.
>
> Great crowds to see us off. Nearly ran over several in effort to reach starting post. Very careless. People ought not to get in the way on these occasions. Noise appalling. Cheers, snatches of *Marseillaise,* snorts of motors, curses of competitors, cries of bystanders knocked down by enthusiastic *chauffeurs,* shouts of *gendarmes* clearing the course. Spectators seem to find glare of acetylene lamps very confusing. Several more or less injured through not getting out of the way sufficiently quickly. At last the flag drops. We are off.
>
> Pull lever, and car leaps forward. Wonder if wiser to start full speed or begin gently? Decide on latter. Result, nearly blinded by dust of competitors in front, and suffocated by stench of petroleum. Fellow just ahead particularly objectionable in both respects. Decide to quicken up and pass him. Can't see a foot before me on account of his dust. Suddenly run into the stern of his car. Apologise. Can't I look where I'm going? Of course I can. Not my fault at all. Surly fellow! Proceed to go slower. Fellow behind runs into *me.* Confound him, can't he be more careful? Says he couldn't see me. Idiot!
>
> Put on speed again. Car in front just visible through haze of dust. Hear distant crash. Confound the man, he's run into a dray! Just time to swerve to the right, and miss wreck of his car by an inch. Clumsy fellow, blocking my road in that way. At last clear space before me. Go up with a rush. Wind whistles past rny ears. Glorious! What's that? Run over an old woman? Very annoying. Almost upset my car. Awkward for next chap. Body right across the road. Spill him to a certainty.
>
> Morning growing light, but. dust thicker than ever. Scarcely see a yard in front of me. Must trust to luck. Fortunately road pretty straight here. Just missed big tree. Collided with small one. Knocked it over like a ninepin. Lucky I was going so fast. Car uninjured, but tree done for. Man in car just ahead very much in my way. Shout to him to get out of the light. Turns round and grins malevolently. Movement fatal. He forgets to steer and goes crash into ditch. What's that he says? Help? Silly fellow, does he think I can stop at this pace? Curious how ignorant people seem to be of simplest mechanical laws.
>
> Magnificent piece of road here. Nothing in sight but a dog. Run over it. Put on full speed. Seventy miles an hour at least. Can no longer see or hear anything. Trees, villages, fields rush by in lightning succession. Fancy a child is knocked down. Am vaguely conscious of upsetting old gentleman in gig. Seem to notice a bump on part of car, indicating that it has passed over prostrate fellow citizen, but not sure. Sensation most exhilarating. Immolate another child. Really most careless of parents leaving children loose like this in the country. Some day there will be an accident. Might have punctured my tyre.
>
> Chap in front of me comes in sight. Catching him up fast. He puts on full speed. Still gaining on him. Pace terrific. Sudden flash just ahead, followed by loud explosion. Fellow's

Opposite: **Henry Farman and his wife in their *aéroplane* (Library of Congress).**

benzine reservoir blown up apparently. Pass over smoking ruins of car. Driver nowhere to be seen. Probably lying in neighbouring field. That puts him out of the race.

Eh? What's that? Aix in sight? Gallop, says Browning. Better not, perhaps. Road ahead crowded with spectators. Great temptation to charge through them in style. Mightn't be popular, though. Slow down to fifteen miles an hour, and enter town amid frantic cheering. Most interesting. Wonderfully few casualties. Dismount at door of hotel dusty but triumphant.

Henry Fournier and his partner Édouard Rabourdin were directors of the Société Anonyme Paris-Automobile at 48 and 50 Rue d'Anjou. Georges-Marie Haardt, an Italian born in Naples who was to be behind Citroën's *croisière* expeditions in the 1920s, spent a few years as Fournier's assistant. Paris-Automobile was initially a Mors agency which occasionally sold a Panhard, Mercedes, Germain or Napier. In 1904 a Hotchkiss agency was added, and in October 1905 the French representation of Itala, Fabbrica di Automobili. At the same time in the Autumn of 1905, Pierre and Georges de Caters were named *administrateurs* and replaced Messieurs Gautier, Civet and Dertelle. Fournier was involved in the design, the development and the *mise au point* of the Mors, Hotchkiss and Itala racers. In April 1905, while testing his power boat *Hotchkiss* on the Seine near Maisons-Laffitte, he was seriously injured when he had his left ankle jammed by the drive shaft. In 1910 he changed fronts and took up a remunerative position in the champagne trade. His brother Achille drove a Hotchkiss in the 1904 French Bennett elimination. A second brother, Maurice, was killed in an accident in the 1911 Grand Prix de France at Le Mans.

Henry Léon Tart was Berliet agent in Paris, at 25 Rue Duret. Tart was born in Orléans on 28 May 1868. Georges Robert Teste was born on 30 March 1874 in Pacy-sur-Eure. Once a foreman at De Dion, in 1908 he was head of Teste & Cie., a Panhard, Mercedes and Renault agency at 144 Rue de Courcelles. Maurice Fabry was Itala agent in London. Edmund T. Stead, who drove a Brasier in the 1904 and in the 1905 French Bennett eliminations, ran a car dealership in the London Radipole Road. René Loysel was director at L'Intermédiaire, "voitures de toutes marques," 136 Avenue Malakoff. The Farman brothers, Henry and Maurice, sold Panhard, Renault and Delaunay-Belleville at 22 Avenue de la Grande Armée. Henri Rougier and his partner E. Pérignon had a shop at 13 Rue Descombes where they sold Isotta-Fraschini and Lorraine-Dietrich, the Lorraines only second-hand after close inspection in the Lorraine repair shops at Neuilly. In the 1910s and after the Great War, Rougier directed the Turcat-Méry shop at 122 Avenue des Champs-Élysées. Rougier's *garage* at 10 Rue Cormeilles, Levallois, was closed in 1936. It was on 4 March 1905 that "De Diétrich et Cie., Constructions Mécaniques, Lunéville," was reorganized into the "Société Lorraine des Anciens Établissements De Diétrich de Lunéville," so that from then on the cars were named Lorraine-Diétrich instead of De Diétrich. In January 1909, Rougier delivered a Lorraine special to Prince Alexis Orloff, a three-seater powered by a 1908 Grand Prix engine. Rougier and the Farman brothers were among the first aviators, Henry Farman obtaining the Aéro Club de France pilot certificate no. 5; his brother Maurice no. 6; and Rougier no. 11. Victor Rigal had no. 60; Louis Wagner no. 83; Adolphe Clément no. 108 and his son Maurice no. 100; René Hanriot no. 368 and his son Marcel no. 95; Armand de Langhe, who won the 1907 Coupe de la Commission Sportive, no 204; René Thomas no. 116; the Thieulin voiturette manufacturer and Rochet-Schneider driver Joseph Thieulin no. 459; and Louis Gaubert no. 159.

Gaubert drove a 6-cylinder Porthos in the 1908 Grand Prix at Dieppe. The Société Générale des Automobiles Porthos was launched in November 1905, located at 12 Rue du

Dôme, Billancourt, with Armand and Michel Farkas and J.-N. Kieffer as directors. It was in November 1909 that the first Hanriot monoplane was put into Louis Wagner's hands. It had never been tested and was fitted with an engine that Wagner designated as "vieux clou" (old nail). Wagner changed the engine, learned to fly, and taught his young pupil Marcel Hanriot to fly also. Then he took part with conspicuous success in the Budapest meeting: "Lithe and agile, Wagner is possessed of remarkable coolness and nerve."[5] Arthur Duray was known to his friends as "le sympathique Duray." He was cheerful and smiling under all circumstances. In 1906, on the hottest day of a very hot Summer, he drove a Lorraine-Dietrich in the first Grand Prix at Le Mans. He had to change eleven tires and was asked whether this experience did not convert him to the new-fangled *jante amovible*, the detachable Michelin rim. Duray replied that he preferred the old-fashioned method and that tire changes, even eleven in a day, were merely *agréments du métier* with which every professional motorist had to put up. In 1909 Duray learned to get off the earth in the Voisin biplane of his friend Henri Rougier. Duray bought his own biplane, a Farman, in 1910 and won a lot of money in aviation prizes at Nice. He had a severe accident at Verona: "It is difficult to understand how a man's body can break the propeller of a 50-hp Gnome engine without fatal consequences, and he must be tough indeed if he is to recover as quickly as some journals are prophesying."[6] In January 1911 Duray joined Girardot's Société Française Daimler as *metteur au point*. Rougier abandoned aviation after an accident during the Monaco meeting in April 1910: "Where the machine fell the water was seventy feet deep. Recounting

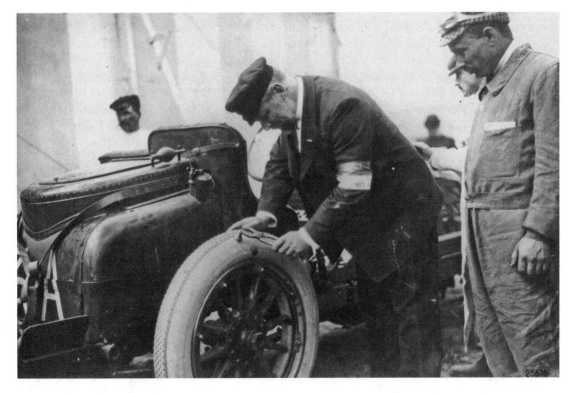

June 1906 — Grand Prix de l'ACF, Le Mans. Commissaire Desson inspecting the wheels and tires of Szisz' Renault during the *pesage*, the scrutineering before the race (Renault Communications/D.R.).

his experiences, the aeronaut said that for some unknown reason the motor suddenly failed and the machine dropped like a stone. It struck the water with considerable force and sank almost immediately. Rougier became entangled in a stay, but succeeded in breaking it, and rose to the surface."[7]

René Roch-Brault and his partner Degrais ran the Germain agency at 30 Place Saint-Ferdinand, with a repair shop at 35 Rue Brunel. Roch-Brault's father Maurice had driven a Belgian Vincke in the 1898 Paris-Amsterdam race and launched the Société Franco-Belge d'Automobile before the turn of the century. Darracq and Bayard driver Louis Villemain's father had a motorcycle shop at 35 Rue Arago, Puteaux, and designed single-cylinder motorcycle engines mounted in frames built by Henri Chanon in the Rue Duret. Émile de Brou, who drove a De Dietrich to third in the 1903 Circuit des Ardennes, had a Bianchi agency at 56 Avenue des Champs-Élysées. At number 93 of the same Avenue was located the Fiat agency of Ernest Loste who drove a 650-kg CGV in the 1903 Paris-Madrid. In February 1907 Loste opened a splendid new shop at 9 Rue de la Paix. Victor Rigal drove a Mors "Dauphin" in the 1903 Paris-Madrid and had a Lion-Peugeot agency at 3 Rue Mozart, Paris-Passy. In 1911 Rigal secured the "Représentation d'Automobiles Sunbeam" at 8 Rue Lesueur, and sold it in October 1913. In the 1920s, he was Panhard agent at 3 Rue Édouard-VII. Émile Ouzou, the bicycle champion who won the 1898 Paris-Dieppe, was the Florentia agent at 241 Boulevard Pereire. In 1900 his Ouzou et Cie. had produced a voiturette powered by a water cooled Soncin engine. Paul Faure was known as *médecin automobile*, or automobile doctor. Faure was *garagiste* at 79 Boulevard Gouvion-Saint-Cyr. In 1904 he prepared Francis Terry's Mercedes for the Circuit des Ardennes, then Pierre de Caters' Mercedes for the 1905 Bennett Cup and the 1907 Circuit des Ardennes. On 29 September 1907 Faure won the Château-Thierry hillclimb at the wheel of the 125-hp Mercedes owned by the Duc de Montpensier. Mariaux, who drove a Mercedes in the 1906 Grand Prix, came into public notice on the 1905 Brescia circuit, and won some local popularity by a series of wild early morning dashes from Paris to the seacoast during the summer of 1905.

Victor Hémery, like Fournier a former bicycle rider and like Fournier involved in the development of his race cars, left Darracq in the autumn of 1906 after he had been replaced by Louis Wagner for the Vanderbilt race. In December, with Félix Gresse, Hémery opened a Tourand agency at 22 Rue Taitbout, Paris. Tourand & Cie. had just begun production in a new factory, Rue de Longchamp, Suresnes. But the 100-hp Tourand racer disappointed and had too little potential. The engine was an 11.8-liter *Vautour*, an L-head of 153 × 160 mm. Power was transmitted via a 3-speed gearbox and shaft drive, wheelbase 285 cm, track 135 cm, tires 810 × 90 front, 820 × 120 rear, dry weight 980 kg. Hémery drove for Mercedes and then for Benz during the 1907 season. Between the autumn of 1907 and the spring of 1908, Hémery superintended the building of the 1908 Benz Grand Prix cars. In the 1908 Grand Prix at Dieppe, "Hemery gave the pluckiest exhibition ever shown by a driver on any course. When the race was half over a stone thrown by a flying wheel struck the goggles he was wearing and drove a bit of glass into his eye. He continued to the tribune and called for a physician. A hurried examination was made, but the piece could not be removed. Hemery refused to stop, and an injection of cocaine was administered to kill the pain while he continued at the wheel to the end. He received an ovation every time he passed the stand thereafter, and the cheers which greeted Lautenschlager on winning were not greater than

C.L. Charley bought no. 70 of the Champs-Élysées in March 1904, after the 1903 Bennett victory spurred an increase in orders (Mercedes-Benz Classic).

Mercedes-Palace

70, Champs-Elysées
=== PARIS ===

Téléphone
509,36.

Adr.-tel.:
Amcharley, Paris.

MERCEDES PALACE

C.L. CHARLEY — 70, Avenue des Champs-Elysées

C. L. Charley

Agent Général pour la France, la Belgique et les Etats-Unis.

General Agent for France, Belgium and America.

General-Agent für Frankreich, Belgien und Amerika.

those which welcomed the defeated Frenchman."[8] On 5 November 1907, the Benz agency in Paris opened a new *magasin d'exposition* at 8 Place de l'Opéra. The Société des Automobiles Benz, directed by Clemente de Bojano and his partner Hutin, exhibited a 50-hp phaeton and a 40-hp chassis. The cars were presented by Hémery and Stoecker. The Benz repair shop remained at 29 Avenue Bugeaud. On 23 July 1911, Hémery and his riding mechanic Antonio Fagnano drove a Fiat to victory in the first Grand Prix de France at Le Mans. On the previous day, at 8 o'clock in the morning, Hémery had picked up the Fiat in Chambéry and reached Le Mans in the late evening. The Fiat was described as a stripped touring car.

A 15-liter Benz racer (155 × 200 mm), the last one of the 1908 Grand Prix type built by the Mannheim factory, was delivered in 1913 by the Paris agency to de Moraes, an amateur driver from Milan. De Moraes was coached by Hémery and started in the 1913 Grand Prix de France at Le Mans. But he did not finish. The last 21-liter Benz (185 × 200 mm) of the "Blitzen" type was delivered to Spain, to Juan Ratés and his two sons Miguel and Ludgardo, 28–30 Illas y Vidal, San Gervasio, Barcelona.[9] In 1907 Juan Ratés had bought a few Hispanos from Abadal y Ca. and in 1908 started in the reliability run between Barcelona and Zaragoza. The 21-liter Benz was ordered in February 1912 at the Barcelona Benz agency of Francisco Ardiz, 4 Ronda de San Pedro, and delivered with a magnificent 4-seat torpedo body via the Madrid Benz importers Enrique Traumann and Paul Anderssen.[10]

Many drivers who started in the last Bennett and the first Grand Prix races began their careers as a riding mechanic, factory tester and *metteur au point*. Ferenc "François" Szisz, the winner of the first Grand Prix, had been riding mechanic for Louis Renault and was head tester at Renault Frères, Boulogne. Szisz had the opportunity to drive his racing car for three or four months before the date of the race. He took the Renault racer out on the road for weeks at a time. Back at the factory, it was taken down and every part was examined for wear and replaced whenever necessary. To win the first Grand Prix in 1906, Szisz had to change tires 19 times during the 12 laps. Renault used detachable Michelin rims, permitting changes in about five minutes. Vinet, the inventor of the detachable rims, caused the Renault to be seized after the race, claiming that Michelin had no right to sell them. There were two rims, differing only in detail. The Vinet rim was produced by Gaston Vinet at 61 Rue de Villiers, Neuilly, and sold by Henry Kapferer et Cie. at 24 Rue de la Rochefoucault. The Vinet rim patent application was filed in November 1904 and accepted in April 1906. The M.L. rim appeared in the Fall of 1905 at the Paris Salon and was produced by the Société Anonyme des Jantes Amoviles M.L., which was formed on 8 November 1905 at 112 Rue Richelieu. Renault mounted M.L.s supplied by Michelin. In 1909 Szisz switched to Delaunay-Belleville, and just before the Great War, with his partners Giboulot and Joly, he opened a Garage d'Automobiles at 103 Route de la Reine, Boulogne. Renault drivers Richez and Sergey "Georges" Dimitrievitch continued to work as *metteurs au point* after 1908. Felice Nazzaro and Louis Wagner were constantly in the employ of the Fiat factories, and spent the entire year practically doing nothing but preparing for races.

Joseph Collomb was a well-known *vélocipédiste*, a bicycle and tricycle star of the 1890s, and a member of the *Cyclophiles Lyonnais*. In 1890 he held the 100-km record in 3 h 45 min. After the turn of the century, Collomb preferred to drive motorized vehicles and took over the Mors, Pilain and Rochet-Schneider agencies at Lyon where he was born. On 14 September 1905, Collomb and his Mors won the 5-km Coupe de Rothschild between Salon and Arles at 149.76 km/h. Three days later he finished fourth in the 1000-kg class in the Mont Ventoux hillclimb.

After taking some photos near the top of Mont Ventoux, the photographers Marcel

Rol and Louis Meurisse wanted to ride back down with Collomb. Rol won a coin toss and took the place beside Collomb in the mechanic's seat while the mechanic sat somehow on the back of the car. At Carpentras, the village at the base of the mountain where the starting line was, the Mors turned over. Collomb and his mechanic were slightly injured but Rol was killed on the spot. Rol, who supplied photographs for *L'Auto* and *La Vie au Grand Air* in particular, had launched the Rol, Tresca et Cie. in December 1903 and one year later the Marcel Rol et Cie., Agence de Reportage Photographique, 37 Rue Joubert. Louis Meurisse had founded his Agence Rapid in 1904 at 9 Faubourg Montmartre but continued to work as *photographe opérateur* with Maurice-Louis Branger, 5 Rue Cambon. In the spring of 1905, when the well-established Branger agency was in financial difficulties, a part of it was renamed Société Branger et Cie., Photographies, and moved to 75 Rue Cambon. At the same time, Maurice Branger launched his Coupe Branger, a race for 1- to 1.5-meter model boats which was run for the first time on the Lac du Bois de Boulogne on 26 October 1905. In 1912, Branger's agency was named Agence d'Informations Photographiques *Photo-Presse*, "the oldest and the most important press agency,"[11] again located at 5 Rue Cambon. In the 1930s the Rol, Meurisse and Branger agencies were merged and later became France Reportage.

Collomb drove his last races in 1906. He was developing his *Orthoptère*, a flying machine named for the class of insects (grasshoppers, crickets and others) whose wing arrangement it mimicked. In 1907 he tested his machine on the race track at Lyon. Joseph Collomb committed suicide on 25 February 1908. Nathan Lazarnick was Branger's counterpart in America and was the "first photographer to specialize in automobile work."[12] Lazarnick was born in Russia on 7 September 1879 and had his New York office at 29 West 42nd Street.

The Mont Ventoux, 25 kilometers in the nordeast of Avignon, was the high-water mark of hillclimbing, starting at an altitude of 290 meters, rising in 21.6 kilometers to 1860 meters, with 4 kilometers at a grade of 6 percent, 10 kilometers at 9 percent, 6 kilometers at 10 percent, and the remaining portion beginning at 10 and ending at 13 percent. The first meeting up the Mont Ventoux was held in 1902 and won by Paul Chauchard in a Panhard in 27 min 17 sec. In 1903 Danjean in a Richard-Brasier climbed the 21.6 kilometers in 25 min 25 sec. Henri Rougier and his Turcat-Méry achieved 21 min 12⅖ sec in 1904, Alessandro Cagno and his F.I.A.T. 19 min 30 sec in 1905. In 1906 Collomb in a Rochet-Schneider was the winner in 24 min 40 sec. In 1907 Rougier and his Lorraine-Dietrich drove up in 19 min 30⅖ sec, and missed Cagno's record by only ⅖ second. Paul Bablot in his Grand Prix Brasier succeeded in breaking the record, in 1908 in 19 min 8⅗ sec, and in 1909 in 18 min 41 sec. In August 1910, Georges Boillot and his single-cylinder Lion-Peugeot beat all comers by racing to the top in 21 min 30⅘ sec. The Lion engine, supplied by the specialists Louis Boudreaux and Louis Verdet, was remarkable, in addition to its long stroke of 250 millimeters, for the use of three horizontal intake and exhaust valves. An accident made victory easy for Boillot. While taking a sharp turn at nearly 100 km/h, Gasté's six-cylinder Rossel skidded and went over into the ditch, with a broken arm for the driver.

A new generation of drivers came up with the voiturette races. Philippe Barriaux and the Vulpès voiturette appeared in the autumn of 1905, in the Gaillon hillclimb, then in the first Coupe de l'Auto, and in the Salon of the Grand Palais. Barriaux was *directeur sportif* at the Société des Automobiles Vulpès, 170 Boulevard National, Clichy. In March 1906 Vulpès entered a 1000-kg racer in the first Grand Prix, a 15.25-liter (180 × 150 mm) with the 3-speed gearbox in the back axle and a "Stabilia" underslung frame. The French magazine *Omnia* published a photograph a few days before the Grand Prix, showing the racer without

November 1907, Paris Salon, Grand Palais. The sumptuous Itala stand (*L'Automobile*).

its body. The 15-liter Vulpès was too heavy and did not appear at the *pesage*, the scrutineering. In the last months of the year it was entered in the sprints of Dourdan, Gaillon and Origny but did not start. One year later, in November 1907, Vulpès was named purveyor to the court of Romania. Vulpès disappeared in 1908. The Société des Automobiles Stabilia entered an underslung chassis in the 1908 Grand Prix des Voiturettes, wheelbase 210 cm, track 115 cm. It was powered by a De Dion single, and the driver's name was Géraldy. But the Stabilia did not appear. When Guyot and his Delage won the 1908 Grand Prix des Voiturettes at Dieppe, Le Petit Parisien titled: "Parti premier, Guyot arrive premier!"[13] Albert Guyot ran the Delage and Gladiator agency at Boulevard Alexandre Martin in his native town Orléans. His riding mechanic in the Grand Prix, Reyrol, opened the Automobiles Reyrol, Carrel et Mourier in 1915, at 23 Rue Louis-Blanc, Levallois-Perret; and the Compagnie Parisienne de Garages d'Automobiles in 1924, at 25 Rue Constantinople.

The Martini driver Boris was also the agent of the Swiss manufacturer at 18 Rue Sartrouville, Argenteuil. The Martinis were built at Saint-Blaise, on the northern end of Lake Neuchâtel. The 1908 voiturette racer was designed by Charles Baehni, in the dimensions of 62 × 90 mm (1.1 liter) for the Grand Prix des Voiturettes at Dieppe and later 65 × 90 mm (1.2 liter) for the Coupe de l'Auto at Compiègne. A single overhead camshaft was driven via helical gears and operated two valves per cylinder. The crankshaft ran in two ball bearings. Output was 12 hp at 1300 rpm, 17 at 2000, and 21 at 2500, transmitted by a Hele-Shaw clutch and a three-speed gearbox. Wheelbase was 220 cm, track 120 cm, tires 710 × 90, or 700 × 85 on the production model offered in the fall of 1908. Dry weights of the cars driven by Beck, Boris and Sonvico at Dieppe were 603, 627 and 601 kg.

Antoine d'Avaray drove a Guillemin-Le Gui voiturette in 1908, and a De Bazelaire in

1909. He was the son of the Marquis d'Avaray and the Duchesse d'Avaray, née Merty-Argenteau. The "La Joyeuse" voiturettes were built at 4 Rue Duchesnay, Asnières, by Émile Taine and Paul Ménard. In the 1908 Grand Prix des Voiturettes they used a De Dion single (100 × 160 mm). Output was 20 hp at 2400 rpm, transmitted via Hele-Shaw clutch and 3-speed gearbox. Wheelbase was 215 cm, track 115 cm, tires front and rear 815 × 105. Émile Taine was the son of Hippolyte Taine, the well-known French critic and historian. In the 1920s, Ménard had a garage at 3 Boulevard Gouvion-Saint-Cyr.

Émile Lamberjack was a former professional racing cyclist, born in Paris on 17 July 1869. He was engaged in the Manège Humber-Gladiator and the Garage Mouter & Lamberjack, and had been the sole export agent of Michelin products for several years. In Paris, Lamberjack's Société Franco-Américaine at Boulevard Gouvion-Saint-Cyr secured the exclusive Fiat agency for France and Belgium in 1907. Lamberjack was married to Virginie Bossu, an embroiderer from the Faubourg Saint-Honoré. With material success, the happiness of the Lamberjacks came to an end. Madame Lamberjack reproached her husband with infidelity, their quarrels became frequent, and finally they were divorced. Yet they continued to live under the same roof. In June 1912 Lamberjack decided to remove his share of the furniture. Madame reproached him, and then shot him fatally with a revolver. Two eminent physicians who examined her said that she was the victim of "Paris life" and its harassing effect upon the nerves. The acquittal of Madame Lamberjack raised a storm of protest among the public and the press. Émile's brother, Dominique Lamberjack, was a Griffon motorcycle rider who started at Ormond, Florida, in January 1904, and became a well-known Bugatti dealer in Paris.

The 11th Salon de l'Automobile opened on 28 November 1908 in the Grand Palais. Armand Fallières, Président de la République, stopped at the Sizaire et Naudin stand and marvelled at the voiturette racer which finished second at Dieppe and won at Compiègne:

"Prodigious!" the president said. "It is tailored to cut the air. It seems that it wants to roll up the space."

"It rolls it up indeed," Maurice Sizaire replied, "it runs at 106 kilometers per hour."[14]

The crisis which had begun in the fall of 1907 was still in full swing. The manufacturers were still producing more cars than there were customers to buy them. Most of the French manufacturers decided to boycott the 1909 Grand Prix de l'ACF. It was to be run on the Circuit de l'Anjou on 2 and 3 July 1909, for cars with a maximum bore of 130 mm and a minimum weight of 900 kg. Panhard, Brasier, Clément-Bayard, Darracq, Renault, Lorraine-Dietrich, and even Léon Desjoyeaux and Edmond de Weisweiller for the Société Française Mercédès agreed to the pact: No race in France in 1909 and hence no Grand Prix de l'ACF, under penalty of 100,000 francs. On 9 December 1908, the ACF's *Commission Sportive* decided to run the Grand Prix if 40 entries could be recorded by 31 December. Mors entered three cars on 18 December. Three cars followed from Cottin-Desgouttes, two from Rolland-Pilain and one from Guillemin-Le Gui. But the foreign entries failed to materialize. On 2 January 1909 the Automobile Club de France cancelled its Grand Prix. One year later, in November 1909, the situation was better. Mors, Rolland-Pilain, Delage, Grégoire, De Dion-Bouton and Benz agreed to enter a three-car team in a 1910 Grand Prix. Not enough! The sportsmen had to wait until 1912 for a revived Grand Prix de l'ACF.

Desjoyeaux and de Weisweiller were directors of the "Société Française d'Automobiles Mercédès" at Puteaux, 6 Quai National. The company was formed on 15 December 1904, and took over the repair and spare part shop "Ateliers Mercédès-Daimler" and the "Societa Italiana dei Motori" at Milan. It was a first step in the rearrangement of Emil Jellinek's and

C.-L. Charley's exclusive selling rights for the Mercedes in France. Desjoyeaux was born in 1866, and was a former director of the Crédit Lyonnais bank. In 1896 he had married Jeanne Burgensis-Desgaultières. His brother Noël was a well-known composer. De Weisweiller was a cousin of Mathilde de Weisweiller, who had married "Dr. Pascal" Henri de Rothschild in 1895.

6

Specials

The Marmon "Wasp" in which Ray Harroun won the 1910 Wheeler & Schebler Trophy at Indianapolis was the first pure speedway special. The Marmon made its appearence in a three-day meet which was held between Thursday, 5 May and Saturday, 7 May 1910, on the 2-mile dirt track at Hopeville, Atlanta, Georgia. The 2-miler was owned by Asa Candler, Jr., the son of the founder of the Coca-Cola Co. and well-known amateur driver at the wheel of his Lozier Briarcliff and Fiat Sixty. The track had been inaugurated in November 1909 with a show in Atlanta's Auditorium-Armory and a complete race meeting. The feature was a 200-mile stock car race won by Louis Chevrolet in a Buick. The track was surfaced with a mixture of clay and Augusta gravel. The Marmon came from Indianapolis where it was built by the Nordyke & Marmon Co. The special was designed by Ray Harroun. "The Marmon six made its initial appearance and is a fast car, using three pairs of the regular Marmon cylinders, 4½ × 5 inches. The car is made without a differential, and because of this holds the track well on the turns."[1] Its T-head six displaced 477 cubic inches. The crankshaft was carried in seven plain bearings. Output was 105 hp at 2000 rpm, transmitted via a cone clutch to a three-speed gearbox in unit with the rear axle, with a final ratio of 2.16 to 1. Harroun mounted sheet metal disks on the spokes of the wood wheels and mounted a narrow streamlined single-seat body with the steering wheel in the middle. The column of the steering wheel ended at dash level and was connected to the regular mechanism on the right-hand side by a train of three gears. Wheelbase was 116 inches, track 56½ inches, tires 34 × 4½ front, 35 × 5 rear, dry weight 2800 pounds. Because of its yellow paint and pointed tail, the Marmon was described in March 1910 as the "Yellow Jacket" or the "Hornet": "The new Marmon Hornet is said to be the first gasoline car built to comply with the new racing rules for class C having limited piston displacement regardless of weight. The body is built along the new lines of wind resistance, and the car is eligible to compete in the 451–600 class."[2] But the Atlantans quickly called it the "Wasp," since "it resembles this insect as it skims up the backstretch."[3]

The Wasp's first race in the Atlanta meet was a 10-mile free-for-all. Harroun was slow in getting under way. DePalma in a Fiat, an 8-liter 1907 Kaiserpreis racer (140 × 130 mm), took the lead until the third lap. Then Harroun pushed the Wasp in front and won in 7 min 43⁵⁄₁₀ sec, with DePalma two minutes back. The best race on Friday was the 50-mile free-for-all. DePalma started in the latest Grand Prix Fiat, the 10-liter tipo S61 (130 × 190 mm). Herb Lytle drove an American, an F-head displacing 571 cubic inches (5¾ × 5½ inches). Like the Marmon, the American was built at Indianapolis. Its underslung frame was designed by Fred Tone, and its specifications were as follows: wheelbase 110 inches, track 56 inches, tires 36 × 4 front, 36 × 4½ rear, dry weight 2400 pounds. Tom Kincade drove a National (5 × 5¹¹⁄₁₆ inches). DePalma got away first, with Lytle, Harroun and Kincade following. Lap 4 saw the Fiat slow down on the backstretch, DePalma's heavily bandaged forearms having cramped. This put Lytle's American in the lead since Harroun was forced to stop with the magneto lead broken. Lytle won in 40 min 20 sec. The 12-mile free-for-all was a race among the three fastest cars, Harroun's Marmon Wasp, DePalma's Grand Prix Fiat and Lytle's American. The Marmon was able to take the turns faster than either of the other cars, although often losing out to the Fiat on the stretches. The first five laps saw all off in a bunch. Then Harroun passed to the front on the back stretch and won in 8 min 59¹⁵⁄₁₀₀ sec, with Lytle 3 seconds back and DePalma a half-minute back.

Harroun's victory in the Wheeler & Schebler Cup in the Indianapolis meet in May 1910 was a mere formality. Harroun was "running on a schedule and as calm as if he were taking a spin on the boulevards.... At the end of the forty-third lap Harroun stopped at the pits.... But there was nothing the matter with the Wasp — It just was a stop to take on fuel and oil and while Harroun lost a lap it didn't upset him and soon the Marmon was plowing away again."[4] The main competitors, the new 624-inch Buicks driven by Bob Burman and Louis Chevrolet, fell out: "Two cars of absolutely new design ... were the Buick Model 100, two special racing machines of the four-cylinder type with 6-inch bore and 5¼-inch stroke. They are not stock, as only two of them have been constructed. They are chain driven constructions and are heavily built racing machines employing the valve-in-the-head construction used on the Buick line."[5] On 10 July 1910, in Cincinnati, Ohio, "Ray Harroun, in his Marmon Six, was the star of the afternoon at the Grand Circuit automobile races at the

30 May 1912 — second Indianapolis 500. Joe Dawson, mechanic Harry Martin, and the winning National flagged by Fred Wagner (Library of Congress).

Latonia track…. In an endeavor to lower the track record of 57⅖ seconds, made by Barney Oldfield last year, he covered the distance over the mile track in 1:00⅖."[6]

Another Marmon special turned up in the third 1910 Indianapolis meet, a two-day affair on Saturday, 3 September and Monday, 5 September, the Sunday remaining free as usual. Ray Harroun had mounted a new long-stroke engine, a 413-inch F-head, a 4-cylinder in the dimensions of 4½ × 6½ inches, into the 116-inch frame of the Wasp six. The F-head four delivered 100 hp at 2000 rpm, saved nearly 100 pounds in comparison to the T-head six, and avoided one of the annoying valve pockets, the overhead intake being located exactly above the exhaust. At the same time, a second long-stroke four was tested in Howard Marmon's touring car, and was intended to be

30 May 1912 — second Indianapolis 500. *Top right*: Joe Dawson. *Bottom*: Ralph DePalma and mechanic Rupert Jeffkins pushing their Mercedes, the Grey Ghost (Library of Congress).

mounted in a 120-inch frame to make a road race special in view of the Vanderbilt, Fairmount Park and Savannah races which closed the 1910 season. At Indianapolis, Harroun drove the four-cylinder special in Monday's feature event, a 200-miler for cars of 600 cubic inches or less. Starter Fred Wagner sent away twelve cars. After 30 miles Johnny Aitken in a National (5 × 5¹¹⁄₁₆ inches), Clemens in a McFarlan six (3¾ × 4 inches) and Harroun were fighting for the lead while Al Livingstone in the second National and Dawson in a pepped up production Marmon (4½ × 5 inches) were having it out for fourth position. Harroun and Aitken completed 100 miles side by side in 1 h 24 min 15 sec. After 170 miles Harroun dropped out on the backstretch. Aitken won in 2 h 47 min 54 sec, 5 min 32 sec ahead of his teammate Livingstone, then Barndollar in a McFarlan and Greiner in another National. "Johnny Aitken is the clown of the game. He injected a laugh in every race, always had a quip or antic to relieve the most tense situation. Howdy Wilcox was Aitken's foil; a Joe Weber to Johnny's Lew Fields; a modern Job in khaki racing suit."[7] The 50-mile free-for-all was won by Eddie Hearne in a freshly imported 15-liter Grand Prix Benz (155 × 200 mm) in 38 min 3 sec, with Harroun in the long-stroke Marmon second at 1 min 30 sec, Livingstone in a National third, and DePalma in a big 18-liter Fiat (190 × 160 mm) fourth after three stops for tires. The Italian sprint racer was a twin brother of "Mephisto" in which Felice Nazzaro had averaged 108 miles per hour over one lap of the concrete oval at Brooklands near London, in 1908. Its feature was an OHV-head with three vertical valves per

1 October 1910 — sixth Vanderbilt Cup, Mineola Circuit, Long Island. Shortly before the start: No. 1, Al Livingstone's National; no. 2, Ralph Mulford's Lozier; no. 3, Arthur Chevrolet's Marquette-Buick; no. 4, Spencer Wishart's Mercedes (Library of Congress).

cylinder, one 108-mm intake and two 66-mm exhaust valves, enabling the engine to develop 175 hp at 1400 rpm.

The first race for Harroun and the long-stroke Marmon in the 120-inch frame was "the sixth competition for the William K. Vanderbilt, Jr. Automobile Cup."[8] The Vanderbilt was run for the last time on Long Island, on Saturday, 1 October 1910, over a distance of 22 laps of 12.64 miles or 278.08 miles. It was open to class C, divisions 4C and 5C: "gasoline cars or chassis made by a factory which has during the last 12 months prior to the date of the contest produced at least fifty motor cars, not necessarily of the same model, eligible for entry under piston displacement limitations of class B, but without minimum weight restrictions."[9] Division 4C was from 301 to 450 cubic inches, 5C from 451 to 600. The 1910 Vanderbilt was not a stock car event as it was in 1909. It was a class C fixture from which the weight restrictions were removed. It was a race for 600-inch non-stock cars. Joe Dawson drove a stripped production Marmon, a 318-inch four in the dimension of 4½ × 5 inches with T-head on a 120 inch-wheelbase. Tires were 34 × 4 all around, on both Marmons. In lap 16 Harroun and the long-stroke special retired because of a broken crankshaft. Harry Grant, mechanic Frank Lee and the Alco "Bête Noire" won the Vanderbilt in 4 h 15 min 58 sec, just 25 seconds ahead of Dawson.

The black Alco beast was a combination of the Model 60 six-cylinder T-head engine

1 October 1910— sixth Vanderbilt Cup, Mineola Circuit, Long Island. The back rows: No. 29, Louis Chevrolet's Marquette-Buick; no. 30, P.H. Jardine's Royal Tourist; no. 31 Louis Disbrow's National; and no. 32, Fred Belcher's Knox six (Library of Congress).

(4¾ × 5½ inches), normally mounted in a long 134-inch chassis, and the shorter 126-inch frame of the four-cylinder Model 40. The Alco was built by the American Locomotive Co. in Providence, Rhode Island. In practice, one week before the race, Grant was tooling his Alco along a level straight stretch of the Parkway at 80 miles an hour when both the right tires came unseated. With his characteristic coolness, Grant managed to hold the big Alco fairly steady and brought it to a standstill. Grant jumped from the seat and regarded the bare rims where the tires should have been with an expression indicative of intense amazement. "Those who follow the racing game now reckon Harry F. Grant ... as one of the really great drivers," read a news report. "This is not only because of what he has accomplished, but because of the heady character of his work. His driving is distinguished by great steadiness and coolness. Always he is calm and deliberate whether winning or losing. When not busy with racing Grant is a salesman of Alco cars at the Boston agency.... Grant is of an exceptionally happy disposition. He is usually smiling, and there is a lilt of cheeriness in his voice as he talks, so it is not surprising that he weighs 200 pounds. He was born at Cambridge, Mass., on July 10, 1877."[10]

One week later, on Saturday, 8 October 1910, Harroun started in Philadelphia's third Fairmount Park road race of the Quaker City Motor Club, a competition of 25 laps of 8.1 miles or 202.5 miles. In 1908 George Robertson in a Locomobile had won at Fairmount Park in 4 h 2 min 30 sec; in 1909 it was again Robertson, this time at the wheel of a Simplex, in 3 h 38 min 13 sec. In 1910 the race was open to non-stock class C cars, subdivided into five displacement classes, a race for 750-inch non-stock cars. This time, Harroun was forced

1 October 1910 — sixth Vanderbilt Cup, Mineola Circuit, Long Island. Harry Grant, mechanic Frank Lee and the winning Alco "Bête Noire" (Library of Congress).

1 October 1910—sixth Vanderbilt Cup, Mineola Circuit, Long Island. *Top*: Joe Dawson and his Marmon finished second. *Bottom*: Ralph Mulford's Lozier being serviced (Library of Congress).

to park his long-stroke Marmon with a defective rear axle housing, in lap 13, just after having broken the lap record in 7 min 38 sec. Erwin Bergdoll in his 12-liter Grand Prix Benz (155 × 160 mm) was the leader between laps 6 and 16, until the Benz broke an oil feed. Len Zengle in a Chadwick won in 3 h 29 min 7 sec, just 5.5 seconds ahead of Mulford in a Lozier (5⅜ × 6 inches), 8 min 35 sec ahead of de Hymel in a Stoddard-Dayton (5 × 5½ inches). Zengle's best lap was 7 min 57 sec.

It was a Philadelphia victory since the driver, Zengle, was a native son and the car, the Chadwick, was made not far from the Quaker City, at Pottstown, Pennsylvania. The Chadwick was an F-head six cast in pairs, 5 × 6 inches, 707 cubic inches, having a crankshaft in four plain bearings, power transmission via expanding band clutch to a four-speed gearbox, chain drive, a wheelbase of 112 inches, and 36 × 4½ tires all around. It was an expensive car, the three-seat runabout being offered at $5500. Tobin de Hymel came from San Antonio, Texas. His parents were French and Spanish. His Stoddard-Dayton was owned by G.A.C. Halff. In November, in a 12-mile handicap race in San Antonio, "Tobin de Hymel ... was killed in the races ... when his car lost a wheel and was wrecked. He drove in the last Vanderbilt cup race in New York and was known as the Aztec indian driver."[11]

On 12 November 1910, Joe Dawson, with Bruce Keene as riding mechanic, took the wheel of the long-stroke Marmon in the Grand Prize at Savannah over 24 laps of 17.3 miles. "There is no restriction placed upon the size of cars entered other than that of the overall width of chassis, which must not exceed 68.8 inches. Any size bore and stroke is permitted."[12] In lap 5 the Marmon broke its crankshaft, just as Howard Marmon had predicted. In lap 15 Dawson replaced Harroun in the stripped 318-inch production Marmon (4½ × 5 inches) and finished sixth. David Bruce-Brown in a 15-liter Benz (155 × 200 mm) won in 5 h 53 min 5 sec, with teammate Victor Hémery second, and Bob Burman in a Marquette-Buick 100 (6 × 5¼ inches) third. Fred Wagner remembered:

> The grand prize race of 1910 was the most thrilling struggle I ever witnessed.... Hemery was the first to cross the wire. For a moment the cheering crowd thought that the Frenchman had won. Then came the announcement that Bruce-Brown had a starting handicap of 3 minutes, that if he finished inside that time, an American, not a foreigner, would take the grand prize. The announcers began to toll off the seconds, fleeting seconds that were cutting down Davey's lead. "Five! 10! 15!"—and then before another count could be announced came the cry "No. 15 car is on the home stretch!" It was the Benz and Bruce-Brown. No New York multitude ever called upon Mathewson to strike out an opposing batter in a pinch; no Yale host ever implored its wavering linemen to "hold 'em" in a gridiron crisis with as great frenzy and desperation as that with which the stands at Savannah urged Bruce-Brown on, urge him on with screams, yells and curses, urged him on with voice and arms. Even I, an official, forgot that I was clothed in the vestments of impartiality and frantically waved him in, with the sweat of terror pouring from every pore in my body and dancing like a madman. Bruce-Brown heard the prayer of patriotic thousands. Cautiously he swung around a turn into view and then opening up the throttle of the giant Benz to the limit, thundered over the finishing line a victor by the narrow margin of 1.42 seconds. He was a public idol, showered with flowers torn from the bosoms of worshipping women.[13]

Dawson's best lap in the long-stroke Marmon was 14 min 30 sec, while Brown's best lap was 14 min 1 sec, Hémery's 13 min 50 sec, and Burman's 14 min 20 sec. Compared to Hémery's big Benz, the Marmon lost 2.3 seconds per mile. Actually, this was no surprise since the Benz was a pure racer displacing 911 cubic inches, twice as much as the Marmon.

Both Marmons, the Wasp and the long-stroke special, started in the first Indianapolis

500 on Tuesday, 30 May 1911. The Wasp six was now fully developed. Ray Harroun and mechanic Harry Goetz fitted two sets of shock absorbers, eight in all: "With these the car held the track beautifully and there was not any of the pounding of the front wheels that was noticeable on several other cars."[14] The Wasp was equipped with Firestone tires, Remy magneto and Schebler carburetor. Since Harroun was alone in the single seater, with Goetz acting as pit manager, he mounted a rear-view mirror on the cowl to keep an eye on his pursuers. The long-stroke four was driven by Joe Dawson with Bruce Keene as riding mechanic. The stroke was lengthened from 6½ to 7 inches, giving 445 cubic inches, and the crankshaft reinforced and better balanced. Both Marmons delivered about 110 hp at 2200 rpm. Cyrus Patschke and W.L. Studebaker acted as reliefs.

To facilitate the scoring, the number disks appearing head high and about 12 inches behind the drivers were made in different color schemes: black disks with white numbers for nos. 1 to 9; white disks with black numbers for nos. 10 to 19; red disks with white numbers for nos. 20 to 29; and yellow disks with black numbers for nos. 30 to 46. Dawson had no. 31, Harroun no. 32. On race day, the gates of the speedway were opened at 6 o'clock in the morning. Special train service to the speedway had been arranged with the Big Four Railway Co. Trains left the Union Station every half-hour from 6:30 to 8:30 A.M. and every 15 minutes thereafter. The fare one way was 10 cents, and 20 cents for the round trip. By 8:30 the special train of the Chicago Automobile Club pulled in. There were 80,000 spectators, 50,000 of whom were seated, while the others either were standing or in cars parked in and about the grounds. At 8:30 the track was cleared. Bob Burman was handed his speed king title and presented with the crown offered by the Firestone Tire and Rubber Co. for the straightaway records in Florida. The crown was a most elaborate affair, made in New York, an exact duplicate of the crown used at the coronation of King George IV, embellished with diamonds, rubies and emeralds. Burman looked embarrassed. Half an hour later he felt better. At the wheel of the Blitzen he went the quarter mile in 8.16 sec, the half-mile in 16.83 sec, the kilometer in 21.4 sec, and the mile in 35.35 sec. At 10 o'clock Carl Fisher, at the wheel of a white Stoddard-Dayton, started at the head of the field, setting a pace of 40 miles an hour. The 40 cars were lined five cars to the row in the order they were entered, with the pole car as pacemaker for each squad.

After 20 laps DePalma in the Simplex (5¾ × 5¾ inches) and Bruce-Brown in the Fiat S61 were the leaders, having completed 50 miles in 39 min 5 sec. In lap 24 Bragg's Fiat dropped out with a broken crankshaft, while Aitken stopped for a right rear tire. After 40 laps Brown was the leader, then DePalma, Harroun, Aitken and Mulford. After 64 laps, Harroun stopped for tires and was relieved by Cyrus Patschke. "The drivers had studied the track and knew what parts were smoothest and wore the tires least. The smooth qualities were nearly the undoing of many about the middle of the race, before the management started putting sand on the course. It was so slippery that the drivers could not open the throttle wide on the backstretch; if they did, the rear wheels wanted to get in front of the forward ones. After the sand was applied slipping was over and the speed average increased."[15] Brown completed 100 laps or 250 miles in 3 h 17 min 49 sec, 56 seconds ahead of Patschke who was still relieving Harroun in the Wasp, 2 min 41 sec ahead of Mulford, then DePalma in the Simplex and Dawson in the Marmon four. After 150 laps or 400 miles Harroun in the Wasp was in the lead, 1 min 28 sec ahead of Mulford, 6 min 32 sec ahead of Brown and Dawson. The yellow Wasp stayed the pace and won in 6 h 42 min 8 sec, average 74.59 miles per hour. The Wasp made four stops for tires, one for water, oil and gas, and never raised the hood. "Harroun perhaps was wise in taking the rest he did, for he has not the robust constitution some of his rivals have. Indeed, it hardly is likely he could have continued much farther. On the other hand, Mulford and Bruce-Brown apparently were in prime condition, neither man having suffered from the long grind. Both of them had gone the entire distance and evidently could have kept on for some time. Wishart showed the strain of the long drive and at the end was nervous and inclined to be morose."[16] Mulford finished second, then Brown, Wishart, Dawson and DePalma, who made ten stops for tires. Brown's Fiat made four stops for tires, two for taking on oil, water and gas, and three stops because of engine trouble, Wishart's Mercedes six stops for tires and one stop for suspected engine trouble. By the end of the race Dawson, who was also relieved by Patschke, bumped another car and poked a big hole in the radiator of his Marmon. He stopped for oil but did not put any water in because he figured the leaky radiator would not hold it. The experiment turned out well, but only after a revision of the checker's report which lasted for more than 24 hours: Dawson was ranked fifth instead of being reckoned as not finishing. The winner received $10,000 and the remaining eleven finishers split $15,000. Mulford filed a protest of the official finish, claiming that he was the winner and that he lapped Harroun when the Wasp limped in on a blown tire. The protest was denied.

Ralph Mulford's Lozier was a stripped Model 46, a 544-inch T-head, $5\frac{3}{8} \times 6$ inches, with a wheelbase of 124 inches. The open 4-seater on the Lozier 46 chassis was called "Briarcliff," the 5-seater "Lakewood," both quoted at $4600. The Lozier Motor Co. had just moved operations from Plattsburgh, New York, to a new plant in Detroit, 3703 Mack Avenue. John G. Perrin, who had designed the first Lozier in 1905, remained in the position of chief engineer. Spencer Wishart's Mercedes was brand-new, a freshly imported 9.5-liter, 130×180 mm, originally intended for the 130-mm formula of the 1909 Grand Prix de l'ACF. In contrast to the older F-head Mercedes racers, this engine, designed by Paul Daimler and Eugen Link, had an OHV head with a huge 86-mm intake and two 50-mm exhausts and developed 130 hp at 2000 rpm. The 270-cm frame was derived from the successful 1908 Grand Prix car and was improved only in details. The three-valve Mercedes was the direct competitor of the four-valve Fiat S61 which had received a small-bore block in the dimensions of 128×190 mm to comply with the 600-inch limit.

On Saturday, 9 September 1911, Burman in the Blitzen and Ray Harroun in the Wasp were the stars of the state fair meet at Minneapolis. Heavy rains had placed the track in a treacherous condition. Burman covered a mile in 50 seconds, unable to match the old track record of $49\frac{2}{5}$ sec. Harroun made a 3-mile exhibition including a front tire change in 4 min 45 sec. During the summer of 1911, Harroun had assembled two additional road race Marmons, with their long-stroke fours rebored from $4\frac{1}{2}$ to $4\frac{3}{4}$ inches, the stroke remaining unchanged at 7 inches. On Sunday, 15 October 1911, the new Marmons started at Santa Monica, California, in the Dick Ferris Cup, a 24-lap 202-mile free-for-all. Cyrus Patschke and Joe Dawson finished second and third, behind Harvey Herrick in a National ($5 \times 5\frac{11}{16}$ inches) entered by the local coast agent. Herrick won at an average of 74.62 mph, smashing Nazzaro's 1908 world road racing record of 74.3 mph. Patschke led until lap 21 but finished on three cylinders. On Monday, Harroun and his crew of ten men left for the east to prepare the Marmons for Georgia, for the Savannah Challenge Cup, the Vanderbilt and the Grand Prize.

The Savannah Challenge for 300-inch non-stock cars was run on Monday, 27 November 1911. The race was to cover 13 laps of 17.14 miles, or 222.82 miles, with an 8 A.M. start. The Savannah Automobile Club had invested $50,000 in the improvement of the course. For several months the Chatham County convict force had been at work, widening the roads, eliminating many of the S turns and the serpentine curve at Thunderbolt. The oil wagons of the Indian Refining Co. followed close behind, using a heavy grade of oil that solidified the road surface until it was almost as hard as asphalt. Bruce Keene and Joe Nikrent were at the wheel of two 300-inch Marmons, with T-head engines, $4^{23}\!/_{64} \times 5$ inches. Hughes in a Mercer won the Savannah Challenge Cup. Keene took second, Nikrent third.

The Vanderbilt for 600-inch non-stock cars was run on the same day at 11:45 A.M. over 17 laps or 291.38 miles. The long-stroke Marmons were driven by Cyrus Patschke and Bob Burman, who switched over from a Prince Henry Benz. Burman's Marmon was eliminated in lap 8 with magneto trouble, and Patschke's car one lap later with a disabled water pump. Mulford in a Lozier won the Vanderbilt ahead of DePalma in a Mercedes. "The Loziers are chain-driven machines and have a pronounced racing appearance, due to shrouding the radiator by continuing the hood forward beyond it and curving it in."[17] DePalma's Mercedes was freshly imported, a 9.5-liter owned by Edward Schroeder, similar to Wishart's Indianapolis car. The Schroeder Mercedes was painted in battleship gray and quickly became known as the "Grey Ghost."

The Grand Prize followed on Thanksgiving, Thursday, 30 November 1911, over a distance of 24 laps or 411.36 miles. In lap 5 Burman's Marmon fell out with a broken magneto shaft sprocket. Cyrus Patschke was able to put his Marmon to the front, but only for a few miles. In lap 10 the cylinders of the yellow racer loosened from the crankcase. Bruce-Brown won his second Grand Prize ahead of Eddie Hearne in a Benz and DePalma in the Grey Ghost. Brown's car was the latest Grand Prix Fiat, the 14-liter S74 (150 × 200 mm). Hémery in the Benz turned the fastest lap in 12 min 36 sec. Brown's fastest lap was 12 min 47 sec, Hearne's 13 min 6 sec, DePalma's 13 min 10 sec, Patschke's 13 min 21 sec, and Burman's 13 min 23 sec.

The Marmon specials spent the 1912 season in the storeroom. In 1913, two of the long-stroke specials ended up in the hands of Charles Erbstein, Chicago's famous criminal lawyer:

> Charles E. Erbstein compiled a record of having defended more than a hundred persons accused of murder without having the death penalty imposed. Three times he was threatened with disbarment, and on each occasion, acting as his own impassioned attorney, he was acquitted and emerged full of fight for another battle. Erbstein would run up and down in front of the jury box, shouting his arguments and excoriating the prosecution. His inexhaustible energy, droll wit, and legal brilliance ranked him with Clarence Darrow, and his income grew with his notoriety.[18]

In 1915 Erbstein purchased two hundred acres near Elgin, erected a large residence with riding stable and his own golf course, and named his estate Villa Olivia after his daughter. Erbstein entered one of the specials, a yellow 445-inch racer ($4\frac{1}{2} \times 7$ inches), in the 1913 Elgin National Trophy for Joe Dawson. The Marmon was flagged sixth, one lap and 31 minutes behind the winner, Anderson in a Stutz.

In February 1914, in the Grand Prize at Santa Monica, Guy Ball drove a long-stroke Marmon to second, 40 minutes behind Pullen in a Mercer. The Marmon had its troubles bunched. In lap 19 it was at the pits for 19 minutes. Ball put on a new float chamber in the carburetor, changed three plugs, took on fuel and water, adjusted the magneto mounting and plugged up a hole in the water pump casting.

In May 1914, the Erbstein Marmon started in the Indianapolis 500, on Houk wire wheels, with Joe Dawson at the wheel. Pat King, brother-in-law of Charles Erbstein, intended to ride beside Dawson, but failed to pass the medical examination. He was replaced by Vere Barnes. In lap 46, Ray Gilhooley swung into the south turn, running high up, when a tire blew, capsizing his green Isotta. Gilhooley's dazed mechanic, Lino Bonini, was crawling up the bank. Wilcox in a Gray Fox dodged him. Dawson in the Marmon started to cut through between the mechanic and the outside wall when he saw he could not make it without hitting the man. To avoid this, Dawson swung down the bank and tried to cut back again, but the Marmon turned over, flinging Dawson and his mechanic out. Dawson was the most seriously hurt of the four involved in the wreck, but he had saved the life of poor Bonini.

In August 1914, three long-stroke Marmons appeared at Elgin. A first car (4½ × 7 inches) was entered by Erbstein for Lou Heinemann. Erbstein had sold his second car (4¾ × 7 inches) to W.H. Harris, of Chicago, inventor of the Harris drive which did away with the differential. For the purpose of demonstrating his device, Harris entered the Marmon for Mel Stringer. The third Marmon (4¾ × 7 inches) was nominated by Ernie Moross for Wilbur D'Alene. Heinemann finished sixth in the CAC Trophy and went out in the Elgin National because of a broken transmission. Stringer's Marmon took a rest in the garage, wrecked by a spill in practice, Stringer sitting in the pits with his arm in a sling. In the CAC Trophy, D'Alene's Marmon was ruled out by the technical committee because its displacement exceeded 450 inches. In the Elgin National, D'Alene was too fast in Hornbeek's turn, crashed into a tree and broke the frame and radiator of the Marmon.

Back in 1911, in the first Indianapolis 500, there was another special of the long-stroke F-head variety. Built by the the National Motor Vehicle Co. of Indianapolis and driven by Howdy Wilcox with riding mechanic J.P. Walker, it boasted a bore of 5 inches and a stroke of 7½ inches for a displacement of 589 cubic inches. Power transmission was via cone clutch to a three-speed gearbox and then to a Hotchkiss type rear axle. Wheelbase was 112 inches, track 56 inches, tires 34 × 4 front, 34 × 5 rear, dry weight 2850 pounds. Wilcox's relief, Arthur Beck, was a wealthy young chap from the east aspiring to become a race driver. He had enough money to purchase a dozen cars, but upon applying for a position as a driver at the National factory he was told that he would have to start from the bottom. Not daunted, he joined the testing force for six months and wore the overalls of a mechanic before being appointed relief driver. Two 446-inch T-head Nationals (5 × 5¹¹⁄₁₆ inches) were driven by Johnny Aitken and Charlie Merz, with L.E. Banks and W.F. Kepner as riding mechanics. During practice Howdy Wilcox and Johnny Aitken covered 275 miles to test out tire wear, with a fastest lap in 1 min 38 sec. In lap 125 of the race, Aitken retired with a broken connecting rod. Merz finished seventh, while Wilcox in the special was delayed by "thirteen cases of tire trouble" and was flagged. Two Nationals and a Marquette-Buick were entered in the French Grand Prix, which was scheduled for 9 July 1911 but was cancelled once again. In October 1911, Len Zengle drove the National special to third in the Fairmount Park race.

The second Indianapolis 500-mile race was run on Thursday, 30 May 1912, as a race for 600-inch non-stock cars with a minimum weight of 2000 pounds. The prizes were doubled: a total of $50,000 with $20,000 as grand prize for the victor. National nominated three racers for Joe Dawson, who was loaned for the occasion by Marmon, Howdy Wilcox and David Bruce-Brown. Dawson's blue National was powered by a conventional T-head engine with displacement of 490 cubic inches and bore and stroke of 5 × 6¼ inches, with 2¾-inch valves and a two-spark Splitdorf magneto, producing 124 hp at 2100 rpm. Wheelbase was 108 inches, dry weight 2615 pounds. The other two Nationals were similar to the long-stroke racer of the previous year, F-head specials, 5 × 7½ inches. Valve diameter was 3 inches, valve lift ⁷⁄₁₆ inch. Two Bosch magnetos supplied four plugs per cylinder: "In the two Nationals, driven by Wilcox and Bruce-Brown, two separate magnetos are employed, each having two-point ignition so that there are four spark plugs in each cylinder."[19] All three Nationals used a double set of Hartford shock absorbers both front and rear.

The pace was set by Ralph DePalma and his Grey Ghost. After 400 miles DePalma was nearly 8 minutes ahead of Dawson. But with two laps to go the Mercedes began hitting only on two cylinders and at the 1.5-mile post it stopped altogether, with a broken connecting rod and a hole in the crankcase: "Finally around the last turn the gray bonnet showed but it only was a crawl. There was no roar of exhaust, no skid on the corner, for gasoline was not furnishing the motive power — the car was being propelled by the weary de Palma and his mechanic Jeffkins, the driver steering and pushing and the helper shoving from the rear. Inch by inch they came and as they neared the pits one could read the tragedy in de Palma's face, from which the perspiration was running in big beads."[20] Dawson, riding mechanic Harry Martin and the National won in 6 h 21 min 6 sec, with Tetzlaff in a Fiat S61 second. Dawson lost a total of 14 minutes at the pits. As one spectator put it, the feature of the race was not the victory of Dawson but the defeat of DePalma. During February and March 1912, the Grey Ghost had been overhauled at Untertürkheim. In April, DePalma received a wire stating that the Mercedes had been shipped back on the *Titanic*. This was not the case. The Grey Ghost reached New York on 25 April. DePalma's Mercedes bettered all existing speedway records with the exception of the 500-mile mark. But the contest board of the AAA announced that according to rule 79 "no record at an intermediate distance is allowable unless the car finished the event. The Mercedes discontinued the race in the one hundred and ninety-ninth or next to last lap."[21] The records were awarded to Tetzlaff and Dawson. Brown's National broke a piston ring in lap 25, seemingly because of lubrication trouble. The engine misfired so badly that it was impracticable to continue. Later it was found that a hose connecting the oil tank with the crankcase was stuffed with waste.[22] Wilcox finished ninth. On 4 June, Brown and DePalma sailed for Europe, to drive two 14-liter S74 Fiats in the French Grand Prix at Dieppe.

George Dickson, manager of the National team, estimated the costs to prepare a car and get it ready for the 500-mile race at $8,000. "National detailed twenty picked mechanics to prepare the three blue cars for the 1912 Indianapolis race.... Two weeks before the contest, this force was increased until there were as many as twenty men toiling over a single mount."[23] On 17 June 1912, the National Motor Vehicle Co. announced "that it has been decided to withdraw from competion so far as the factory is concerned. The reason given is rush of business after the victories gained by the National within the last year, including the 500-mile race."[24]

Both the Wasp from Marmon and the Bête Noire from Alco were specials combining a big production engine with a light short-wheelbase frame. In fact, the combination was a result of the preceding stock car mania which was replaced by another style of racing, the free-for-all type. It was a transition solution but was really effective and bred the first successful sixes in auto racing. The next step involved a purpose-built engine whereby both Marmon and National relied on an F-headed long-stroke four. The special engine saved weight. The concept was on the right path although, a few years later, the F-head became obsolete owing to bitter experience with its capacity as a detonation inducer. To prevent this detonation, National used four spark plugs per cylinder. A third approach came from a fresh New Jersey factory which offered a jewel of a sports car, needing only to be tuned up for racing: the Mercer.

7

Mercer

The Mercer was the 1911 car of the year. The 300-inch racer was not only fast enough to win its class but repeatedly showed that it had the speed of much bigger bores. The Mercer appeared in January 1910:

> The Mercer is one of the most interesting newcomers on Broadway. The car is manufactured at Trenton by the Mercer Automobile Company, of which F.W. Roebling is the head. The Roeblings have been known to be experimenting with automobiles for some time, and it has been expected that some startling developments would follow the introduction of their car on the market. The Mercer is regarded as their product, although they are not the sole owners of the license formerly held by the Walter Automobile Company, in which the Roeblings were interested. There is probably no concern in the country which has had as wide an experience with the study of structural materials as the Roeblings. The car in which they are interested can fairly be regarded as a construction of undoubted strength and capable of the greatest endurance. The Mercer is a four and five passenger car. It is made in toy tonneau, close coupled, and regular touring body, besides limousine and landaulet. Its construction is standard throughout, no principle being employed that is not recognized as standard good practice. The touring car weights 2,500 pounds, and the closed bodies are proportionately light. The lines of the car are very graceful and the fitting very attractive. It has Circassian walnut dash, seventeen-inch hard rubber rim on the steering wheel, and aluminium spider. The upholstery is best buffed leather, and the painting in standard colors with best grade of coach work. Altogether the car makes a very smart appearance, and is a distinct addition to the medium-priced cars that Broadway offers.[1]

On 15 May 1910, Charles Bigelow and his Mercer "left Times Square for a transcontinental trip to Los Angeles."[2] The Mercer arrived in Los Angeles on 13 June having covered 3,288 miles in 327 hours, a new record. On 1 October 1910, two Mercers were entered in the Wheatley Hills Trophy on Long Island, the race for 300-inch cars run simultaneously with the Vanderbilt, for W. Howard Frey and E.H. Sherwood. Frey hit a telegraph pole and Sherwood did not start. On 11 November 1910, Washington Roebling, with Felix Geschwantner as riding mechanic, took second in the 300-inch Savannah Trophy, a curtain raiser of the Grand Prize. Roebling was lucky to finish: During the race, his goggles got so dirty and befogged that he misjudged the turn on Norwood Avenue and went off the road, streaking a palmetto tree and losing between 5 and 6 minutes.

The 1911 season opened in California on Wednesday, 22 February, George Washington's birthday, with the Oakland Panama-Pacific road race which was run over the Alameda County Boulevard course between San Leandro and Hayward, lap length 10.923 miles. Fully 100,000 people lined the course. The Mercer driven by Charles Bigelow had no trouble in capturing the 9-lap event for 300-inch cars, with Earl Cooper in a Maxwell second. It

Spring 1914. Spencer Wishart and Eddie Pullen, accompanied by mechanics, at the wheels of the two 450-inch Mercers used for the Grand Prize at Santa Monica (Library of Congress).

was the first victory of a Mercer, and the first appearance of Earl Cooper in a big race. In May 1911, two Mercers started in the first Indianapolis 500, driven by Hughie Hughes and Charles Bigelow, with L.P. Firmin and Charles Illingsworth as riding mechanics. Hughes finished twelfth; Bigelow was flagged. In August, the Mercer duo driven by Hughie Hughes and W.F. Barnes took first and second in the 300-inch Kane County Cup at Elgin, whereby Hughes stole a march on his teammate by treating his monkey mascot to a new red coat. Hughes also finished third in the 600-inch Elgin National. In October, the same Hughes took sixth overall and the 300-inch division in the Fairmount Park race, and in November he won the Savannah Trophy.

The Mercer was built at Trenton, Mercer County, New Jersey, where the Mercer Automobile Co. had been founded in May 1909 by a handful members of the prominent Roebling and Kuser families. Young Washington Roebling, born in 1881, was general manager. After working at his father's business, he got involved in the small automobile plant of William Walter, a Swiss immigrant. In 1906 production was moved from New York to a vacant brewery owned by the Kusers, on Whithead Road, Hamilton, New Jersey. In 1909 the Roeblings and Kusers bought Walter out and renamed the company after Mercer County. In October 1908 Washington Roebling appeared at the wheel of a 140-hp racer: "It is built of Krupp steel wherever possible, and after designs of M. Etienne Planche, an expert in building fast racing cars. It is understood that the morning test showed 120 miles an hour easy of accomplishment, even when conditions were not ideal."[3] The Roebling-Planche was powered by a T-head engine of 7 × 6 inches, displacing 923 cubic inches, on a 115-inch wheelbase chassis. In the spring of 1912 Washington Roebling sailed for Europe. In Turin he tested and bought one of the latest Fiats, then booked passage on White Star's *Titanic* while the Fiat and his chauffeur, Frank Stanley, were sent on another liner. Washington Roebling was lost at sea in the *Titanic* disaster.

The Mercer was designed by Finley Robertson Porter. Born on 28 December 1872 in Lowell, Ohio, Porter left school aged 11 and took mail courses in mechanical engineering. Before moving to Mercer in 1910, he worked as general manager of the Empire Brass Works in East Stroudsburg, Pennsylvania. The engine of the Mercer was composed of cast iron pairs, with integral T-heads and water jackets. The cast iron pairs "were subjected to two grinding processes, the final grind being after they have had time to age. The limit on this work is .01 inch."[4] The cylinder dimensions of $4\frac{3}{8} \times 5$ inches resulted in 300.5 cubic inches, just below the displacement limit of the 300-inch class. The intake was on the right, the exhaust on the left hand side. The valves, made of tungsten steel had a diameter of $2\frac{1}{4}$ inches and lift of $\frac{7}{16}$ inch. The connecting rods were of H-section, but turned opposite to that generally used to provide extra wide flanges. The 2-inch crankshaft ran in three plain bearings, their width $3\frac{1}{2}$ inches front, 3 inches center and 4 inches rear. The cylinders were not offset. Camshaft diameter was $1\frac{1}{4}$ inch. The front bearing of each camshaft was of the annular ball type, while the center and rear bearings were plain, $1\frac{7}{16} \times 3$ inches and $1\frac{7}{16} \times 1\frac{1}{2}$ respectively. The lubricating system was a combination of early pressure-feed and splash. A gear-driven rotary pump carried the oil from the sump through a sight feed on the dash back to the crankshaft main bearings. The overflowing oil was picked up by pockets on the crankshaft and thrown by centrifugal force to the cranks. Oil capacity was $1\frac{3}{4}$ gallons. A Bosch ZR-4 magneto supplied two sets of plugs, one over the intake and the other over the exhaust valves. A $1\frac{3}{4}$-inch Rayfield carburetor was responsible for the mixture. The 300-inch engine delivered 58 hp at 1700 rpm, in racing trim 85 hp at 2500 rpm. Power was transmitted by means of a multidisk clutch running in oil, with 44 steel-to-steel plates engaged by a single helical spring. Wheelbase was 108 inches, track 56 inches, tires 32×4 all around, dry weight 2300 pounds. The rear springs were shackled at both ends, the driving stress being taken by two radius rods.

During the 1911 season, "Lord" Hughie Hughes, who was born in London in 1886, used to carry a toy monkey in his yellow Mercer so that his mount became known as the "Monk." Ralph DePalma appeared at the wheel of a Mercer in October 1911 in Philadelphia's Fairmount Park race, but withdrew because of a broken steering knuckle. On 4 May 1912, he was luckier and drove the ex–Hughes Monk to victory in the 300-inch race over 18 laps of the 8.4-mile Santa Monica road course. After the race the yellow Monk was sold to Huntley Gordon, a used car dealer and southern California Stearns distributor. Gordon was born in New York but lived in Los Angeles. In the meantime, Lord Hughes was preparing a revamped 300-inch Mercer for the second Indianapolis 500 held a few weeks later on 30 May 1912. In fact, Hughes made best practice time in 1 min 41 sec. The engine was fitted with forged steel pistons and tubular connecting rods; the camshafts ran in three ball bearings, with hollow pushrods and larger $2\frac{1}{2}$-inch valves. In front of the forward cylinder there was a transverse shaft for the magneto and the water pump, driven by silent chain and worm gear from the crankshaft. Altogether the modifications were good for 95 hp at 2800 rpm. An enveloping body with narrow radiator, tapering tail and smooth pan enclosing the entire bottom, and Rudge-Whitworth wire wheels gave the Mercer a completely new look. Dry weight was reduced to 2200 pounds. In the middle of the race, the Mercer ran out of gasoline at the beginning of the homestretch, and Hughes had to push the racer to the pits.

Nevertheless, he finished third at 76.13 mph, 12 minutes behind Dawson's 490-inch National, 4 minutes behind Tetzlaff's 597-inch Fiat. In August 1912, Hughes drove the revamped Mercer to victory in the 300-inch Aurora Trophy over 18 laps of the 8.5-mile road course at Elgin, Illinois.

In preparation for the eighth Vanderbilt Cup, a non-stock event for 600-inch cars, Hughes' Mercer was slightly rebored to 4.39 × 5 inches in order to displace 302.6 inches. On 29 July 1912, it was announced that the Vanderbilt and the Grand Prize were to be run on the Wauwatosa course, Milwaukee County, Wisconsin, and that the originally scheduled Greenfield course was abandoned. After signing up all but two of the property owners and residing tenants, the Milwaukee Automobile Dealers' Association, promoter of the great speed carnival, believed everything secure for the Greenfield course when it was discovered that Chicago and eastern concessionaires were bidding for rights along the roads. When the situation was investigated it was found that almost every foot of the course would be covered with peanut stands and soda water bars. Just at this time the town board of Wauwatosa approached the association with an offer to build a course and insure titles to every foot of ground provided the association would keep it a secret until all details were completed. Two days later the board had received the signatures of 99 of the 101 property owners. The meet was scheduled for 17, 20 and 21 September. In the second week of August, E.G. Williams, Willie Vanderbilt's personal representative, inspected the new course: "It is fine. It is much better than the Greenfield course you Milwaukeeans first thought of using for the big races. Those two 3-mile straightaways will add a touch of the real sport of motor racing, and I think some new marks will be hung up if the course proves as fast as it looks today."[5] The course was directly approached by three trunk streetcar lines, one of which had been extended to the homestretch for the purpose. The start and finish line was on Burleigh Street, midway between the North and South Fond du Lac roads. The Wauwatosa course was the first which actually touched the city limits of a large metropolis such as Milwaukee with its 410,000 inhabitants. The course was a four-legged speedway, almost a parallelogram, "all sides of which are straight as arrows."[6]

Heavy rains caused the postponement of the races. The Vanderbilt was held on Wednesday, 2 October 1912, covering 38 laps of 7 miles 4658 feet, or 299 miles. The Grand Prize followed on Saturday, 5 October, over 52 laps. During practice on Tuesday, 1 October, David Bruce-Brown at the wheel of the Fiat S74 he had driven in the French Grand Prix established a new unofficial world's road record when he turned a lap in 5 min 53.82 sec or 80.2 miles per hour. A few minutes later he lost his life:

> The accident occured on the back stretch shortly before 1 P.M., when the entrants were at the height of the day's practice. While speeding at the remarkable rate of 82 miles an hour, one of the rear tires of the big Fiat exploded, causing the car to lurch into the ditch. In a vain attempt to right the machine, Brown jerked the wheel in the other direction, causing the car to jump to the other side of the road. Both driver and mechanician were pitched out of the car, turning completely over, crushed through a fence. Brown and his mechanician were picked up unconscious by farmers who had witnessed the accident. Word was immediately conveyed to the officials and both men were rushed to the Trinity hospital, where they were operated upon. Brown never regained consciousness.[7]

Tony Scudelari, "mechanician for Bruce-Brown,"[8] died on 8 October.

Despite the gloom cast by the death of Bruce-Brown, a crowd of 50,000 came for the Vanderbilt. DePalma in the Grey Ghost entered by Edward Schroeder was the first to line up, with Hughie Hughes in the yellow Mercer beside him. Teddy Tetzlaff's red Fiat S61 entered by Eugene Hewlett brought up the rear of the lineup. DePalma got a bad start and did not jump into motion as he usually did. On the other hand, Hughes was off like a shot. After the first lap Tetzlaff was in the lead with 6 min 27 sec, Mulford in a Knox six (4.8 × 5½ inches) second at 4 seconds back, Wishart in his 9.5-liter Mercedes third at 25 seconds, DePalma fourth at 30 seconds.

In lap 2 Hughes stopped at the pits to change a tire. In lap 3 Mulford and the Knox withdrew because of magneto trouble. DePalma took second 1 min 11 sec behind Tetzlaff, 47 seconds ahead of Clark in a third 9.5-liter Mercedes, 1 min 22 sec ahead of Wishart. Harry C. Nelson's Lozier, entered by Richard H. Knowles, scion of a wealthy Milwaukee family, developed brake trouble but on the stretches he appeared to be going well. In lap 5 Clark was forced to change a tire on the back stretch, falling back to fifth behind Tetzlaff, DePalma, Wishart and Anderson. In lap 12 Clark misjudged his stop at the pit and was forced to back up. He changed both rear tires and took on gasoline. In lap 15 DePalma stopped at the pits for fuel, oil and a tire. Wishart took second, 22 seconds ahead of the Grey Ghost. Tetzlaff completed 19 laps in 2 h 3 min 4 sec, 7 min 8 sec ahead of Wishart, 7 min 34 sec ahead of DePalma, 8 min 48 sec ahead of Hughes. It was also after 19 laps that Tetzlaff made his first stop for fuel, oil, water and a left rear tire. In lap 21 Wishart took 28 seconds to replace a rear tire, a record for this operation.

In lap 26 misfortune overtook Tetzlaff when the driveshaft of the Fiat broke on the backstretch. There was a murmur of dismay from the crowd when the husky voice of the announcer proclaimed that Tetzlaff, easily a favorite with them all, was out of the running. Tetzlaff's fastest laps, his second and fourth, were the fastest of the race at 6 min 15 sec. DePalma took the lead, with Hughes second 3 minutes back and Wishart third 5 minutes back. In lap 26 Nelson's Lozier retired because he was too far behind, more than 70 minutes. In lap 29 Wishart was forced to put a new chain on his Mercedes on the backstretch, while at the same time DePalma, Anderson and Clark stopped at the pits for new rear tires. After 32 laps Hughes had cut DePalma's lead down to 39 seconds. At the end of lap 35 DePalma had the better of his rival in the yellow Mercer by 46 seconds. Three laps later DePalma flashed across the tape winner of the eighth Vanderbilt in 4 h 20 min 31 sec, averaging 68.9 miles per hour, with Hughes second, just 43 seconds back.

On Wednesday, Caleb Bragg announced his withdrawal from the Grand Prize out of respect to his friend Bruce-Brown. But on Saturday he could not resist the entreaties of his teammates and took the wheel of his big 14-liter Fiat, being persuaded at the last minute to compete. Hughes was at the wheel of his rebored Vanderbilt Mercer (4.39 × 5 inches). There was a crowd of 100,000, including fully 10,000 people completely filling the immense grandstand. At the last minute, Barney Oldfield succeeded in getting Brown's big Fiat, which had won the 1911 Grand Prize at Savannah and was owned by the Los Angeles attorney and society man Eugene Hewlett. After three laps Hughes stopped to replace a spark plug. In lap 14 the Mercer was still worrying along in last place, threw a wheel but Hughes controlled the car, keeping it on the road. In lap 17 the Mercer went out for good with a broken fuel line. The end of the race was a struggle between Bragg and DePalma. With four laps to go, DePalma was 4 min 19 sec to the bad. He made lap 50 in 6 min 28 to Bragg's 7 min 21 sec and cut the margin to 3 min 26 sec. Lap 51 was made in 6 min 36 sec by DePalma and 7 min 27 sec by Bragg. The gap was reduced to 2 min 42 sec when starter Wagner waved his green flag for both of them.

DePalma was chasing his rival with deadly intensity and upon receiving a signal from his pit to "beat it" he stepped on the throttle and had the accelerator flat with the boards

Spring 1914. Caleb Bragg at the wheel of his 450-inch Mercer. No. 21 was his number in the 1914 Indy 500. The Mercer dropped out because of a broken magneto driveshaft (Library of Congress).

when he swung into the North Fond du Lac road. He crept up on the Fiat with great leaps and bounds and at station 11 he had caught his rival. But it was necessary for him to do more than catch him — he had to pass and beat him to the tape by the margin that Bragg had over him at the start. DePalma attempted to pass Bragg, but did not allow enough room to clear the other car, hitting the big Fiat with sufficient force to overturn his speeding Mercedes, throwing him and mechanic Tom Alley out of the car. Their injuries at first were thought to be serious, but did not prove so grave. Bragg won in 5 h 59 min 27 sec, averaging 69.3 miles per hour, with Bergdoll in the 12-liter Benz second at 15 min 31 sec, after a hot finish with Anderson in the Stutz who lost second in the next to the last lap when he was forced to stop for fuel. Oldfield took fourth.

DePalma was rushed to the Trinity Hospital, suffering from abdominal injuries. When he was lifted from the ambulance at the doors of the hospital, he said to the newspaper men: "Boys, don't forget that Caley Bragg wasn't to blame. He gave me all the road."[9] On 22 October it was reported that "Ralph DePalma ... is driving a wheeled chair around Trinity Hospital and the neighborhood these days. DePalma made his first public appearance on Saturday night, when he wheeled himself into the banquet hall of the Deutscher Club amid the cheers of 500.... His physicians say DePalma will be ready to leave the hospital for good in about 10 days."[10]

During the winter of 1912–1913, Bragg and DePalma switched over to Mercer since at Trenton, Finley Porter had designed new 450-inch racers for the 1913 season. Bragg was born in 1888, the son of a wealthy Cincinnati publisher, Lewis Van Antwerp's partner in the Van Antwerp, Bragg & Co., which was in 1890 the largest schoolbook publishing concern in the world. "He is a most remarkable youngster. He weighs only 127 pounds, is slight, and has no dare-devil look in his mild eyes."[11] He came to the fore in April 1910 when, at the wheel of his Fiat S61, he defeated Oldfield in the Lightning Benz in a 2-mile match race on the new board motordrome at Playa del Rey near Los Angeles. Starter Wagner remembered: "There is Caley Bragg, the Chesterfield of the speed circuit and most unostentatious of all drivers. Two years ago, when Bragg, a tyro, defeated Oldfield, the veteran, at the Los Angeles speedway and shattered several of Barney's records, he was the most down-hearted kid I ever saw. 'On the level, Wag,' he said 'I'm sorry I beat Barney. He makes a living out of this game and I don't need the money or the prestige.'"[12]

The displacement limit for the 1913 Indianapolis 500 was reduced from 600 to 450 cubic inches, and the minimum weight from 2000 to 1600 pounds. Trenton entered two 450-inch cars for Bragg and DePalma, and a 300-inch racer for Wishart, with Roy Thatcher, Andy Vollman and Johnny Jenter acting as riding mechanics. In principle, the 450-inch Mercer was a scaled up version of Hughes' 1912 racer. The new Mercer displaced 448 cubic inches with the dimensions of 4.8 × 6.189 inches. Valve diameter was 3¼ inches, valve lift ⁷⁄₁₆ inch. The camshafts were driven by skewed spur gears. The pistons were made of cast steel. A 2¼-inch Rayfield carburetor supplied the mixture. The big T-head delivered 138 hp at 2500 rpm, 150 at 2800, and weighed 782 pounds. The wheelbase was 112 inches, four inches longer than the 300-inch car and dry weight was 2700 pounds.

Bragg's Mercer rolled on wood wheels, DePalma's and Wishart's 300-inch car (4⅜ × 5 inches) on American Rudge Whitworth wire wheels made under license by the George W. Houk Wire Wheel Co., Buffalo, New York. Concerning the wire wheels, "Porter stated that the saving in weight was small but that there was less mass concentrated at the rim and more at the hub, the result being that the gyroscopic action of the wire construction is considerably less."[13] The torque of the rear axle was transmitted by the springs: "Where a shaft-drive construction is used without radius rods the driving stress must be taken by the springs, and as it is usual to shackle the springs at the rear the driving is done through the front. Thus the spring members are in compression and tend to buckle. Heavier spring members must be employed with this construction than are necessary when the shackles are at the front and the fixed ends are at the rear. It has been demonstrated on the recent Mercer racing models that springs of the latter type give better results as they may be made lighter. There is less strain on them, due to the fact that the spring members are in tension."[14]

With the big Mercer, Finley Porter had produced the final development step of the T-head racer. Of course, the difficult combustion within the valve pockets reduced the output, especially at high engine speeds. But the T-head engine as such was fully developed, sound and reliable. As in the smaller forerunner, the weight distribution was perfect, the engine being mounted as far back as possible. The Mercer marked the endpoint of a line whose highlights included the first Mercedes, the Grand Prix Panhard, the Hispano-Suiza voiturette racer, and the American Lozier and Stutz.

As usual, the 500-mile race was held on 30 May, a Friday in 1913. In lap 15 DePalma parked his big Mercer with burned out bearings. In lap 128 Bragg withdrew the second 450-inch Mercer because of a twisted pump shaft. With the race half over, DePalma took the wheel of Wishart's 300-inch machine and brought the small Mercer from ninth to third before turning it over to Wishart for the final laps. The 300-inch Mercer finished second,

13 minutes behind Goux's Peugeot. The little Mercer made the run with five tire changes, losing about 5 min 30 sec.

On Friday, 29 August 1913, the Chicago Automobile Club Trophy was held near Elgin, Illinois, open to non-stock cars of 300 inches and under. It covered 36 laps of 8 miles 2030 feet, a total of 301 miles. The Kane County course had been discovered by Frank Wood and had been proposed in 1910 for the stock chassis championships, the "Western Vanderbilt," the original lap length being 8 miles 2499 feet. In 1913 the Elgin course was shortened after a change made at McQueen's turn. To get away from the bad left-hand corner, the promoters cut between two small hills and made a big bend which could be taken wide open. Additional improvements were made in the backstretch where some of the narrow bits were widened. DePalma and Wishart drove the latest evolution of the 300-inch Mercer with 2¾-inch valves. DePalma started with an axle ratio of 2.5:1, with front tires from Firestone measuring 32 × 4 and rear tires from Prowodnik, also 32 × 4. Wishart preferred steel-studded Michelins, 32 × 4 front and 32 × 4½ rear. DePalma's racer had a 40-gallon fuel tank and a 15-gallon oil tank, Wishart's a 30-gallon fuel tank. The wheelbase was the usual 108 inches, and dry weight was 2400 pounds. A third Mercer, a tuned up production car, was driven by Guy Luttrell.

The CAC Trophy was starter Wagner's first big race meet of the 1913 season. "Wagner, who had started every race at Elgin since the Kane County course was discovered by Frank Wood, made his annual entrance in a new makeup. Some 'ole clo'se man' has Wag's grease spotted knickerbockers and bicycle cap of prehistoric vintage, and the king of all starters appeared freshly accoutred."[15] In lap 2 Wishart was forced to stop for tires. In lap 7 Luttrell was in the pits to repair a leaky water pump, and one lap later to change spark plugs. In lap 15 he retired with a burned out bearing. After 15 laps DePalma made his first pit stop to change the right rear wheel as the tire was beginning to show the effect of the furious pace. He was in the lead and completed 20 laps in 2 h 29 min 46 sec, 2 min 27 sec ahead of Joe Dawson in the Deltal.

Dawson celebrated his return to the speed game after 15 months of retirement. The Mercer and the Deltal, one a veteran and the other a novice, were about equal in speed. Neither was hard on tires. Each stopped for gasoline and oil. But the Deltal constantly demanded water while the radiator cap of the Mercer was never removed. After 22 laps Dawson made his second stop to take on fresh supplies of gasoline and water and a new set of spare wheels, losing 2 min 18 sec. Dawson never got the Deltal close enough to the Mercer to worry DePalma. In lap 24 Wishart retired the Mercer with a broken spring. After 27 laps Dawson was forced to stop at the pits because of the loosening of the throttle lever connection. At the same time the shock absorbers were tightened up. Dawson was held for 2 min 11 sec.

At the end of round 30, DePalma stopped for a can of gasoline, losing 25 seconds. DePalma won in 4 h 31 min 56.90 sec, averaging 66.8 mph and beating Dawson by 7 min 56 sec. "Harry Goetz, the Lilliputanian mechanician who rode beside Dawson Friday, had two blistered and swollen hands as souvenir of the futile pursuit of de Palma. The blisters are the result of Harry's attempts to keep his seat in the bouncing Deltal."[16]

The Deltal? It was entered in the 1913 Indianapolis 500 and took part in the qualifying trials on 27 May: "The Deltal was a veritable dark horse, a mysterious unknown, until it appeared at the track on Tuesday, and caused the wise ones to open their eyes. The car is a very racy looking creation with streamline body and is to be driven by Joe Dawson, winner of last year's race. It is a four-cylinder car 4 × 5⁵⁄₁₆ inches bore and stroke. Cylinders are cast in block and the valves are on the right side and are $2^{11}/_{16}$ inches in diameter. Pistons are forged steel and weigh but 1¾ pounds and have but one ring. At 2,500 revolutions per minute the motor shows 118 horsepower. Oil is forced to motor bearings under 50 pounds pressure."[17] The Deltal was designed by Eric Herman "E.H." Delling, a consulting engineer from Brooklyn, New York, and Paul Friedrich "P.F." Hackethal, its name being a combination of these names, and "was built in a small town in Connecticut."[18] Both engineers were born in Germany, Delling on 7 July 1884, Hackethal on 26 October 1883.[19] The Deltal was not ready for the 500 and did not start. In view of the Elgin race, the stroke was lengthened to 5.945 inches resulting in 298.6 cubic inches, and valve diameter was increased to $2^{13}/_{16}$ inches with ½ inch lift. The crankshaft ran in five plain bearings. Output was 122 hp at 3250 rpm, with the ability to rev briefly to 4000 rpm, and engine weight was 570 pounds. "Simplicity is the feature of this car.... A glance at the motor shows nothing but eight wires leading to the spark plugs and the bare cylinders. The magneto and water pump are hardly visible, being driven by a transverse shaft at the front of the motor."[20] The wheelbase was 109 inches, tires from Diamond were 34 × 4½ all around, and dry weight was 2300 pounds. It cost Delling and Hackethal close to $11,000 to place the Deltal on the track at Elgin.

The Elgin National Trophy for non-stock cars of 450 inches and under was run one day after the CAC Trophy, on Saturday, 30 August, again over a distance of 36 laps or 301 miles. DePalma and Wishart changed their mounts, taking the wheel of two 450-inch Mercers. DePalma's big Mercer rolled on wire wheels equipped with Firestone tires — 32 × 4 front, 34 × 5 rear. Wishart's racer started on wood wheels with 34 × 4½ front tires, 34 × 5 rear. The axle ratio on both cars was 2.25:1. Anderson in a Stutz won the race while Wishart made the fastest lap in 6 min 38 sec and finished third, with DePalma fifth. Encouraged by the showing of his cars, Finley Porter immediately shipped the two 450-inch Mercers to California to participate in the Corona road race.

On Tuesday, 9 September 1913, Corona celebrated the anniversary of California's admittance to the union by hosting to the motor speed kings. Corona was a little city lying on the north slope of the foothills of the Santa Ana moutains, 15 miles west of Riverside and 50 miles southeast of Los Angeles. In the spring of 1913 a motor club of 600 members was formed and Teddy Tetzlaff, Barney Oldfield and prominent motorists from Los Angeles were called in for consultation. The course was the boundary road of Corona known as Grand Boulevard, a perfect circle 2.769 miles in circumference, 70 feet wide from curb to curb, lined on both sides by luxuriant pepper and palm trees. The club decided to issue $86,000 worth of bonds for the purpose of macadamizing Grand Boulevard. The prize money totalled $15,000. Three races were run simultaneously: a 302-mile free-for-all over 109 laps, a 252-mile medium car race for 450-inch cars over 91 laps, and a 102.5-mile light car race for 230-inch cars over 37 laps.

Before a holiday throng of 200,000 spectators, Earl Cooper in a Stutz and Barney Oldfield in the Mercer owned by his backer George Settle jumped to the front at the start. At the end of 10 laps Oldfield was leading by 19 seconds. In lap 12 Wishart withdrew his Mercer because of a burned out bearing. Oldfield changed a tire in lap 14, and Cooper in lap 15, rapid pit work giving Cooper a slight lead which he increased to a half lap in five more circuits. When Cooper stopped in lap 23 for a tire, Oldfield went to the front but he held that position for only one lap since he was forced to halt at his pit for a rear shoe the next time around. DePalma parked his Mercer with a cracked cylinder. In lap 27, after gradually crawling up on the Stutz, Oldfield passed Cooper in front of the stand. Suddenly, at the end of lap 30, Felix Magone in another Stutz had a slight lead on Cooper. Magone withdrew in lap 41 because of magneto trouble. With 50 laps completed Oldfield was leading Cooper by two laps and when the race was half over he had an advantage of 2 minutes. But in lap 60 a rear tire of the Mercer left the rim. The wheel collapsed. The Mercer turned over and and piled up against a pepper tree. Barney, still chewing his cigar, walked calmly to the stands. Mechanic H. Sandhoffer suffered a slight concussion of the brain. With Oldfield out, Tetzlaff in the Fiat S74 went up into second place. In lap 90 the Fiat went out with a cracked crankcase. From then on Cooper had the race well in hand, although the Fiats of George Hill and Frank Verbeck were always within hailing distance. Cooper won the free-for-all in 4 h 2 min 38 sec, averaging 74.63 miles per hour, with Verbeck second at 7 min 42 sec and Hill flagged after 105 laps. Cooper also won the 450-inch race in 3 h 21 min 29 sec, 48 minutes ahead of Caldwell in a Marmon.

On 7 October 1913, the Grand Prize and the Vanderbilt were called off by the Savannah club due to lack of interest. Six weeks later it was announced that the two classics would be run at Santa Monica in February 1914. The Vanderbilt was booked for Saturday, 21 February, the Grand Prize for the following Monday, 23 February. But when heavy rains came, followed by inundations and washouts, Chairman Leon Shettler called a meeting of the drivers and proposed to hold the Grand Prize on Monday and the Vanderbilt on the following Wednesday. The Stutz and Mercer people objected as they were after Vanderbilt Cup honors and did not want to take any chances with their cars by starting them first in the Grand Prize. So the Vanderbilt was rescheduled for Thursday, 26 February, and the Grand Prize for Saturday, 28 February.

The Vanderbilt was open to 600-inch cars and consisted of 35 laps of 8.4 miles. Ralph DePalma had just resigned from the Mercer team because of his objection to teaming with Barney Oldfield: "Ralph DePalma and I had a squabble in 1914 that made us enemies for years," Oldfield explained. "Ralph was captain of the Mercer factory racing team, and a good captain he was. I was asked by the factory management to come on the team, but DePalma was not consulted in the matter. I accepted and Ralph said if I was taken on, he would get off the team. I was not asked to stay off the team because of DePalma's attitude, so DePalma left. This happened in the early spring of 1914. DePalma said several uncomplimentary things about me and I wasn't backward with my tongue either."[21] DePalma had soon hooked up with Edward Schroeder and drove the Grey Ghost to victory, the old Mercedes which had received fresh bearings and a Master carburetor built by Harry Miller. "De Palma's race was the best the veteran ever drove and probably is the most remarkable of all the Vanderbilts, for de Palma never stopped from the time starter Wagner patted him on the back and sent him away on the 294-mile journey."[22] DePalma had a mighty foe in Barney Oldfield who drove his 450-inch Mercer before his own townsmen and was determined to add the Vanderbilt to his long list of motoring honors. Barney was handicapped by three stops at the pits and two others on the course because of tire trouble. He lost by just 1 minute and 20 seconds. DePalma rode with Tom Alley as mechanic, Oldfield with George Hill, "the best man I ever had at my right."[23]

The Grand Prize was a 48-lap unlimited free-for-all. Wishart in the Mercer led for the first 22 laps before dropping out in lap 23 with a burned-out main bearing. DePalma in the Grey Ghost led for seven laps before being forced to stop at the pits because of a broken intake valve. The Grey Ghost finished the race on three cylinders. Johnny Marquis in a Sunbeam six took over as the new leader, until lap 33 when he turned turtle in Death Curve. Now Eddie Pullen in the 450-inch Mercer was three minutes ahead of Anderson in a Stutz. Eliminations came fast so that Pullen had absolutely no competition and jogged home, completing the distance in 5 h 13 min 30 sec. Born on 16 August 1883 in Trenton, Edwin "Eddie" Pullen joined Mercer in 1910 as mechanic. In 1914 he lived on Norway Avenue in nearby Hamilton, Mercer County, New Jersey. On 4 April, he and his Mercer were welcomed home:

> Hurrah for Pullen, whoop 'er up!
> For Eddie is a dandy.
> Yes, he 's the guy that won the Cup.
> Just have the Mercer handy.[24]

In the second week of March 1914, Finley Porter resigned from his position as factory manager and chief engineer at Mercer. Porter was replaced by Eric Delling, one of the Deltal designers. On 30 March 1914, Mercer filed its entry for the Indianapolis 500, two 450-inch racers (4.8 × 6.189 inch) for Wishart and Bragg. "The third Mercer, to be driven by Pullen, is the design of engineer Delling and is strongly reminiscent of the Deltal that ran second at Elgin last year. It has an L-head motor on four cylinders with a bore and stroke of 3¾ × 6¾ inches. It is equipped with a Bosch double distributor magneto and a Rayfield carbureter, the valves are 2¹³⁄₁₆ inches in diameter and have a ½-inch lift. The wheel-base is 110 inches."[25] Steering was on the left-hand side, the exhaust pipe on the right. The new car was not ready and did not start. But the 450-inch cars initially ran well. At 104

30 September 1916 — second Astor Cup, Sheepshead Bay, Brooklyn. Eddie Pullen and his 300-inch Mercer finished fifth (Library of Congress).

laps or 260 miles, Duray in a little 3-liter Peugeot was leading the field with Wishart second and Bragg fifth. At 280 miles Wishart took the lead, ahead of Boillot in a 5.6-liter Peugeot. In lap 117 Bragg's Mercer was eliminated with a broken magneto driveshaft. The speed demanded by Wishart was too much for the second Mercer: In lap 124 it broke a camshaft. A few weeks later, in July, the big Mercer held together and Wishart took second in the 300-miler at Sioux City.

The 1914 Elgin meet was composed of two races, as usual: the Chicago Automobile Club Trophy on Friday, 21 August, for 450-inch cars, consisting of 36 laps of 8 miles and 2030 feet, and the free-for-all Elgin National Trophy on the following day, Saturday, 22 August, over the same distance. The Mercer Automobile Co. nominated a 450-inch racer for Wishart and the latest 300-inch L-head car (3¾ × 6¼ inches) for Pullen. The local Mercer agent, Ed Schillo, entered a slightly modified Raceabout (4⅜ × 5 inches) for Otto Henning. In lap 11 of the CAC Trophy, Pullen dropped out because of transmission trouble. Wishart completed 12 laps, one-third of the distance, in 1 h 15 min 23 sec, 4 min 13 sec ahead of DePalma in the latest 4.5-liter Grand Prix Mercedes. In lap 22, Otto Henning parked his Mercer with a broken water manifold. One lap later, Wishart stopped to tighten the fuel tank which had been jolted loose. But he lost only 1 min 10 sec and completed 200 miles or 24 laps in 2 h 34 min 26 sec, 6 min 30 sec ahead of DePalma. Although leading by a wide margin, Wishart was in trouble. The fuel tank of the Mercer was leaking badly as he passed the stands and, at the end of lap 26, he stopped once more in a futile endeavor to fix the tank. During the next lap he abandoned the Mercer in disgust. DePalma won the CAC Trophy. Wishart and his mechanic Johnny Jenter labored far into the night to make repairs and prepare the 450-inch Mercer for the Elgin National. Wishart showed his car no mercy, and, after 100 miles, he led Bob Burman in a 5.6-liter Peugeot by 2 min 49 sec. In lap 14, on the backstretch of the course, one mile from the second turn, near the Coombs' farm, Wishart attempted to go by Otto Henning's Mercer. The hub cap of Wishart's Mercer grazed the front wheel of Henning's. Wishart's car swerved, shot off the road, tore through a fence, crashed against an elm tree, and rolled over twice before stopping. Wishart sat unconscious at the steering wheel, his leg broken and his chest crushed. Mechanic Jenter had been thrown to the side of the road, one arm broken and hanging limp, and having sustained internal injuries. Six of the many spectators in the path of the hurtling Mercer were bruised and cut. An ambulance sped to the scene and carried Wishart and Jenter to St. Joseph's Hospital in Elgin. DePalma won again, with Pullen in the 300-inch Mercer finishing second.

Spencer Wishart had announced his engagement to Ruth McGowan, the daughter of Hugh McGowan, an Indianapolis railroad magnate, immediately after the Indianapolis 500-mile race. The wedding had taken place on 23 June. The young couple spent their honeymoon in Europe and sailed home for America with DePalma, just two days before war was declared. The young Mrs. Wishart watched Saturday's Elgin race from the Mercer camp at Gurnett's farm. After the accident in lap 14, she was taken in the referee's car to her husband's bedside when an examination showed that he could not survive, and was with him when he passed away two hours later. Mechanic Johnny Jenter died of his injuries on Wednesday morning, 26 August. From the days of his youth, Wishart had tinkered with cars. In 1905, when he was but 18 years old, he had a Maxwell raceabout in which he burned up the streets of Greenwich, Connecticut. His father, a mining engineer, encouraged him in his speed whim and bought him a 60-hp Mercedes in which he made his racing debut in 1909. Wishart drove his own cars for two years, but in 1911, when his father lost his fortune, he became affiliated with the Simplex company, and in 1912 switched to the Mercer. Starter Fred Wagner recalled:

> The car that would survive under Wishart would survive under any other driver.... Wishart did not know the meaning of fear. I remember the first race he ever drove, the Vanderbilt of 1909. A day or so before the race he came to me and asked me to explain the rules to him and to give him any advice that I could. The morning of the race I expected to send a trembling, nervous boy away. Imagine my surprise when he behaved like the oldest head in the business! I recall another incident that illustrates his daring. After the Santa Monica races this year, Glenn Martin, the aviator, asked me to fly with him. I accepted the invitation, but with little relish. Just before we started, Martin turned to the crowd and said, 'I've room for one more.' The 'one more' was Wishart, who grasped the opportunity to soar among the clouds without a moment's hesitation. After we had been flying about 5 minutes and I was wondering whether I would ever reach earth again, Martin said that we were up 2,500 feet. 'Is that all?' Wishart asked, as if a trifle disappointed. Then he added, after looking at the foggy sky calmly, 'It isn't a very good day for flying, is it?' ... Except when his car failed him, Wishart usually was in the money. He finished third in the Vanderbilt cup races of 1911 and 1912, runner-up to Jules Goux in the Indianapolis international sweepstakes of last year and beaten only by a few seconds by Rickenbacher at Sioux City. Wishart's seeming indifference also was a byword in the racing camps. A stop at the pits at a crucial stage of a race, a delay that causes other drivers to swear and sweat, made no impression on him. While his helpers were slaving to save precious seconds, he drank water, examined his car calmly and carefully pulled on his gloves and adjusted his goggles. He never vaulted to his seat, but stepped in with a nonchalance worthy of a Beau Brummel entering a drawing room.[26]

DePalma said: "The only thing that seemed to wake him up was the popping of the exhausts."[27] DePalma, Caleb Bragg and David Bruce-Brown were Wishart's closest friends. Before the death of Bruce-Brown, the four took a trip to Europe annually.

The 1914 season closed in California with the "second annual Corona gasoline classic"[28] on Thanksgiving, 26 November, a 109-lap race on the Grand Boulevard course or 300.84 miles. The Bentel & Mackey Co., the Mercer distributor for California, entered three cars for Eddie Pullen, who took the wheel of the 450-inch racer that Wishart drove at Indianapolis, Sioux City and Elgin; Louis Nikrent; and Grover "Guy" Ruckstell. Nineteen cars started, lined up four abreast. Owing to the fine gravel on the course, most of the drivers wore face masks. Rickenbacher and his mechanic Fred McCarthy, in a 5.6-liter Peugeot, wore weird-looking helmets with speaking tubes connecting from mouth to ear and back again. Grant and Babcock, in their Sunbeams, wore black masks which made them look like train bandits. Others did not even wear racing caps and trusted alone to goggles. Pullen and his Mercer, once yellow but painted crimson now, completed ten laps in 18 min 10 sec, 15 seconds ahead of Rickenbacher. In lap 30 Pullen dropped back to eighth after blowing a tire and skidding off the course. In lap 50 he was back to second, 1 min 52 sec behind Babcock. After 60 laps Earl Cooper in a Stutz took the lead. Babcock had caught a white bulldog crossing the road, damaging a steering arm of the Sunbeam. Pullen was second, just a minute behind Cooper. After 80 laps Pullen was in the lead again, in front of Cooper, with Oldfield in a Maxwell third. In the last laps Cooper battled with Ruckstell for second. Then, in lap 107, Cooper went out with broken timing gears. One lap later, Nikrent ran out of gas. And in the last lap, just one mile from the finish, it was the turn of Ruckstell. Pullen was the winner, in 3 h 26 min 2 sec, averaging 87.86 mph, nearly three minutes ahead of Oldfield. The Grand Prize at Santa Monica and the Corona race were to be the last great victories of a T-head racer.

"World's Road Racing Record Smashed by Pullen"[29] was the headline. Pullen collected $6,000 as first prize and and an additional $2,000 for breaking the world record. Pullen shared the honors of the day with Barney Oldfield, who two weeks earlier earned the title of "the master driver of the world" by winning the Cactus Derby, the road race from Los Angeles to Phoenix. The veteran of them all covered the 300 miles without a single stop for fuel, water, tires or mechanical adjustments. "Barney was in poor condition physically, not having recovered from the strain and tortures endured in piloting the Stutz across the desert in the Cactus derby; he had only 2 days of practice before he was sent away by Starter Wagner and knew very little about the mechanicism of the car which he drove for more than 3 hours without a single stop. If there was any doubt about Barney's right to the title of 'master driver of the world,' he dispelled them in his wonderful achievement today."[30] Oldfield was not happy with the classification of Corona as road race:

> Placing a course like that at Corona, Cal., on a par with that of Santa Monica or Elgin, Ill., is ridiculous. Corona is a speedway, as Indianapolis, in spite of its being a public highway and not fenced in, yet the time made at Corona is looked up as the world's official road racing record. The course is an almost perfect circle. Its surface is as well paved as any city street. From the beginning to the end of the race it was not necessary to shift gears once, and not once did I vary the pressure of my foot on the throttle. Why should a course like this be classed with Elgin or Santa Monica, where the surface is rough, where gear shifts at several turns are necessary? It seems to me that a special classification, perhaps to be known as 'semi-speedways' should be made for courses of this kind. Then Santa Monica, Elgin and the other bona fide road courses of the country could offer drivers inducements to break the old world's road racing record of 78.72 miles an hour.[31]

The 28-year-old Ruckstell was born in San Francisco where he attended high school. In 1910 he opened a garage at Bakersfield and one year later he started in the 430-mile Bakersfield road race at the wheel of a Stutz. In 1912 he drove a Mercer in the Panama-Pacific road race. The Mercer was owned by George Fiester, through whom Ruckstell met George Bentel, the partner of Charles Mackey in the Bentel & Mackey Co., the Simplex and Mercer agency located at 1053 South Grand Avenue, Los Angeles. Moreover, Bentel made a fortune with his Geo. R. Bentel Co. at 1015 South Grand Avenue which designed and trimmed new cars out of old ones and sold the result for as high as $10,000. Bentel was also chairman of the Ascot speedway. He was Ruckstell's backer in 1915. In April 1915, Ruckstell paid a visit to the Mercer factory and was promptly offered a car for the Indianapolis 500.

On 27 April Mercer entered three cars in the 500, for Pullen, Ruckstell and Louis Nikrent. Eric Delling continued to rely on simplicity, and hence on his beloved L-head. The new cars were developed from the 1914 300-inch racer using the same dimensions of $3\frac{3}{4} \times 6\frac{3}{4}$ inches. But the Mercers had done scarcely 100 miles before reaching the speedway. Only one of them came out to qualify, driven by Ruckstell and making its lap in 1 min 47.4 sec. Each of the other two cars broke a connecting rod and tore a hole in the cylinder casting and the crankcase. On 28 May the complete team was scratched. Because of the war in Europe, Delling was unable to secure the famous BND steel from Belgium for the rods: "No material to be had in this country will do."[32] On 4 July, Ruckstell drove a Mercer to victory in the 250-mile Montamarathon Trophy on the new Tacoma board track in 2 h 57 min 3 sec, while Pullen in another Mercer finished third.

The Mais and the Cino-Purcell used modified Mercer engines during the 1915 season. Johnny Mais' Mais Special was powered by a Mercer engine (4.373 × 4.985 inches) fitted with an OHV head. The Cino-Purcell, built by William Purcell of Ludlow, Kentucky, and driven by Charles Cox, relied on a modified Mercer T-head (4.37 × 4.97 inches).

The T-head tradition was not only continued by Mercer but also by the main competitor, Stutz. In contrast to Mercer, Stutz did not built its own engine. The T-head for the Stutz was supplied by a specialist and mounted into a Stutz frame. The Mercer-Stutz rivalry took place on the tracks as well as in the salesrooms where it was hard for the wealthy young sportsmen to decide in favor of the Mercer Raceabout or the Stutz Bearcat. In 1913, the Raceabout with 300-inch engine and 108-inch frame was offered at $2600. The Bearcats were less expensive, the 390-inch four (4¾ × 5½ inches) in a 120-inch frame being offered at $2000, and the 425-inch six (4¼ × 5 inches) in a 124-inch frame at $2125. At the same time a Ford Model T Runabout was quoted at $525, a 318-inch Marmon Speedster (4½ × 5 inches) at $2750, and a 448-inch National Semi-Racing Roadster (4.88 × 6 inches) also at $2750. Mercer produced 891 cars in 1913, Stutz 759, Ford more than 220,000, Marmon 599, and National 1710.

8

Stutz

The day on which the "car that made good in a day"[1] made good was Tuesday, 30 May 1911. The event was the first Indianapolis 500. The car was the first Stutz. Gil Anderson was the driver, and Frank Agan the riding mechanic.[2] They finished eleventh, 40 minutes behind Harroun's Marmon Wasp. Harry Clayton Stutz was born on 12 September 1876 in Ansonia, Ohio, near Dayton, the second of four children born to Henry J. Stutz, who had a small farm, and Elizabeth née Snyder. Harry learned the machinist trade, repaired bicycles, built gas engines, sold Schebler carburetors, and in 1906 was appointed factory manager and chief engineer at the Marion Motor Car Co. in Indianapolis. In November 1909, he opened the Stutz Auto Parts Co. at Indianapolis acting as specialized manufacturer of his transaxle design. Of course, a three-speed transaxle was mounted on Anderson's racer, the rear axle being of the semi-floating type. The engine was supplied by the Wisconsin Motor Mfg. Co. which was located at 53rd and Burnham Street, West Allis, Milwaukee County, Wisconsin. The technical director at Wisconsin was Arthur F. Milbrath, one of the men who had founded the company in March 1909. Milbrath had began his career with the A.O. Smith Co., an engine part manufacturer in Milwaukee. Stutz used the Wisconsin Type A, a 390-inch T-head, 4¾ × 5½ inches. The chassis of the 1911 Indianapolis racer had a wheelbase of 110 inches, track of 56 inches, 34 × 4 front tires and 34 × 4½ rear, and a dry weight of 2390 pounds.

On 9 September 1911, Cincinatti made its first attempt at road racing on the occasion of the opening of the Fernbank Dam across the Ohio river. The course was a 7.9-mile triangle between Silverton, Blue Ash and Montgomery, near Rossmoyne about 15 miles from Cincinnati. Two races were run simultaneously, the 150-mile, 19-lap Hamilton County Trophy for 300-inch non-stock cars and the 200-mile, 25-lap Cincinnati Trophy for 600-inch non-stock cars. At 11:40 A.M. Fred Wagner sent away twelve starters at 30-second intervals. The Stutz driven by Gil Anderson withdrew after a few yards because of transmission trouble. Eddie Hearne in the 8-liter Kaiserpreis Fiat won the $2000 Cincinnati silver cup in 3 h 29 min 3 sec, while the former prize-fighter Johnny Jenkins in a 300-inch Cole took second 11 minutes back, and at the same time won the Hamilton County in 2 h 46 min 29 sec. On 9 October, Anderson started in the Fairmount Park race, but again his Stutz fell out. On 15 October, at Santa Monica, California, Dave Lewis drove a Stutz (4¾ × 5½ inches) to third in the Leon Shettler Cup for non-stock 450-inch class C cars, behind Charlie Merz in a National (5 × 5¹¹⁄₁₆ inches) and Bert Dingley in a Pope-Hartford.

The 8.4-mile road course at Santa Monica was also the location of the first big meet of the 1912 season, the windup being a free-for-all on Saturday, 4 May over 36 laps or 302.4 miles, starting at 1 o'clock. There were only seven starters, but seven strong starters. Three ex–Savannah Fiats, 14-liter *tipi S74* (150 × 200 mm), were driven by Caleb Bragg, a resurrected Barney Oldfield whose suspension had just ended, and "Terrible" Teddy Tetzlaff. Oldfield handled the ex–Bruce-Brown Fiat and Tetzlaff the ex–Wagner car. The Fiats were entered by three Los Angeles society men, Bragg's by Eugene E. Hewlett, Oldfield's by Edward R. "Eddie" Maier, and Tetzlaff's by Dr. Edwin Janss: "Dr. Edwin Janss, of the Janss Investment Company, of this city, purchased the 'Owensmouth Baby,' the big Fiat which Teddy Tetzlaff drove into a world record, and entered the car in the Santa Monica Road Race. Eddie Maier, of the Maier Brewing Company, purchased the 'Select Kid,' the big Fiat Barney Oldfield drove, and made it possible for the former world's speed king to be a drawing card for the big road battle. Attorney Eugene E. Hewlett, the Fiat agent, sold the cars to Dr. Janss and to Eddie Maier."[3] Attorney Hewlett was the heaviest stockholder of the Pacific Coast Motor Car Co., the West Coast Fiat agents. Maier was involved in the Maier Pier Co. and the Maier Brewing Co., and was "the enterprising president of the Vernon baseball association."[4] Janss of the Janss Investment Co. was a prominent Los Angeles realty man who lived in the Wilshire district, Windsor Square, in a "pure Italian Renaissance"[5] house designed by architect J. Martyn Haenke. Two Stutzes (4¾ × 5½ inches) were handled by Earl Cooper and Dave Lewis; a 15-liter Benz (155 × 200 mm) by David Bruce-Brown who was back in the car of his first great success; and a Simplex (5¾ × 5¾ inches) by Bert Dingley. The crowd was estimated at 150,000. Bruce-Brown was the early leader until he stopped in lap 4 to renew two tires. Then Tetzlaff was in front, with Bragg second. Bragg lost valuable minutes in lap 8 when he stopped for tires. Oldfield took second until lap 12 when a spring bolt broke and put him out of the running. Tetzlaff completed 18 laps in 1 h 57 min 58 sec, with Brown trailing by 3 min 9 sec, Bragg by 5 min 9 sec, Dingley by 8 min 44 sec, and the Stutzes more than 12 minutes back. In the last lap Tetzlaff swept down Ocean Front too fast into the right angle turn at Nevada Avenue and went into the iron rail. Bragg in the second Fiat stopped, but a hasty examination showed nothing more serious than a damaged tire and a dent in the fuel tank. Tetzlaff changed the tire and won in 3 h 50 min 57 sec, a new record average of 78.7 miles per hour, 2 min 8 sec ahead of Bragg and 4 min 35 sec ahead of Brown, who was slowed by tire trouble. Tetzlaff's Fiat rolled on Michelins on the front and Millers (made in Seattle) on the rear. Lewis and Cooper were flagged after 34 laps, fourth and fifth: "The Stutzes ran consistently throughout the race and for lap after lap were not separated by over 25 feet."[6] Lewis averaged 71.4 miles per hour, his mate Cooper 71.3.

While the "car that made good in a day" had been nominated by the Stutz Auto Parts Co., the Stutz entries for the 1912 Indianapolis race were made by the Ideal Motor Car Co., which had just been founded by Harry Stutz and his backer Henry Campbell to manufacture the Stutz model A, more or less a duplicate of the 1911 Indianapolis car. The factory was located at 221 West 10th Street, Indianapolis. Three cars were entered for Gil Anderson, Len Zengle and Charlie Merz, with Billy Knipper as relief. The cylinder dimensions of the Wisconsin T-head were unchanged at 4¾ × 5½ inches, with 2⅜-inch valves; the wheelbase remained 110 inches; and dry weight was up to 2440 pounds. The Stutz pits used box-like funnels built according to Knipper's design, with turned-in edges to prevent the fuel from splashing out. After 200 miles, Anderson left the track when a front wheel collapsed. Merz finished fourth, 12 minutes behind Dawson in the National, and Zengle sixth.

The next big meet took place on the new 5-mile course at Lake View near Tacoma, Washington, on Friday and Saturday, 5 and 6 July 1912, with 65,000 persons watching the sport. On Friday, Bob Evans in an EMF-Flanders won the 100-miler for 230-inch cars.

STUTZ WRECKED — INDIANAPOLIS

30 May 1912 — second Indianapolis 500. After 200 miles, Gil Anderson's Stutz left the track when the right front wheel collapsed (Library of Congress).

Earl Cooper in a Stutz was the winner of the 150-miler for 450-inch cars, in which Pollem in a Mercer took third and the 300-inch division. Erwin Bergdoll, for once in a Mercer and not in his Benz, retired with a broken universal joint. The 200-miler for 600-inch cars was won by Teddy Tetzlaff at the wheel of a Fiat S61 in 2 h 54 min 31 sec. A Knox six finished second, 3 min 41 sec back, driven by Billy Chandler and Ralph Mulford, who was forced to come in with a bleeding head caused by a flying stone. Earl Devore in a National was third over 11 minutes back. Hughie Hughes in the factory Mercer withdrew in the 150-miler with a burned-out clutch and in the 200-miler with a broken connecting rod. On Saturday, Tetzlaff in the Fiat won the 250-mile free-for-all in 3 h 47 min, 3 min 49 sec ahead of Erwin Bergdoll, now at the wheel of his 12-liter Benz, then Devore in the National, and Frank Verbeck in a second Fiat S61. Bergdoll lost 12 minutes because of a broken chain. Hughes in the 300-inch Mercer retained the lead until the third lap when clutch trouble caused his third withdrawal in the contest. On the same weekend, Louis Disbrow was the star performer at Old Orchard Beach, Maine. Disbrow drove his Jay-Eye-See, a highly modified 18-liter Fiat, and his Simplex Zip, a short-chassis 450-inch Simplex (5 × 5¾ inches). In the Jay-Eye-See he made a mile in 35.1 seconds. In the Zip he covered five miles in 4 min 4.5 sec, and won two 10-milers in 8 min 36 sec and 8 min 53 sec. Dave Lewis in a Stutz won a 100-miler in 1 h 32 min 43 sec.

As usual there were two days of racing at Elgin. In 1912 the races were open to class C non-stock cars, instead of the previous year's class B stock. Three curtain-raisers were run simultaneously on Friday, 30 August: the Fred W. Jencks Trophy for cars under 230 inches, covering 12 laps of 8 miles 2499 feet or 101 miles; the Aurora Trophy for the 231–300 inch division 18 laps or 152.5 miles; and the Illinois Cup for the 301–450 division, 24 laps or 203 miles. The turns at Hornbeek's, McQueen's and McLean's were cemented. As an additional safety factor the Elginites tried out a proposition of Tetzlaff's and put straw bales on the turns. There were only four contenders in the Illinois: two Stutzes (4¾ × 5½ inches) with Gil Anderson and Charlie Merz, a National (5 × 5¹¹⁄₁₆ inches) with Neil Whalen, and a Rayfield six (4 × 5½ inches) with W. Hobbs. They were the first to be sent off by starter Wagner, at 11 o'clock. Charlie Merz in the Stutz led the race from the start while Neil Whalen in the National was a close second until lap 7. The Rayfield was out in lap 3 with a burned out crankshaft bearing. In lap 8 Anderson took second, ahead of Whalen who dropped out in lap 10 with a broken magneto drive. This left the race entirely in the hands of the Stutzes. Merz won the Illinois in 3 h 4 min 32 sec, averaging 66.11 miles per hour, finishing 1 min 42 sec ahead of his teammate Gil Anderson. Merz' Stutz consumed 21 gallons of fuel, Anderson's 20 gallons.

The main events followed on Saturday, 31 August: the Elgin National Watch Co. Trophy for class C 600-inch cars, over a distance of 30 laps or 254 miles, and the concurrent 36-lap free-for-all, measuring 305 miles. On Friday afternoon, in his garage, DePalma went over the Grey Ghost with a drop light and discovered at 4 P.M. that his clutch case was cracked. It was 2 A.M. Saturday when he finished the repair. But when the Mercedes was pushed to the tape, DePalma was forced to do more work. In fact, it was necessary to delay

9 October 1915 — first Astor Cup, Sheepshead Bay, Brooklyn. Gil Anderson (Library of Congress).

the start of the Elgin National 15 minutes in order to give his pitmen a chance to tinker with the stubborn Mercedes clutch. A crowd of 50,000 lined the course. The weather was the hottest which had visited the middle west in 1912 and the boiling sun beat down furiously upon the speeding drivers, much to their discomfiture. Erwin Bergdoll, mechanic Fritz Craemer and their 12-liter Grand Prix Benz, which rolled on rare Fisk tires, 36 × 4 front and 36 × 4½ rear, completed 30 laps in 3 h 39 min 4 sec but were ineligible to win the Elgin National because the car's displacement exceeded 600 inches. DePalma won that race in 3 h 43 min 20 sec, averaging 68.4 miles per hour, with Ralph Mulford in a Knox six placing second, Charlie Merz in the Stutz third, Mortimer Roberts in a Mason-Duesenberg fourth and Anderson in the second Stutz fifth. In the succeeding six laps of the free-for-all, Bergdoll was delayed by tire problems, enabling DePalma to win the 36-lap free-for-all as well, in 4 h 25 min 36 sec, with Bergdoll second.

According to DePalma the backstretch was the hottest, and was very much like an oven, despite the fact that the big Mercedes was travelling at nearly 70 miles an hour. The heat from the engine swept directly back to the occupants to add to the sun's rays. DePalma used a total of 29 gallons of fuel for the 36 laps thus averaging 10.5 miles to the gallon. His tank had a capacity of 49 gallons, and while at the pit on one occasion he took on 10 gallons. Meanwhile the Mercedes block was bored to 131.8 mm, with the stroke unchanged at 180 mm, displacing 599.2 cubic inches. "Speaking of the course, de Palma stated that it was one of the best on which he has driven, and that it was an easy matter to pass any other car, the width being amply sufficient. At 90 miles an hour the slight roughness of the road surface is not noticeable at all, he stated, while at 60 miles, the unevenness is only slightly perceptible, and is by no means a disturbing factor. The course is better than that over which the French Grand Prix is run in that respect, in the recent French event he being obliged to run along for some 15 miles at certain parts of the French course before he was able to pass any other car."[7]

Stutz closed the 1912 season at Milwaukee with Anderson's fourth in the Vanderbilt and third in the Grand Prize. The Stutz ran on wire wheels and "looked small beside the immense foreign machines."[8] In the Grand Prize, Anderson held the palm of the longest non-stop run of the day. He made only two stops during the entire 410 miles and ran the first 215 miles without a halt. He had no mechanical trouble and changed but one tire, the left rear. At the same time he took on gasoline and oil. His only other stop was on the next to the last lap when he refilled his fuel tank. His best lap was 6 min 41 sec.

Early in 1913 two road races were held in San Diego, California. The first one, on New Year's day, 1 January, covered two long laps of 91.7 miles. George Hill drove a Fiat to victory in 3 h 58 min 12 sec, with Smith in a Mercer second at 14 minutes and Carlson in a Stutz third at 18 minutes. The second race took place on 1 March, over a 5.9-mile course on the Point Loma peninsula, a distance of 34 laps or 200.6 miles. Billy Carlson in a Benz won in 3 h 23 min 9 sec, 1 min 41 sec ahead of Earl Cooper in a Stutz.

In May 1913, at Indianapolis, the Ideal Motor Car Co. turned up with three cars for Charlie Merz, Gil Anderson and Don Herr, with Harry Martin, Frank Agan and Roy Vernon as riding mechanics, and Earl Cooper as relief. In February there had been negotiations with Joe Dawson as driver of the third car, but finally Don Herr took its wheel. The displacement of the Wisconsin T-heads was slightly increased from 389 to 436 cubic inches, the bore now being 4.813 instead of 4¾ inches and the stroke 6 instead of 5½ inches. Wheelbase was 112 inches, tires 34 × 4½ all around, and dry weight was 2350 pounds. In lap 7 Herr parked his Stutz with a broken clutch shaft. After 400 miles or 160 laps Goux in the

Peugeot was in the lead, with Anderson, who had been relieved by Cooper, second at 4 min 18 sec. In lap 187 Anderson coasted into the pits, lifted the hood, gave a few turns of the starting crank and pushed the white Stutz into the paddock with a broken camshaft. Now Merz, who had also been relieved by Cooper, was third, behind Goux and Wishart in the 300-inch Mercer. "Starting his last lap, Merz's Stutz was a flaming torch of gasoline under the bonnet. If he stopped at the pits to extinguish it he lost his chance of beating out the Mercer for second place, so he pluckily continued for the lap which ended with the checkered flag. Coming down the stretch for the last time, the Stutz, a mass of flames in front, coasted over the line and to the pits, with the mechanic sprawled over the bonnet fighting the fire. And Merz lost second place by just 36 seconds."[9] He was given a cheer that rarely is accorded to a third-place car. On 26 June, Harry Martin, Merz's riding mechanic, was killed and Frank Agan was severely injured when trying out a new Stutz at the Indianapolis Speedway.

On Saturday, 5 July 1913, Earl Cooper in a Stutz took the 200-mile Potlatch trophy at Tacoma, Washington. The road course was new and lap length was now 3.5 miles instead of the previous year's 5 miles, while the number of laps increased to 57. Cooper's time was 2 h 49 min 32 sec, over 20 minutes ahead of Burman whose Keeton was slowed by cylinder trouble. On the following Monday, Cooper won the 250-mile Montamarathon free-for-all in 3 h 38 min 8 sec, averaging 70.71 miles per hour, and finishing 2 min 52 sec ahead of Dave Lewis in a Fiat S61, and 7 min 47 sec ahead of Hughie Hughes in the Tulsa. Tetzlaff and his big Fiat S74 went out in lap 14 because of a broken oil pump; Burman and his Grand Prix Benz followed suit in lap 49 because of a broken gas line. On 9 August, Earl Cooper and his Stutz continued their clean sweep in the 450-miler at Santa Monica, California, covering 53 laps of 8.4 miles in 6 h 1 min 52 sec, averaging 73.77 mph to finish 5 min 53 sec ahead of Barney Oldfield in a 450-inch Mercer entered by George F. Settle, and 27 minutes ahead of Louis Nikrent in the 300-inch Mercer Monk entered by Huntley Gordon.

On Saturday, 30 August 1913, Anderson drove his Indianapolis car in the Elgin National Trophy for non-stock cars of 450 inches and under, a race of 36 laps of 8 miles 2030 feet. The Stutz was entered by the local agent, Robert E. Maypole. Some 40,000 spectators witnessed the start. "Reports of the Elgin National trophy race may be anticipated by the readers of Vogue, the Ladies' Home Journal, the Woman's Home Companion and the Delineator. The press stand was aflutter with female reporters Saturday."[10] There were twelve starters. The red Isotta driven by Harry Grant was the only foreign car in the field. "Harry Grant, in blue jersey, white helmet and yellow silk handkerchief fluttering in the breeze, was as resplendent as a medieval crusader.... Barney Oldfield should swear a warant for Erwin Bergdoll on the charge of stealing his stuff and sue the Philadelphian for infringement of copyright. When the Erwin Special was sent away in the Elgin National trophy race, the millionaire driver and his mechanician, Mercedes Fritz Kramer, carried cigars as part of their racing equipment. They were not satisfied with chewing them as is Barney, but had the Havana panatellas ignited."[11] The Erwin Special was a mixture of Bergdoll chassis and Benz engine, prepared by Fritz Craemer,[12] the former star mechanic of the Benz Auto Import Co. who had pumped oil near Bruce-Brown during the 1910 Grand Prize at Savannah. The frame was a stripped Bergdoll stock chassis, wheelbase 108 inches, tires 34 × 4 front, 34 × 4½ rear. The 7-liter Benz engine came from a 1910 Prinz Heinrich racer, measuring 115 × 175 mm, with OHV 4-valve head. Craemer had fitted magnalium pistons and a 2-inch Rayfield carburetor: "Magnalium is made of a combination of magnesium and aluminum primarily and the coefficient of expansion is very nearly that of grey iron."[13] At 3000 pounds the Erwin Special was the heaviest car in the race.

Wishart in the big Mercer took the lead after a first lap in 6 min 51 sec, 16 seconds ahead of Anderson. Bergdoll stopped for a new plug and taped one of the petcocks. In lap 4 Anderson took the lead. After a stop for fuel and oil, Anderson completed 18 laps in 2 h 4 min 33 sec. The plucky Norwegian was 4 min 26 sec ahead of Mulford in a Mason, 4 min 39 sec ahead of Wishart, then Burman in the Keeton and Bergdoll. In lap 19 Burman came in to take on oil and tighten his shock absorbers. He signalled for a relief driver, but before Harry Endicott could get into his khaki knickerbockers and white flannel norfolk jacket, the Keeton was eliminated with a cracked cylinder. "When Anderson applied the brakes previous to his first stop on the twenty-first lap of Saturday's race, the left rear tire was partly off the rim. Rooney, the mechanician, picked out a soft spot on the gasoline tank, reclined there and landed a solar plexus blow on the wabbling casing. The tire rolled 100 yards down the course, broke up a heart-to-heart conference between three soldiers and then hurdled the fence in front of the press stand."[14] In lap 23 Anderson changed a tire on the backstretch and came to the pit to put a new spare on the rack. One lap later, "Farmer Bill Endicott's mascot, from the pig-stye of the Brown County farm, squealed in disgust when the Case Tornado ceased to blow in Saturday's race and 20 minutes were lost in installing a new breaker box. Then he (or she) drowned his (or her) sorrows in a bottle of milk."[15] After 26 laps Bergdoll took third behind Anderson and Mulford, in front of Wishart. In lap 32 Bergdoll ran out of gasoline on the backstretch. Anderson kept increasing his pace, much to the surprise of the spectators who had expected him to play safe. Each of his last 11 laps was under 7 minutes and he wound up with a lap of 6 min 48 sec, which was only 10 seconds slower than Wishart's $200 lap record. Anderson won in 4 h 13 min 38.97 sec, an average of 71.5 miles per hour, with Mulford in the Mason second, 6 min 53 sec behind, and Wishart third, trailing by 16 min 20 sec. Anderson lost a total of 3 min 45 sec at the pits. "The course was far from first class and toward the end became slippery in spots. There was also terrific heat to contend with. Anderson's race under the circumstances was marvellous and he deserved to win. He beat it from the start and had us all standing on our heads."[16]

At the end of the year, Earl Cooper was awarded the title of 1913 road racing champion. Fred Wagner summarized:

> Earl Cooper is our most meteoric driver. Tooling the car "that made good in a day," he has made good in one season. Last year he was practically unknown except on the Pacific coast.... Cooper is a great judge of pace. In this respect he has few equals. Add to this brains and gameness and you have an excellent three-point suspension for fame. Of the stars of 1913, Gil Anderson, to my mind, has overcome the most obstacles. When I first saw him I did not think that he would ever be a great driver. He seemed to lack several qualities that make for greatness in the speed game. These qualities, however, were not lacking. They were only latent. Anderson has developed wonderfully. No man ever drove a headier race than did Gil in the Elgin trophy this year. Nor do I think that he has reached the top of fame's crest.[17]

Earl Cooper was a native of Nebraska, born in Broken Bow on 2 December 1886. Five years later his parents went to California. In 1913 Cooper was a resident of Los Angeles, where he was in the employ of the Walter M. Brown Co., the local Stutz agent. As in the case of Harry Grant, Cooper never started in a race without his plan of action having been worked out to the most minute detail before lining up at the tape. Cooper was only 17 years old when he drove his first race in 1904, and his victory on that occasion lost him his job. At that time he was working for C.H. Letcher, later a prominent dealer in San Jose, California. Letcher and Cooper had worked hard in putting a one-cylinder Cadillac in shape for racing at Agricultural Park, San Jose.

Letcher had elected to drive the car himself. But Cooper likewise was filled with racing enthusiasm and so, unknown to his boss, he borrowed another one-cylinder Cadillac, owned by a San Jose woman, and entered it in the same meet. Cooper went to the tape in fear and trembling, finding his boss already there. Letcher took it as a joke and laughed at the boy. The race was a 5-mile event and Cooper, knowing that Letcher's car was the faster of the two, resorted to strategy. Letcher took the lead at the start, but after running a couple of miles he slowed down in order that Cooper might catch up and make the finish an interesting one. Cooper, however, lagged behind until the 3.5-mile post was reached, whereupon he made his run from the rear with the throttle wide open. Cooper caught his boss napping and passed him in a whirl of dust, gaining a lead that his boss was unable to overcome and winning the race hands down. Cooper reported for work at the garage the next morning, only to find that his victory of the day before had been a costly one, for Letcher declared that no boy could turn a trick like that on him and continue in his employ. Cooper lost his job.

In February 1914, at Santa Monica, Cooper and the Stutz finished fourth in the Vanderbilt while Anderson went out with a broken driveshaft. In the Grand Prize both Stutzes failed to finish, Anderson's because of a cracked cylinder, Cooper's because of a broken valve. It was at Santa Monica that Harry Stutz became enthused over Oldfield when he saw the enthusiasm of the veteran, admired his cool and daring driving. Stutz was convinced that the Oldfield of the Santa Monica meeting was a far different chap than the Oldfield who used to barnstorm it through the country. Oldfield was anxious to get hold of a foreign car, was negotiating with three foreign concerns, and had his eye on a Mercedes. But he decided in favor of Stutz and expected to arrive at Indianapolis during the first week of May to begin with practice work.

Stutz had built three new cars for the 1914 Indianapolis race, being satisfied to relegate the two 1913 racers of Cooper and Anderson to minor events. Meanwhile the Stutz Auto Parts Co. and the Ideal Motor Car Co. had merged into the Stutz Motor Car Co., which entered the three new racers for Anderson, Cooper and Oldfield. Anderson's engine displaced 418 cubic inches with dimensions of 4.813 × 5¾ inches; Cooper's and Oldfield's were 436 cubic inches with 4.813 × 6 inches. Wheelbase was 112 inches as on the older chassis; tires from Firestone were 34 × 4½ front, 35 × 5 rear, on wood wheels. After 50 laps Anderson's Stutz went out with a broken crankshaft, then in lap 119 Cooper's followed with a broken wheel. After 300 miles Anderson relieved Oldfield, and drove for 1 h 10 min. The Oldfield-Anderson Stutz finished fifth, 20 minutes behind Thomas's Delage. The Stutz stopped only three times and lost only 3 min 36 sec. "It must have been most gratifying to the former speed king to add to his racing laurels by being the first American to finish in the 500-mile race. Also Barney gained distinction by having led the scramble at one time. Oldfield and his Stutz were prominent at all stages of the race."[18]

On Friday, 3 July 1914, Hughie Hughes driving one of the new 450-inch Maxwells won the 200-mile Potlatch trophy on the new 2-mile speedway at Tacoma, Washington. Hughes' time was 2 h 41 min 32 sec. Klein's King was 4 seconds back, Cooper's Stutz 2 min 29 sec back. Next day, Earl Cooper in a Stutz captured the 250-mile Montamarathon race in 3 h 24 min 34 sec, 6 minutes ahead of Ruckstell's Mercer, 10 minutes ahead of

Klein's King. Bert Dingley wrecked his Ono and was so seriously injured that he spent several weeks hospitalized. Ono? The Ono was owned by Frank Young, a Los Angeles society man who acted as mechanic for Dingley in the 1913 desert race to Phoenix. In April 1914, Young bought the 14-liter S74 Fiat which had been driven by Wagner at Savannah in 1911 and by Tetzlaff at Santa Monica in 1912 and 1914. Its block, perforated by a broken connecting rod, was irreparable. But its frame was in good condition. In July 1913, Dingley took charge of the sales department at the Los Angeles Pope-Hartford agency of William "Wild Bill" Ruess. So it was no surprise that the Fiat frame received a Pope-Hartford OHV engine. Young, Dingley and Ruess tried to find a name for their creation: "After every suggestion, one of the group would exclaim 'Oh no!' Late in the evening, one of the members announced 'I'm going home. You can name the car 'Oh no' for all I care."[19]

On 4 July, Anderson and his Stutz finished fifth in the 300-miler at Sioux City while Oldfield retired his racer with a cracked cylinder. Then it was time for Elgin. "At Elgin there is a waviness on the backstretch that slows the speeds while Santa Monica is like a boulevard all the way. Elgin's turns seem as easy to negotiate as Santa Monica's, but the surface gives California the edge.... Elgin's finishing straight, to a Chicagoan, seems better than Santa Monica's, for it is more like one imagines a road race should be — out in the country, with green fields everywhere and no signs of a city. At Santa Monica one cannot get away from the city. One feels as if he were standing alongside of a city boulevard watching the cars speed by, while at Elgin one is near to Nature's heart."[20] The 1914 meet was composed of two races, the 36-lap, 301-mile Chicago Automobile Club Trophy on Friday, 21 August, for 450-inch cars, and the free-for-all Elgin National Trophy on Saturday, 22 August, over the same distance.

The Stutz Motor Car Co. entered the 418-inch car for Anderson and a 436-inch car for Oldfield. William Ziegler, Jr. nominated an older Stutz racer (4¾ × 5½ inches) for Frank H. Dearborn. In lap 20 of the CAC Trophy, Anderson lost a spare wheel on the backstretch. Fearing to be disqualified, he sent his mechanic after it. The delay cost him 7 minutes. Moreover, he stopped at the pits to have the spare strapped up and to take on fuel and oil, losing 1 min 16 sec more. After 24 laps Anderson was third behind Wishart in the Mercer and DePalma in the 4.5-liter Grand Prix Mercedes. In lap 27 Anderson took the lead, with Oldfield fourth. After 30 laps Anderson stopped a second time to change a right rear tire, losing 1 min 2 sec. In lap 31 DePalma passed Anderson and assumed a lead of 44 seconds. This was enough for the last laps. Anderson finished second in the CAC Trophy, Oldfield fourth. In lap 5 of the Elgin National, Anderson was forced to stop at the pits to repair the broken off radiator cap by plugging up the hole with cloth, losing almost 4 minutes in the affair and falling back to fourteenth. In lap 20 he withdrew his Stutz because of the missing radiator cap and transmission trouble. Oldfield finished third behind DePalma and Pullen in the Mercer.

Three Stutzes started at Corona, on Thanksgiving, 24 November 1914, two of them being entered by Walter M. Brown for Arthur Klein and Dave Lewis, and a third racer by Earl Cooper for himself. Originally Oldfield had been entered by Walter Brown in a Stutz. But the Corona Racing Association did not meet the speedking's demands. Maxwell offered a large amount for Oldfield's services and on 20 November he agreed to drive one of the Maxwells. Klein went out with a cracked cylinder, which had been welded only a day before. Lewis withdrew because of a broken bearing, and Cooper, while battling for second during the last laps, went out because of a broken timing gear.

Not only the Stutzes were powered by T-heads from the Wisconsin Motor Mfg. Co.

In the 1913 Indianapolis 500, George Clark started at the wheel of a Tulsa, an Oklahoma entry taking the name of its home city and owned by Carden Green and J.B. Levey, both of Broken Arrow, Arkansas. The Tulsa was powered by the 390-inch Wisconsin, 4¾ × 5½ inches. The Tulsa was short, with a wheelbase of 100 inches, wore 34 × 4½ tires all around, and had a dry weight of 2150 pounds. Clark, riding mechanic Bob Moore and the Tulsa finished in the money, taking tenth.

In the same 1913 Indianapolis 500, Bob Burman appeared with his Keeton powered by a 448-inch Wisconsin T-head, 5.094 × 5.5 inches, with 3-inch valves. The radiator of the Keaton was located behind the engine, Renault fashion. Wheelbase was 108.3 inches, tires were 33 × 4½ front and 34 × 4½ rear, and dry weight was 2,350 pounds. Before the start, Burman had to work all night to replace a broken steering knuckle and arrived at the last moment. But after 40 miles he was the leader, ahead of Zuccarelli in the Peugeot. And after 100 miles he was still in the lead, having covered 40 laps in 1 h 16 min 35 sec, with Goux in the other Peugeot second. In lap 50 he was forced to change the carburetor of the Keeton which had caught fire, losing 21 minutes. Later he was relieved by Hughie Hughes and flagged after 184 laps in 7 h 52 min 37 sec. In 1914 the same car reappeared at Indianapolis with Billy Knipper at the wheel, finishing thirteenth. The Keeton made thirteen pit stops, changing seven tires. It lost considerable time near the end. Knipper and Burman suspected ignition trouble and put in a new coil, later finding a stuck valve was the trouble. The car had a very complicated spark control connection which ran from one side of the engine around the front to the magneto on the other side. Some of these connections loosened up and this caused trouble for a time. "Mercedes Fritz" Walker, Knipper's mechanic, got after it with his Speednut wrench which he carried throughout the race, and he "was very proud of the speed with which the repair was made."[21] A few weeks later the Keeton was driven by Jesse Callaghan at Elgin, and ordered out because of bad brakes. At the same time the Keeton Motor Co., Detroit, advertised the "48" six, as the only true French type of car built in America, with the radiator at the rear of the engine, Renault fashion. The Keeton 48 was powered by a 364-inch L-head six, 3¾ × 5½ inches. The completely equipped Riverside Touring and the Meadowbrook Roadster were offered for $2750, the Tuxedo Coupé for $3000.

It was in February 1914 that Alex Sloan, manager of the Case racing team, agreed to act as Bob Burman's business adviser during 1914. Burman planned to make his 1914 premiere at Indianapolis, then to drive in the 300-miler at Sioux City, go to the Pacific coast to compete at Seattle and Tacoma and return to Chicago in time for the annual Elgin meet. During the winter of 1913–1914 Burman broke off relations with Ernie Moross, who had chaperoned him in his dirt track migrations for two years, and decided to assist Horace Thompson of Battle Creek, Michigan, in building two specials for the 500-mile race on Memorial day: "The motor is a four-cylinder engine, having sixteen valves, two inlets and two exhausts in the head of each cylinder. This engine was calculated by Burman and Mr. Milbrath of the Wisconsin Motor Co. the evening after last year's Indianapolis race. So well were their calculations and the construction carried out that both engines developed 134 horsepower at 2,250 rpm.... The wheelbase is 107 inches and the tread is standard. Burman and Disbrow will drive the Burmans."[22] The four-cylinder was cast in pairs, displacing 449 cubic inches with the dimensions of 5.1 × 5.5 inches. Four inclined overhead valves per cylinder were operated by two side camshafts, via pushrods and forked rockers, the rockers being carried in their center by rather high pillars. The 2-inch valves were inclined at about 30 degrees to the cylinder axis, with lift of ½ inch. In principle it was the well-known 450-inch Wisconsin block refined by Burman's OHV head. A similar system had been tried out in France but was discarded because of poor valve operation due to unequal warping of the forked rockers. Pistons were steel. Rayfield supplied the carburetor, Remy the magneto. Tank capacity was 35 gallons, good for 350 miles. Tires were 33 × 4½ from Nassau, wire wheels were from Houk, and shock absorbers were from Hartford. In lap 48 Burman retired his Burman with a broken connecting rod. He relieved Knipper in the Keeton. In lap 136 Disbrow went out with the second Burman because of a broken valve. In August 1914, Eddie Hearne drove one of the Burmans to fifth in the Elgin National.

In the 1914 Indianapolis race, the 450-inch Wisconsin T-head turned up in four other cars, in Keene's Beaver Bullet, Klein's King, Clark's Texas, and Brock's Ray. The Beaver Bullet was designed and built by Charles L. Rogers and Charles F. Keene for the Beaver Automobile Co. of Beaver Falls, Pennsylvania. Like the Keeton, it used the 450-inch Wisconsin of 5.1 × 5.5 inches, with 3-inch valves. The wheelbase was 101 inches and tires were 35 × 4. "It is conventional in design except for the fact that the oil tank is carried under the frame lenghtwise of the right frame member.... A streamline effect is gained in the front by a pointed nose and tapered hood. S.R.O. bearings are used throughout."[23] Rogers acted as relief, "a pioneer driver, having started as a road tester in the Pope Motor Car Co.'s plant at Toledo in 1903. Rogers has been connected with the motor car and the aeronautic industries for a number of years as experimental man and road mechanic and has been connected with several prominent racing teams."[24] Keene finished eighth.

The King was a special built by the Detroit concern and young Arthur Klein:

> Although heralded by his press agent as the youngest speed king in captivity, Klein is 26 years of age. He was born in Cleveland, O., and served his apprenticeship in the assembly room of the Peerless factory and as a road tester for the Stearns and Stoddard-Dayton. He drove his first race in 1909 at Atlanta, Ga., where his mount was a stock Stoddard-Dayton. The following year, he was at the steering wheel of a Flanders in a brief barnstorming campaign and in the fall of 1911 and the spring of 1912, drove a Mercer in some dirt track events in Ohio. Klein quit the racing game in 1912 to go to work for his brother-in-law as a cigar clerk in Youngstown, O. Selling stogies and shaking dice was not speedy enough for him, however, and at the New York motor show of 1914, he decided to don the khaki once more when the King company asked him to design and build a car for the Indianapolis race.[25]

The engine was the 450-inch Wisconsin. Built on a 112-inch wheelbase, the King used the patented King cantilever springs at the rear and wore 33 × 4½ tires from Empire all around. In lap 78 Klein's King went out with a broken valve.

The Texas was the renamed and modified Tulsa of the previous year, entered by George Clark, now "made in Fort Worth, Texas,"[26] and powered by a 450-inch Wisconsin. "The car has a 100-inch wheelbase, 2⅓ to 1 gear ratio and carries 35 gallons of gasoline and 15 gallons of oil, the latter being sufficient to carry him throughout the entire race, Clark believes. At present wire wheels and Miller tires, 35 × 5 all around, will be used, but this equipment has not been definitely decided upon."[27] The Texas did not show the necessary speed in the qualifying trials.

The Ray came from Portland, Oregon, was entered by the Los Angeles sportsman Huntley Gordon and was to be driven by Fred Brock, a power boat expert owning the *Wisconsin* and *Oregon Kid*. The Ray was a combination of Gordon's Mercer Monk frame and 450-inch Wisconsin T-head. In lap 5 Brock went out with a broken camshaft.

The 450-inch racers from Mercer and Stutz marked the end of the T-head era. They were relics of the stone age, T-head racers in the last development stage. They had been able to survive because of the relatively high displacement limit of 450 cubic inches or 7.4 liters, which was enough to balance the reluctance of the T-head for high engine speeds. Despite the bad combustion, the engines delivered enough power to take advantage of the frame and tire potential. With the advent of the new displacement limits in 1914 and 1915, 4.5 liters in Europe and 300 cubic inches in America, the side-valve show was over. The turnaround in Europe had its origins in the voiturette movement. In America, the lightweight racer was the brainchild of the Duesenberg brothers.

9

Mason-Duesenberg

The Mason was put in the limelight during the 1912 Elgin races, in the curtain-raiser run on Friday, 30 August. In the Fred W. Jencks Trophy, a 100-miler for cars under 230 inches, Harry Endicott drove a Mason to victory in 1 h 40 min 43 sec. The little Mason displaced 228 cubic inches with cylinder dimensions of $3^{13}/_{16} \times 5$ inches. In the Aurora Trophy, a 150-miler for the 231–300 inch division, Mortimer Roberts was at the wheel of a rebored Mason, $3^7/_8 \times 5$ inches, and finished fourth. Mortimer was a brother of Montague Roberts of New York–Paris fame. On Saturday, Roberts started in the Elgin National for 450-inch cars and took fourth, between the Stutzes of Merz and Anderson.

On Friday, 4 October 1912, the Masons started in the small car races of the Milwaukee meet. Two races were run simultaneously: the Pabst Blue Ribbon Trophy, sponsored by Colonel Gustave Pabst of Milwaukee, open to class C non-stock, division 3C for cars of 231 to 300 inches, over 28 laps of 7 miles 4658 feet; and the 22-lap Wisconsin Challenge Trophy, sponsored by the Wisconsin Motor Mfg. Co. of Milwaukee, open to class C non-stock, division 2C for cars of 161 to 230 inches. In the Pabst race, Roberts in the rebored Mason took the lead with a lap in 7 min 35 sec, 10 seconds ahead of Hughes in his Mercer, 24 seconds ahead of Pullen in another Mercer, followed by Nikrent in a Case ($4^{23}/_{64} \times 5$ inches), Rooney in a Bergdoll ($4 \times 5^1/_{16}$ inches), the Falcar duo of Chandler and Hastings, and Wishart whose Mercer was feeling bad. In lap 4 Hughes slipped from second to fourth when he was forced to stop at the pit for water. One of the water connections of his Mercer had been jarred loose, letting all the coolant run out. In lap 5 Nikrent docked the Case with a broken crankcase and Tom Rooney the Bergdoll with a broken connecting rod. Now the order was Roberts, Pullen, Hughes, Wishart, Chandler and Hastings. In lap 9 Roberts stopped on the backstretch to repair a break in the fuel supply pipe of his Mason. He fixed it temporarily and came back to the pit slowly, losing about 5 minutes and thereby first place. Pullen succeeded to the premier position, with Hughes at 52 seconds after making the lap in 7 min 2 seconds. Roberts got away, but just below the grandstand he stopped again. He had forgotten to turn on his gasoline, having shut it off when making the repair to the pipe. In lap 13 he stopped again on the backstretch for a few seconds. In lap 15 Wishart, in third place, parked his Mercer with a broken crankshaft. Hughes completed 15 laps or 118 miles in 1 h 52 min 36 seconds, with Pullen just 6 seconds back, and Roberts 11 min 58 sec back. Hughes negotiated lap 16 in 6 min 53 sec, the record for the day. In lap 17 Hughes blew a tire which put Pullen in the lead by 15 seconds. Hughes did not stop to replace the damaged tire on the backstretch but drove on the rim to the pit. In lap 22 Hughes' Mercer broke a universal joint. And in the next lap Pullen was out with a broken gearset. Now Roberts was more than 23 minutes ahead of the two FALs. Roberts finished the race in 3 h 45 min 8 sec, averaging 58.8 miles per hour, with Hastings second, 29 min 57 sec back, and Chandler stopped and given third place owing to darkness. Roberts' best lap was his 21st in 7 minutes flat.

Three Masons were the only starters in the Wisconsin, Kulick having retired his Ford special and Heber his EMF. Harry Endicott's car was entered by F.S. Duesenberg, Snyder's and Mason's cars by the Mason Auto Co. In lap 1 Endicott stopped to change a spark plug. In lap 4 Snyder's Mason withdrew with clutch trouble. George Mason's car was a remodelled touring car and had no chance against Endicott's racer. Endicott won "the farcical contest" in 3 h 6 min 44 sec, averaging 55.6 miles per hour, with Mason second and trailing by 35 min 56 sec. Endicott's fastest lap was the fifth, at 7 min 29 sec.

"There is one motor that has leaped into prominence simply through its performance in the closing season's contests," read an October 1912 article. "This is the Duesenberg motor which pulled the Mason cars over the finish line as class winners in many of the important events of the year.... 'What is there to these cars which causes them to perform so well?' was asked. There are several things which help to make a good racing car, and one of these is undoubtedly the power plant or motor. The motor used in the Mason specials which have come into the limelight of late is of most peculiar construction and is exclusively the design of F.S. Duesenberg and his brother, both of Marshalltown, Ia."[1] Actually the Duesenberg brothers, Fred and Augie, were born in Kirchheide near Lemgo, Germany, Friedrich on 6 December 1877, August on 11 December 1879, the younger brothers of Conrad, Wilhelmine, Caroline, and Amalie. Their father, Konrad Düsenberg, died at the beginning of the 1880s. Their mother, Luise Conradine, decided to leave Germany and try her luck in America.[2] In 1895, she crossed the Atlantic, then took the train to Iowa in the company of her six children. Friedrich, now called Fred, took a job with a farm implement dealer, set up windmills and repaired all possible machinery, built bicycles for a couple of years, and opened a garage in Des Moines which in 1906 turned into the initial Mason Motor Car Co. by taking over the name of the financial backer, the local attorney Edward R. Mason. The car, powered by a two-cylinder, horizontally opposed engine with bore and stroke of 5 × 5 inches, designed by Fred and Augie, was built in a plant at East Fifth and Vine streets and was advertised as the "Hill Climber." In 1909 Fred Maytag's washing machine company purchased the Mason majority and in 1910 production moved to the former Waterloo Motor Works in Waterloo, Iowa. In January 1912 Maytag sold the stocks so that Edward Mason and his son George were again in control.

The Mason racer developed in Marshalltown and driven to victory by Roberts in the Pabst race was powered by a monobloc four, $3\frac{7}{8}$ × 5 inches, giving a displacement of 235 cubic inches. The monobloc casting measured $18\frac{1}{2}$ inches long, 14 inches high, and 6 inches wide. The crankshaft ran within a one-piece barrel-type crankcase, carried by two large plain bearings, $1\frac{7}{8}$ inches in diameter, the front being 4 inches wide and the rear $4\frac{1}{2}$ inches. The big ends had a diameter of 2 inches and width of $2\frac{1}{4}$ inches, the wrist pin bearings a diameter of $1\frac{1}{8}$ inches and width of $2\frac{5}{8}$ inches, with a connecting rod length of $10\frac{3}{16}$ inches. The cast iron pistons had a length of $4\frac{3}{4}$ inches, and carried three bull-ring type rings, $\frac{5}{8}$ inch wide for the lower one and $\frac{5}{16}$ inch for the two upper ones.

The valves were "placed horizontally opening directly into the explosion chamber, thus doing away with the valve pockets. The inlet valves have a diameter of $1\frac{7}{8}$ inch, while the exhausts are $\frac{1}{16}$-inch less, and the lift of both is $\frac{11}{32}$ inch.... The valves are of the conventional poppet variety and have a 30-degree bevel. The stems are 5 inches in length and $\frac{7}{16}$ inch in diameter. The ordinary type of coil spring serves to close the valves."[3] The valves were operated by a low mounted camshaft via 14-inch-long vertical rocker arms, the famous "walking beams." The camshaft ran in three plain bearings, 1⅛ inch in diameter, their width 4 inches front, 2 inches center and rear. The distance from the point of cam contact to the arm pivot was 6 inches, and 8 inches from the pivot to the valves. The rocker shaft was provided with four bronze-bushed bearings, one between each pair of rockers. Four short vertical pipes carried the exhaust gases through the top of the hood. Two spark plugs per cylinder were located on the opposite side of the valves, in caps which could also be used to inspect the cylinder head and the piston faces.

The crankcase contained two gallons of oil which was pumped up into the hollow rocker arm shaft. Then the oil was sent to the cams through oil leads and flowed to the oil troughs under the connecting rod ends. The main bearings of the crankshaft, the big ends, and the cylinder walls were supplied by the splashing of the connecting rod ends into the troughs, which also resulted in a mist of oil going up through the slots in the top of the crankcase where it lubricated the valve stems. The oil level in the troughs was regulated for 1 inch. The cooling system used a combination of pump and thermosyphon circulation, two water pipes being taken from the lower part of the radiator, one going directly to the engine by thermal action and the other passing through a light pump. The Duesenberg engine delivered 58 hp at 2300 rpm, 65 hp at 2600 rpm.

The power was transmitted via a cone clutch and torque tube to the tree-speed gearbox mounted at the rear axle, which had a gear ratio of 2⅗:1. "The drive shaft is enclosed within a torque tube, the rear end of which bolts to the forward end of the transmission gearset case. Two radius rods run from the front end of the torque tube to the axle housing in the conventional way."[4] The front axle was of the I-beam type, with a 3½-inch drop at its center. The springs were half-elliptic in front and elliptic in the rear. The wheelbase was 104 inches, tires were 32 × 3½, and dry weight was 2000 pounds. "The racy type car is a special speedy creation and is built to order only at a price of $8000, with left drive and center control."[5] Did the Duesenberg brothers originally intend to start in the 1911 or 1912 Coupe de l'Auto in France, with the cylinder dimensions of 3.4 × 5 inches to comply with the 3-liter limit? Probably not. Yet the Mason-Duesenberg came very close to a French *voiture légère* racer.

In 1912, the Mason Motor Co. entered a car for Lee Oldfield in the Indianapolis 500. Cylinder dimensions were quoted as 3¹⁵⁄₁₆ × 5 inches, 243 cubic inches. The Mason failed to qualify and was scratched. In 1913 there were two Masons and one Duesenberg at Indianapolis, for Bob Evans, Jack Tower and Willie Haupt. Haupt's car was initially entered as a Mason but renamed Duesenberg. In 1912, Evans and Tower had raced for EMF, and in 1911, Tower had driven a Jackson in the 500-mile race with Evans as mechanic. The 1913 Mason engines displaced 350 cubic inches with dimensions of 4.316 × 6 inches, with steel pistons replacing the cast iron ones. The crankshaft ran in two large ball bearings, lubrication was via dry sump, and output increased to 110 hp at 3000 rpm. The wheelbase was lengthened by 2½ to 106½ inches and tires were now 32 × 4 front, 34 × 4½ rear, but dry weight remained 2000 pounds. There was another car in this 1913 Indianapolis race powered by a 350-inch Duesenberg engine: Billy Knipper's Henderson. The Henderson had a wheelbase of 108 inches, 35 × 4½ tires all around, and dry weight of 2200 pounds. Harry Goetz acted as Knipper's pit manager, while Frank Jones, who had charge of Knipper's service shop at Rochester, New York, was Knipper's mechanic. In the second trial session on 28 May, Tower made fastest time in 1 min 42 sec. The speed of the Mason was confirmed during the beginning of the race. For the second and the third lap, Evans put the little Mason into the lead.

30 May 1913 — third Indianapolis 500. *Top*: Jack Tower at the wheel of his Mason-Duesenberg, with his mechanic. In the second practice session on 28 May, Tower was the fastest in 1 min 42.00 sec. In lap 51 of the race, Tower and the Mason skidded off the track on the south curve and turned over. Tower suffered a broken leg, his mechanic some fractured ribs. *Bottom*: Front row from left: Bob Evans in no. 5 Mason-Duesenberg, Billy Liesaw in No. 17 Anel, Albert Guyot in no. 9 Sunbeam "Toodles IV," and Caleb Bragg in no. 19 Mercer. In the second row, Jules Goux in no. 16 Peugeot, Harry Grant in no. 26 Isotta-Fraschini, and Don Herr in no. 8 Stutz (Library of Congress).

In lap 51 Tower skidded off the track in the south curve and turned over, suffering a broken leg. In lap 125 the Henderson retired with a slipping clutch. Every few laps Knipper had been on his back under the car, treating the cone of the clutch with a squirt gun of gasoline and driving in pieces of saw blade in the facing. In lap 158 Evans, who was relieved by Lee Oldfield, parked his Mason for unknown reasons. Haupt, who was also relieved by Oldfield, finished ninth. Lee Oldfield was a young driver from Lone Tree, Kansas, and was not related to Barney.

On 4 July 1913 the third annual 200-mile race was held at Columbus, Ohio. Ralph Mulford drove a Mason to victory in 3 h 21 min 48 sec, with Madden in a Nyberg second by 23 minutes. The race was marred by an accident, in which Harry C. Knight and mechanic Milton Michealis in the Rovan Special lost their lives. The Rovan was a new front-drive racer made by the Kinnear Mfg. Co. of Columbus. It blew the right rear tire and turned turtle, throwing out its crew. On the same day George Mason in a Mason scored a native son victory on the Sioux City 2-mile dirt track, winning the 40-mile free-for-all in 32 min 36 sec, ahead of Jack Newhouse in the Case Tornado and Louis Disbrow in the Simplex Zip handicapped by tire trouble. Mason also took a 16-miler in 13 min 39 sec.

On 29 August 1913, at Elgin, three Masons started in the 300-inch CAC Trophy, a race of 36 laps or 301 miles. The drivers were Eddie Rickenbacher, Billy Chandler and Ralph Mulford. Mulford's and Rickenbacher's Masons were powered by 300-inch Duesenberg engines measuring 3.985 × 6 inches, with 2³⁄₁₆-inch valves. The wheelbase was 106 inches, dry weight was 2000 pounds, the rear axle ratio was 2.25:1, and tires were 32 × 4 front and 34 × 5 rear. Rickenbacher started on Michelins mounted on wire wheels, Mulford on Braenders mounted on wood wheels. Chandler's racer displaced 275 inches with the dimensions of 3.819 × 5 inches and 1¹³⁄₁₆-inch valves. The wheelbase was 104 inches, dry weight 1875 pounds, axle ratio 2.6:1, and tires from Michelin were 32 × 4 all around. From the very first the Masons started to beat it. Mulford took the lead after a first lap in 7 min 19 sec and completed 8 laps in 57 min 18 sec, with Rickenbacher 22 seconds back. At the end of lap 9 Rickenbacher came in to replace a valve. At the same time he took on oil and water, losing 5 minutes. He stopped again after lap 10 to look at the valves but did not work on them. In lap 13 Mulford shook his head over a sheared flywheel bolt and came back to the pit as a spectator. In lap 18 Rickenbacher pulled up at the pit and poured nearly a gallon of gasoline into the oil tank thinking that the oil was too thick. In lap 22 he stopped to cut down the gasoline feed in the carburetor. In lap 23 Chandler stopped when Fred Horey relieved Jones as mechanic. DePalma in the Mercer won. Chandler and Rickenbacher were still running when a flagman over the backstretch became confused and wig-wagged that the race was over so that the crowd came out on the course. Chandler was given third place with 32 laps in 5 h 2 min 33 sec, while Rickenbacher was flagged with 27 laps in 4 h 51 min 27 sec.

Next day, in the 450-inch Elgin National over the same distance, Eddie Rickenbacher and Willie Haupt started with 350-inch Masons, with bore and stroke dimensions of 4.315 × 6 inches, while Mulford drove the 300-inch car of the CAC trophy. Rickenbacher's engine used a 1¾-inch Schebler carburetor, Haupt's a 2-inch Schebler, and Mulford's a 1¾-inch Rayfield. All three Masons rolled on 32 × 4 tires front; Rickenbacher and Mulford used 35 × 5 in the rear, while Haupt ran on 34 × 5 rear tires. Mulford finished second behind Anderson in the Stutz. Rickenbacher went out with a bent axle. Haupt's Mason caught on fire.

In February 1914, at Santa Monica, Billy Carlson and his Mason took third in the Van-

26 February 1914 — Vanderbilt Cup, Santa Monica, California. Billy Carlson's no. 10 Mason-Duesenberg finished third, nine minutes behind DePalma's winning no. 12 Mercedes (Library of Congress).

derbilt, while Dave Lewis' sister car went out with a broken piston. Lewis' Mason and Frank Verbeck's Fiat were entered by film director Mack Sennett, the man of the Keystone comedies. In 1913 Sennett had produced *Barney Oldfield's Race for a Life*. Oldfield recalled:

> I had done a lot of things, but had never been in the movies. Mack Sennett stopped me on the street in Los Angeles one day in 1913 while I was giving exhibitions on the West Coast.
> "Barney" he said, "why don't you go into the movies?"
> "Nobody ever asked me," I replied.
> "Well, you are asked now," Mack went on. "I've got a big idea."
> And he told it to me. So I went into the movies for a few reels.[6]

Oldfield played himself, Ford Sterling the villain, Sennett a youthful suitor and Mabel Normand "Mabel Sweet and Lovely." The movie provided the typical damsel–in–distress story, with Mabel ending up tied to the railroad tracks, while the villain twirled his mustache and Mack and Barney raced to the rescue.

In May 1914, at Indianapolis, there were four cars using engines from Duesenberg, Mason's Mason, Rickenbacher's and Haupt's Duesenbergs and Chandler's Braender Bulldog. The first three were "alike in practically every respect and simply were refinements of the Masons, which made such a fine showing within the past few years."[7] The horizontal-valve Duesenberg engine now had dimensions of 4.40 × 6 inches, for displacement of 360 cubic inches. On the Mason, the exhaust ended in a sheet metal header open at both ends, while the Duesenbergs had separate pipes carried out of the hood. Mason's and Haupt's engines had Schebler carburetors, Rickenbacher's a Master instrument from Miller. With a wheelbase of 106 inches and fitted with 34 × 4½ tires, the Mason rolled on wood wheels, the two Duesenbergs on Rudge Whitworth wire wheels. "The Duesenbergs looked as if they were George M. Cohan's entries. They were red, white and blue striped."[8] The Bulldog was the Braender tire entry, designed by Ralph Mulford and Billy Chandler.

> It is a very sturdy and well-designed appearing car. The radiator is about 4 feet high, by less than half as wide and has a visor at the top. The bonnet ends at the rear in a cowl that almost conceals the driver and the mechanic. The streamline idea was carried out very thoroughly, the body being made by William Woop, New York, whose son, Charles Woop, is Chandler's mechanic on his car. Young Woop was so anxious that the car would make a good appearance upon its arrrival at the speedway that he spent the entire time of the journey from New York in the express car painting his pet. Both cowl and back are so high that the car could turn over completely without injuring the driver or mechanic.... The transmission is a Brown-Lipe and the axle is a Timken. Chandler carries 40 gallons of gasoline and 15 gallons of oil, sufficient to carry him 400 miles. The car, though it looks speedy, will probably not be driven to the limit as it is the intention of the Braender tire people to repeat on Mulford's record of last year of running the entire 500 miles on one set of tires.[9]

Wheelbase of the Braender Bulldog was 105 inches and the tires were from Braender, of course, in the size of 35 × 5.

In lap 66, Mason's Mason retired with a "caved-in piston head."[10] The Bulldog went out three laps later with a broken connecting rod. Rickenbacher finished tenth, Haupt twelfth. Rickenbacher made nineteen stops, although he changed only four tires. Most of his stops were due to engine trouble. He lost a great deal of time in trying to restart the engine after each stop, as four or five men usually had to take turns at the crank. A great deal of his trouble was with the plugs. His last stop was occasioned by a change of the left rear tire and he was all ready to go in about 40 seconds, but it took four men 7 minutes to get the engine started. He lost, in all, 36 minutes at the pits.

> Willie Haupt in the Duesenberg made fifteen stops before he finished. The first four were to take on water, as were a number of the others. Every time the radiator cap was taken off the steam and hot water spouted out like a geyser. The engine seemed to be heating up more than the other Duesenbergs; the clutch was slipping; the pump was not working properly. Five different times new spark plugs were put in the motor. It seemed that the high compression caused them to break. Nine tires were changed during the race. The clutch was not disengaged on stopping — seemingly it had been wedged to prevent slipping — and the rear wheels were jacked up on starting. When the engine got going at a good speed, the car was pushed off the jacks and started out on high.[11]

On Saturday, 4 July 1914, Mason, Rickenbacher and Alley started on the 2-mile track of the Sioux City Automobile Club and Speedway Association, located just over the state line in Union County, South Dakota, for a race of 150 laps or 300 miles. The three cars had 360-inch engines, 4.4 × 6 inches, Schebler carburetors, and Riverside tires measuring 33 × 4½ front, 35 × 5 rear. Mason's rear axle ratio was 2.3:1, Alley's 2.5:1 and Rick's 2.6:1. Burman in the 5.6-liter Peugeot that Goux had driven at Indianapolis had the satisfaction of leading the first 20-mile post. But after 32 miles he stopped to change a tire and make a carburetor adjustment. At 40 miles Wishart in his 450-inch Mercer was the new leader, with Mel Stringer in an older 7.4-liter Peugeot second and Rickenbacher in the Duesenberg third. Mason's Mason went out with a broken drive shaft. After 144 miles Rickenbacher stopped for a new right rear tire, losing 35 seconds. "Tom Alley, in Duesenberg No. 12, had a narrow escape from severe injury when he made his first stop after running 156 miles. The car was filled with water and oil and as soon as the pitman started to fill the tank with gasoline the car caught fire and a merry blaze continued for about 15 seconds. It was extinguished with three Pyrenen extinguishers. The rear of the car was all ablaze and the fuel in the tank was just beginning to burn. The burning funnel and can, used in pouring, were thrown first into the pit and then outside, where the flame was extinguished. The moment the blaze was out, a roar was heard and away went Mulford in Alley's car."[12] What had happened? Mulford's 5.6-liter Peugeot had been eliminated with a leaking oil tank. Mulford saw that Alley was incapacitated and jumped into the vacant Duesenberg seat, without informing the pit attendants. "It was a good example of quick thinking and it brought both Alley and Mulford credit and money as well."[13]

At 180 miles Rickenbacher climbed out in front and once there he never relinquished his advantage. The foreign cars from Europe were tired and broke down. Wishart lost 8 minutes to replace a broken valve spring so that Rickenbacher could stop for fuel and oil without worry. Rickenbacher won in 3 h 49 min 2 sec, blowing a right rear tire in his last assurance lap just as he crossed the finish line. Wishart finished second, 48 seconds back, and the Alley-Mulford Duesenberg was third, 3 minutes back. Billy Chandler's Braender Bulldog was flagged after 126 laps. "In a way America was avenged for the Indianapolis slaughter, for of the six foreign cars that started only one finished and that only limped home with a cracked cylinder."[14] Rick's knowledge of the track where he had raced for the last two years stood him in great stead and the way he took the turns picked up many seconds for him. Edward Rickenbacher was born in 1890, in Columbus, Ohio. His father, William, and his mother Elizabeth, née Basler, were Swiss immigrants who met and married in Columbus. Eddie was the third of eight children.

On the very same day, "the French Grand Prix produced a big surprise party, in that the French cars met with an overwhelming defeat. Germany ran one, two, three with three Mercedes, Lautenschlager the winner."[15] Promptly *Motor Age*'s J.C. Burton put "Lautenschlager"[16] into rhyme:

> In Paris gay the Glooms hold sway,
> No cock of vict'ry's crowing;
> The car Delage is termed fromage,
> And wine, like glue, is flowing;
> Monsieur Boillot is rated slow,
> No tender kiss is planted
> Upon his lips, and as he sips
> His absinthe, dirge is chanted.
>
> All Gemany is on a spree
> And other lands is scorning;
> The Teuton clan now leads the van
> While France is wearing mourning:
> One, two and three in the grand prix,
> First also at Sioux City —
> Just quaff your beer, don't shed a tear
> The Dutch ask not for pity.
>
> Great Kaiser Bill has had his fill
> Of Pilsener and lager;
> He loudly boasts and drinks deep toasts
> In praise of Lautenschlager:
> Across the sea a victory

Has led this peace-plan knocker
To plan to knight in his delight
That Deutscher, Rickenbacher.

In August 1914, in the CAC Trophy at Elgin, Rickenbacher went out with a broken gearshift lever, Alley with a broken gearset. In the Elgin National, Rickenbacher retired his Duesenberg with a cracked cylinder. Then, "Alley stops for fuel on his twentieth lap and is relieved by Rickenbacher who steps on the throttle and sends the Duesenberg in pursuit of Burman. He gradually gains on the blue Peugeot until at the end of the twenty-fourth lap he has cut down Burman's lead to 26 seconds. Rickenbacher passes Burman on the thirtieth lap, but is fated. With only 33 miles more to go, a driveshaft of the Duesenberg breaks and Rickenbacher and his mechanician walk to the pits, eliminated at the very dawn of their hour of triumph."[17]

On 24 October 1914, a 100-miler was held on the Hamline Park track, located midway between St. Paul and Minneapolis. The meet was run under the management of Fred Duesenberg who was about to move his factory to the Twin Cities. Alley in a Duesenberg won in 1 h 31 min 30 sec, ahead of his teammates Mulford and O'Donnell. In November, at Corona, O'Donnell finished third, while Alley retired his Duesenberg with a broken clutch spring and Callaghan with engine trouble.

The 1915 season opened in California on the occasion of the Pan-American Exposition in San Diego. On Saturday, 9 January, a 305-miler was run on a 5.98-mile road course on the Point Loma peninsula. There were 18 starters. Tom Alley driving a Duesenberg was in the lead until lap 18, then Rickenbacher in a 5.6-liter Peugeot. In lap 24 Earl Cooper in a Stutz took the lead and held it until the finish, winning in 4 h 40 min 10 sec, 1 min 37 sec ahead of Billy Carlson in a Maxwell, then Tom Alley in the Duesenberg 11 min 45 sec back, Grover Ruckstell in a Mercer at 37 minutes back and Bill Taylor in an Alco at nearly one hour. On Wednesday, 3 February, the Duesenbergs of Eddie O'Donnell and Jesse Callaghan scored a double victory in the Tropico race at Glendale, California. O'Donnell covered 53 laps of 1.9 miles in 2 h 7 min 7 sec and finished 3 min 18 sec ahead of his teammate. Four days later, on 7 February, there was again a double of the Duesenbergs in the 100-miler on the 1-mile dirt oval of Ascot, Los Angeles. O'Donnell won in 1 h 41 min 15 sec, beating his teammate Alley by 16 seconds.

> Two years ago, Tom Alley was a humble repairman in the shop of the Chicago Locomobile agency. Today he is a thirty-third degree knight of the khaki, a driver respected for his skill and daring.... Ralph de Palma was Alley's teacher. In 1912, when the Italian was without a mechanician, de Palma took Alley out of the Chicago Locomobile shop and gave him a job pumping oil. He rode to dual victory with de Palma at Elgin and was Ralph's mechanic in the Milwaukee classics of that year, sharing in the Vanderbilt Cup triumph and suffering injuries in the Grand Prize accident. Last year, when DePalma was captain of the Mercer team, Alley was a member of the crew but did not serve as a mechanician.... Fred Duesenberg gave him a chance to drive and it is apparent that Alley has made good.[18]

In lap 14 of the Ascot race, Jesse Callaghan in the third Duesenberg skidded through the fence and was impaled in the chest by a board. Next day he died from his injuries.

The 1915 Indianapolis 500 was the first race of the new 300-inch formula. There were five Duesenberg engined cars. The Duesenberg brothers entered three racers for Tom Alley, Eddie O'Donnell and Ralph Mulford. In order to comply with the 300-inch limit, the bore was reduced from 4.4 to 3.98 inches, the stroke remaining at 6.0 inches. Fuel mixture was supplied by a Master carburetor, and the lubrication relied on a two-pump dry sump. The rear axle ratio was 2.6:1, with 33 × 5 Goodrich Silvertown cord tires all around. Mulford's Duesenberg was the only car of the field rolling on wood wheels. The Sebring was a mixture of modified Marmon frame and Duesenberg engine. Wheelbase was 102 inches, tires 33 × 5. It was built at Sebring, Ohio, entered by E.E. Miles and J.W. Gwin, two sportsmen of Youngstown, Ohio, and driven by Joe Cooper, a Hoosier. The fifth Duesenberg engine worked in Arthur Klein's Kleinart, and was mounted into the frame of the King he drove in 1914. Wheelbase was 109 inches, tires 33 × 4.5.

The race was between Resta's Peugeot, DePalma's Mercedes and the Stutz team with Anderson, Wilcox and Earl Cooper. In the second lap Resta was in the lead, closely followed by Wilcox, DePalma, Cooper, Anderson and Rickenbacher in the best Duesenberg. Mulford stopped in lap 25 for a new right rear tire. Rickenbacher went out in lap 102 with a broken connecting rod which went through the crankcase. In lap 112 the Kleinart was ordered off the course for excessive smoke. The connection between the oil and gasoline tanks had given way, causing the lubricant and fuel to mix, à la two-cycle practice. In lap 124 Mulford retired with a broken connecting rod. In lap 155 Joe Cooper, who had stopped eight times at the pits and lost 42 minutes to replace the overheated spark plugs of his Sebring, skidded into the inside safety wall and broke a wheel. O'Donnell came in for his first stop in lap 171 and changed a rear tire. He finished fifth, 35 minutes behind DePalma in the 4.5-liter Mercedes. Alley was eighth after riding the entire distance on one set of Silvertowns. Billy Chandler acted as relief, took the wheel of Mulford's Duesenberg twice, and then rushed to the aid of Art Klein.

On Saturday, 26 June 1915, a 500-mile race was held on the new 2-mile board speedway at Chicago. Alley in the Duesenberg finished ninth. O'Donnell went out in lap 140 with a burned-out bearing, and Haupt in lap 147 with clutch trouble. Joe Cooper in the Duesenberg engined Sebring was tenth, and Mulford in his Mulford engined Mulford was flagged fifteenth after 238 laps. The upcoming 300-miler at Sioux City was open to 450-inch cars. On 3 July, Eddie Rickenbacher repeated his victory of the previous year, this time at the wheel of a Maxwell. He won in 4 h 57 sec, ahead of O'Donnell, Alley and Chandler in Duesenbergs. The 300-miler held two days later on the new 1.25-mile board track at Omaha, Nebraska, was open to 300-inch cars. Again Rickenbacher in the Maxwell was the winner, his time being 3 h 17 min 39 sec, with O'Donnell in the Duesenberg 2 min 48 sec back, then Orr in another Maxwell and Grant Donaldson in his Emden. On 9 July, Burman and his Peugeot special won a 100-miler on the half-mile dirt oval at Burlington, Iowa, in 2 h 7 min 30 sec, seven minutes ahead of Chandler, O'Donnell and Alley in Duesenbergs.

In the 300-miler on the fresh Des Moines Auto Speedway, a 1-mile board track, Ralph DePalma did not drive his Mercedes but a 300-inch Stutz: "The 500-mile mill at the Indiana city burned out the Mercedes to such an extent that it is no longer the same car."[19] On Saturday, 31 July, in the elimination trials, he promptly turned the fastest lap in 36.98 sec. Burman in his special achieved 37 seconds, Joe Cooper in the Sebring 38.60 sec. Because of inclement weather the race was postponed to Saturday, 7 August. Burman did not start; he had shipped his special to the Chicago speedway where he took part in a 100-mile challenge race. After an all-night session untangling a mix-up in their scoring system, the officials gave the victory to Ralph Mulford in a Duesenberg. His time was announced at 3 h 27 min 5 sec, 1 min 7 sec ahead of DePalma in the Stutz and 4 min 40 sec ahead of O'Donnell in a Duesenberg. In lap 39 Joe Cooper's Sebring turned turtle after crashing through the railing in front of the grandstand, two laps after the treads of his left rear tire had flown off. Cooper was instantly killed. "The reason for Cooper's popularity outside of his ability, which is

30 September 1916 — Second Astor Cup, Sheepshead Bay, Brooklyn. George Buzane at the wheel of his Duesenberg. The Duesy did not finish because of a broken wrist pin (Library of Congress).

1 June 1918 —100-mile Harkness Handicap, Sheepshead Bay, Brooklyn. Tommy Milton's Duesenberg finished second in 58 min 31 sec (Library of Congress).

exceptional, is that he is one of the easiest men to befriend that ever lived. He never tires of explaining the intricate details of his racer to the layman, nor refuses to back up his statements by actual demonstration. As a result, he is always surrounded by the curious, with more than one man his debtor for having cleared up some knotty point."[20] Cooper's mechanic George Piero escaped with several broken ribs. In lap 239 Chandler's Duesenberg also turned over after the rear left wheel broke. Chandler was seriously injured. Mechanic Morris Keller died a few hours later at Mercy Hospital.

In May 1916, Wilbur D'Alene, with Eddie Miller as riding mechanic, took second in the Indianapolis classic which was run over 300 miles only. In September, he was second in a 300-miler at Cincinnati, Ohio. In July, Tommy Milton finished third in a 150-miler on the 1.25-mile board speedway at Omaha, Nebraska. In August, he was second in a 300-miler at Tacoma. On 30 November 1916, Rickenbacher won a 150-miler on the 1-mile dirt oval at Ascot, Los Angeles. Rickenbacher's Duesenberg was owned by 21-year-old William Weightman. Weightman had bought a second Duesenberg for himself. In the 1916 Vanderbilt, with Jimmy Murphy as riding mechanic, he finished third, nearly 30 minutes behind Resta in the Peugeot. At the same time, during the 1916 season, Weightman had a 300-inch Wisconsin engine (4.34 × 5 inches) mounted in a short Stutz frame: the Weightman Special. The head of the Wisconsin engine was more or less a copy of the 6.2-liter Delage in which René Thomas had won the 1914 Indianapolis 500, with two low-mounted camshafts and four horizontal valves. The Wisconsin's crankshaft ran in three plain bearings instead of the Delage's five ball bearings. According to a factory brochure the Wisconsin engine was good for 100 hp at 3000 rpm. Had it been commissioned by Harry Stutz in the summer of 1914 in view of the upcoming 300-inch formula? In any case Stutz finally decided in favor of an overhead-camshaft design.

Could a blue painted Duesenberg pass for a genuine French racer? In fact, it was surprising that the early Duesenbergs were built in America's Middle West by two brothers of German origin, and not in France, in the west of Paris, in a shop at Levallois-Perret or Courbevoie, assembled by a group of former voiturette specialists. Maybe the Duesenberg lacked a solid gearbox with one or two additional speeds for twisty road courses. But the general layout of the car, the short cylinder block with the two-bearing crankshaft and the rocker-operated horizontal valves, reflected Coupe de l'Auto and French Grand Prix approach. It was a pity that Rickenbacher and Mulford were not entered in the 1913 Grand Prix at Amiens to stir up a purely French race between Peugeot and Delage.

10

Camshaft Handlers

The engineer responsible for the Grand Prix Peugeots, the technical director of the Peugeot racing department at Levallois-Perret between 1912 and 1914, was not French but Swiss. His name was Ernest Henry. He was born in Geneva, Switzerland, on 2 January 1885, the son of Louis Henry and Julie Decombes. His first job, after graduation at the vocational college in Geneva, was with the Picker brothers within the Mégevet company. Charles-Jules "C.-J." Mégevet was involved in several factories in and around Geneva and at Bellegarde, 20 kilometers in the west across the frontier in France to avoid customs. The Mégevet group produced tires, bicycles, motorcycles, boat hulls, combustion engines, and the famous *radiateur Mégevet* which was a Swiss interpretation of the Mercedes honeycomb radiator.

In 1902 Lucien Picker built a small boat engine, a twin of 90 mm bore and 110 mm stroke with automatic intake valves and Bosch ignition. In 1903 a four (60 × 80 mm) was mounted in a four-wheeled chassis and the car was named "Lucia." The first customer, Charles Moccand, was so impressed that he suggested to Lucien Picker that he found his own company. The resulting "L. Picker, Moccand & Cie." in 1904 moved into a small factory building at 78 Route de Chêne-Bougeries in the eastern part of Geneva. Lucien Picker employed fifty workmen in his company and focused on the production of L-head engines for boats and Lucia cars. Guillaume Busson, the Picker-Moccand agent in Paris, who like Ernest Henry was born in 1885, entered a Lucia in the 1907 Targa Florio on Sicily and the Kaiserpreis through the Taunus mountains. But he did not start. In Paris, the cars were sold as Lucia EGA by Busson's Entrepot Général d'Automobiles at 209 Boulevard Pereire. In 1908, Picker, Moccand & Cie. was shut down. Lucien Picker declined an offer to work for the Fiat engineering department at Turin, preferring to join the Mégevet company.[1]

While Lucien Picker concentrated on conventional L-head engines and cars, his brother Charles worked on high-speed T-heads and hulls for power boats. Charles Picker was born on 28 February 1881 in Geneva. With C.-J. Mégevet he had founded the "Société Anonyme de Constructions Mécaniques Système Charles Picker" at Genève-Acacias. In the 1906 boat meetings at Monaco and Évian, the 8-meter cruiser *Mais-je-vais-Piquer*, wordplay of "Mégevet-Picker," met with success so that the orders from France began to fill up. In the fall of 1908 Charles Picker moved from Eaux-Vives, Geneva, to Maisons-Laffitte, in the west of Paris. Ernest Henry came along as Picker's right-hand man, and on 8 June 1909 was *immatriculé à Paris*; that is he became an inhabitant of Paris. Charles Picker opened his Picker et Cie., Fabrication de Moteurs, at 51 Rue de Colombes, Courbevoie, with a large workshop a few hundred meters away on the Île de la Jatte, the Jatte island in the river Seine.

9 September 1912 — GP de France, Le Mans. Paul Rivière and his 3-liter Hispano finished fifth. The Hispano was a 1910 racing voiturette rebored to 69 × 200 mm from 65 × 200 mm (Mercedes-Benz Classic).

Immediately Picker landed a big fish, an order from Hispano-Suiza for a batch of racers for the 1909 Coupe des Voiturettes. The Hispano factory, the *Fábrica de Automóviles La Hispano-Suiza*, was located at 54–60 Calle Floridablanca, Barcelona, with offices at 59 Calle de Calabria. The factory was directed by Geneva-born Marc Birkigt. All Hispanos were equipped with Mégevet radiators. A small Picker T-head with the dimensions of 65 × 140 mm according to the latest regulation of the Monaco boat meeting was waiting on the shelf, ready for pickup. It happened to match the specifications for the 1909 Coupe de l'Auto race for voiturettes. The Hispano voiturette racers debuted on 20 May 1909 in the Copa Catalunya near Sitges, their engines having dimensions of 65 × 180 mm. The drivers were Paolo Zuccarelli with mechanic Ravelli, Louis Pilleverdier with Castanera, and Louis Derny with Reus. The race distance was 13 laps of 28 km, a total of 364 km. On site, the Hispanos were prepared in a "splendid garage"[2] at Villanueva under the direction of Birkigt and Isidoro de Salazar, the marketing director. Derny was second in lap 5, and Zuccarelli was in the lead in lap 6, but broken crankshafts forced both Hispanos out. Pilleverdier finished fourth in 7 h 55 min 29 sec, an hour and a half behind the winner, Jules Goux in a Lion-Peugeot. Zuccarelli, "Zucca" to his friends, was born on 24 August 1886 in Milan, the son of a painter. In Italy he worked for Florentia, when Derny met him in Milan and brought him to Hispano as *metteur au point*, or development engineer. Derny was a well-known motorcycle rider who had ridden in 1902 for Clément, in 1904 for Werner, and in 1906 on a Peugeot, for Francisco "Paco" Abadal's Auto Garage Central, the Peugeot motorcycle and Hispano *concessionario* in Barcelona. A few weeks later, on 20 June 1909 in the Coupe des

Voiturettes at Boulogne, Pilleverdier and mechanic Lisà finished fifth, Zuccarelli and Ravelli sixth, Derny and Soler seventh.

It was also in 1909 that Labor, a company specializing in the production of bicycles, motorcycle frames and aeroplane components, decided to manufacture the Picker T-heads under license as Labor-Picker in 65 × 210 mm, 90 × 210 mm, and 100 × 210 mm versions. The Société des Moteurs Labor Aviation was formed at 29 Route de la Révolte, Levallois-Perret. The 90 × 210 mm Labor-Picker engine was most successful in the spring of 1910 in the Monaco power boat races. Later in 1910, the engine was produced in series for

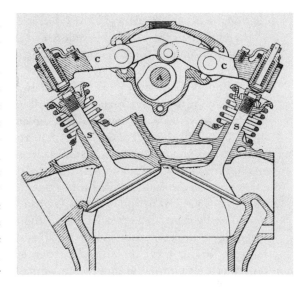

Top right: Cylinder head of the 1908 Clément-Bayard (155 × 185 mm, 14 liters, 138 hp at 1450 rpm) designed by Samuel Guillelmon and Louis Sabathier. Victor Rigal and his Bayard finished fourth in the 1908 Grand Prix de l'ACF at Dieppe. The Bayard was the first overhead-cam Grand Prix car which achieved good results (*La Vie Automobile*, 1909). *Bottom*: October 1907 — third Coupe de l'Auto pour Voiturettes, Rambouillet. Giosue Giuppone and his Lion-Peugeot voiturette coming through the Rambouillet hairpin. They finished sixth, 13 minutes behind Naudin's Sizaire-et-Naudin (Mercedes-Benz Classic).

Blériot and other aeroplanes. "The valves are carried in outstanding ports on opposite sides of the motor. With the double object of keeping down the amount of metal and also of obtaining a suitable form of combustion chamber for high efficiency, the valve chambers are made so small that the valve stems have to be considerably inclined from the vertical. The cylinders are offset from the crankshaft 25 mm. The connecting rods are tubular, while the cast iron pistons have been drilled until not a superfluous ounce of metal has been left."[3] The 5.35-liter (90 × 210 mm) gave 62 hp at 1350 rpm, and weighed 130 kg dry. The 6.6-liter (100 × 210 mm) gave 80 hp at 1330 rpm. The Labor-Picker was mounted in power boats for the Monaco meeting, in Guillaume Busson's Blériot monoplane and in the Zodiac airship *Tschaïka*. On 2 October 1910 a pair of Labor-Picker powered Pierron production cars started in the Gaillon hillclimb, a 5.6 liter (95 × 200 mm) driven by Hutton and a 3.8 liter (90 × 150 mm) driven by Louis Pierron: "Among French cars the best performance was undoubtedly that of the two Labors in the 95 mm class. These two cars were fitted with special long-stroke aviation motors, well known by reason of their performances at Monaco. Hutton, driving a car on which no attempt whatever had been made to cut down head resistance, got up the hill in 40⅘ sec, while Pierron covered the distance in 41⅕ sec."[4] But commercially, Labor Aviation was not successful and was closed in June 1913.

During the same period, Picker sold slightly different T-heads with other partners under the name Picker-Janvier and Bignan-Picker. Albert Guyot drove a 3-liter Picker-Janvier (78 × 156 mm) in the 1912 Grand Prix de France at Le Mans. The Picker started

Lion-Peugeot engine for the 1911 Coupe de l'Auto, a 20-degree V-4 with dimensions of 78 × 156 mm, displacement of 3 liters, and OHV-head (*La Vie Automobile*, 1911).

two hours late because of a defective clutch. Then it caught fire in front of the grandstand, but could be saved. In the autumn of 1913 the Picker-Janvier reappeared as Anasagati and started for Argentina. Antoine d'Avaray drove it in the 1913 Coupe de l'Auto and the Gaillon hillclimb. Jacques Bignan began to assemble a range of "Moteurs de Rendement,"[5] meaning Bignan-Picker high-performance engines, during the fall of 1913, in a shop at Rue du Chemin-de-Fer, Courbevoie. The Bignan-Pickers were available with dimensions of 62 × 124 mm, 70 × 140, 80 × 160, 90 × 180, and 105 × 210 mm. In the autumn of 1913 a Despagna "15 HP, 80/180, type Sport"[6] appeared in London and Paris, in the Olympia and Grand Palais shows. The Despagna was assembled in Paris by Messieurs Despaigne and Sauvalle. It was powered by an 80 × 180 mm Picker T-head. Wheelbase was 280 cm, track 135 cm, tires 820 × 120. In October, Despaigne drove his Despagna in the Gaillon hillclimb and won his "catégorie"[7] or displacement class (3 to 3.75 liters) in 51⅕ sec.

Ernest Henry adjusted the 65 × 210 mm Labor-Picker so that it could be used in the Hispano voiturette racer during the 1910 season. The T-head displaced 2.65 liters with 65 × 200 mm bore and stroke, valve diameter 55 mm, two-piece crankshaft running in three ball bearings, tubular connecting rods, and pistons made of BND steel from Dérihon. Output was 45 hp at 2500 rpm, transmitted via a multiple disk clutch and a three-speed gearbox to the Hotchkiss type rear axle. The chassis remained unchanged with a wheelbase of 240 cm, track of 124 cm, and 810 × 90 front and rear tires. The wooden artillery wheels of 1909 were replaced by Rudge Whitworth wire wheels. Four Hispanos started on 29 May 1910 in the Copa Catalunya, running 22 laps of 14.938 km: three factory entries driven by Zuccarelli, Pilleverdier and the new teammate Chassagne, and an older voiturette driven by Carreras. Giuppone and his Lion-Peugeot were in the lead until lap 4, then Zuccarelli until lap 15 when he was forced to withdraw because of lubrication problems. Goux won for Lion-Peugeot in 4 h 12 min 26 sec, followed by Giuppone, Carreras and Chassagne. In August 1910, Zuccarelli achieved 21 min 50 sec up to the Mont Ventoux, besting Chassagne's 22 min 21 sec and Pilleverdier's 24 min 38 sec. On 4 September 1910 Zuccarelli won the Coupe d'Ostende, with Pilleverdier third, while Chassagne withdrew. Two weeks later, on 18 September 1910, Zuccarelli and mechanic Ernesto Fanelli won the European race of the year, the Coupe des Voiturettes at Boulogne, with Chassagne third and Pilleverdier sixth.

Driver Giosue Giuppone was born on 29 September 1878 in Calco, Lombardy. He was a bicycle and motorcycle star before taking the wheel of the Lion-Peugeot voiturette racers. On 16 September 1910 he was practicing with the new V-4 for the Coupe de l'Auto on the Boulogne course. Near Wirwignes, "on approaching the foot of a hill, he observed two cyclists ahead of him. One of the two pedalled ahead quickly and pulled in to the right.... The second one, fearing that there was not enough room on the right-hand side of the road, suddenly attempted to cut across to the left. Giuppone, who was approaching at 60 miles an hour, saw that an accident was inevitable, and with admirable coolness throttled his motor and applied the brakes hard. It was too late, however, for the cyclist was hit and thrown into the ditch, with very slight injury. The racing car spun round like a top at least half a dozen times. Giuppone was thrown out, alighting on the back of his head and sustaining such injuries that he died a few minutes later without regaining consciousness."[8] Mechanic Paul Péan escaped with superficial injuries. In November 1910, the Peugeot racing team hired Paolo Zuccarelli and mechanic Ernesto Fanelli as replacement for Giuppone.

In the spring of 1911, Ernest Henry moved from Courbevoie to the other side of the river Seine, to Levallois, and began to work for the Peugeot racing department as "directeur du bureau de dessin et des ateliers"[9] (director of the drawing office and workshop). It was

Zuccarelli who suggested engaging Henry and not Picker. In Charles Picker's eyes, the T-head with slightly inclined valves was the optimal solution, "avoiding the pockets and the inconvenients of valves in the head."[10] Nevertheless, Zuccarelli and Henry knew quite well that the Picker T-heads had a tendency to misfire at engine speed above 2000 rpm because of overheating exhaust pockets.

In 1909 and 1910 the racing department of Peugeot Frères ordered the engines for the voiturette racers from long-stroke specialists, just like Hispano. The six-valve single (100 × 250 mm) used in 1909 was designed by the engineering shop of Louis Boudreaux and Louis Verdet at 8 Rue Hautefeuille, Paris. The 20° V-2 (80 × 280 mm) and V-4 (65 × 260 mm) of 1910 came from Gratien Michaux who had his shop at 35 Boulevard Magenta, Paris. The output of the V-4 engine was excellent:

> This motor ought to have won the race, for it developed 45 horse-power on the bench and undoubtedly was the fastest on the straightaway. Boillot lost a certain amount of time through the breakage of his gasoline feed pipe and the disarrangement of his foot brake, but the real cause of his defeat was overheating. The exact cause of this is not known except to the engineers of the firm, but it doubtless can be traced to the inefficient cooling of the exhaust valve chambers. The car showed extraordinary speed; it was wonderfully flexible, and despite the defect mentioned there never was any mechanical breakage on the road. The number of revolutions is given at about 3,000 to 3,500 a minute, and it has been ascertained on good authority that the lineal piston speed is from 4,250 to 4,900 feet a minute.[11]

25 and 26 June 1912 — Grand Prix de l'ACF, Dieppe. Georges Boillot, mechanic Prévost and their 7.6-liter Peugeot (Peugeot).

Zuccarelli, Henry, Boillot and Goux preferred the more homogenous Hispano concept and decided in favor of a pepped up Hispano racer, powered by a 7.6-liter with dimensions of 110 × 200 mm. These dimensions were retained for the 1910 Grand Prix de l'ACF which was cancelled once again, then were carried over for a class in the 1911 Grand Prix de France at Le Mans, and were originally intended for the 1912 Grand Prix de l'ACF. Somehow the troublesome valve pockets of the T-head had to disappear. Henry simply turned the valves and their low mounted camshafts upwards. He was forced to maintain the previous valve area in order to secure the breathing of the long-stroke cylinders so that he replaced the eight side valves of the T-head by 16 smaller overhead valves inclined at 30 degrees. The result was a pent roof combustion chamber with four valves per cylinder operated by two overhead camshafts. Valve diameter was 60 mm. The tappet guide turned out to be Henry's hobby: A ring in the form of a semicircle or stirrup surrounded the cams, connecting the tappet guides above and below the camshaft. An included valve angle of 60 degrees was to be a feature of all DOHC engines designed by Henry. Peugeot claimed in the autumn of 1912: "The valve design is a Peugeot patent, for although the inclined position of the valves is not unusual, the method of operating them by means of independent overhead camshafts is altogether original."[12] Wasn't a twin-cam head the feature of the *Titan*, a huge 62-liter Delahaye engine (300 × 220 mm) which propelled the *Dubonnet* of liqueur magnate Marius Dubonnet during the 1905 Monaco power boat meeting? With its displacement of 7.6 liters the first Grand Prix Peugeot was named L76 or EX1 for Étude Expérimentale no. 1. The

25 and 26 June 1912 — Grand Prix de l'ACF, Dieppe. Boillot's 7.6-liter Peugeot passing the grandstand (Peugeot).

9 September 1912 — Grand Prix de France, Le Mans. Paolo Zuccarelli, mechanic Fanelli and the 3-liter Peugeot about to start. Actually, the 3-liter Peugeots were still entered under the name "Lion-Peugeot." In the background Barriaux's Alcyon (Mercedes-Benz Classic).

crankshaft ran in five plain bearings. The camshafts were driven by a vertical shaft. The L76 delivered 135 hp at 2200 rpm, or for a short time 148 at 2500, with a compression ratio of 5.5:1. The engine, the multidisk clutch and the separated four-speed gearbox were mounted in a U-shaped subframe which was attached by three ball and socket joints to the main frame. The combination of three-point mounting of the engine-gearbox complex with a simple rear axle of Hotchkiss type founded a new school of chassis design. Wheelbase was 275 cm, track was 135 cm, Continental tires were 875 × 105 front and 880 × 120 rear, and dry weight was 1000 kg. In addition, Henry designed a smaller 3-liter for the *voiture légère* class. Cylinder dimensions were 78 × 156 mm. The camshafts were driven by a vertical shaft at the front of the engine, just as in the 7.6-liter, but in contrast to the big brother they operated only two valves per cylinder. Wheelbase was 256 cm.

Georges Boillot won the revived Grand Prix de l'ACF on 25 and 26 July 1912, which consisted of ten laps each day of the old 77-km course near Dieppe. Goux's Peugeot went out with a punctured tank, and Zuccarelli's sister car with a broken fuel line. Just after the Grand Prix, the Chicago sportsman Ellmore Patterson and the publisher Robert Collier had cabled an offer to Peugeot agreeing to finance the shipment and the entry of three Peugeots in the upcoming Elgin and Milwaukee races. On 21 August, "A cablegram received by Paul Lacroix, American representative of the Peugeot, announced ... that the three cars that raced in the French grand prix were already on the water, accompanied by three drivers, with the intention of taking part in the American road races. It is anticipated that they will reach

30 May 1913. Jules Goux and the 7.4-liter Peugeot (108 × 200 mm to comply with the 450-inch formula, instead of 110 × 200 mm for the 7.6-liter) winning the third Indianapolis 500 (Library of Congress).

New York Saturday and be shipped immediately to Chicago, reaching Elgin on Tuesday, which will give a couple of days for practice. Just who the drivers are is not known, but it is anticipated that they are Boillot, winner of the grand prix, and Goux and Zuccarelli."[13] But when French Line's *La Provence* arrived on 24 August, the Peugeots were not aboard. On 9 September 1912 at Le Mans, Goux in the 7.6-liter won the Coupe de la Sarthe, and Zuccarelli in the 3-liter the Grand Prix de France.

In the spring of 1913, two Peugeots crossed the Atlantic. In order to comply with the 450-inch limit of the 1913 Indianapolis race, the L76 duo received new blocks, with a 108 mm bore. The two racers were shipped on 30 April 1913 on the North German Lloyd liner *Kronprinzessin Cecilie*. Goux, Zuccarelli and the mechanics Émile Begin and Ernesto Fanelli sailed on the morning of 3 May from Le Havre on the French liner *La France*. Begin and Fanelli mounted Firestone tires, 35 × 4 front and 34 × 4½ rear. The dry weight of the Peugeots was quoted as 2200 pounds. Hadn't Goux's record car of the same type been checked at 3220 pounds, in April, at Brooklands? The team was managed by Charles Faroux,[14] the editor of *La Vie Automobile*. Arthur Newby, of the National company, placed his whole factory at the Peugeot team's disposition. Immediately Goux was put into the limelight:

> Although a veritable pigmy, Jules Goux is supreme in the Peugeot camp. He is the master, feared and respected — as powerful as a king in the gray garage where the fleet blue cars are housed. Europe hails him as the greatest of all speedway drivers. He is deserving of such homage because of his spectacular feat at Brooklands in April when he covered 106 miles

12 July 1913 — Grand Prix de l'ACF, Amiens. Boillot, mechanic Prévost and the 5.6-liter Peugeot winning their second French Grand Prix (Peugeot).

307 yards within an hour. Georges Boillot, his absent teammate and winner of the Grand Prix, is said to be his superior in a road race but Goux is without parallel on a banked track, they say. Scarcely 5 feet 6 inches in height and as straight and slender as a cotter pin, Goux seems anything but a great racing driver. He appears to be a typical Parisian boulevardier, more fitted to promenade the Champs Elysée than to sit at the wheel of a roaring monster of steel. Even when driving he is faultlessly dressed. His puttees are of soft tan doeskin, his black and white checked knickerbockers are unspotted by grease. Compared with his Yankee foemen in dirty, but businesslike khaki, he is a Beau Brummel, a motoring dandy.[15]

The Stutz men remained confident that the Peugeots would drop out soon after 400 miles.

"The car having the most features of interest to American eyes is the English Sunbeam."[16] It was driven by Albert Guyot. The Sunbeam was a Brooklands special known as *Toodles IV*, powered by a 6.1-liter L-head six, 90 × 160 mm. Wheelbase was 126 inches. Guyot booked passage on the French liner *La Provence*, sailing from Le Havre on 10 May, and was accompanied by R.F.L. Crossmann, "of the English navy, who, after being wounded in the Boxer rebellion, took up motor racing when invalided out of the service."[17] The Sunbeam was shipped on a cargo boat from Liverpool.

During practice on 19 May, Goux gave the railbirds a thrill when he drove high up on the banks during an exciting brush with DePalma in the Mercer: "Goux is said to hold the record for driving higher on the banks at Brooklands than any other driver that ever appeared there."[18] Some 96,000 worshippers were gathered on Friday, 30 May 1913, at 10 o'clock, when starter Charles Root sent away a field of 27 cars. After eight laps Jules Goux in the Peugeot led in front of Haupt in the Mason and DePalma in the Mercer. Ten laps later Zuccarelli pushed his Peugeot into the garage after a fuel line gave way and the carburetor caught fire. Johnny Aitken, former National racing manager, was in the Peugeot pit and acted as a governing valve on Goux's impetuosity. When "Retardez" showed in letters of white on the black board, the Frenchman restrained his desires and slowed down. At the signal "Allons," he smiled and stepped on the throttle. Goux won in 6 h 35 min 5 sec, averaging 75.92 mph, followed by Wishart in the Mercer, Merz in the Stutz and Guyot in the Sunbeam. Goux's Peugeot wore out seven tires in all, three on the right rear, two on the left rear and two on the right front wheel, the left front tire going through without a change. Time lost during these changes totaled 11 minutes; of course, the stops were also used to fill up fuel, oil and water. Goux used 50.7 gallons of fuel and 8.5 gallons of oil:

> I was handicapped by being geared too high. My ratio was 2 to 1, which was the ratio adopted for road work with a cylinder bore of 110 millimeters. We had cut the bore down to 108 millimeters and had not changed the ratio. I found that in order to make my right rear tire last a reasonable length of time I could start my turns at 85 miles an hour, but had to finish them at not more than 73 miles. After being cut out on the bends the straightaways were not long enough to get the motor up to its highest number of revolutions. The fastest I could get on the straightaways, without considering the life of tires, was 99 miles an hour; with a suitable gear ratio I could have done 112 miles an hour. In consequence of this, the motor always was running at a lower number of revolutions than that for which it was designed. At first I did my laps in 1:40 and could have kept to 1:45 throughout the race if it had been necessary. When I had got a couple of laps lead on my

12 July 1913 — Grand Prix de l'ACF, Amiens. Boillot's 5.6-liter Peugeot entering the village of Boves (Peugeot).

nearest competitor I considered there was nothing to be gained by going faster than 1:50 per lap. I could have broken the record if there had been anybody really dangerous behind me.[19]

After the race, Aitken and Wilcox sailed from New York to France in company of the Peugeot team to witness the Grand Prix at Amiens.

Edward Schroeder bought Goux's winning Peugeot. Zuccarelli's 7.6-liter went to Armour Ferguson of New York, "the latest of millionaire amateurs to enter the professional fold.... The latest discovery in racing circles is the youngest registered driver on the list of the American Automobile Association — Armour Ferguson, 21 years of age. He has a keen eye and a 'head,' say those who have watched his work at the wheel. He is a student at the same Connecticut school at which Bruce-Brown was educated."[20] At the Galveston beach meet on 29 July 1913, Ferguson in his Peugeot was "a warm favorite with the spectators in every event in which he was entered."[21] Obviously the Peugeot was in fine form since Ferguson won a 15-miler in 11 min 59.29 sec, ahead of Mulford in a Mason, and a 100-miler in 1 h 23 min 30 sec, ahead of Disbrow in the Simplex Zip. But a few days later, on 9 August at Brighton Beach, the Peugeot was the disappointment of the afternoon: "Ferguson was unable to keep the car running at any speed."[22] The millionaire amateur took the wheel of his Mercer and finished second in a 5-miler behind Wishart. Schroeder entered the ex–Goux Peugeot in the 1913 Elgin National, but the car did not start since a new front axle, ordered by cable from France, did not arrive in time. Ralph Mulford, who was to drive the French racer, took the wheel of a Mason.

In the autumn of 1912, Louis Pilleverdier was the third technician switching over from the Hispano racing department to Peugeot. And Robert Peugeot made available an additional larger shop for the assembling of the racers: Frédéric Rossel's former aero-engine factory at Suresnes, two kilometers away from Levallois. The 1913 regulations of the Grand Prix de l'ACF limited fuel consumption to 20 liters per 100 km. Ernest Henry reduced the cylinder dimensions to 100 × 180 mm, 5.6 liters. The two overhead camshafts were driven by a train of spur pinions now, and operated the four valves per cylinder via L-shaped tappets, the vertical member of the L acting as an upper guide. The two-piece crankshaft ran in three ball bearings, within a one-piece barrel-type crankcase. The 5.6-liter delivered 110 hp at 2500 rpm, 130 at 3000. The frame was slightly shorter, having a 270 cm wheelbase. The rounded radiator edges and the closed underpan were the result of trials in Gustave Eiffel's wind tunnel, the latest *soufflerie* in his Laboratoire d'Auteuil, which had just been built at 27 Rue Boileau, Paris. The tunnel boasted a test section two meters in diameter and a wind velocity of 32 meters per second or 115 kilometers per hour.

On Thursday, 19 June 1913, just a few days after coming back from Indianapolis, Zuccarelli and Fanelli were testing the 5.6-liter on the dead straight *Route Nationale* between Nonancourt and Évreux, 80 km in the west of Paris. Just after passing the crossroad to Marcilly-la-Campagne, the Peugeot collided at top speed with a hay cart. Zuccarelli died on the spot. Fanelli was severely injured, but survived. For the Grand Prix, which was run on 12 July 1913 near Amiens, Zuccarelli was replaced by Jean Delpierre, a rather unknown driver from Boulogne-sur-Mer. Delpierre drove a Corre-La Licorne voiturette in the 1910 Coupe de Normandie and the Coupe de l'Auto, a Côte in 1911, and a Motobloc in some secondary events. In the 1912 Grand Prix de l'ACF he was replacement driver in the Sunbeam team. At Amiens, Delpierre did not finish the first lap and ended up in the ditch at the Boves corner. Boillot and Goux took the first two places in the Grand Prix. Boillot made himself the idol of the crowd: "Boillot's two consecutive triumphs have erased from the

26 February 1914 — Vanderbilt Cup, Santa Monica, California. Harry Grant and his Isotta just after the start. They did not complete the first lap because of a broken piston. The Isotta was powered by a 7.2-liter (120 × 160 mm) with an overhead camshaft and four valves per cylinder. It was one of the first racers with front wheel brakes. Three cars came to America for the 1913 Indianapolis 500 and were driven by Trucco, Tetzlaff and Grant (Library of Congress).

French mind the humiliating memory of Nazzaro's victory in 1907 and the success of Lautenschlager the year following, smarting French defeats that resulted in the abandonment of the grand prix for three years."[23]

In the first weeks of February 1914, Peugeot and Goux, who was learning English in England, held off the works entries for Indianapolis. The development of the latest 4.5-liter racer for the French Grand Prix had priority. The 4.5-liter was to be on the road within the first weeks of February. Boillot had decided "not to race in America, at least not in 1914."[24] But the assembly and first testing of the new Peugeot went better than expected so that, on 17 February, the Indianapolis management received two works entries: "The Peugeot cars to be used at Indianapolis are those having finished first and second at the Amiens grand prix."[25]

For Indianapolis, the 5.6-liter engine was practically unchanged, a Zenith carburetor replacing the original Claudel unit. But the chassis was set several inches lower, with the front and rear springs mounted below the axles. "To enable them to make their turns at a higher speed, the Peugeot men have filled the left hand frame member with lead.... An egg-shaped tail, with the gasoline tank carried inside it, has been fitted to both cars. The underpan also gives as clean a run as possible, but a wind cutter is not fitted on the front axle."[26] Houdaille supplied the shock absorbers, Rudge Whitworth the wheels. "The Peugeot contract calls for the use of English Dunlop tires throughout the 1914 racing season. These tires will therefore be used on both cars at Indianapolis. Size selected is 880 × 120 front and 895

21 September 1913. Boillot on his way to victory in the "Coupe des Trois-Litres," the 3-liter Coupe de l'Auto at Boulogne-sur-Mer. His 3-liter "baby Peugeot" was sold to Georges and Jacques Menier, and driven by Arthur Duray in the 1914 Indianapolis 500 (Peugeot).

× 135 millimeters rear."[27] Nevertheless, Boillot and Goux somehow arranged to start on Palmer cord tires bought privately from the French factory, 34 × 4½ front inflated to 80 pounds (5.5 bar), 35 × 6 rear inflated to 87 pounds (6 bar).

A third Peugeot was entered for Arthur Duray, privately. In February 1914, Duray had been nominated in a 6.2-liter Delage. But on 3 March, William Bradley, the European representative of the Indianapolis Speedway and well-known correspondent of *Motor Age* and *The Automobile*, reverted to the original proposition. Duray was entered at the wheel of the 3-liter "baby Peugeot" driven to victory by Boillot in the 1913 Coupe de l'Auto at Boulogne.[28] "Duray is to the French racing game what Rube Waddell was to the American base-ball, a most eccentric character.... Duray is a jolly good fellow, never serious and always playing practical jokes."[29] Arthur Duray was born on 9 February 1882 in Brussels, Belgium. The little Peugeot was owned by Georges and Jacques Menier, the sons of Gaston Menier, the French chocolate king. In a fabulous Belle

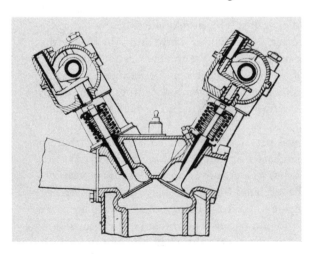

Cylinder head of the 1913 Peugeot, featuring the L-shaped tappets (*La Vie Automobile*).

Époque factory at Noisiel, around 20 km to the east of Paris in the Marne valley, the Meniers would produce 17,500 tons of chocolate in 1914, more than 50 percent of the French market, certainly enough turnover to afford the Coupe de l'Auto racer. The Meniers had bought the little Peugeot soon after the *Coupe des Trois-Litres*, the 3-liter race at Boulogne in October 1913. They had driven it in a few local hill-climbs and done a small amount of touring with it. Duray's baby Peugeot displaced 3 liters with dimensions of 78 × 156 mm. As on the 5.6-liter, the camshafts were driven by spur gears and operated four valves per cylinder. Output was 92 hp at 2870 rpm. Wheelbase was 256 cm, dry weight 880 kg. Duray and his mechanic Henry Matthys fitted 33 × 4½ English Palmer tires.

On 22 April, two 6.2-liter Delages, an Excelsior six and the 3-liter Peugeot were shipped to America on White Star's *Oceanic* sailing from Cherbourg via Queenstown to New York. On 29 April, Goux and Boillot secretly sailed on White Star's *Olympic*, thereby stealing a clean march on their compatriots who were under the impression that they were all to embark together on 9 May. As planned, William Bradley, who looked after the interests of the Delage and Excelsior teams in America, followed with Duray, Matthys and the other foreigners on Compagnie Générale Transatlantique's *La Provence* from Le Havre. Goux, Boillot and their mechanics Begin and Prévost reached Indianapolis on Monday, 11 May 1914, and were given a dinner that same night by speedway manager C.G. Sedwick.

On Sunday afternoon, 17 May 1914, Boillot was out for practice, turned a record lap in 1 min 35.80 sec, more firmly entrenching the Peugeot in its position as favorite. Before, Joe Dawson and the old long-stroke Marmon had boasted 1 min 36.40 sec. "Joe swept

30 May 1914 — fourth Indianapolis 500. Jules Goux at the wheel of the 5.6-liter Peugeot (Library of Congress).

around the curves with the throttle wide open. Boillot, on the other hand, rolled the turns, shutting off before he went into the embankments. The American cars now at the speedway have yet to show the speed of the blue invaders from across the Atlantic. They are not as well prepared at the present time as are the Peugeots."[30] The surprise of the first day of the trials, on Monday, 25 May, was the showing of Duray's little Peugeot, "the baby of the speed pack, with a motor as small as a Ford."[31] Duray achieved 1 min 40 sec or 90 mph. Fastest on this first day were Bragg's Mercer in 1 min 36.80 sec, 93.25 miles per hour, and Wilcox's Gray Fox in 1 min 39.16 sec, 91.1 miles per hour. The feature on Tuesday, 26 May, was the whirlwind drive of Goux who encircled the track in the new record time of 1 min 31.71 sec or 98.3 mph. Dawson made 1 min 36.20 sec, René Thomas in the 6.2-liter Delage 1 min 35.20 sec. "The sensation of the last day of the trials was the performance of Boillot, who made good on his declaration that a speed of 100 miles an hour was possible on the Indianapolis speedway."[32] Boillot made his lap in 1 min 30.13 sec, equal to 99.85 miles per hour.

On 28 May, *Motor Age* pictured "The Foreigners":

> Boillot was born to tame racing cars, to fight the obdurate steel monsters on dangerous turns and master them. Except for a slight preponderance of girth, he has the appearance of a trained athlete. He is of average height and heavily built. His complexion is ruddy and his hair and moustache black. He is a typical Frenchman, good natured and of a nervous temperament. There is a touch of vanity in his make-up. He glories in the crowd's applause. Each cheer spurs him on to more speed, more daring. Because he is so highly strung, critics believe that Boillot may not finish Saturday's grind. The monotonous circling of the brick oval may wear on him. He may take chances under the strain that will prove disastrous. His smile is that of the master musician who delights in the changing motifs of a sonata but tires in the practicing of scales. Jules Goux, Boillot's teammate and fides Achates, is of an entirely different type. For a Frenchman, he is cold. He hails from the France-Comté, famous as the home of hard-headed, unemotional men. This inheritant calmness, this splendid control of his nerves aids him in his track driving, in which he has proven himself a master at Brooklands. Before the start of a race, Goux is cool and determined. Boillot is just as determined, but is excited. His heart beats faster. He is impetuous to be off. In stature Goux is not as formidable appearing as Boillot, but he is just as finely trained and as strong. He gives one the impression that he is a dandy, a boulevardier. He is immaculate in his dress and looks more like a young Englishman than a Frenchman. Like Boillot, he is very jovial and a bit of a humorist in a quiet and satirical way. Goux is Boillot's guide in the latter's first invasion of America. He has taken him to the circus, introduced him to pie à la mode and ice cream soda and taught him to whistle ragtime tunes. Their favorite selection is 'You Made Me Love You, I Didn't Want To Do It.' They also have picked up a few choice bits of American slang. Except when tuning up their cars or discussing race details with Johnny Aitken, their pit manager, they conduct themselves like two boys out for a lark.[33]

After 24 laps, Duray's baby Peugeot was second, just 19 seconds behind Thomas in the Delage. And there was more to come. Duray overtook Thomas and during 32 laps played the role of mechanical David humiliating the trailing Goliaths. Thomas dropped back to seventh. His teammate Guyot took upon himself the task of clinging to Duray, who completed 100 miles in 1 h 10 min 46 sec, averaging 85 mph. After 120 laps, Thomas again swept to the front and took the Prest-O-Lite trophy offered to the leader at 300 miles. Wishart in the 450-inch Mercer was just 3 seconds back, Duray 25 seconds and Boillot in the works Peugeot 50 seconds. Then Boillot took second. But not for long! At the completion of 340 miles, the Peugeot blew a tire on the far turn. The tire flew up, hit Boillot on the arm. The great Boillot lost control of the Peugeot for a moment. Not satisfied with this, the casing again struck him, this time on the head. Boillot did not give up, but gave the steering wheel a sharp twist. A side frame member cracked, putting Boillot out of the race. Boillot and his no. 7 Peugeot had made five stops. During one of the stops Boillot took on 10 gallons of gasoline, at another time 15 gallons more. The Peugeot pit men changed one tire in 40 seconds, two tires in 1 min 2 sec. After 375 miles Duray was in for gasoline, oil, both rear tires and a front one. Duray finished second, Goux fourth.

Bob Burman's backer Louis C. Erbes, a wealthy gentleman from St. Paul, Minnesota, bought Goux's 5.6-liter. The New York Peugeot Auto Import Co. of Alphonse Kaufmann took over the Boillot car. And Harry Stutz bought the baby Peugeot from the Menier family for $10,000, in view of a close inspection. In July 1914 in the 300-miler at Sioux City, Burman's 5.6-liter was put out after 150 miles with a broken piston, connecting rod and crankcase, and Mulford's Peugeot Auto Import car after 26 miles with a broken oil tank: "Mulford's elimination in the Peugeot came about in a peculiar way. One thing he evidently overlooked when he took over the car, which was the same Boillot had at Indianapolis, was to check up on the oil tank. Evidently the vibration at Indianapolis and Boillot's accident had loosened the rivets and when Mulford opened up in the Sioux City race these rivets, or rather some of them, rattled loose and fell inside the tank, permitting the oil to escape."[34] Until 1 August, the Peugeot was repaired and Mulford's perpetual smile was broader than ever when he captured all three of the 50-mile events of the Cotton Carnival sweepstakes at Galveston, Texas. In the 1914 CAC Trophy at Elgin, Mulford finished third.

Was the trend-setting Peugeot head over-engineered? Probably a simpler single-cam layout did not even cross cam handler Henry's mind since the Peugeot had its roots in the T-head. Two camshafts were present from the outset. In 1914, when the pent roof combustion chamber was adopted as Grand Prix standard, the competitors saw it under a different point of view. Most of them regarded a single overhead camshaft as sufficient. The 6.2-liter Delage, Peugeot's main competitor in 1913, also relied on two camshafts, on two low mounted camshafts operating four horizontal valves per cylinder. In the 1913 French Grand Prix, the Delage was the fastest car on the track but lost the race because of bad luck. In the 1914 Indianapolis 500, Delage was luckier.

11

Indy Expedition

The idea was not bad: revive last year's Grand Prix cars, ship them across the big pond to Indianapolis, beat the Americans on home soil, collect the big prize money, and finally sell the worn-out racers on site. While the Hoosier crowd would have preferred a domestic victory, it was a good deal, not only for the French. The Peugeot victory was to induce a technical turnaround within the American scene and attracted further exotic entries for the upcoming race, first and foremost Peugeot's main competitor Delage. It was in California that the Delage was in the limelight for the first time. In January 1914 wealthy Los Angeles sportswoman Leotia Northam entered her chauffeur Omar Toft in the Santa Monica races: "She sent her chauffeur to Europe to buy the car, and he has cabled he made the purchase."[1] Mrs. Northam planned "to enter all the important meets of the season.... Failing to get a Delage, she will buy some other car, she says. In the past she has used a Simplex. To indulge in her racing hobby, Mrs. Northam had to have herself incorporated. The A.A.A.'s definition of 'entrant, contestant, or competitor' is 'any man or organization which makes an entry of a motor car for a contest.' No mention being made of woman, Mrs. Northam had only the alternative of becoming an organization."[2]

In fact the Delage was entered but never did turn up in California: "A veil of mystery surrounds this entry. It has not arrived as yet and no one seems to know whether it is in this country or not. One story has been published in the local papers to the effect that Omar Toft, displaced as the Delage driver at the eleventh hour by Bert Dingley, had stopped the car in New York because he was not going to be at the wheel of the importation from France. It is intimated by Oldfield and his backer, George Settle, that Toft never went to France to get the car and they offer a reward of $100 for proof that the purchase was made."[3] The purchase was not made and Barney could save his money. Toft was suspended until January 1916 because there was no sincere intention to have the car compete. A few weeks after the end of his suspension, on 30 March 1916, Omar Toft married Leotia Northam.

On 17 January 1914, Albert Guyot announced from Paris that he was about to make an official entry in the Indianapolis 500 "with the Delage 120-horsepower racer driven by him in the last French Grand Prix.... There is a possibility of a second Delage entry being made, the car to be driven by René Thomas, the crack driver of Schneider cars."[4] Guyot's Delage was the 6.2-liter in which Paul Bablot had won the 1913 Grand Prix de France at Le Mans. Thomas' car was said to be the same one which Mrs. Northam was supposed to have bought for the recent Santa Monica races: "Omar Toft, reported to have been injured while driving the Delage in France, had not even seen it. Several cables had been sent from Los Angeles, and the Delage factory, considering the proposition a serious one, had kept the machine out of the Indianapolis race. As soon as it was clear that there was nothing to

25 June 1911— Coupe de l'Auto pour Voitures légères, Boulogne-sur-Mer. Paul Bablot and the winning 3-liter Delage at the Saint-Martin hairpin (Mercedes-Benz Classic).

the American offer, Delage signed the entry blank for Indianapolis and gave instructions to Thomas to be ready to sail with Guyot on 9 May. The cars are for sale, but they cannot pass out of Delage's hands until after the Indianapolis race."[5]

The "120-horsepower" Delage, the 6.2-liter type Y, was a direct descendant of the *Trois Litres*, the 3-liter type X (80 × 149 mm) in which Paul Bablot had won the 1911 Coupe de l'Auto at Boulogne. The cylinder dimensions of the 6.2-liter were 105 × 180 mm, nearly the same as the Peugeot's with the exception of the slightly bigger bore. But the head was different. Designer Arthur Michelat continued to rely on his successful solution used in the Trois Litres: Two low mounted camshafts operated the horizontal valves via pushrods and rockers. The 6.2-liter had four valves per cylinder, each 55 mm in diameter, with valve lift of 9 mm. Each camshaft and the four-piece crankshaft ran in five ball bearings from M & B, the specialist Malicet & Blin. The big ends ran in plain bearings. The famous BND chrome-nickel steel from the Dérihon brothers was used for the crankshaft, the conical connecting rods, the camshafts and the valve gear.

> Steel pistons are used with two rings, having bayonet-type joints. The pistons are drilled, the central portion is of smaller diameter than the top and bottom, and oil grooves are provided. There is a cylinder offset of 25 millimeters. Two independent magnetos are fitted, one of these is driven off the cross shaft operating the water pump, and the other is set fore and aft on the exhaust side of the motor. The eight plugs are mounted in the head of the cylinders, but as far apart as possible. Each magneto has its own switch, mounted on the dashboard, thus enabling the driver to cut out either magneto for purposes of test-

3-liter Delage engine for the 1911 Coupe de l'Auto: 80 × 149 mm, two horizontal valves per cylinder, design by Arthur Michelat (*La Vie Automobile*, 1911).

12 July 1913 — Grand Prix de l'ACF, Amiens. Albert Guyot and his 6.2-liter Delage at Moreuil (Mercedes-Benz Classic).

ing. While the failure of either magneto would not stop the running of the car, it is found that much better results are obtained with the two magnetos firing simultaneously. Lubrication is an interesting feature. A gear pump in the base chamber is driven off the intake camshaft. It delivers oil through a collector to the main bearings, ... the overhead valve gear and ... to the dashboard pressure indicator.... There is a cage around each ball bearing. This insures a constant batch of oil for each bearing, and also enables the bearing to drive out the lubricant centrifugally into collectors delivering it to the connecting rod ends and to the camshafts and piston walls. The system can be described as a centrifugal one, the function of the pump being limited to keeping a supply of oil in the housings around each main bearing.... In all their French races these cars have been fitted with Claudel carbureters and Bosch magnetos.[6]

Output of the Delage was 115 hp at 2500 rpm, transmitted via a multiple-disk clutch to a five-speed gearbox: "The first speed is really an emergency and like the reverse is kept covered by a clip on the gate."[7] The engine was rigidly mounted on four points; the gearbox, however, was suspended at three point from a couple of transverse frame members. The gearbox and the rear axle housings were of aluminum and the shafts of BND steel, carried on M & B bearings. The rear axle, of the Hotchkiss type, weighed 170 pounds, including the brake drums. Wheelbase was 275 cm. In the French Grand Prix at Amiens, the Delages rolled on German Continental tires, 875 × 105 front and 880 × 120 rear.

The two Delages spent Easter Monday and Tuesday on the road testing the 3 to 1 gear ratio to be used at Indianapolis. This was the ratio originally adopted for the 1913 French races, but changed later for a higher ratio: "At Amiens and Le Mans, the only two big races in which these cars have been run, the Delage machines held the whole field in the matter of rapid pick-up. This week's tests with the lower gear ratio showed that the cars were amazingly rapid in getting away after slowing down. Not many mechanical changes have been made on the Delage cars. Guyot has fitted a streamline tail enclosing his gasoline tank and has got rid of a little superfluous weight."[8] For Indianapolis, Guyot, Thomas and the mechanics Achille Secuws and Robert Laly mounted English Palmer cord tires, 35 × 5 front and 35 × 6 rear, inflated at 58 pounds (4 bar).

The Delage team was managed by William Bradley who found additional cars for Indianapolis: Duray's 3-liter baby Peugeot, a Sunbeam for Chassagne, an Excelsior for Christiaens, and a Bugatti for Friderich. The great Felice Nazzaro, who was to drive one of his Nazzaros, backed out. Chassagne's Sunbeam was a 4.5-liter L-head six (80 × 150 mm), a 1913 Grand Prix racer with the wheelbase extremely shortened from 300 to 211 cm or 83 inches:

> In all except the engine, the new special car is smaller than the older ones, and it is reported that the Sunbeam company offered it to Grant for the same price as he paid for the one he bought. Sunbeam either will enter its new special machine itself or is willing to consider the offer of any private sportsman to buy the car and run it under his own name, but it wants Chassagne to drive the car. The new car embodies features which are the result of last year's experience at Indianapolis. While the chassis is specially prepared, the motor is the one with which Chassagne made the 12-hour record at Brooklands, averaging 89.85 miles per hour. According to Louis Coatalen, chief engineer of the Sunbeam company, the motor develops 18 horsepower more than do those of the two larger cars. A special feature is that it is fitted with two carburetors and two inlet pipes. The short wheelbase of 83 inches has necessitated designing a special gearbox, with very short shafts, giving two speeds only. It is carried on the same subframe as the engine, hung from the main frame by three universal hangers. Modifications in the oiling have been made with a view to cooling, the bulk of the oil, instead of being carried in the base chamber, is carried in a tank at the back of the chassis.[9]

Albert Guyot and mechanic Achille Secuws in the 6.2-liter Delage (Library of Congress).

The Sunbeam special started on Dunlops, 34 × 4½ all around, pumped at 65 pounds (4.5 bar).

Harry Grant's Sunbeam was a former 1913 Grand Prix car entered by William Ziegler. The Sunbeam had finished third at Amiens. In the autumn of 1913, Grant and Johnny Marquis bought the car for Ziegler at the Olympia Show in London. The Grand Prix Sunbeam had a wheelbase of 300 cm. Grant mounted 35 × 5 Palmer tires. Ziegler's Isotta entry was left dangling. The 23-year-old William Ziegler, Jr. was the adopted son of the baking powder tycoon and patron of arctic expeditions, William Ziegler, who died in May 1905. The biological son of the capitalist's half-brother, William Jr. was "heir to $30.000.000."[10]

Ernest Friderich's Bugatti was entered by cable on 28 April 1914, three days before the deadline of 1 May. The Bugatti came from Molsheim in Alsace, Germany, at the time. The most notable feature of the 5.65-liter (100 × 180 mm) was its 3-valve head, with two intakes and one exhaust operated by a single overhead camshaft. The chassis dimensions of the Bugatti were rather small, with a wheelbase of 255 cm and track of 125 cm and the tires were 33 × 5 Continentals. The Excelsior had finished eighth in the 1913 Grand Prix de l'ACF at Amiens. It came from Zaventem, a northeastern suburb of Brussels, and was powered by a pepped-up stock engine, an L-head six built up in two sets of three and displacing 6.1 liters with the dimensions of 90 × 160 mm. The crankshaft ran in seven plain bearings with lubrication under pressure. Wheelbase was 265 cm. The detachable wheels were supplied by Adex, the 34 × 5½ tires by Palmer.

> Guyot drives motor cars for sport and sells them as a business.... Thomas is a graduate of the school of hard knocks.... Unlike most French drivers, Thomas works on his car from

morning until night before a race instead of permitting his mechanic to wield file and hammer under his direction. He is a born mechanician and can do a thing quicker and better than he can explain to another. For a Frenchman, Thomas is very serious, but life always has been serious for him. He never has had time to play. One look at Joseph Christiaens, the driver of the Excelsior, and you would know he is a Belgian. He has the bulky frame and fair complexion of the north countryman and is slow, methodical and careful. He has the temperament that makes him a dangerous contender in a race. He is too calm to get excited, and too good an engineer to abuse his car.... Ernest Friderich comes to America with the 'Made in Germany' label on him. He was born in Paris of German parents but has spent the greater part of his life in the Fatherland. After serving in the kaiser's army, he secured employment in the Bugatti shops and has always been identified with that company. He is the dark horse of the foreign contingent.[11]

The qualifying trials were held on Monday, Tuesday and Wednesday, 25, 26 and 27 May 1914, starting at 10 o'clock in the morning and finishing at sundown. All cars had to qualify within these three days and those not ready were eliminated. The last car to enter was the first to take its trials and the first entry was the last to be given a trial. The trials had become eliminating trials since according to the official entry blank "only thirty cars will be allowed to start. In the event more than thirty cars are entered, after three-car teams have been reduced to two cars each, the thirty fastest cars in a speed trial of one lap of the track will be eligible."[12] In the previous years a car had only to demonstrate its capability to make a circuit of the speedway at 75 miles an hour. A commendable change in 1914 was the rule requiring the changing of steering knuckles and tie rods two days previous to the race. The technical committee had been instructed to see that this was carried out and that new parts were installed on every car. On Tuesday evening, 26 May, there was a medical examination of all drivers and mechanics, of the heart, eyes, lungs and other organs of the body; and on Thursday, 28 May, there was an instruction meeting for drivers, mechanics and officials.

On race day, Saturday, 30 May 1914, the sky was clear of clouds and as early as 7 o'clock a huge crowd was clamoring at the gates for admittance. With 10,000 additional seats having been provided in the huge stands, attendance was estimated at close to 125,000. Among the notables were Owen Johnson, the author, and Howard Chandler Christy, the artist. The usual brake tests were held and everyone qualified. Then came the grouping of the drivers, mechanics and officials for the big photograph, and the parade of the drivers, each being followed by an introduction to the crowd, after which the cars were located in position for the start itself. Instead of dancing around in the smoke and dodging the cars, starter Tom Hay was safely located on a bridge that ran high over the track where every driver could see him. As usual Carl Fisher acted as pacemaker, with Finley Porter, the Mercer engineer, by his side holding a watch in order to bring the real start as close to 10 o'clock as possible.

Favored by his position in the first row, Howdy Wilcox in the Gray Fox shot over the wire in the lead. Not for long. After two laps, the Excelsior of Christiaens was in front with the Maxwells of Carlson and Tetzlaff 300 yards behind. After 20 miles the Sunbeam of Chassagne blew a tire, dished a wheel and turned over. The Frenchman, who was not seriously hurt, sought refreshment at a lemonade stand before being escorted by Gaston Morris to the hospital tent, where a few beauty patches were applied to some cuts on his face. After 24 laps, Thomas' Delage hurtled to the front, having covered 60 miles in 38 min 52 sec, an average of 83.6 mph. After 140 miles, Thomas made a second stop to change both rear tires, losing 1 min 30 sec. After 170 miles, the new leader, Guyot in no. 10 Delage, covered 72 laps or 180 miles in 2 h 7 min 20 sec. But after 190 miles he too had to stop to change two tires and fill up gasoline and oil, losing 8 min 20 sec since the engine refused to restart. After 215 miles Thomas came in for his second stop, changed a left rear, and got away in 50 seconds. Guyot and Duray were playing Alphonse and Gaston and alternating in setting the pace, with Thomas third. After 240 miles Christiaens came in for his first stop, changed both rear tires and a front one, and took on gasoline and oil. He got away after 4 min 39 sec. After 120 laps, Thomas swept to the front and took the Prest-O-Lite trophy offered to the leader at 300 miles. Then Christiaens pulled up at the pits, completely exhausted, falling out of the car. The gasoline tank of the Excelsior was filled in 1 min 15 sec. The moment's rest did wonders since the Belgian took the wheel briskly and finished the race in good condition. Friderich abandoned his Bugatti when one of the ball bearings of the driving pinion gave way. Friderich had changed 14 tires, most of these on the right rear, getting an average of 25 miles on a tire. The Bugatti boomed the rubber market the most. In all, the Bugatti lost 34 min 34 sec at the pits. Thomas stopped after 350 miles for gasoline, water and oil, and took the opportunity to change both right tires. It held him 2 min 25 sec. Teammate Guyot halted after 375 miles to take on gasoline, losing 55 seconds, and Duray, too, was in for gasoline, oil, both rear tires and a front one. After 380 miles the order was Thomas in 4 h 37 min 45 sec, then Duray 2 min 25 sec back, Guyot 2 min 33 sec back, and Goux 8 min back. In the remaining 140 miles, Thomas increased his lead over Duray's Peugeot to 6 min 44 sec and won in 6 h 3 min 46 sec.

Wearing his checkered cap hindside before, Thomas had won his first classic:

> If his heart was bursting with joy, his smileless face did not show it. If there was a flush of pride on his cheeks, it was not discernible because of the grease and grime that covered his features. He was as unimpassioned as an ancient stoic, as calm and cold in victory as in strife, the very antithesis of what a Frenchman is supposed to be. When Jules Goux won the 500-mile race of 1913, he shook with emotion and surrendered to his joy. Kisses were imprinted on his grimy cheeks. He grabbed with his numbed fingers a bottle of champagne and drained it at one gulp. But there were no kisses, no wine for René Thomas. Had there been, he probably would have resented and spurned them. He was deaf to the applause that shook the gray stands. His joyous pitmen and compatriots had to reach for the hand that they wished to shake. It never was offered to them. This reserve, this coldness, this modesty of the Delage driver was somewhat depressing. In victory, heroes should not act like this. For 6 tortuous, fatiguing hours, Thomas drove with a nonchalance that must have been maddening to the desperate rivals who were pursuing the snub-nosed, defiantly roaring Delage. Although driving at a death-inviting speed, he seemed as unconcerned and peaceful as if he were sitting in a rocking chair on his veranda at home.... If he had marked his course on the track with chalk, he could not have kept to the line any better. He went into the turns neither high nor low. He always was travelling were the track was blackest with oil — treacherous, slippery oil.... Even when Boillot and the hated Peugeot overtook and passed him, Thomas restrained himself and refused to allow impulse to get the better of judgment.[13]

The foreigners not only won the race, but also captured second, third, fourth and sixth, while another foreign car, the Sunbeam, driven by an American, Grant, was seventh. Counting actual cash as pulled from the speedway purse of $50,000, the foreign drivers captured $40,700, leaving only a scant $9,300 to be divided among the five American pilots. Added to this was still another humiliation: The 500-mile speedway record of 78.7 miles per hour was smashed not only by the winner but by the three other foreigners who followed him home, the top notch being 82.47 miles per hour. George M. Dickson, general manager of the National company, derived some consolation out of the fact that no American car broke

Joe Dawson's 500-mile record. Oldfield in the Stutz, first American to finish, missed it by more than 2 minutes. "It's all the more remarkable, that record, because it was made 2 years ago and yet no American car can beat it,"[14] said Dickson. Ralph DePalma watched the race from the judges' stand. On Monday, 2 June, he sailed for England to drive an English Vauxhall in the French Grand Prix near Lyon.

During the race, over $14,000 was burned up in tires as 138 casings were ground to shreds or blown into the air, each of the racing tires costing over $100 on average. Guyot's Delage had the least tire trouble, with only two of its English Palmer tires having to be replaced. Oldfield's Stutz was next, with three casings, Firestones. Christiaens' Excelsior wore out four of the cord tires, Rickenbacher's Duesenberg five Michelins. The winning Delage and the baby Peugeot each used up five Palmer, and Grant's Sunbeam used six cord tires, as did Mulford's Mercedes special. The Beaver Bullet held the record among the finishers for the greatest number of tires changed, having lost 13. Goux, who finished fourth, claimed a record almost as bad, with 11 tire changes. Some rather unconventional tire sizes and tire inflation pressures were developed by the drivers: Burman used 35 × 5-inch tires all around, carrying 90 pounds (6.2 bar) pressure on the right or outer tires, and 85 pounds (5.8 bar) on the left. Wilcox, in the Gray Fox, carried from 70 to 80 pounds (4.8 to 5.5 bar) in his Silvertown cords, and Keene, in the Beaver Bullet, carried 75 pounds (5.2 bar). Goux and Boillot had French Palmers, 34 × 4½-inch in front and 35 × 6-inch in the rear, the latter a somewhat unusual size. They carried 80 pound (5.5 bar) in front and 85 pounds (5.8 bar) in the rear. The Delages carried 58 pounds (4 bar), and their tires were also of an unusual size, being 35 × 5-inch in front and 35 × 6 in the rear. Chassagne's Sunbeam used 34 × 4½-inch all around, inflated to 65 pounds (4.5 bar). Mason had 32 × 4-inch tires in front and 34 × 4½-inch in the rear, inflated to 60 pounds (4.1 bar). Duray, with his 32 × 5-inch tires, also an unusual size, carried between 60 and 65 pounds (4.1 and 4.5 bar). Carlson, in the Maxwell, carried only 40 pounds (2.75 bar) pressure with 32 × 4½ tires in front and 33 × 5 inches in the rear. This was the lowest pressure used: "Harroun's selection of this was based on his experience in last summer's transcontinental trip, in which he used 34 × 6-inch tires inflated to only 30 pounds pressure. Judging from the results of observations at the pits it seemed that the lower tire pressures gave somewhat longer life to the tires in this high-speed work, particularly when tires of rather large cross-section were used in the race."[15] Haupt had his tires pumped to three different pressures, 65 pounds (4.5 bar) on the right rear tire, 80 pounds (5.5 bar) on the left rear tire and 75 pounds (5.2 bar) on the two front tires. "The cord tire was used in much larger sizes than ever before, there being several 36 × 6-inch tires fitted on the rear, and these with air pressures of 70 pounds or under, instead of pressures of 90 or 100 pounds used in the same size of fabric tire."[16]

René Thomas and his teammates sailed home on the German *Imperator*. From Cherbourg the drivers were allowed to take first-class compartments to Paris, while the mechanics were relegated to second class, on separate trains. Louis Delage, his wife, chief engineer Arthur Michelat and a huge crowd of racing fans packed the inside and outside of the Gare Saint-Lazare. Flowers were presented, flags were waved, and men and women alike struggled to kiss the somewhat bashful and embarrassed Thomas. It was in the new 4.5-liter racer that Thomas was given a triumphal joy ride through Paris to the Delage showrooms on Boulevard Pereire, where champagne flowed freely. In the meantime war was raging in Paris between Delage and Peugeot partisans: "An inferior grade of tire was sold to Boillot and Goux, and had they been given the same high quality as supplied to Thomas, one of the Peugeots would have won the race. The Palmer Tire Co. keeps out of the discussion, merely

René Thomas at the wheel of the 6.2-liter Delage (Library of Congress).

stating that Delage men were supplied from the London stock and the two Peugeot men bought privately from the French factory, but that the English and the French tires are identical."[17] Tire experts explained the failure of the Peugeots by defective fitting.

W.E. Wilson bought the Indianapolis winning Delage. In August 1914, Billy Knipper drove it in the 300-miler at Sioux City. After running 198 miles, cylinder no. 4 of the Delage became cracked, allowing water to run out. Nevertheless, Knipper decided to continue, stopping eight times to fill with water. Knipper finished sixth, 42 minutes behind Rickenbacher in the Duesenberg. On 28 September, Claude Newhouse was at the wheel of the Delage in the 100-mile dirt track race at Kalamazoo, Michigan. He finished third behind Burman in his special and O'Donnell in a Duesenberg.

In view of the 300-inch limit, the Delage received a new 93-mm block (93 × 180 mm). In the 1915 Indianapolis 500 it was driven by John DePalma, Ralph's younger brother. When taking his second trial in the afternoon of Sunday, 23 May, the young DePalma skidded entering the homestretch, struck the inside wall, and rolled over three times. The front end of the frame was broken, but the engine and transmission were not damaged. The Delage was repaired while John DePalma and his mechanic Phillips were slightly hors de combat but were able to start. "John de Palma had extremely bad luck and the failure which caused him to retire in the forty-second lap could not be blamed upon his accident in practice. After making a good pace till his first and only stop, he found the flywheel running out of truth, owing either to it being loose on the shaft or to the built-up crankshaft having loosened at the flywheel end."[18] By the end of June 1915, Louis Chevrolet drove the Delage to seventh in the 500-miler at Chicago.

In June 1915 René Thomas tried to secure an option on the purchase of a 4.5-liter Delage and to prepare the racer for track work. He had applied for his discharge but could not find a backer and continued to be on army service. The 4.5-liter Delage, the type S, was built in view of the displacement limit of the 1914 Grand Prix de l'ACF. In principle, it was an evolution of the 6.2-liter which won at Le Mans and Indianapolis. Delage engineer Arthur Michelat relocated the two low mounted camshafts to the top of the head and had combined them with a desmo operation. As in the Peugeot, the four valves per cylinder formed a pent roof, with an intake diameter of 48 mm, and an exhaust of 46 mm. The cylinder dimensions were 94 × 160 mm and output was 115 hp at 3000 rpm. Wheelbase was 270 cm, 5 cm shorter than on the previous year's car; track was 135 cm, 5 cm wider; and the tires used in the Grand Prix at Lyon were 875 × 105 front, 895 × 135 rear. Just before the race at Lyon, all three Delages driven by Bablot, Guyot and Duray experienced backfiring into the carburetors, attributed to a slightly imperfect seating of the desmo valves. A new adjustment was made a few hours before the start, but the engines lost their power. The Delage trio, among the hot favorites before the start, came down to earth. Bablot and Guyot withdrew while Duray finished eighth.

In the first week of August 1915, a 4.5-liter Delage arrived in America, bought by David Joyce. On 7 August, Barney Oldfield started in a 100-miler on the Maywood speedway, although "Oldfield had been unable to adjust carburetor trouble and did not consider

9 October 1915 — first Astor Cup, Sheepshead Bay, Brooklyn. Barney Oldfield leaning against the rear wheel of his 4.5-liter Delage. By his side, at the back, Johnny Aitken and Dario Resta. At the front, mechanics Maurice Becker, Fred McCarthy and Ray Dasbach (Library of Congress).

30 September 1916 — second Astor Cup, Sheepshead Bay, Brooklyn. Jack LeCain drove one of the 4.5-liter Delages owned by Harry Harkness (Library of Congress).

himself a real contender when he started.... Oldfield had the pole at the start and showed the way in the pacemaking lap. That was the only time he was in front, for the other three flashed past him when the flag fell, and tire troubles early put him out of the running."[19] At Elgin, Oldfield took third in the CAC Trophy and fifth in the Elgin National, and in September eighth in the Minneapolis 500. In October 1915, in the Astor Cup at Sheepshead Bay, Oldfield's 4.5-liter broke a connecting rod after 12 miles. In the same Astor Cup Carl Limberg drove the ex–Guyot 6.2-liter Delage which had been reduced to 300-cid and finished sixth. During the winter of 1915–1916, Harry Harkness imported the three remaining 4.5-liters.

Immediately after arriving in America the 6.2-liter Delage gave proof of its potential by winning the 1914 Indianapolis 500. Compared to the Peugeot, it had a displacement advantage of 0.6 liter, and an outmoded cylinder head. But two low-mounted camshafts and horizontal valves were still good enough to ensure an effective combustion at engine speeds up to 3000 rpm. The success at Indianapolis was due to the perfect preparation in the Courbevoie factory in France. Later, when it finished in private hands, the French racer lost its competitiveness and was not a front-runner anymore. The 4.5-liter desmo team of the Harkness stable met the same fate. In America, the Delages lacked an adequate racing car department. One of the Peugeots, in particular, was in a better situation. It was prepared and developed like a factory car by the New York importer with input and assistance of a Los Angeles carburetor shop.

12

Peugeot Career

On Saturday, 27 February and Saturday, 6 March 1915, the Grand Prize and the Vanderbilt were held at San Francisco, on a 3.905-mile course within the grounds of the Panama-Pacific International Exposition celebrating the opening of the Panama Canal in August 1914. The fair featured a reproduction of the Panama Canal that covered five acres. Visitors rode around the model on a moving platform, listening to information over a telephone receiver. An actual Ford assembly line was set up in the Palace of Transportation and turned out one car every 10 minutes for three hours every afternoon except Sunday, producing 4400 cars during the Exposition. The Grand Prize attracted 30 starters and the Vanderbilt 31. The only really new car was the no. 5 Stutz driven by Gil Anderson, the prototype of the future 300-inch racer. Dario Resta won both races in the Peugeot Auto Import Co.'s 5.6-liter which had been brushed up in the shops of Harry Miller, Los Angeles. In the Grand Prize, Resta completed 104 laps of 3.905 miles, a total of 406 miles, in 7 h 7 min 53 sec, nearly 7 minutes ahead of Howdy Wilcox in the older 450-inch T-head Stutz, 14 minutes ahead of Hughie Hughes in the Ono, and 22 minutes ahead of Anderson in the 300-inch Stutz. The Vanderbilt was run over 77 laps or 300 miles. Resta's time was 4 h 27 min 37 sec. Again Wilcox finished second 7 minutes back, with Pullen in a Mercer third 8 minutes back, and DePalma in the 4.5-liter Mercedes 11 minutes back. "With the same courage and skill which carried him to victory in the Grand Prize race a week ago, Resta, in his high-powered, snorting Peugeot racer, won the Vanderbilt Cup race, America's blue ribbon auto classic, here today. Resta's feat in winning the two big races in eight days is one of the most remarkable performances in the history of auto racing."[1]

After the San Francisco races, Resta was immediately promoted as "Racing's Latest Sensation — The Man from Over the Sea," just what *Motor Age's* J.C. Burton was waiting for:

> Dario Resta is small in stature. There is nothing commanding about him. He does not typify the great strength as does Georges Boillot, the French champion, or did the late David Bruce-Brown. He is built more on the lines of Jules Goux or Ralph de Palma. He would have to stand on tip-toe to knock off the hat of a 6-foot antagonist and could train down to the lightweight limit after a week of road work. Yet there is nothing about him that could be mistaken for physical weakness. He is well proportioned. His shoulders are broad. He is a personification of the carefully trained athlete.... He is a living lie to the fallacy that it takes a big man to tame a powerful motor car when it runs wild. He proved that he was master of his mount in the grand prize race when the Peugeot skidded on the slippery macadam and swung completely around in making the treacherous right-angle turns. His hands alone give a hint of his vocation. They are big and powerful, somewhat out of proportion to the rest of his body. Perhaps his hands are the best life insurance that

9 October 1915 — first Astor Cup, Sheepshead Bay, Brooklyn. In the first row no. 1 Peugeot with Dario Resta and mechanic Fred McCarthy, no. 2 Peugeot with Johnny Aitken and Maurice Becker, no. 3 Delage with Barney Oldfield and Ray Dasbach, and no. 4 Peugeot special with Bob Burman and Jack Gable. In the second row a batch of Stutzes (Library of Congress).

he carries, for they are gripping. It is somewhat difficult to classify Dario Resta nationally. He looks what he is, an Italian, for his skin is dark, his hair is wavy and his eyes are large and deep, eyes such as one associates with a native of a southern country. Still, were you blind and unable to see him, you would wager that he was an Englishman. He has all the mannerisms of speech that identifies a Briton. The day that I talked with him, the weather in Chicago was 'beastly.' He told me that Carlson drove 'jolly well.' He said he would 'rahther' not divulge his future plans. This paradox can be explained, however. Resta was born in the land of Garibaldi. He is a native of Livorno, or Leghorn.... His parents emigrated to England.... He was educated in the English public schools. He served his apprenticeship in the Panhard shops, where he learned the mechanics of motor car construction. He raced first in England. He went into business in London. What he knows of Italy has been told him, or he has read.... Resta is a sportsman in every sense of the word. Next to driving racing cars, his favorite pastime is roller skating. Three years ago, he won the international championship at figure skating and holds several challenge bowls which he captured in competition on the floors of London rinks. The Italian plays golf to steady his nerves and boxes a little.[2]

Resta was born in Faenza, between Bologna and Rimini, Italy, on 19 August 1882.[3] His parents emigrated to London where young Dario served an apprenticeship in the Panhard shops. Resta made his racing debut on the Brooklands track in 1907, driving the Mercedes owned by F.R. Fry, a wealthy chocolate manufacturer of Bristol and prominent British turfman. In 1908 he drove an Austin six in the Grand Prix de l'ACF at Dieppe. Between 1912 and 1914 Resta drove for Sunbeam and was the heaviest stockholder in the Dario Resta Co., a motor car agency at no. 27 Haymarket, London. When war was declared he accepted a contract offered by Alphonse Kaufmann's Peugeot Auto Import Co. Resta came to America to conquer, but instead was conquered. Soon after landing he married Spencer Wishart's sister Mary.

The New York Peugeot Auto Import Co. was located at 1809 Broadway and 57th Street, and was managed by Alphonse Kaufmann and Arthur Hill. On 20 April 1915, the Peugeot Import entered one of the latest 4.5-liter Peugeot racers for Resta in the upcoming Indianapolis 500, alongside two older Coupe de l'Auto 3-liters. The man from over the sea was promoted to favorite. The 4.5-liter Peugeot for Resta was said to be the car that Georges Boillot handled in the 1914 French Grand Prix at Lyon. But when the racer arrived at the speedway this was quickly corrected: "Resta's car was the spare mount of the Peugeot team at Lyon last year. It is identical to the car that Boillot drove nearly to victory."[4]

In 1914, the Automobile Club de France limited the maximum displacement to 4.5 liters and the maximum weight to 1100 kilograms. The Peugeot racing department built four 4.5-liters (92 × 169 mm), factory designation EX5/L45, the fifth model of the new twin-cam generation. The general layout of the engine remained unchanged: two-piece crankshaft running in three ball bearings, two overhead camshafts driven by spur gears, four valves per cylinder, intake diameter 52 mm, exhaust 46 mm. The carburetor was supplied by Zenith. The 4.5-liter developed 115 hp at 3000 rpm. In April 1914, Georges Boillot tested an Isotta with four-wheel brakes, and was delighted. The 37.6-km road course near Lyon comprised a hilly and windy part so that the Peugeots were equipped with four-wheel brakes. They were operated via hand lever, the additional transmission brake via foot pedal. As a result of further tests in Gustave Eiffel's *soufflerie* and in view of the endless 12-km straight, the Peugeots received a streamlined tail carrying a couple of spare wheels. The wheelbase remained unchanged, 270 cm as in 1913 on the 5.6-liter; track was 135 cm; and tires were from Dunlop, 875 × 105 front and 880 × 120 rear.

After 18 laps of the 20-lap Grand Prix de l'ACF, Georges Boillot's Peugeot and Christian Lautenschlager's Mercedes were exactly on the same level, with Lautenschlager on the upgrade. But Boillot, the typical French driver, spirited and proud, the reincarnation of d'Artagnan having emerged from a Pierre Souvestre novel, wanted the victory and nothing else. He tried to get the impossible out of the Peugeot which broke down. Teammate Jules Goux finished fourth behind the Mercedes trio driven by Lautenschlager, Wagner and Salzer, 11 minutes behind the winner.

"According to Johnny Aitken, ... the Peugeot engineers have come nearer to solving completely the problem of overcoming wind resistance than any other designers of the new or old world. In the 1914 grand prix, Aitken tore up his program into small bits and scattered it along the home stretch When the Peugeots rushed past, the paper was not blown a fraction of an inch but there was a regular stage snowstorm when the other cars swept by the pits."[5] For the 1915 Indianapolis race the humped camel back to accommodate the spares was cut as there was no need to carry wheels on the track. Resta, who had won the San Francisco races on Nassau tires, now mounted Goodrich Silvertown Cords, 34 × 4½. In the first week of May, it was announced that Peugeot had shipped a second 4.5-liter to America, but the car did not arrive. Resta was forced to practice at the wheel of the 5.6-liter used in the San Francisco races. There was no new axle for the 4.5-liter and he did not want to infringe the rule that all cars must be equipped with new axles two days before the contest. Resta qualified the 4.5-liter in 1 min 30.4 sec, the third best time. One of the 3-liters entered by the Peugeot Auto Import was the car which Arthur Duray had driven in 1914 and which Harry Stutz had bought with the objective of disclosing its mechanical secrets. The other one was freshly imported. The 3-liter Peugeots (78 × 156 mm) still used their original French Claudel carburetors. Wheelbase was 256 cm, with 33 × 4½ Silvertown tires.

In January 1915, in the San Diego race, the older 5.6-liter of the Peugeot Auto Import had been driven by Rickenbacher. Afterwards, it was overhauled in Harry Miller's shops at Los Angeles and fitted with alloyanum pistons. Then Resta took the wheel in the San Francisco races, and enthusiastically praised the new piston metal. As a consequence all three Indianapolis Peugeots were equipped with alloyanum pistons. According to the original entry Bob Burman had the choice to drive either one of the 3-liters or his own Peugeot special. The third driver was not named. On 11 May 1915, Frank Galvin and George Babcock were at Indianapolis to drive the two 3-liters. Galvin had an accident and turned over, suffering a broken collarbone and contusions about the head. Mechanic Ray Dasbach's arm was in splints. The little Peugeot sustained a bent frame and a stripped off front axle but could be repaired. Kaufmann attempted to sign up Caleb Bragg as replacement for Galvin, but finally nominated Jack LeCain. On 25 May, the Peugeot Auto Import Co. lodged a protest with the AAA against the decision requiring Burman's special to start as a Peugeot or not at all. The AAA rules allowed only three cars of any one make to compete. If Burman's car started as Peugeot, then one of the 3-liters had to be scratched. Of course, Burman's car originally was a Peugeot. But a lot of parts had been replaced since the 1914 Indianapolis race so that the Peugeot people tried to place it as a special. The referee was adamant and one 3-liter entry was cancelled. It was a fight between George Babcock and Jack LeCain to see which would qualify. LeCain achieved 1 min 40.6 sec, but Babcock took the wheel in the race.

Burman had to enter his rebuilt 5.6-liter Peugeot as a Peugeot and not as the Burman Special. "The story of how Burman prepared for the great speedway event is the story of 3 months of hard labor on the part of the speed king and long hours spent over the drafting table. In the rear shop of a Los Angeles accessory house the foreign speed creation was remodeled and turned out in better condition than when it left the shores of France."[6] At Corona, in the practice session on 20 November 1914, Burman had turned a record lap at 103 miles an hour. But when warming up the Peugeot on the eve of the race, the engine broke a wrist pin and connecting rod and drove a piston through the cylinder. After this misfortune, Burman tried to patch up his car for the San Diego race in January 1915. But again the Peugeot left him in the lurch with a blistered piston and broken connecting rod. Burman continued to trust in his French mount and decided to rebuild it on his own lines, in the shops of Harry Miller's Master Carburetor Co., Los Angeles. Of course he relied on the assistance of Miller's star machinist Fred Offenhauser and draftsman John Edwards. Burman made a flying trip to Chicago to purchase the steel for the axles. Then, "with the exception of 12 days spent at San Francisco where he drove a Case car, the driver wore greasy overalls 7 days a week until he had a car which he claims is the peer of any racing machine in America."[7]

The old, original 5.6-liter Peugeot block was repaired. In addition Burman had two new 300-inch blocks cast, with bore and stroke dimensions of 3.66 × 7.10 inches, 93 × 180 mm. The pistons, the inlet manifold and the sideplates of the water jackets were made of alloyanum, Miller's latest wonder metal, nothing else than a pepped up form of magnalium with specific gravity of 3.532. "Harry A. Miller, inventor of the Master carbureter, has given the motor industry a light-weight piston metal which mechanical experts claim will do much for the American high-speed motor. The Los Angeles man calls his metal, which is an aluminum alloy, Alloyanum.... If a 4-pound cast iron piston is replaced by one of Alloyanum 2 pounds are eliminated."[8] The plates bore "Bob Burman" in large letters. The new inlet manifold was anchored by means of four large bolts instead of the original seventeen small ones. Two sets of pistons and connecting rods were made for each new block, the piston rings with oil grooves being of Burman's own design. The wrist pins and the tubular connecting rods were made of chrome-vanadium steel, the 2-inch valves of rich-tungsten steel. The new connecting rods, which replaced the older I-beam rods, were fitted with scoops for the oil. The cylinder walls, which had just received a few drops of oil from the splash system, were now directly lubricated via ducts. "The new pistons are alloyanum and have but a single ring apiece, this being very wide, with a deep half-round groove cut in the face. This groove catches oil and cares for cylinder lubrication, which Burman says was inefficient when first he had the car. The pistons have small holes drilled in them that lead to the wrist-pin, which bears in the casting direct, and there is a new oil lead which takes lubricant to the cylinder walls. This lead has three branches and each branch terminates in a double head between a pair of cylinders, so that two are fed from each pipe, while there are separate leads to care for the ends of the motor block. Oil is fed under a pressure of 8 pounds per square inch."[9]

Of course the new engine was fitted with Miller's Master carburetor, rigged with a covered air inlet. All the components of the rebuilt power transmission were made of chrome-vanadium steel. Two front axles, steering arms and knuckles were turned in a Los Angeles shop. When the body was repainted the finishing touch was the emblem of the Chicago Automobile Club, Burman's mascot. Material cost and mechanical labor, exclusive of Burman's time, was figured at $2,000. In any case, later in the season, he did not want to sell his special for less than $15,000. For the Indianapolis race, Burman mounted Goodrich Silvertown tires, 34 × 4½ all around. Wire wheels were supplied by McCue.

Burman used the repaired 5.6-liter block on 4 April 1915, when he easily defeated Louis Disbrow in the Simplex Zip and Earl Cooper in the Stutz in a three-cornered 50-mile match race at Ascot Park, Los Angeles. With the same repaired engine he won the 200-miler at Oklahoma City on 29 April: "The Burman jinx was on the job, however. Bob won in spite of it. No one knew the handicap under which the victor drove until after the race was over. When he vaulted from his triumphant car after completing the eighty-third and last lap, Burman asked for a physician. He had driven from the seventh lap on with a piece of glass in his right eye and with nothing to protect the injured optic from the terrific pressure of the wind. The right lens of Burman's goggles had been broken by a pebble hurled by the wheels of Eddie Hearne's car when Bob was passing the Case on Rainbow curve. A peculiar feature of the accident was that when the Peugeot swept by the Case, it also threw a stone that shattered the glass in Hearne's goggles."[10]

Burman's Indianapolis qualifying time was 1 min 37.4 sec. The ruling that all cars should be fitted with new front axles two days prior to the contest was much protested. It was amended to refer only to steering arms and spindles. But Burman had already spent $300 for a new front axle after the speedway management had announced that it would make no exception. On race day, Burman wore trousers and blouse of blue serge with his initials, B.B., embroidered in yellow silk on the right sleeve. Babcock's 3-liter Peugeot went out in lap 118 with a cracked cylinder. Resta in the 4.5-liter finished second behind DePalma in the Mercedes, and Burman in his special was sixth. Barney Oldfield offered $12,000 for Resta's 4.5-liter, but the offer was not accepted.

On 28 May 1915, representatives of seven speedways held a conference at Indianapolis and organized the Speedway Association of America, including Sheepshead Bay (2 miles, board), Indianapolis (2.5 miles, brick), Chicago (2 miles, board), Minneapolis (2 miles, cement), Omaha (2 miles, dirt), Omaha (1.25 miles, board), and Tacoma (2 miles, board). In April the new Maywood speedway near Chicago had jumped from project on paper to actuality. Active work on the construction of the 2-mile board track at Burnside on the western edge of the windy city began on Tuesday, 21 April. A few days later, three 8-hour shifts were at work. A 500-mile race was set for 19 June and contest director F.E. Edwards wanted to have the track ready for practice until June 5. The construction was of wood throughout, except for the concrete footings: "Upon these are set 12 × 18-inch sleepers lengthwise of the track. The sleepers carry 2 × 12-inch beams placed radially and the top surface is of 2 × 4-inch lumber lengthwise of the track. The width is 56 feet on the straight-aways, except the homestretch, which is 66 feet, and 75 feet on the turns. The track is to be banked on the turns for speeds up to 95 miles an hour or better. The grandstands will seat between 45,000 and 50,000 spectators."[11] A contract signed on 14 May by J.T. Brown of the Chicago Automobile Club and David F. Reid of the Speedway Park Association gave the CAC complete control of the 500-mile race. On Monday, 8 June 1915, after 36 actual working days, the 9 million feet of lumber were laid and spiked down with 150,000 tons of nails. By closing day on 10 June there were 29 entries.

Because of poor weather and a street car strike, the elimination trials, originally sched-uled for the week of 8 June, were postponed to Tuesday and Wednesday, 15 and 16 June, and a final session on Tuesday, 22 June. Referee Harry Vissering rescheduled the race for Saturday, 26 June. In order that Earl Cooper and Bob Burman could start and also drive at Tacoma a week later, the speedway management chartered a special express car to take Burman's Peugeot special to the Pacific coast and allow him to work on the machine en route. Cooper did not have to ship as he had a 450-inch Stutz at Los Angeles which he intended to drive at Tacoma. Finally, to avoid any overlapping, Tacoma was postponed to 4 July.

An 85 mph lap was necessary in order to start. In the first trial on Tuesday, 15 June, 15 of the 29 entries qualified. Resta in the 4.5-liter Peugeot was the fastest with a record lap in 1 min 5.4 sec, or 110.1 miles per hour. On Sunday, 20 June, in the presence of more than 40,000 spectators who turned out to witness practice, Barney Oldfield established a lap record for the wooden bowl. Taking the wheel of his front-drive Christie for a demon-stration run, he covered two miles in 1 min 4.4 sec, 111.5 miles per hour. Bob Burman believed that at the wheel of his 21-liter Benz he easily could make a lap in one minute or 120 miles an hour. The order of start was determined by the elimination times. Consequently several drivers tried to improve their times in the last trial on Tuesday, 22 June:

Make	Driver	Time	Mph	Best lap at Indianapolis mph
Peugeot	Resta	1:05.4	110.1	98.5
Stutz	Wilcox	1:08.7	104.75	98.9
Stutz	Earl Cooper	1:08.8	104.6	96.75
Stutz	Anderson	1:08.8	104.6	96.4
Maxwell	Carlson	1:09.78	103.2	84.1
Maxwell	Rickenbacher	1:09.9	103.0	82.0
Peugeot	Burman	1:11.3	101.0	92.4
Sunbeam	van Raalte	1:11.45	100.8	93.75
Sunbeam	Porporato	1:12.96	98.65	95.1
Delage	Chevrolet	1:14.3	96.9	87.2

FRP	Keene	1:14.3	96.9	–
Duesenberg	O'Donnell	1:14.7	96.4	89.0
Sunbeam	Grant	1:14.8	96.3	89.3
Duesenberg	Alley	1:15.9	95.0	90.0
Mercer	Henning	1:16.0	94.8	–
Duesenberg	Haupt	1:16.71	93.9	82.7
Peugeot	Babcock	1:17.0	93.5	89.9
Sebring	Joe Cooper	1:18.0	92.3	85.5
Ogren	Rawlings	1:18.3	92.0	–
FRP	Hughes	1:18.98	91.15	–
Maxwell	Orr	1:20.5	89.6	83.5
FRP	DeVore	1:21.3	89.55	–
Mulford	Mulford	1:23.75	86.05	–

All cars had to carry approved mud aprons so that grease could not leak onto the boards. The usual changing of steering spindles and parts prior to the race was insisted upon, but the changing of the axle proper was not required. The drivers expected an unusual amount of engine trouble since there was no opportunity to close the throttle. At Indianapolis and all other courses in America, it was necessary to close the throttle in order to take the turns. Sunbeam driver Jean Porporato said that his car held the turn at whatever level it entered it, and that little if any steering was necessary to keep the car on its course. The Illinois Central erected a $25,000 station at the main entrance and ran special trains on a 15-minute schedule. All the roads within a 2-mile radius had been covered with crushed stone and oiled. With the consent of the drivers, the start was postponed from 10 A.M. to 10:30 since Bob Burman had to replace a piston.

Twenty-one cars started, lined-up in rows of four each. After a preliminary lap at 75 miles an hour, more than 80,000 spectators witnessed a perfect start. Resta and the three Stutzes of Wilcox, Cooper and Anderson struck the wire within the same fraction of a second. During the first ten laps, Resta's blue Peugeot was trailed by the white Stutz trio and Porporato's green Sunbeam. It was Porporato who averaged 99.05 miles an hour and took the $1,000 prize for the completion of the first century, with Cooper's Stutz second. Porporato's Sunbeam was fitted with screens over the carburetor to prevent the air inlet from sucking in dust, and with stronger hood straps. Two stops for tires had put Resta in third place. Rawlings docked his Duesenberg engined Ogren with a broken bevel pinion housing in lap 12; Henning's Mercer went out with ignition trouble in lap 21; and Wilcox's Stutz suffered a broken piston in lap 45. In lap 61 Resta took the lead definitively and was never challenged again, although he was forced to change a tire two laps from the finish. Resta covered 200 miles in 2 h 2 min 17 sec (98.1 mph), 300 miles in 3 h 3 min 19 sec (98.2 mph), and 400 miles in 4 h 4 min 49 sec (98 mph). After 250 miles Cooper's Stutz was slowed by a leaking radiator. Grant in a 4.5-liter Sunbeam six finished the distance nonstop, with 50 gallons of gasoline, 7 gallons of oil and one set of Silvertown tires. He sucked oranges, drank water and ate hard boiled eggs while traveling at a speed of 95 miles per hour. "Two laps from the finish Resta stopped for oil and gas and then proceeded to speed up in the last rounds, winning at 3:38 P.M., or just 5 hours, 7 minutes and 27/100ths of a second after the start."[12] Porporato finished 3 min 23 sec behind Resta, after driving the entire 500 miles with gases from the Sunbeam's breather pipe putting smoke in his face.

On 26 March 1916, Burman and his Peugeot special won the Panama-California Exposition Cup at San Diego, covering 50 laps of 1.136 miles in 57 min 30 sec. A few days later, on 8 April 1916, in the 300-miler at Corona, Burman's Peugeot special blew a tire and crashed through a barrier against a parked car. Burman, mechanic Eric Schroeder and a

30 May 1916 — Indianapolis 300. Ralph Mulford, riding mechanic Fred McCarthy and their 4.5-liter Peugeot. They finished third, behind Resta's sister car and Wilbur D'Alene's Duesenberg. Tires were "Goodrich Silvertown Cord" (Peugeot).

track guard were killed and five spectators were injured. "Burman died in a hospital at Riverside, twelve miles away. His wife was with him when he died."[13]

The 1916 Indianapolis classic was shortened to 300 miles. It was believed that the shorter race would prove more popular as many persons held that it was too wearisome to sit through nearly six hours of racing. Expectations were that the 1916 race would develop into another duel between DePalma and Resta, but DePalma smashed his Mercedes the previous week at Chicago and was therefore unable to start. "Late information from Indianapolis about the International Sweepstakes, which is to be run there 30 May, is that Dario Resta is the bookmakers' favorite, being the only driver slated at even money. Josef Christiaens, the British war aviator, with the Sunbeam ranks second; with Eddie Rickenbacher in his Maxwell third, and Johnny Aitken in his Peugeot fourth. The mystery car from Cleveland, the Richard, with Delno, of Fresno, Cal., driving, is a 100 to 1 shot."[14] The Indianapolis Speedway had just founded its own team and bought two 4.5-liter Peugeots, which it entered for Johnny Aitken and Charlie Merz. A fourth Peugeot was nominated by Ralph Mulford for himself.

In addition to the Aitken and Merz Peugeots, the Speedway team entered three brand-new Premiers for Gil Anderson, Tom Rooney and Howdy Wilcox, who replaced the originally nominated Harry Stillman. The Premiers were more or less closely modeled after the 4.5-liter Peugeot and Bob Burman's special: "Burman was to drive one of the new Premier specials which are being built in factories at Indianapolis. Who will take his place is not known. Burman is credited with having incorporated in these new cars many of his pet theories and constructional features that experience had taught him. There is considerable sentiment associated with these Premier cars in Indianapolis. They say they are looked upon as monuments to the late Burman."[15] Many components for the Premier were supplied by Miller and other Los Angeles specialists. Starting from the blueprints by the end of January 1916, the cars were finished within three months. They were financed by the Premier Motor Mfg. Co., Indianapolis, and originally painted green. The engines followed Peugeot practice, with the usual twin-camshaft four-valve head. Cylinder dimensions were 3.66 × 6.65 inches or 93 × 169 mm, combining the bore used in Burman's special with the stroke of the 4.5-liter Peugeots. Was the shorter stroke of the 4.5-liter good for less engine weight and more crankshaft speed? In any case the Premiers displaced 280 cubic inches, 20 inches below the limit. The frame featured details of Burman's special as well as of the 3- and 4.5-liter Peugeot. The Premiers rolled on small 32-inch front wheels with the axles mounted below the springs, in contrast to the 4.5-liter Peugeot.

The new Premiers were no match for Resta, mechanic Bob Dahnke and their 4.5-liter: "A French Peugeot, driven by Dario Resta, won the international sweepstakes gasoline derby at the Indianapolis Motor Speedway this afternoon, covering the 300 miles in 3 hours 36 minutes 10.82 seconds. Less than two minutes behind him came the American-made Duesenberg, driven by Wilbur D'Alene. Third honors went to another Peugeot, which was piloted by Ralph Mulford."[16] Wilcox in the best Premier finished seventh.

30 September 1916 — second Astor Cup, Sheepshead Bay, Brooklyn. Dario Resta. In the background, mechanic Bob Dahnke (Library of Congress).

30 September 1916 — second Astor Cup, Sheepshead Bay, Brooklyn. Dario Resta at the wheel of his 4.5-liter Peugeot, with mechanic Bob Dahnke changing the rear tire (Library of Congress).

30 September 1916 — second Astor Cup, Sheepshead Bay, Brooklyn. Johnny Aitken at the wheel of the winning 4.5-liter Peugeot (Library of Congress).

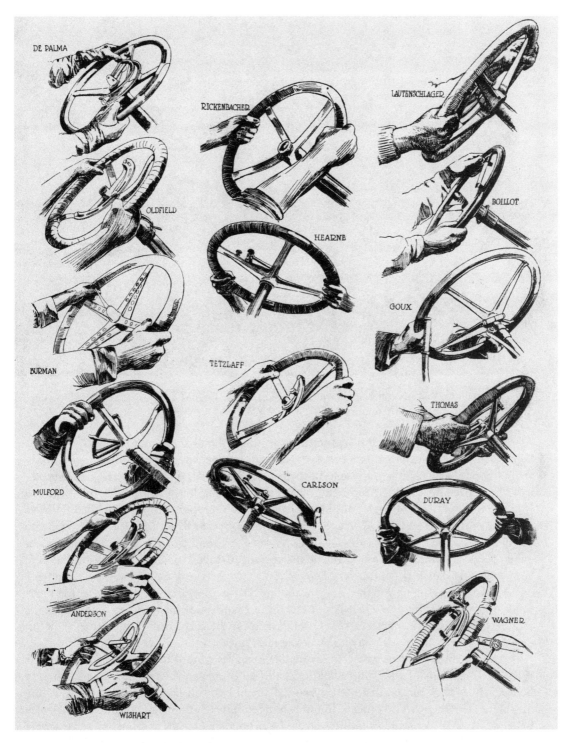

"Master Touches of Speed Virtuosos — Various Ways in Which Race Drivers Grip Wheel. Like Kubelik or Paderewski, each virtuoso of speed has a master touch that is distinctive, a method of gripping the wheel which individualizes his driving as the technique of the violinist or pianist individualizes his playing" (*Motor Age*, October 1914).

30 September 1916 — second Astor Cup, Sheepshead Bay, Brooklyn. Dave Lewis at the wheel of his Premier (Library of Congress).

The 4.5-liter Peugeots finished the 1916 season in good shape. Resta's car was owned by the Peugeot Auto Import, two other 4.5-liters driven by Aitken and Wilcox by the Indianapolis Speedway Team Co. In June, Resta won the 300-miler on the Chicago board speedway. In September, Aitken took the 300-miler at Cincinnati, Ohio, the 100-miler at Indianapolis and the 250-miler at Sheepshead Bay. In October, Resta and Aitken finished one-two in the 250-miler in Chicago. And in November, at Santa Monica, Resta won the Vanderbilt despite a cracked cylinder, and Wilcox the Grand Prize. But the season as such ended tragically, on 2 December, in the inaugural 100-mile Universal Trophy on the new 1.125-mile board oval at Uniontown, Pennsylvania. After stalling their Hoskins Duesenberg on the banking, Hughie Hughes and mechanic Gaston Weigle were walking to the press office near the starting line when Frank Galvin lost control of his Premier. The car struck Hughes, Weigle and a spectator. They were killed on the spot. Galvin died the following day. Louis Chevrolet in a Frontenac won the race, ahead of Dave Lewis in a Premier.

The 4.5-liter Peugeot was Henry's masterpiece. Its American career was to last until 1919, until the end of the 300-inch formula. Ten Peugeot racers were sold to America between May 1913 and October 1915, two 7.4-liters, two 5.6-liters, two 3-liters and four 4.5-liters. The French cars quickly found a suitable service and repair shop in Los Angeles where Harry Miller and his suppliers created a proper small-scale industry to secure their well-being. The influence exerted by these Peugeots on subsequent American designs was in accordance with the number of imported cars and the number of their successes: It was immense. The other benchmark was set by the German racer which was able to beat the Peugeot in the 1914 French Grand Prix: the Mercedes.

13

Aero-Engines

In DePalma's and Wishart's hands, the 9.5-liter three-valve Mercedes was extremely successful in America. Initially intended for the 130-mm formula of the 1909 Grand Prix de l'ACF, its career was expiring in 1913. It played a transitional role between the stone age machines and the new wave racers which used aero-engine methods. Mercedes did not start in the 1913 Grand Prix de l'ACF at Amiens but four cars appeared a few weeks later, in August 1913, in the Grand Prix de France at Le Mans: a new 9.2-liter overhead-camshaft four-cylinder (140 × 150 mm) for Théo Pilette, and two new 7.2-liter OHC sixes (105 × 140 mm) for Christian Lautenschlager and Otto Salzer. An older 9.5-liter four (130 × 180 mm) for Leon Elskamp was a late entry and served as comparison. Paul Daimler, since 1907 technical director of the DMG, the Daimler-Motoren-Gesellschaft at Stuttgart-Untertürkheim, looked on the 1913 Le Mans race as a test run. The new overhead-cam engines were made up of steel pairs, came from Untertürkheim's aero-engine department, and were mounted in updated 270-cm chain-drive frames as used in the 1908 Grand Prix at Dieppe. At Le Mans, Pilette, Salzer and Lautenschlager finished third, fourth and sixth, with a Delage trio taking first, second and fifth. Now, *Direktor* Daimler, Eugen Link and Karl Schnaitmann, his engine and chassis experts, were convinced: The 4.5-liter for the 1914 Grand Prix was to feature an aero-engine composed of steel cylinders and a shaft-drive frame.

In February 1914, at the time when Ralph DePalma was negotiating with Stutz and his former backer Edward Schroeder, Untertürkheim sent a cablegram announcing a factory entry in the upcoming Indianapolis race and wanting him to drive it. Mercedes importer Paul Lacroix informed him that a six-cylinder was to be shipped, "one of those that ran in the last Grand Prix de France,"[1] and that he was under discussion to drive one of the new 4.5-liters in the Grand Prix near Lyon on 4 July. On his way home from the Santa Monica races, DePalma passed through Chicago on 9 March and announced that he planned to sail for Germany shortly. He wanted to get one of the latest racers and commented that "he will not drive a six-cylinder as Mercedes wanted him to, but that he must have a four-cylin-der."[2] On 21 March 1914, Ellmore Patterson entered a Mercedes six in the Indianapolis 500, "and named for his driver none other than Ralph de Palma, twice winner of the Vanderbilt cup, who has abandonned his trip to Germany, decided not to drive in the French grand prix, and who will devote the entire summer to carrying the Patterson colors in the leading racing events on this side of the Atlantic.... Patterson's deal with de Palma followed an interview Thursday between the Vanderbilt cup winner and the officials of the Mercer company. For a time it looked as if de Palma would return to his old love, but there was a hitch over terms which was followed by Ralph tying up with Patterson."[3] The Mercedes was the 7.2-

26 February 1914 — Vanderbilt Cup, Santa Monica, California. Ralph DePalma, mechanic Tom Alley and the Grey Ghost Mercedes winning the Vanderbilt Cup, 1 min 20 sec ahead of Barney Oldfield and his Mercer (Library of Congress).

liter in which Salzer had finished fourth at Le Mans.[4] An additional Mercedes entry from Patterson, intended for Pilette, was cancelled. Ellmore "E.C." Patterson, aged 47, was a "gentleman sportsman of New York and Chicago"[5] who was an advertising executive of *Collier's Weekly*, one of the best-selling illustrated magazines with a circulation of nearly one million.

"DePalma's new six-cylinder Mercedes is one of the speediest looking cars in the race. It has a long-pointed nose and pointed radiator and streamline, the hood being shaped somewhat like the hull of a speed boat with a reverse curve to throw the wind out. The radiator is hung on trunnions and there is a screen in front. The cylinders are cast in pairs and the valves are over-head in the old Mercedes style. The car is chain drive and a spout is provided from the oil system which shoots oil on each chain at the front sprocket. The pistons are of cast iron, but the cylinders are of steel and a block of two cylinders weighs just 22 pounds. Wind resistance is cared for even to pointing the starting crank."[6] On 29 May, DePalma and Patterson withdrew the speedy looking Mercedes because of excessive engine vibration. The technical committee examined the car and excused him. In fact, at high speed it was found impossible to keep the fuel tank in place.

Nonetheless, there was a Mercedes in the 1914 Indianapolis race, or more exactly, a Mercedes chassis. Ralph Mulford, Edward Schroeder's driver, could pick and choose, either the Peugeot driven by Goux in 1913 or the Grey Ghost which had just won the Vanderbilt at Santa Monica. But an entry of the Peugeot was quickly declined because of the rule forbidding more than three cars of one make. Schroeder promptly nominated the Mercedes,

Ralph Mulford at the wheel of the Grey Ghost Mercedes (Library of Congress).

stating that he probably would fit it with the engine of the Peugeot. Mulford liked the Mercedes but found it a trifle slow since the engine had been cut to 450 inches: "He reconstructed the motor and fitted it to de Palma's old war horse in place of the Mercedes engine."[7] The Peugeot engine had been rebuilt, with the new cylinder dimensions of 112 × 183 mm instead of the original 108 × 200 mm. "The engine is practically the same as last year except that the bore has been increased slightly and the stroke lessened a little. The old Mercedes chassis is practically the same as always, being one of the few with chain drive and having 180-inch wheelbase."[8] The Mercedes-Peugeot started as Mercedes Special and finished eleventh.

DePalma revised his decision not to drive in the Grand Prix de l'ACF. In 1914, the French motoring classic took place at Givors, a few kilometers south of Lyon, on Saturday, 4 July, over 20 laps of 37.6 km. DePalma took the wheel of an English Vauxhall. The Vauxhalls were unprepared: "It is doubtful if there was any set of drivers more seriously handicapped in the matter of road knowledge than Messrs. Hancock, Watson and De Palma. By mere hazard the cars were not ready to leave when the word came from Paris, with the result that the drivers were unable to get round the course on their racing mounts. Their familiarity with the many difficult turns had to be obtained from the seat of a touring car."[9] DePalma "struggled hard against fate, covering the first lap in 26:29, as compared with 21:11, the best time for the initial circuit, made by Sailer in the Mercedes. De Palma completed the second circuit in about the same time, was a little faster on the third and fourth, and after he had completed the fifth, he pushed his car off to the side of the road after passing the pits."[10]

The Grand Prix was an overwhelming success for the new 4.5-liter Mercedes which took the first three places with Lautenschlager, Wagner and Salzer. Technical details did not come to light until after the race: "Elaborate precautions are being taken to prevent secrets leaking out. The Mercedes cars are housed in a completely inclosed stone garage, with an 8-foot thick wall around it. One guardian sleeps inside and another outside the garage while as a final precaution a heavy chain is padlocked round the bonnet when the cars are not in service."[11] The 4.5-liter was composed of four steel singles, 93 × 165 mm, with welded on water jackets and periphery. A single overhead camshaft was driven by a vertical shaft at the rear, via bevel gears. It operated two 43-mm intake and two 40.5-mm exhaust valves per cylinder. Intake and exhaust were inclined at 30 degrees to the cylinder axis. The crankshaft ran in five plain bearings, and lubrication was provided by an arsenal of three piston pumps. "Provision is made for the use of four spark plugs, placed almost horizontally around the cylinder, just below the valves. As a matter of fact, the cars only used three plugs — of Eisemann construction — in the race."[12] Output was 115 hp at 2800 rpm, 105 at 3100. During tests under the supervision of Rudolf Slaby, the engine was even pushed up to 5340 rpm. Power was transmitted via a double-cone clutch to a four-speed gearbox and a torque-tube rear axle. Concerning the chassis layout, the Mercedes was the opposite pole of the flexible Peugeot, having a rigid four-point attachment of the engine and the gearbox in combination with an X-bracing member and a torque-tube axle. Wheelbase was 285 cm, track 135 cm, and the tires used in the Grand Prix were from Continental, 815 × 105 front, 835 × 135 rear. Dry weight was 900 kg. "The cars were beautifully finished off. A thermos flask was mounted at the rear of the driver, and the mechanic could feed him through the medium of a tube. Under the dashboard was attached a neat little satchel containing sandwiches."[13]

Quite deliberately, Paul Daimler and his chassisman Karl Schnaitmann did without front-wheel brakes although Peugeot, Delage, Fiat and Piccard-Pictet used them in the Grand Prix. Daimler and Schnaitmann preferred to save unsprung weight and to mount softer springs and smaller wheels than the competitors. And it was precisely the front-wheel brakes that decided the finish in the Grand Prix at Lyon: Winner Lautenschlager stopped only once for tires, fitting a new set at half-distance, while Georges Boillot in the Peugeot stopped every three laps and changed four more times on the course. The correspondent of *The Motor* saw it differently: "It is almost impossible in so many words to explain the braking action of these front-wheel-brake-fitted cars. Four firms had them on their cars — Delage, Peugeot, F.I.A.T. and Piccard-Pictet.... The Peugeots were certainly better than the others. They came swooping down the corner as one thought to certain catastrophe. Then they seemed to be drawn up on their 'haunches' by some wondrous and invisible power, as if the whole forces of 'levitation' had been thrust at them. One is led to wonder how the Mercédès cars would have fared if they had fitted front-wheel brakes. Personally, I believe it would have saved them a quarter of an hour to 20 minutes."[14]

William Bradley wrote:

> Much of the success of Mercedes in this race may be attributed to the very thorough manner in which the race was entered and prepared for.... The drivers were sent to study the roads as early as last January and two entirely different types of cars were built. One set of cars had six-cylinder motors built to the maximum piston displacement and the other set were those which ran in the race, and had four-cylinder motors. Both sets were completely ready 2 months before the date of the race. In addition to the five cars run in the race, a sixth reserve car was prepared and was even weighed in with the others so that it could start if an accident occurred just before the start of the contest. Further, a complete chassis without motor was brought to the racing headquarters, to be used in case of emergency, a week before the start of the race. It is estimated that 30,000 miles were covered in road tests before the Mercedes came to the starting line.[15]

Immediately after the Grand Prix, DePalma travelled to Untertürkheim and paid $6000 for a 4.5-liter. Was it a refreshed racer, or the reserve car? According to press reports it was the Wagner car, and it was his own money although Patterson continued to back him. The Mercedes was shipped from Cuxhaven on Hapag's (Hamburg-America line) *Vaterland* which was ordered to stay at her Hoboken pier when the war broke out in Europe.

DePalma's first race in the 4.5-liter followed on Friday, 21 August 1914: the CAC Trophy for 450-inch cars at Elgin, over a distance of 36 laps of 8 miles 2030 feet, a total of 301 miles. The Chicago Automobile Club came up with two innovations, the two-car start which was used for the first time in the 1914 French Grand Prix, and the Pendleton scoreboard. Designed by E.H. Pendleton of Los Angeles, it recorded the exact position of each car at each mile of the course, and as soon as a car finished a lap, the lap number also was posted. The information was secured by a telephone system with a station for each mile. The girl operators had to do a good job, each telephoning when a car passed her station. Twenty cars lined up, in ten rows of two each. DePalma won the CAC Trophy in 4 h 5 min 1 sec, averaging 73.9 mph, with a fastest lap of 6 min 29 sec. He halted three times, losing a total of 1 min 29 sec at the pits and around 3 minutes to change a tire on the back stretch. This was in accordance with the opinion of the railbirds who had predicted that the winner would be held up at least 3 minutes, based on the experience of former years. DePalma's pit attendants were his younger brother John, Gordon and James Murdock, E.C. Cheney and Harrison H. Boyce. On Saturday, 28 cars lined up for the free-for-all Elgin National over the same 301-mile distance. Again DePalma and the Mercedes were the winners, in 4 h 6 min 18 sec, with a fastest lap in 6 min 28 sec. DePalma changed no tires, and used the Nassau front tires from Friday's race.

There was another Mercedes in the Elgin National: Walker's Rae. "Never before in the history of the sport has such a unique mount been prepared for a racing classic."[16] In 1903, "Mercedes Fritz" Walker served as mechanic in Camille Jenatzy's Mercedes in the ill-fated Paris-Madrid race before riding to victory in the Bennett Cup near Ballyshannon, Ireland. Walker was born in Holland and had served his apprenticeship in the Daimler factory, laboring three years for nothing, and earning enough in the fourth year "to buy two cigars on Sunday."[17] His parents sent him to the university at Bonn, but after three months, Fritz ran away and joined the navy. He served for two years and eight months, participated in the Boxer rebellion, walked from Shanghai to Peking when his boat, the armoured cruiser *Hela*, was shot to pieces and beached.

In 1904, he emigrated to America, escorting Foxhall Keene. He pumped oil for the New York stock broker in the 1904 and 1905 Vanderbilts. In the latter race, the Mercedes ran into a tree, turned over and caught fire. Keene's mustache suffered the most, being singed. Fritz assisted in the building of Joe Tracy's 1906 Locomobile, the Vanderbilt racer. He also rode beside Tracy, but only for a few laps, before he was canned by the driver for urging him to hit it up. Later in the year, Fritz began to work for White as a traveling repairman in Texas and Louisiana. In 1907, Fritz selected St. Louis as his permanent place of residence and opened a repair shop. But the shop was not destined to last long. Fritz took in a lot of work, but little money, and eventually closed the doors to join Oldfield and Christie in their barnstorming campaign of 1908. In the fall, he went to Savannah where he was slated to take the wheel of Keene's Mercedes in the Grand Prize, but was forced to withdraw because of cracked cylinders two days before the race. Victor Hémery immediately engaged Fritz as his mechanic in the Benz. In 1911 and 1912, Walker was a member of the Mercer crew. In 1913 he served as mechanic for Mulford and Rickenbacher in the Mason, in 1914 for Knipper in the Keeton at Indianapolis and in the Delage at Sioux City. At the same time he decided to prepare a racer for himself: "I am going back to the fateful Mercedes. It's the only wagon I've ever had any luck with. I'd be the happiest Dutchman in the world if I could win the Vanderbilt Cup with that old boat."[18]

Walker called his mount the Rae. It was an assembled job, with components from all parts of the United States. The frame and the engine were the property of Elmer Ray, a St. Louis engineer connected with the Central Welding Co. and the Superior Oxygen Co., and came from a 1903 Mercedes doomed to spend the remainder of its days in the asylum for superannuated machines. Ray had purchased the touring car when he was a student at Cornell University. "Incorporate my ideas in that motor and that car will show better than 100 miles an hour," Fritz told the owner. "How will I do it? I will do what all the foreign engineers are doing. The motor has only one set of intake and exhaust valves now, but I will reconstruct it so that it will have two sets of exhaust valves."[19] Ray first thought that the excessive heat of St. Louis had affected Walker's brain. As an engineer, he knew that the conversion of a T-head into a valve-in-head engine would be a costly job and that the results might not be satisfactory. Moreover, it would be an impossible job for a man like Walker, who had little money with which to buy new parts. But Walker finally secured the owner's consent. With his helper Frank Allen, formerly mechanic for Frank Verbeck, he started to work in a small shop near the Anheuser-Busch brewery. The tools they lacked they borrowed from the brewery machine shop. The rear axle was borrowed from some philanthropic friend, Walker couldn't recall who. The same mystery surrounded the source of the spark plugs, shock absorbers and flywheel. Bob Burman supplied the wire wheels; August Busch, the brewer, the clutch spring; Dwight Davis, a St. Louis millionaire, the chains and sprockets; Bosch the magneto; J.E. Duffield, western manager of the Thermoid Rubber Co., the Nassau tires; the Ahlbred Bearing Co. of Chicago the bearings. An anonymous benefactor furnished the macadamite metal of which the upper part of the crankcase was made. All Walker knew was that it came from the Philadelphia navy yard. And then there was Rudolph, a humble restaurant keeper of St. Louis, who supplied the nourishment, three square meals per day. Rudolph did not contribute voluntarily. He was the victim of a frameup. He owned an antiquated car.

"Try to fix it," he told Walker and Allen.

"It will be an expensive job," they warned him.

"I love this car and cannot see it suffer"[20] was Rudolph's reply.

They put the pistons in splints, tightened the bearings and bolts, polished the steering post, and presented their bill, $20: "We'll take two steaks smothered in onions, German fried potatoes, some apple pie and a couple of cups of coffee as part payment," they declared, "and you can give us meal tickets for the balance."[21] Rudolph's car was most obliging. By a peculiar coincidence, it became afflicted with some fatal malady that required immediate and costly attention just at the time the supply of meal tickets was exhausted. Walker had few tools with which to work, but he never gave up hope. He came up smiling after each reverse with a plan of remedy. And he had supreme confidence in the ability of his car to make good. It was a question whether any man with as few resources had worked harder to prepare a car for a race than he. In the first lap of the Elgin National, a disappointed Fritz Walker docked his Rae with a broken clutch.

DePalma's legendary jinx rejoined him in the 100-mile dirt track race at Kalamazoo, Michigan, on 28 September 1914. He found that all of the gasoline in town was too low proof for use in the Mercedes. Consequently he sent to Grand Rapids for a supply of higher proof gas. As it turned out, he overplayed it, for in practice, an hour before the race started, DePalma blew out a copper gasket of the carburetor, the car caught fire on the backstretch and several drivers went to the rescue with fire extinguishers. The car was not badly damaged and after putting in a new gasket, DePalma was ready to start. After thirty-six laps in the lead, despite the fact that the Mercedes was equipped with offset steering knuckles, a decided disadvantage in a race over a mile track, he was forced to quit on account of trouble with his eyes. A pair of defective goggles had allowed the dust to work inside and fill his eyes with calcium chloride, which burned the optics. Several doctors came to DePalma and removed the irritants. Burman in his 5.6-liter Peugeot won in 1 h 34 min 29 sec. Another 100-miler followed on 23 October, at Galesburg, Illinois. Burman in his Peugeot led the field from the 20-mile post. DePalma drove the 7.2-liter Mercedes six and was forced to go into dry dock because of dirt clogging the fuel line. Burman ran out of gas within a quarter mile of the finish. Mulford in a Duesenberg won in 1 h 32 min 54 sec, 14 seconds ahead of Burman. In lap 31, Jack Gable who drove one of Burman's 1914 Indianapolis specials turned partly over when a rear wheel collapsed on the backstretch. Gable escaped with a few bruises, but Fritz Walker, his riding mechanic, was severely hurt. Walker was taken to the Galesburg hospital where he died on 28 October.

DePalma concluded the 1914 season at Corona where he drove the 4.5-liter to fourth. He did not spend the winter in California but went home. It was said that at Detroit he would put a new body on his Mercedes six. *Motor Age* selected DePalma as the American road racing champion of 1914, "because of the exceptionally fine showing which he made during the season just closed, winning three of the important road races and finishing fourth in two others.... Yet the most ardent admirers of the Mercedes pilot must admit that Pullen stands very close to the throne."[22]

DePalma did not work on the 7.2-liter six but prepared the 4.5-liter four in view of the 1915 Indianapolis race. On the morning of 15 May 1915, he arrived at the speedway: "Ralph has been working on the car at the Packard shops in Detroit for the past 3 weeks and has fitted it with a new body of very extreme streamline design. The new body is much narrower than the old one, the cowl has been cut down to minimize wind resistance and the tail resembles the rear end of an aeroplane."[23] He unloaded the Mercedes, drove it to the speedway under its own power and without lifting the hood, covered a lap at 90 miles per hour: "He already has decided on his gear ratio and to obtain sufficient engine revolutions to insure maximum power must use $33 \times 4\frac{1}{2}$ casings."[24] Jesse G. Vincent, the Packard chief engineer, had assisted DePalma in overhauling the Mercedes and came to Indianapolis to help the Italian to get it in shape for the race and served as pit manager. A Packard carburetor of standard type was substituted for the original Mercedes: "It is understood that this change has cut some two or three seconds off the possible lap time on the speedway and onlookers can observe that there is no misfiring or popping when the throttle is shut off for the turns, as is common with many racing carburetors. Despite the presence of an air valve, which is supposed generally to be bad for highspeed work, the Packard carburetor certainly works wonderfully well and if it does as well in the race as it has in practice, the details will be worthy of the closest study."[25] According to DePalma the Mercedes was four seconds faster per lap with the new carburetor. Obviously the Packard air valve instrument was better suited to American gasoline than the Mercedes mixer. "A particularly striking feature is the abolute steadiness of the front wheels when the car is traveling over 100 miles an hour on the straightaways, this being due to a caster wheel system worked out by Mecedes for the French road-racing classic."[26] DePalma's qualifying time was 1 min 30.3 sec, ahead of Resta in the 4.5-liter Peugeot, behind Wilcox in the Stutz: "Resta drove the track well, but shut off on all four turns, whereas de Palma did not throttle down on any of them. Resta's car was designed to carry two extra tires on the rear for road racing and without these on the speedway, the tail is a little light and skids on the turns."[27]

The postponement of the 500-mile race from Saturday, 29 May to Monday, 31 May 1915 because of inclement weather resulted in reduced attendance. The crowd was not as large as in 1913 and 1914. About 60,000 spectators witnessed the race. Because of the marshy condition of the infield, only a few cars were permitted to park inside the track, holders of parking places being given grandstand seats free by the management. The roads and walks inside the enclosure were ankle-deep in mud and the Beau Brummels who wore white silk hose wished that they hadn't. Barney Oldfield played the humble role of spectator. His heart was with the Stutz team and his money was on Anderson. Starter Fred Wagner watched the race from the judge's stand. For the preliminary lap before the flying start, the 24 cars were lined-up in rows of four, according to the qualifying speed. Carl Fisher led the race off at a merry pace, bearing down on the throttle of his white Packard six in order to avoid being run down. When he turned off the track to allow the flock of fame chasers to pass, he was averaging better than 60 miles an hour.

Resta completed 40 laps or 100 miles in 1 h 7 min 30 sec, an average of 88.88 miles an hour, just one second ahead of DePalma. The race was a match between two Italians. Resta was watching DePalma and DePalma was watching Resta. The Peugeot driver completed 60 laps in 1 h 40 min 38 sec with DePalma a car length behind. In lap 63 the Mercedes came in for two right tires, losing one minute. This gave Resta a lead of nearly one lap, with Anderson in the Stutz second, DePalma third and Cooper in another Stutz fourth. At 170 miles DePalma and Anderson passed Resta. DePalma's time for 175 miles was 1 h 58 min 11 sec, one-quarter lap ahead of Resta. The Mercedes driver completed 80 laps or 200 miles in 2 h 14 min 29 sec, averaging 89.22 miles an hour, with Resta trailing by 38 seconds, Anderson 40 seconds, Cooper 1 min 16 sec. At the halfway point DePalma was still 29 seconds ahead of Resta, then the Stutzes with Anderson and Cooper. DePalma had just established a new 300-mile record in 3 h 19 min 32 sec, 90.21 miles per hour, when he came in to change all four tires. Now Resta was in front again. DePalma and Resta were racing neck and neck, with Resta a lap to the good over DePalma. The Mercedes was better in the turns, the Peugeot on the straightaways. Resta had trouble with the Peugeot's steering, a worn-out worm gear causing about four inches free movement on the rim of the steering wheel. He had to drive with caution. Resta and DePalma continued to come down the home stretch hood-to-hood although the Peugeot still held a one-lap lead over the Mercedes. But in lap 136 Resta skidded. DePalma barely missed hitting him. The Peugeot touched the concrete wall and had to stop for new tires. The duel was resumed as this seemed to take the heart out of the speed king of the Panama-Pacific exposition. Resta did not go into the curves at such high speed thereafter. Now DePalma was in the lead. He completed 140 laps or 350 miles in 3 h 54 min 41 sec, with Resta 1 min 20 sec or nearly one lap back. Two laps from the finish the leading Mercedes broke a connecting rod which punched two holes through the crankcase, but good fortune prevented a repetition of the unlucky experience of 1912. DePalma and the crippled Mercedes won in 5 h 33 min 56 sec, one lap ahead of Resta and the Peugeot.

"Both de Palma and Resta ran right through without ever lifting the hood and both had only two stops at the pits, taking on tires and gasoline. De Palma took on some oil, but Resta did not even this. It seems that de Palma was extremely lucky to be able to finish a winner, as a connecting rod broke and punched two holes through the crankcase two laps from the finish."[28] The 24 starters made 102 stops, and the eleven finishers 45 stops, in both cases an average of four stops per car. All the finishers used Goodrich Silvertown cord tires.

Immediately after the Indianapolis race, the Mercedes was sent to the Packard shops at Detroit. The hole in the crankcase was repaired but in the heat-treating process the base chamber was so badly warped that reassembly was impossible. Mechanics labored overtime to construct a new crankcase but could not get it ready in time for the 500-miler on the new Maywood

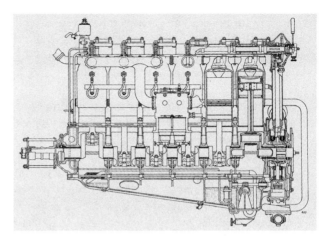

1916 Mercedes aero-engine: six cylinders, 140 × 160 mm, 14.7 liters, OHC-head, 197 hp at 1,700 rpm (*Automobile Engineer*, 1918).

speedway at Chicago. In September 1915, in the 500-miler on the new cement oval at Minneapolis, the Mercedes went out after 190 miles because of magneto trouble. The 4.5-liter was tired now.

In February 1916 it was announced that DePalma was to split up with Patterson. On 2 March DePalma incorporated his own business in Chicago, with the objective to build aero engines. For the 1916 season the Mercedes was rebuilt with new cylinders giving a displacement of 299 inches or 4.9 liters. On 24 June 1916, DePalma won a 150-miler at Des Moines, on 4 July a 150-miler at Minneapolis ahead of Aitken's Peugeot, on 8 July a 112-miler at Grand Rapids, on 15 July a 50-miler at Omaha, and on 22 July a 100-miler at Kansas City. By late summer the Mercedes was tired again. DePalma took the wheel of a Peugeot!

Of course, Packard engineer Jesse Vincent used the Mercedes as sample for new aero-engines. Before 1914, aero engines had merely reached a sufficient power-to-weight ratio to enable aeroplanes to fly. Beyond this, practically no special adaptation to aircraft requirements had been attempted. The war in Europe quickly revealed that the extension of bombing activities at long ranges, easy maintenance, and an increased ceiling to carry out untroubled reconnaissance required more power. The Germans, realizing at an early stage of the war the necessity of large engines, concentrated their attention on the production of a simple type of engine: a straight row of six or eight cylinders of an average weight per horsepower, neither excessively heavy nor particularly light. The policy of the Allies was by no means so definite, and the French, British and American engine designers worked on a number of different types: rotary, radial, and V-type air-cooled designs as well as water-cooled V-8, V-12, and six in line engines. An important factor was the development time, generally 18 months between the commencement of the design and a useful flow of reliable production engines. On 6 April 1917, the United States declared war on Germany. The Signal Corps, which was responsible for aviation, sent a commission to Paris and London to study the French and British aero engines. Contracts were under way to build the Hispano-Suiza V-8 and the 9-cylinder air-cooled rotary Gnôme engines under license.

The Hispano was a 90-degree V-8, composed of steel cylinders within an enamelled aluminum block. The vertical valves were directly operated by one overhead camshaft per bank. Originally the Hispano was produced in the dimensions of 120 × 130 mm, producing 180 hp at 2000 rpm with a compression of 4.7:1, and weighing 475 pounds with coolant and oil. Later the same engine delivered 235 hp at 2300 rpm and 5.3:1, weighing 520 pounds. In the course of the war, the dimensions were stretched to 140 × 150 mm, good for 300 hp at 2100 rpm and 5.3:1, weighing 565 pounds. In France, the Hispano was produced under license by Peugeot, Delaunay-Belleville, Ariès, Ballot, Brasier, DFP, De Dion, Voisin and SCAP; in Italy by Nagliati, SCAT and Itala; in England by Wolseley; and in America by Wright-Martin. Total production of the V-8 during the war was 49,893.

The most powerful Mercedes was a 240-hp straight-eight in the dimensions of 140 × 160 mm, with a single overhead camshaft and two valves per cylinder. It was designed by Paul Daimler and Eugen Link, the team responsible for the 4.5-liter racer. Originally this type of Mercedes aero engine appeared as a 7.2-liter straight-six (105 × 140 mm) in the 1912 Kaiserpreis for aero engines. At the beginning of the war, Daimler and Link stretched the dimensions to 140 × 160 mm and gave the crankshaft seven plain bearings, instead of four previously. Now the six displaced 14.7 liters and developed 174 hp at 1400 rpm and 197 at 1700, with a compression of 4.64:1. Weight was 660 pounds. During the war, an extra pair of cylinders was added. The 19.7-liter straight-eight delivered 242 hp at 1350 rpm, 267 at 1550, and 287 at 1750, with a compression of 4.73:1. Dry weight of the eight was 900 pounds, meaning around 0.27 hp per pound at 1350 rpm. The six and the eight were built up of separate cylinders, machined steel forgings, with the valve pockets screwed and welded into the cylinder head. The water jackets were of sheet steel, 1.5 mm gauge, with all joints being acetylene welded in position. The single intake and exhaust valves were set at 15 degrees to the vertical and operated by an overhead camshaft via rockers. The pistons had concave steel crowns, screwed and welded into the cast iron skirts. Lubrication was under pressure, a multiple plunger pump supplying oil to the main bearings, the big ends and the camshaft bearings.

Overhead-cam sixes with four inclined valves and cylinders made of steel were built by Austro-Daimler and Basse & Selve. The Austrian engine displaced 15 liters with the dimensions of 135 × 175 mm. It delivered 200 hp at 1400 rpm and 222 at 1600 with compression of 5.02:1 and weight of 728 pounds, 0.275 hp per pound. The Basse & Selve was built at Altena, Wesphalia. It displaced 22.6 liters with 155 × 200 mm bore and stroke, exactly the same dimensions as the long-stroke Grand Prix Benz used between 1908 and 1912. Output of the Basse & Selve was 269 hp at 1400 rpm and 302 at 1600, compression 4.34:1, weight 885 pounds, 0.3 hp per pound. The Maybach six was also built up of individual steel cylinders, but in combination with four vertical valves per cylinder operated via two low mounted camshafts, pushrods and rockers, its 165 × 180 mm dimensions resulted in 23.1 liters and 294 hp at 1400 rpm and the high compression of 5.95:1. It weighed 911 pounds, 0.32 hp per pound. The Austro-Daimler and the Basse & Selve used aluminum pistons, the Maybach cast iron pistons. "The grade of the workmanship of every part, including the exterior finish throughout, is exceptionally good, and the working clearances are carried to very fine limits. Compared with any of the other enemy engines, the workmanship is undoubtedly of a much improved character. Every part evidences the usual German effort for strength and reliability, combined with standardisation and simplicity from a manufacturing viewpoint. Effort for saving weight has not been carried to extremes."[29] The most powerful aero engine used in 1917 was a Fiat, known as type A14. It was a 60-degree V-12 built up of separate steel cylinders with a single overhead camshaft per bank and four valves inclined at 25 degrees to the cylinder axis. Bore and stroke were 170 × 210 mm, for 57.2 liters. The big Fiat delivered 600 hp at 1500 rpm and a compression of 4.96:1, weighing 1826 pounds, for 0.33 hp per pound.

In America it was found that the time required to convert from metric measurements and adapt American manufacturing methods to the production of the French engines would be two or three years. In May 1917, the American authorities decided to develop a type of engine with unit cylinders capable of various combinations. Jesse Vincent had offered a V-12 design to the war effort without expectation of a royalty although by then Packard had spent $400,000 on the development. The government accepted and Vincent was joined by Elbert John Hall, the co-owner and chief designer of the Hall Scott Motor Car Co. of Berkeley, California. On 29 May 1917, Vincent, Hall and three draftsmen locked themselves in a suite of rooms at the Villard Hotel in Washington and, according to the legend, within five days and nights designed the "Liberty Engine," an engine calculated to deliver 200 hp in 8-cylinder and 300 hp in 12-cylinder form:

> The idea of developing standard engine types was first thought of about May 25, 1917, and was further developed in a conference with representatives of the British and French Missions held from May 28 to June 1.... The first eight-cylinder model was delivered to the Bureau of Standards on July 3, 1917.... The twelve-cylinder Liberty ... was said to have passed a fifty-hour test on August 25, 1917. Contrary to many rumors circulated at the time, the Liberty engine was not an invention. The design was based on the practice of several well-known American and European manufacturers that had been proven in service.... The Liberty 12-A engine, the only one of the series to be produced in large quantities, has two rows of six cylinders with an included angle of 45 degrees. The bore is 5 in., the stroke 7 in., and the total displacement 1648.92 cu. in.[30]

The individual cylinders were made of steel. A single overhead camshaft per cylinder bank was driven via vertical shaft, and operated two valves per cylinder, intake and exhaust inclined at 13 degrees to the cylinder axis. The crankshaft of the V-12 ran in seven pressure lubricated plain bearings. The first engines used a Delco battery and high-voltage coil ignition instead of a magneto. Later a magneto which could fire a 45-degree V-12 was developed, and proved superior to the Delco system. But in service, the coil ignition system rarely caused engine failures.

During the 50-hour test in August 1917, the V-12 delivered between 301 and 320 hp at 1750 rpm and a compression of 4.5:1, with a dry weight of 850 pounds, around 0.375 hp per pound. On 13 September, it was given its first trial in the air at Minneola, Long Island: "Colonel Roosevelt today tested the new 'Liberty Motor,' with which the United States hopes to attain the war supremacy of the air, and after a flight of half an hour at a speed of more than 100 miles an hour, he pronounced it 'great.'"[31] Ultimately, the Liberty reached 420 hp at 1700 rpm and a compression of 5.4:1 in normal operating mode, with 450 at 2000 available for takeoff, around 0.5 hp per pound. Pistons were made of aluminum, the low compression ones with a flat top, the high compression ones domed with cutouts for the valves. On 29 May 1918, one year after the design of the engine, 1100 units had been produced. The government placed orders for 26,500. By 11 November 1918, Armistice Day, 20,478 Liberty V-12 engines had been produced: 6500 each by Packard and Lincoln, 3950 by Ford, 2528 by Cadillac and Buick and 1000 by Nordyke & Marmon. Up to the spring of 1918, the balance between the air forces of Germany and the Allies was very close. With the advent of the Liberty engine, the Allies took control of the air and this was one of the factors that brought about the surrender of Germany.

1 June 1918—100-mile Harkness Handicap, Sheepshead Bay, Brooklyn. Ralph DePalma and his V-12 Packard. The color was described as "creamy" (Library of Congress).

In order to test the pecularities of the V-12, Packard mounted a small 300-inch version into a racer to be used on the oval tracks, and a 905-inch version into a record car. The small 60-degree V-12 had dimensions of 2.65 × 4.5 inches, output of 100 hp at 2300 rpm and 130 at 3300, and weight of 500 pounds. The bigger 45-degree V-12 had dimensions of 4 × 6 inches, output of 235 hp at 1800 rpm and 250 at 2050, and weight of 800 pounds. Ralph DePalma used the 300-inch racer between May 1917 and October 1919 on the board tracks at Cincinnati, Chicago and Sheepshead Bay, and on the brickyard at Indianapolis. On 3 September 1917, he won a 50-miler at Chicago in 28 min 9 sec, averaging 106.5 mph. On 17 August 1918, he won a 20-, a 30- and a 50-miler at Sheepshead Bay, completing the 50-miler in 27 min 29 sec, averaging 109.1 mph. On 12 February 1919, on the beach at Daytona, DePalma took the wheel of the big 905-inch car, which weighed 3400 pounds. When DePalma left the beach five days later, he had covered the flying mile in 24.02 sec, meaning 149.887 mph; 2 miles in 49.54 sec; 10 miles in 4 min 9.3 sec; and 20 miles in 8 min 54.2 sec. Due to an error in the electric timing, the records were never accepted as official. Later in 1919, DePalma accepted an invitation to drive the "905" in an exhibition at Denver. With traffic and pedestrians carefully controlled, he tooled the Packard down Logan Street through the heart of Denver at 120 mph.

In 1920, DePalma sold the 300-inch Packard to Italy, to Eugenio Silvani. In January 1921, in the hillclimb between Vermicino and Rocca di Papa, the Packard was described as a "racing machine of 12 cylinders and not far away of 200 h.p."[32] In July 1921, Maria Antonietta Avanzo took the wheel of the Packard in a sprint on the Fanø island, Denmark. When the Packard caught fire, she drove it into the North Sea. Legend has it that a young Enzo Ferrari was very impressed. Maria Antonietta Bellan was born in 1889 near Rovigo, and

2 November 1915 —100-mile Harkness Trophy, Sheepshead Bay, Brooklyn. Ralph DePalma at the wheel of his 4.5-liter Mercedes (Library of Congress).

learned to drive on her father's De Dion tricycle. Before the Great War, she married Baron Eustachio Avanzo and moved to Rome. In 1919 she began her racing career at the wheel of an SPA in the Giro di Lazio.

The general layout of all future racing cars was based on a mixture of the ingredients supplied by the 4.5-liter Mercedes and its counterpart from Peugeot. The steel singles, single-cam head, plain bearing crank, and torque tube axle of the Mercedes faced the cast iron block, twin-cam head, ball bearing crank, and Hotchkiss axle of the Peugeot. Both cars were built to compete in the 1914 French Grand Prix, on the 37.6-km road course at Givors which comprised a windy 13-km part with 80 corners and bends as well as an endless 12-km straight. Max Sailer achieved the best Mercedes lap in 20 min 6 sec, Georges Boillot the best Peugeot lap in 20 min 20 sec. The Peugeot lost 0.37 second per kilometer. This virtual equality was confirmed by the subsequent results in America whereby DePalma's lone Mercedes often had to face a well-serviced Peugeot fleet. At all events, the Mercedes pointed out that in 1914 two overhead camshafts were not absolutely necessary to operate the 16 valves of a 4.5-liter four. As a consequence, the single-cam head became widely adopted in the American 300-inch formula.

14

New Wave Racers

Almost all of the new American racers which were designed after the Peugeot victory in the 1913 Indianapolis 500 showed a decided attempt to follow or improve on foreign design. The T- and L-heads, the American standby for many years, gave way to some type of overhead-valve arrangement in nearly every case. Another tendency was the attempt towards light connecting rods and pistons, improved balance and better oiling systems. "The general sloppiness of many of the American racers of the olden days has disappeared in nearly every instance. This may be credited to a certain extent to the showing made by the foreign cars a year ago, whose fine workmanship was generally remarked."[1]

The 1914 Maxwells were the first American racers of the overhead camshaft, long-stroke wave. They were developed and built within four months. It was on 20 December

24 June 1916 — 150-miler, Des Moines, Iowa. When the Maxwell racing department was closed in the Fall of 1915, the fleet of cars was bought by the Prest-O-Lite Co. The Maxwells were upgraded and painted white for the 1916 season. Pete Henderson in no. 3 Maxwell finished second in the 150-miler at Des Moines, and Rickenbacher in no. 12 Maxwell third (Auburn University Libraries Special Collections and Archives).

1913 that Maxwell president Walter E. Flanders came up with the idea of a start in the 1914 Indianapolis 500. On this date he entered into a contract with Ray Harroun, calling for the construction of three racers capable of laping the Indianapolis speedway in 1 min 37 sec. Harroun and his corps of mechanics headed by Harry Goetz went to work in their new "racing car department,"[2] behind the canvas partition of one of the Maxwell plants at Detroit, Milwaukee Avenue. The department consisted of six draftsmen who worked continually on new designs and a special shop department of twelve men for the assembling and fitting of new parts. Construction work began in March 1914. In the last week of April the first racer emerged and "its motor started to bark vociferously at the first turn of the crank."[3] It was a sophisticated cocktail of speedway experience and imported long-stroke technology: "Built upon a 104-inch wheelbase, which is the same as that of the stock Maxwell 25, the Maxwell-Harroun racing cars have motors of unusual construction."[4] The cylinders were cast in one block in the dimensions of 4.2 × 8 inches, for displacement of 445 cubic inches. The head was detachable and carried two vertical valves per cylinder with diameter of 2¾ inches and lift of ½ inch. The overhead camshaft, driven via helical gears by a vertical shaft at the front, ran in three ball bearings and operated the valves through rockers. The crankshaft was counterbalanced, had no flywheel and ran in three main bearings: self-aligning ball bearings at the outer ends, plus a plain bearing 2½ inches in diameter and 3 inches wide in the center. All the ball bearings were double row annulars made by Rhineland. The pistons were made of magnalium: "They weigh 17 ounces while the ordinary cast iron piston of the same dimensions would tip the scales at between 4 and 5 pounds. The pistons are each fitted with two compression rings and one retainer ring for the wrist pin. All rings have a width of ⁵⁄₁₆ inch and are constructed of steel. The usual I-beam rods are made of chrome-vanadium steel."[5] Output of the Maxwell was quoted as an optimistic 140 hp at 2400 rpm, with an engine weight of 650 pounds. The rear axle was of the Hotchkiss type, drive and torque through the springs. Houk supplied the wire wheels, and Palmer the tires, 32 × 4½ front, 33 × 5 rear.

By the beginning of April 1914, Ernie Moross, the manager of the Maxwell team, had contracted only one driver for the Indianapolis 500: Billy Carlson. Moross was after Victor Hémery, Felice Nazzaro and Teddy Tetzlaff for the second and third Maxwells since Dawson, Oldfield and Mulford, with whom Moross had been dickering, slipped away. In fact Moross announced that he received a cablegram from Hémery asking if Moross could use him for the season. The Maxwell man immediately cabled back asking for terms. Obviously Hémery was too expensive. The French star did not cross the Atlantic. Teddy Tetzlaff was definitely signed and was to report at the Indianapolis speedway on 26 April. Practice work with the two Maxwells was not bad, especially since there had been considerable skepticism as to their ability to hold up to their rivals. Harroun, however, had guaranteed that the cars would equal the old track record of 93 miles per hour or he was not to be paid for his work. He more than made good in the first trial when Tetzlaff reeled off a lap in 1 min 33.4 sec at the rate of 96.65 miles per hour. For good measure Harroun contributed another sensation in Carlson's performance of 1 min 36.6 sec or 93.5 miles per hour, the feature being that kerosene was used as fuel. The third Maxwell, the one for which no driver had been selected, was scratched, Harroun giving as a reason that it was not ready for the race. In the race, Tetzlaff parked his Maxwell after 100 miles because of a broken rocker arm. Carlson finished ninth. He made ten stops to change nine tires and take on 12 gallons of kerosene, losing 18 min 13 sec. Carlson used kerosene of 43.3 degrees Baume gravity, which sold at about 6 cents per gallon. He used just a little less than 30 gallons in the 500 miles, a consumption of 16.7 miles per gallon. Gasoline was used to start the engine before the race, but none during the race. One blown out spark plug was the only trouble experienced.

A lot of other American specials were entered in this 1914 Indianapolis race. Horan's Metropol hailed from Port Jefferson, New York, and relied on a T-head, 4.2 × 7.1 inches, 393 cubic inches. Joe Horan was described as having "graduated as mechanic for Ralph Mulford on the Lozier team to a full-fledged race driver of quality."[6] The Stafford was a Kansas City product entered by Terry Stafford, to be driven by the former Case mechanic Jesse Callaghan. With 4.2 × 5.1 inches, the Stafford displaced only 290.7 cubic inches. Two valves per cylinder were set at 30 degrees and operated by a chain driven overhead camshaft. The Great Westerns, to be driven by Johnny Jenkins, Ray Price and Fred Radina, were featured by their Carter piston-valve engines, two of them with 4.2 × 8 inches giving 445 cubic inches, the third one with 3.7 × 5.7 inches giving 254 cubic inches. The wheelbase of all three cars was 106 inches, with Houk wire wheels and Miller tires, 34 × 4½ on the large cars, 34 × 4 on the smaller one. Mortimer Roberts' Pope Bullet used a Pope-Hartford four, 4.7 × 5.7 inches, with 2⅛-inch valves in the head. The Rayfield was designed and built by William Rayfield and Hughie Hughes at the Rayfield Motor Co. factory, Springfield, Illinois. The engine was an L-head six, 4.135 × 5.5 inches, the 2⅛-inch valves being slightly inclined, "placed so close to the bore of the cylinders that though the cylinders are L-head, the effect is almost the same as the over-head system, as there are practically no pockets and the explosion is concentrated above the pistons."[7] Two radiators were placed on the side, just in front of the dash, permitting a very narrow body. The rear axle was of the Hotchkiss type, the wheelbase was 104 inches, and tires were from Riverside, 34 × 4½. Charles Shambaugh's Shambaugh hailed from Lafayette, Indiana. Its engine had three overhead valves per cylinder and water jackets made of copper. A feature of the Shambaugh was a copper coil mounted just behind the radiator and serving as an oil cooler. The details of Mel Stringer's Washington (4.7 × 5.7 inches), Joe Mazzucco's Tatter (4.1 × 5.3 inches) and Fred Melaun's Titze (5.1 × 5.5 inches) remained unknown quantities. The Tatter and the Titze were Chicago entries. The Tatter was entered by Louis and John Tatter, two brothers who made a business out of rebuilding old cars. All these mysterious specials were shut out during the elimination trials.

In August 1914, the Moross Amusement Co. turned up at Elgin with three Maxwells for Tetzlaff, Carlson and Tom Orr, and the older F-head Marmon for D'Alene. Tetzlaff and Carlson started in the CAC Trophy, and both went out with engine trouble. All three Maxwells started in the Elgin National. Orr retired with a broken radiator, Tetzlaff with a broken fuel line, while Carlson was flagged. In view of the Corona race, Maxwell offered a large amount for Barney Oldfield's services. On 20 November the speed king agreed to drive one of the Maxwells. He finished second, and Carlson sixth. Oldfield covered the 301 miles without a single stop for fuel, water, tires or mechanical adjustments.

Maybe Barney's mascot, a worn sheet of paper containing a prayer written by his wife Bess, had displayed its supposed power. "Billy Carlson claims to have no mascot, driving the Maxwell car on his own nerve and judgment; but his mechanic let the story get out. When a young salesman in Los Angeles, Carlson never wore a mustache, but as soon as he stepped out as a contender for honors in the speed game, he cultivated a serious-looking little growth on his upper lip which was a mascot in every race."[8] Pullen's good luck bringer, his baby's little shoe, was always riveted to the cowl of his Mercer. Dave Lewis had only one mascot, his mother, who always was one of the last to say good-bye to him and wish him luck in his races. And he always went to her first after a race. Louis Nikrent also carried one of Bess Oldfield's prayers. Moreover, at least one of the Nikrent brothers or his father was always in the pits. Sometimes the entire pit crew were Nikrents and one of the brothers rode with him. The number 8, a little iron kewpie an inch long with a broken leg, and his wife were Earl Cooper's good luck combination. During Earl's races, Mrs. Cooper always sat in a box opposite his pits holding the iron kewpie in her hand. Grover Ruckstell carried a smiling oriental image on the cowl of his Mercer. The tiny mystic idol came from Canton, China, and was of carved ivory. Arthur Klein had embedded a silver quarter on the top nut of his steering wheel. Harry Grant carried a small rabbit's foot, given to him the night before his first Vanderbilt by an aged negro. A gold ring was A.A. Cadwell's safety omen. "Gaston Morris carries the strangest talisman of all the drivers. It is a clipping from a newspaper in which the driver is referred to as 'the speedy Gaston.' Ralph de Palma commercializes his mascot privileges. He carries a motormeter which has been transferred from one car to another and the 1914 American road race champion says that his motormeter is his best insurance policy."[9]

Most of the drivers who came from the east to Corona stayed in California for the winter. DePalma, however, went home to work on his Mercedes. Billy Carlson stayed in his hometown Los Angeles. In December, Carlson married Miss Margaret Mazzini, "a daughter of one of the prominent old Spanish families which made California history and has lived all her life in Los Angeles and Santa Barbara. Last season Mrs. Carlson created a sensation as a member of the company which played the famous Mission Play. The romance started at the time of the Vanderbilt and Grand Prize races at Santa Monica last February and is declared by the bride and groom to be a real romance of the speedway."[10]

On St. Patrick's Day, 17 March 1915, a 301-miler was held at Venice, California, 97 laps of 3.1 miles down Electric Avenue, Rose Avenue and Compton Road. Resta and DePalma did not start since their demand for appearance money was turned down. "From the start Eddie Rickenbacher, with a Maxwell, took the lead and held it to the fifty-second lap, when he picked up a stone on the back stretch that tore a hole through the crank case and put him out of the race. During part of Rickenbacher's performance he was making more than 100 miles an hour, and his bursts of speed past the stands brought the big crowds to their feet frequently."[11] Then Dave Lewis in a Stutz took the lead until the 96th lap when he went out because of engine trouble. Barney Oldfield in a 450-inch Maxwell burst into the lead and won in 4 h 24 min 9 sec, beating his teammate Carlson by 54 seconds. Grover Ruckstell in a Mercer took third, Johnny Marquis in a Bugatti fourth. The 32-year-old Marquis, born in Bloomington, Delaware, served an apprenticeship with the Searchmont Automobile Co. in Chester, Pennsylvania, before acting as Lewis Strang's mechanic in the Isotta. In 1910 he moved over to the driver's seat of the Isotta and captured several events on the Los Angeles motordrome and a minor league road race at Coalinga. In 1911 he drove a Stearns in 24-hour races at Brighton Beach and Atlanta, before disappearing from the scene. He reemerged when William Ziegler, Jr. sent him to Europe to buy a Sunbeam. His backer in 1915 was Charles W. "Charlie" Fuller of New York and Venice, the owner of the Bugatti.

Meanwhile Ray Harroun had been working on the new 300-inch cars for the 1915 Indianapolis race. One of the 300-inch Maxwells was on the speedway in March 1915. With Billy Carlson at the wheel, it was sent around daily over a two-month period in order to see at what rate of speed it could take the turns with the least tire wear. In April, Eddie Rickenbacher was signed as second driver. Tetzlaff and Dawson were under discussion to take the wheel of the third car, but finally Tom Orr was nominated. Orr was Harroun's assistant at the Maxwell factory and originally was to drive Harroun's Maxwell engined special. Harroun "declared that the machine entered by him under the name of the Harroun Special is a Maxwell in every respect but the name."[12] The only difference was a gear, and the objective was to circumvent the three-car rule.

The cylinder dimensions of the 300-inch Maxwell were 3¾ × 6¾ inches. As in 1914, the Maxwell had a single overhead camshaft, but in 1915 it operated four valves per cylinder, which were not inclined but stood vertically, "being staggered so as to make room for enough cams."[13] Valve diameter was 1¾ inch, valve lift ⁷⁄₁₆ inch. As on the 1914 two-valve engine, the overhead camshaft was driven by a vertical shaft via helical gears. The two-piece crankshaft ran in three ball bearings, with lubrication à la Peugeot: Low pressure force feed taken to each of the three ball bearings, the overflow then being caught inside sheet-metal disks of flat-cup form bolted against the balance weight, the oil being thrown centrifugally and conducted through holes in the crankpins to the big ends. A pure splash system for emergency only was under the control of the mechanic. The pistons were made of magnalium, and weighed 15 ounces. The carburetor was a Master. Wheelbase was 110 inches, gear ratio 2.6:1, tires 33 × 5. Brake spiders and brackets were made of macadamite, an "alloy of great strength and low specific gravity."[14] All the drivers and mechanics in the Maxwells wore leather helmets "similar to the headgear that protects the domes of line-plunging half backs."[15] And Orr's feet were encased in green buckskin shoes.

Rickenbacher's Maxwell went out in lap 102 with a broken connecting rod, and Tom Orr's black racer broke a rear axle bearing in lap 169. But Carlson in the third Maxwell finished ninth. A few weeks later, on 26 June 1915 in the Chicago 500, Rickenbacher and Carlson drove brand new cars with twin-cam engines and a shorter 105-inch wheelbase, weighing 2202 and 2267 pounds. Rickenbacher finished third. Maxwell closed the racing car department in the fall of 1916 and sold the cars to the Prest-O-Lite Co., Indianapolis. Eddie Rickenbacher remained in the position of team captain.

During the winter of 1914–1915 Stutz, too, joined the new wave movement. Immediately after the 1914 Indianapolis race, Harry Stutz had purchased the 3-liter baby Peugeot from the Menier family in order to discover the secrets of the French wonder racer. The result was a Stutz prototype for the 300-inch formula of 1915. In February 1915, Gil Anderson drove the prototype in the Vanderbilt and the Grand Prize held at San Francisco. Stutz was not seeking prize money, although Anderson finished fourth in the Grand Prize. The primary object was to find faults before sending the new car out to cover itself with glory in the race of races, the Indianapolis 500. In fact the ignition was at fault. The spark plugs burned out. The necessary changes were adopted in the machines to be run at Indianapolis by Anderson, Earl Cooper and Howdy Wilcox.

The new 300-inch engine of the Stutz was built by the Wisconsin Motor Co., using a design by Arthur F. Milbrath. In May 1915, at Indianapolis, the cylinder dimensions were quoted as 3.808 × 6.484 inches for the Anderson and Cooper cars and 3.816 × 6.484 for the Wilcox racer. In October, *The Automobile* quoted 3¹³⁄₁₆ × 6½ inches.[16] The 300-inch Stutz followed the long-stroke fashion set in the French Coupe de l'Auto races and the Grand Prix, and by the 1914 Maxwell. But in contrast to the baby Peugeot, the Stutz had only one overhead camshaft, operating four valves per cylinder, via rockers. Had the second camshaft been overlooked? The 1914 French Grand Prix was the showroom for the different head configurations. Sunbeam and Nagant took over the Peugeot solution whereby Sunbeam used finger-type cam followers instead of the L-shaped tappets of the Peugeot. Delage added a desmo operation and Vauxhall used diminutive rockers reducing the inclination of the intake and the exhaust to 9 degrees. Mercedes, Alda, Opel and Nazzaro relied on the single-cam four-valve head. Mercedes won and a Peugeot could have finished second. According to the result in this French Grand Prix, a single overhead camshaft was fully sufficient to operate four valves per cylinder in a long-stroke four displacing 4.5 liters or even 300 cubic inches and topping at 4000 rpm. In fact, the second camshaft brought in unnecessary components, sources of trouble, and weight. The two-piece crankshaft of the Stutz ran in three ball bearings, with the big ends in plain bearings. The camshaft ran in five ball bearings, and the spur gears were also mounted on ball bearings. There were four valves per cylinder, each valve 1½ inch in diameter, with lift of ⅜ inch. "In appearance the engine bears a strong resemblance to the Mercedes, having the same sort of camshaft case with a good deal of bronze work on it. The aluminum casing for the train of spur gears at the front end looks very small, as compared with Peugeot practice, doubtless because there is only one camshaft to drive instead of two."[17] The carburetor was a Stromberg, the magneto an American made Bosch. Output was 130 hp at 3000 rpm, 132 at 3200, 128 at 3400, and maximum engine speed 3800 rpm. The rear axle was of the torque tube type, the wheelbase was 104 inches, and weight was 2400 pounds.[18] Houk supplied the wire wheels and Goodrich the 33 × 5 Silvertown tires.

In the 1915 Indianapolis 500, Howdy Wilcox and his Stutz made the best qualifying time in 1 min 31 sec. Teammate Earl Cooper achieved 1 min 33 sec, and Anderson 1 min 33.4 sec. Right away, the Stutz achieved the same lap times as DePalma's Mercedes and Resta's Peugeot whereby the Stutz had a displacement advantage of 0.4 liter, or 24 cubic inches. In the race, the Stutz trio confirmed the excellent qualification trials, Anderson finishing third, Cooper fourth and Wilcox seventh. Johnny Aitken acted as relief for both Anderson and Cooper.

The Blood Bros. Machine Co. of Allegan, Michigan, entered a little Cornelian in the 1915 Indianapolis 500, for Louis Chevrolet. The veteran had celebrated his return to the racing game in the Cactus Derby, the desert race between Los Angeles and Phoenix, in November 1914. The Cornelian made its "particularly noteworthy" appearance in September 1914 in a 100-miler at Kalamazoo. Described as "not much larger than a cycle car,"[19] it was powered by a 103-inch engine (2⅞ × 4 inches) and weighed 950 pounds. Driven by Kennedy, the Cornelian was flagged after 73 miles. In preparation for the 1915 Indianapolis race, the displacement was increased to 114.6 inches with dimensions of 2.932 × 4.25 inches. It was an overhead-valve engine with 1¼-inch valves, lift ⁹⁄₃₂ inch. The Cornelian's notable feature was its chassis whereby the body acted as frame, an early monocoque: "This grasshopper amongst the elephants has a Sterling motor of a paltry 116-cubic-inch displacement and yet can lap at over 80 miles an hour, owing to the negligible weight and windage of the tiny machine. It has no frame at all, as the sheet-steel body acts as a frame as well; still more extraordinary, it has no axles. This sounds like an impossibility, but it can be explained by the spring system, which replaces the axle proper. At the rear there are three springs placed transversely one above and two below and the extremities of these springs are linked to brackets which carry the rear road wheels. The transmission is fixed to the frame-body."[20]

Joe Boyer, who acted as Chevrolet's relief, qualified the grasshoper in 1 min 51 sec. In the race, the Cornelian was "travelling in fair shape with Chevrolet, its driver, sitting as if in a touring car."[21] In lap 67 the grasshoper ran out of fuel, providing a good opportunity for Chevrolet's oil pumper to warm his feet. C. Kline was his name and he trotted more than a mile to the pits for a can of gasoline. He was so exhausted that Boyer was sent back to the fuming Chevrolet. Ten laps later the Cornelian broke a valve which fell inside the

18 August 1917—20- and 30-mile match races, Sheepshead Bay, Brooklyn. Louis Chevrolet (with headgear) at the wheel of his "chocolate colored" Frontenac. A few weeks later, on 22 September, Chevrolet won the Harkness Trophy (Library of Congress).

cylinder. The Cornelian "seemed to be under-cooled as water was taken in three times during the 3 hours that the car ran."[22]

Three FRPs, or Porter-Knights, were nominated for Hughie Hughes, Charlie Keene and Neil Whalen. FRP stood for Finley Robertson Porter, the former Mercer engineer. The racers were built at Port Jefferson, Long Island, in the shop in which François Richard had built the Only. The FRP engine relied on the Knight double-sleeve principle. In contrast to common practice the FRP used two eccentric shafts located on opposite sides, one reciprocating the inner sleeve and the other the outer one. "In the standard Knight design these sleeves have had intake and exhaust ports near their upper ends but Mr. Porter has in addition introduced lower exhaust ports close to the lower ends of the sleeves, this being a result of experience gained last year with the Minerva-Knight cars which used this lower exhaust in the Isle of Man race. The majority of the hot exhaust escapes through this lower port leaving the upper port to serve merely for scavenging the remaining gases."[23] The sleeves of the FRP were made of iron with a high graphitic carbon, the inner sleeve being $3/32$ inch thick and the outer one $1/8$ inch. The four separate cylinders were made of gray iron and had detachable heads with a single spark plug in the hemispherical dome. The crankcase was an aluminum casing supported at three points: two rigid arm supports to the frame on the carburetor or right hand side, and a central trunnion on the exhaust or left hand side. The crankshaft ran in three plain bearings $2\frac{1}{4}$ inches in diameter, their lengths $3\frac{1}{4}$ inches front, 3 inches center, $4\frac{1}{2}$ inches rear. With dimensions of $3\frac{3}{4} \times 6\frac{1}{8}$ inches, the FRP displaced 270 cubic inches, well under the 300-inch limit of the 1915 season. Output was 122 hp at

3950 rpm with peaks up to 5000. With a 3.25:1 ratio on high, the engine was rotating 1985 rpm at 60 mph, 2650 at 85, and 3250 at 100 mph. The frame was made of ⅛-inch chrome-vanadium steel, with 4⁷⁄₁₆-inch vertical section. Wheelbase was 110 inches, track 56 inches, tires 32 × 4 front and 33 × 4½ rear, dry weight 1910 pounds. The body measured 30 inches overall width at its maximum, resulting in a wind resistance at 100 miles per hour of 50 pounds per square foot of frontal area. Porter calculated that 98 horsepower were needed to drive the car at 100 miles an hour and that 93 of these 98 were needed to overcome wind resistance. There was keen disappointment when none of the FRPs qualified, due to piston rings breaking. The cars were late in reaching the track and the drivers did not have a chance to work out the new engines. New piston rings were made, but failed to reach Indianapolis in time. The fastest FRP lap was turned by Earl DeVore in 1 min 53.7 sec, too slow for qualifying. The three FRPs represented an outlay of $60,000. DePalma valued his 4.5-liter Mercedes at $12,000. The three Stutzes cost $38,000 to build.

The Erwin Motor & Machine Co. of Erwin and Grover Bergdoll entered three Bergdoll Specials (4 × 5.9 inches) in the 1915 Indianapolis 500. Only one of the trio reached the speedway before noon on Tuesday, 25 May. Willie Haupt took the wheel. The Bergdoll was sluggish and stiff and did not fire regularly, missing all the way. Haupt's best lap was 1 min 58.5 sec, considerably above the 1 min 52.25 sec which was the time for a 80-mph average required in qualifying.

On 26 June 1915, in the 500-miler at Chicago, the Stutzes handled by Anderson and Cooper came home fourth and sixth, while the Maxwells of Carlson and Orr were flagged.

9 October 1915 — first Astor Cup, Sheepshead Bay, Brooklyn. Three white Stutzes with Gil Anderson, Tom Rooney and Earl Cooper in a field of Peugeots (Library of Congress).

The upcoming races at Sioux City and Tacoma were open to 450-inch cars. On 3 July 1915, Rickenbacher and Maxwell won the 300-miler at Sioux City. Charles Cox, driving Rawlings' Ogren, was killed in lap 34. One day later, on 4 July, Grover Ruckstell in a Mercer won the 250-mile Montamarathon trophy on the new Tacoma board track in 2 h 57 min 3 sec, 1 min 2 sec ahead of Earl Cooper in a Stutz, then Eddie Pullen in a Mercer, Bob Burman in his Peugeot special, and Barney Oldfield in the Peugeot that Resta had driven in the Panama-Pacific races. In lap 56 Carlson's Maxwell went airborne when a tire blew. Billy Carlson and mechanic Paul Franzan were fatally injured. Next day Pullen won the 200-mile Potlatch trophy in 1 h 21 min 14 sec, just 11 sec ahead of Cooper, with Oldfield third and Ruckstell fourth. The 300-miler held on 5 July on the new 1.25-mile board track at Omaha, Nebraska, was open to 300-inch cars. Rickenbacher in the Maxwell was the winner, his time being 3 h 17 min 39 sec, with O'Donnell in the Duesenberg 2 min 48 sec back, then Orr in another Maxwell and Grant Donaldson in his Emden. The Emden was built by the Donaldson brothers from Milford, Iowa: "The Donaldsons evidently favor the Germans in the European clash, for they have named their Indianapolis 500-mile race entry after the torpedo boat Emden."[24] Cylinder dimensions were 4¼ × 5¼ inches. Willie Haupt had driven the special at Indianapolis, finishing eleventh.

The 1915 Elgin races were a Stutz affair. DePalma had the intention to lease one of the 300-inch Stutzes and was to campain the Stutz along with two Mercedes racers. But he

18 August 1917 — 20- and 30-mile match races, Sheepshead Bay, Brooklyn. Barney Oldfield and his Golden Submarine, "the car that is made of armor plate and so enclosed that the driver will be uninjured if the machine turns turtle. It behaved badly in the amount of power which it gave yesterday, and the remark was soon under way in the first race that the submarine would be sunk" (Library of Congress).

started in the repaired 4.5-liter Mercedes. The CAC trophy was run on Friday, 20 August, open for 300-inch cars, over the same distance as in the previous year: 36 laps of 8 miles and 2030 feet, a total of 301 miles. DePalma in the Mercedes immediately took the lead, but retired in lap 21 with a broken rocker arm. The race was a match between the Stutzes of Earl Cooper and Gil Anderson. Cooper won in 4 h 1 min 32 sec, averaging 74.6 miles per hour, 3 min 32 sec ahead of his teammate Anderson. On Saturday, the Elgin National trophy was open for 450-inch cars, its distance again being 36 laps or 301 miles. This time the winner was Anderson in the Stutz, in 3 h 54 min 26 sec, 3 min 4 sec ahead of Cooper in the second Stutz, then O'Donnell in the Duesenberg and DePalma in the Mercedes. One week later DePalma took the wheel of a Stutz and won a 100-miler on the 1-mile dirt oval at Kalamazoo, Michigan, ahead of Burman in his Peugeot special and Chandler in a Duesenberg. On Saturday, 4 September, the 2-mile cement oval at Minneapolis was opened with a 500-miler for 300-inch cars. There was a fine field of 14 cars. Again it was a Stutz affair. Cooper won in 5 h 47 min 24 sec, averaging 86.35 miles per hour, $^{23}/_{100}$ sec ahead of Anderson. O'Donnell in a Duesenberg was third, 33 minutes back, then Alley in the Ogren, Ora Haibe in the Sebring, and Haupt in a Duesenberg. On 9 October, the Stutzes driven by Anderson and Rooney took the 350-mile Astor Cup at Sheepshead Bay.

After a dispute with his shareholders, Harry Stutz was forced to close his racing car department, his "White Squadron" team. The withdrawal was announced in October 1915. The marvelous Stutzes did not start by the beginning of the 1916 season. One of the 300-inch Stutz racers came back in 1917. Earl Cooper bought one of the 300-inch racers and promptly won the season opener, a 100-miler at Ascot, Los Angeles, and a 250-miler at Chicago. In 1917, Carl Fisher was building Miami, and there was no Indianapolis race, the speedway being used as an aircraft maintenance depot. A new car celebrated two victories: The Frontenac built and driven by Louis Chevrolet won a 250-miler at Cincinnati, a 100-miler at Chicago and the Harkness Trophy at Sheepshead Bay.

Louis and Arthur Chevrolet were born in La Chaux-de-Fonds, in the Swiss Jura just a few miles from the French border, Louis on 25 December 1878, and Arthur on 25 April 1884. By the end of 1887 the Chevrolet family left Switzerland to live on the other side of the border at Beaune, a few miles south of Dijon, where Gaston was born on 26 October 1892. After a short stay in Paris, Louis migrated to Montreal, and then, in 1901, to New York where he worked for the bicycle shop of William Walter and the local De

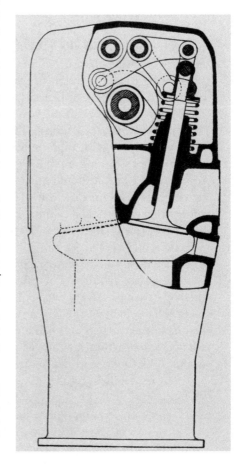

Desmo-head of the 4.5-liter Théo Schneider designed by Gratien Michaux for the 1914 Grand Prix de l'ACF. Harry Miller certainly came across this section view, which was published by the magazine *Motor Age* in August 1914.

Dion agency. In 1905 he was hired by Hollander and Tangeman. In May 1905, driving William Wallace's 90-hp Fiat on the Morris Park track, he dropped Barney Oldfield in the background by making a mile in 52.8 sec. On 3 July 1905, Louis Chevrolet married Suzanne Treyroux in the church of St. Vincent Ferrer, New York. When William Crapo Durant lost control of General Motors for the first time in 1910, he commissioned Louis Chevrolet to design a car able to compete with Ford's Model T. Chevrolet hired Étienne Planche to help him, a French engineer whom he had met at the Walter Automobile Co. in Brooklyn (which was taken over by the Roebling family and evolved into the Mercer Automobile Co.). The original Chevrolet went into production in 1912. But Louis Chevrolet split with Durant in 1914 and founded the Frontenac Motor Co. with the financial assistance of Albert Champion, who was the man behind the AC Spark Plug Co. and had won the Paris-Roubaix bicycle race in 1899. Again the relationship did not last for long, so that a Frontenac racer did not appear before 1916. Still with Planche by his side, Chevrolet designed a 300-inch engine with a twin-cam four-valve head à la Peugeot. The output disappointed. In 1915, Planche moved to the Dort Motor Car Co. Louis Chevrolet decided to build a new engine completely made of aluminum, with a single-cam four-valve head. Bore and stroke were 3.87 × 6.375 inches, the camshaft was driven via a vertical shaft, and valves measured 2 inches (intake) and 1¾ inches (exhaust). The two-piece crankshaft ran in three ball bearings. In 1918, Louis Chevrolet won a 100-miler at Chicago, one of the few important races since America was involved in war.

In the spring of 1915, shortly after the San Francisco classics, Huntley Gordon, who had rebuilt the Mercer Monk as the Gordon Special and sold it to Frank Elliott, was "building a car which is to make its first appearance in the Tacoma races in July. Harry A. Miller, inventor of the Master carbureter, is the designer of the new speed creation and is personally supervising its construction. It is patterned after the Peugeot and will be in the 300-inch class."[25] In fact, one year later, Harry Miller's Los Angeles shops began to assemble a batch of six four-cylinder engines. Two of them were intended for airplanes and four were used to power the first racers bearing the name Miller. In aero-engine form the Miller displaced 352 cubic inches with dimensions of 4 × 7 inches; in racing car form it dropped to 297 inches with a smaller bore of 3.675 inches. The 352-inch Miller developed 139 hp at 2600 rpm and 155 at 2900, and the 297-inch engine gave 130 hp at 2950 rpm. Completely machined vanadium cast iron sleeves were inserted in the water jackets and packed with rubber ring gaskets. The cylinder head held the sleeves in place and was cast from aloyanum. The two-piece crankshaft ran in three double-row ball bearings, with tubular connecting rods, four bolt caps, wrist pins clamped in the upper ends, and a dry sump. The single overhead camshaft was driven by a train of spur gears, ran in five ball bearings, and operated four valves per cylinder. The follower cam caused the rocker to follow the main cam and thereby gave a positive movement to the rocker, later often described as semi-desmo operation. Dry weight of the engine was 410 pounds. The frame of the Miller racer featured rear cantilever springs and had a wheelbase of 104 inches. One car was bought by the cinematographer Arthur A. Cadwell, sponsored by his camera producer Bell & Howell. On 4 March 1917, Omar Toft drove one of the Millers to third in a 100-miler at Ascot.

Barney Oldfield recalled:

> There was a motor builder in my home town, Los Angeles, who was highly touted. So in the Spring of 1916 I had gone to him and discussed the building of a motor with several new ideas. Harry Miller had a small machine shop, where he built motors with the exactitude of a watchmaker. He had ridden as a mechanic in the 1906 Vanderbilt Cup and other

races, and had been in close contact with racing since that time. He knew me and I knew him. We decided together on an inovation in the racing world. Instead of having the driver sit out in the open, where he had a good chance to have his neck broken in case of a turnover, we decided to have the driver sit inside the car. We designed a body with a rounded top so that the car looked much like an egg with a hood at one end of it. The motor was a four-cylinder that would develop 130 horsepower. So strongly built was the car that I felt that if we should turn over neither Stein, my riding mechanic, nor myself could possibly be hurt. The car had small openings in the side, front and rear. There was only one door in the car, and that on the driver's side. Some of the motor editors called it the Golden Submarine, some the Golden Egg, some the Golden Lemon. The car was painted with golden enamel. Personally, I was sure it wasn't a lemon, and so was Harry Miller. In fact, he hasn't forgiven one or two of the motor editors yet for calling it a lemon. During the first part of 1917 I took my Golden Submarine to Milwaukee, where I beat DePalma and his Packard in three match races at ten, fifteen and twenty-five miles. At Detroit he beat me. I beat him at Indianapolis. He beat me at Sheepshead Bay.[26]

The *New York Times* commented: "Oldfield has a new machine which he calls Speed Bug, and, being made with steel ribs, aluminium covered, with an aviation motor, believes he has designed not only the safest, but the speediest racer ever constructed. It is an egg-shaped affair, the mechanician being seated behind him instead of at his side when he drives. Oldfield peeps from his queerlooking racer through screen-covered slits. He thinks the construction makes a serious accident to himself, his mechanician, or his car impossible."[27]

In 1916 Finley Porter's factory at Port Jefferson, Long Island, had produced around ten FRP luxury cars. They were powered by a 450-inch 100-hp engine, a 4-cylinder with single overhead camshaft. The FRP was offered in three different frame lengths, as Raceabout, Runabout or Touring, with wheelbases of 110, 130 or 140 inches. When the United States entered the war, the FRP plant was taken over by the government while Porter became chief engineer of the Army's Air Base at Wright Field, Dayton, Ohio. After the Armistice, Porter was appointed chief engineer of the Curtiss Engineering Co. at Garden City, Long Island, before founding his Porter Engine Development at 2 Rector Street, New York. The FRP production car had a successor in the Porter which was powered by the same overhead-camshaft engine but was available only in a long 142-inch frame. Between 1919 and 1922 the Porter was assembled by the American and British Manufacturing Co. in Bridgeport, Connecticut, and distributed by the Morton W. Smith Co. of New York City. Only 36 Porters were built.

Finley Robertson Porter died on 8 February 1964 at his home in Southampton, Long Island. Eric Delling, Porter's successor at Mercer, left Trenton in June 1916. In February 1918, Delling joined the engineering department of the Stanley Motor Carriage Co. in Newton, Massachusetts. With his brothers as partners, he founded the Delling Motors Co. in 1923, in Collingswood, New Jersey. Later Delling designed steam engines for Alma, Brooks and Stanley. Mercer director Ferdinand W. Roebling died on 16 March 1917, his brother Charles G. on 5 October 1918. As a consequence, the Mercer Automobile Co. was in disarray and was sold off to a group of Wall Street financiers. The last Mercer was assembled in 1925.

15

Sheepshead Bay

It was in the 1880s that horse racing became the passion at Brighton and Manhattan beaches. William Engeman established the first of the resort's three racetracks at Brighton Beach in 1879. The track was a spectacular success. A year later, the Coney Island Jockey Club launched the Sheepshead Bay racetrack. The Jockey Club, headed by Leonard Jerome, enlisted some of New York's most prestigious figures, including J.G.K. Lawrence, William K. Vanderbilt, A.J. Cassat, August Belmont, and Pierre Lorillard. The track occupied 112 acres along Ocean Parkway across the bay from Manhattan Beach and its grounds included an elegant grandstand and a music pavillon. It became the premier racetrack in America.

2 November 1915 — 4- and 6-mile match races, Sheepshead Bay, Brooklyn. Bob Burman in the Blitzen Benz, "which was recently purchased by Harry Harkness," and Ralph DePalma in the V-12 Sunbeam (Library of Congress).

The Futurity Stakes, first held at Sheepshead Bay in 1888, was the richest event of its time, with August Belmont once collecting a purse of $67,675. The Suburban was the first of the great handicaps. The Sheepshead Bay track also staged the Lawrence Realization Stakes, the Century Stakes, and the Annual Champion Stakes. The finest horses of the era, including Henry of Navarre, James P. and son Foxhall Keene's Domino, Roseben, Colin, and Synosby, competed at Sheepshead Bay. They were mounted by such legendary jockeys as Tod Sloan or Edward "Snapper" Garrison. Crowds at the Futurity and Suburban sometimes swelled to 35,000 and the betting-ring on Derby Day attracted gambling luminaries such as Rily Grannon, "Bet-a-Million" Gates, and "Pittsburgh Phil."

The Sheepshead property included 430 acres bounded by Ocean Avenue, Neck Road, Voorhees Avenue and Cedar Woods. When betting on the horses was banned in 1910, the track was put out of operation. Just the stables were kept up. August Belmont had 18 yearlings at Sheepshead. The Coney Island Jockey Club sold the track on 30 March 1915, for $2,400,000, and the Sheepshead Bay Speedway Corporation was incorporated "for the purpose of maintaining at the old Sheepshead race track a park for motor races, automobile shows, and athletic contests of various kinds."[1] New York was to have a 2-mile oval within 35 minutes of Broadway. Harry Harkness was president of the new Speedway Corporation, and prominent stockholders included Carl Fisher, Arthur Newby, starter Fred Wagner, Ralph DePalma, Alphonse Kaufmann and photographer Nathan Lazarnick. In August 1915 Carl Fisher resigned, because "many other duties demanded his attention."[2] The Coney Island Jockey Club was dissolved in May 1917.

18 August 1917 — 20- and 30-mile match races, Sheepshead Bay, Brooklyn. Ralph DePalma in the V-12 Packard, Louis Chevrolet in the Frontenac, and Barney Oldfield in the Golden Submarine (Library of Congress).

Harry Stephen Harkness was born on 17 July 1880, the only son of Lamon Vernon Harkness, the second largest stockholder in the Standard Oil Company. Lamon Harkness died on 17 January 1915, aged 65, at the Paicines Rancho in San Benito County, California. With his sisters, Myrtle Macomber and Lela Edwards, the young Harkness inherited a large share of the $150,000,000 estate left by his father. On 1 May 1902, Harry Harkness took delivery of a 6.5-liter 40-hp Mercedes, chassis number 2434. On 23 August 1902 Harkness and his Mercedes started on the Brighton Beach track, in the "mid–Summer speed contest of the Long Island Automobile Club.... A 2,130-pound gasoline carriage, operated by H.S. Harkness, carried off the lion's share of the honors, being first in the ten-mile free-for-all race and in the pursuit race open to all classes.... Mr. Harkness was so pleased with the success of his machine that he made a try at the world's record on a track of 1:06⅖. Mr. Harkness went twice around the track before he signified his readiness to start. Thirty-five seconds were taken to reach the half-mile post and averaging the same rate of speed, the machine finished in 1:10."[3] On 24 October 1902 Harkness won a 5-miler at the Grosse Pointe track, Detroit. In the spring of 1903 Harkness had a racer of his own built, and was a candidate for the 1903 Bennett team. The engine of the Harkness racer was designed by E.T. Birdsall, a member of the Racing Board of the AAA. It featured four separate cylinders, 5 × 7 inches, and a T-head. The frame was supplied by the Standard Welding Co. of Cleveland, Ohio. "The Harkness car is of eighty horse power, and is a very large machine, having a wheelbase of 8 feet 4 inches."[4] But, in April 1903, the racer failed to appear at the qualifying trial in Garden City "due to an injury to his car." Harkness "left Brooklyn at about 4 o'clock,

1 June 1918—10-mile Futurity Handicap, Sheepshead Bay, Brooklyn. From top, Louis Chevrolet in no. 3 Frontenac, Ralph Mulford in no. 9 Frontenac, Dario Resta in no. 1 Resta Special, Eddie Hearne in no. 8 Duesenberg, and Tommy Milton in no. 7 Duesenberg (Library of Congress).

1 June 1918 — 100-mile Harkness Handicap, Sheepshead Bay, Brooklyn. "More than 40,000 persons were packed in the grandstand at the Speedway and watched the thrilling tests between the daredevil drivers." Barney Oldfield had removed the roof and the tail of the Golden Submarine (Library of Congress).

and in order to escape observation and make better time took the 'back road,' which is not in as good condition as the more traveled route. A rough place in the road threw his car up into the air and it came down upon a sharp stone, perforating the water tank, which is set very low under the body of the car. The injury could not be repaired in time to take part in the trials."[5] In 1904 Harkness was back on the tracks at the wheel of a Mercedes, a Sixty.

In 1910 Harkness bought four Antoinette monoplanes. They were designed and built in Paris by Léon Levavasseur.[6] Both from a workmanship and artistic standpoint, the Antoinette was called the *Queen of the Air*. Three of the Harkness fliers were equipped with 100-hp V-8 Antoinette engines, and the fourth had a 50-hp V-8. On 24 August 1910, Harkness tried one of the Antoinettes on the Hempstead aviation field, Long Island: "The monoplane resembles a mammoth darning needle, with its long, thin body and delicate wings as it skimmed across the grass."[7] On 17 October 1910, he secured his pilot's license, making him the first monoplane pilot in America and licensed pilot no. 16 on the list of American aviators. By the beginning of 1911, he moved his aeroplanes to San Diego, California. With Glenn Curtiss he leased North Island from the Coronado Beach Co., sponsored an aviation venture, and formed the Aero Club of San Diego. On 7 February 1911 Harkness carried the first war message ever taken by an airman by flying to an army camp at Tijuana near the Mexican border. Harkness was married twice, between November 1906 and October 1916 to Marie Moss Marbeck, then from November 1916 to Florence Steuber Gaines, a daughter of Louis Steuber, a shipbuilder.

Originally, the Sheepshead Bay track was to be a 2-mile brick oval, patterned after the

1 June 1918 — 10-mile Futurity Handicap, Sheepshead Bay, Brooklyn. Dario Resta at the wheel of his Resta Special. The Resta Special was a mixture of a Peugeot frame and a twin-cam aero engine of 3¾ × 6¼ inches (Library of Congress).

Indianapolis speedway. But brick was quickly replaced by wood. Work started in April 1915: "The track itself to be built by Blaine H. Miller, engineer of the Indianapolis Speedway, will be of wood, a radical departure from the brick surface at Indianapolis, and the concrete course at Brooklands."[8] There were two straightaways of a half mile each and two turns of the same distance. The track was to be

> 70 feet wide on the straightaways and approximately 76 feet on the curves. The wood used is longleaf yellow pine in 2 × 4-inch pieces laid on edge and running circumferentially or in the same direction as the line of travel of the cars when racing. These planks vary in length, namely, 12, 14, 16, 18 and 20 feet, so as to give lap jointing every place. The planks are soaked in creosote and the track will have a dark brown appearance. The banking is such that at the curves the outer edge is 25 feet 6 inches above the ground, the claim being made that the banking will permit a higher speed than Brooklands track. A cross-section of the track on the curves follows a parabolic curve, the same scheme as employed on Brooklands. On the straightaways of either side, which are practically ½ mile long each, the track is supported on transverse concrete walls 6 feet apart and on the curves it is supported by steel framework.... There is a 30-inch safety wall of 8-inch concrete around the entire outside of the track and a similar wall at the inside.... The main grandstand has accommodations for 30,000 and is a steel structure with a double deck and is located directly opposite the repair pits. Diametrically across on the back stretch is located the bleacher grandstand with a capacity of 25,000.[9]

The first big race was to be the 350-mile Astor Cup scheduled for Saturday, 2 October 1915. The Cup was designed by Black, Starr & Frost, a simple design in the form of a Grecian bowl. The 2-mile board track at Sheepshead Bay was opened on Saturday, 18 September 1915. Harkness took the wheel of Dario Resta's 4.5-liter Peugeot to make the first trip around the track, with C.E. Danforth, the treasurer of the Speedway Co., as riding mechanic. Then Resta and mechanic Fred McCarthy went around a few times to tune the Peugeot, and covered 10 miles in 5 min 32⅘ sec. This was 11 seconds faster than he drove the same distance on the Chicago boards a few weeks earlier. "'This is the finest track in the world,' said Resta, 'and I have driven on them all. These embankments at the ends are so well constructed that I didn't even have to steer my car around the turns. The car took them naturally without an effort at the steering wheel. It is the speediest course I ever drove on and many new records are sure to result in the big races.'"[10] Four days later, on Wednesday, 22 September, three cars were out for practice. Ora Haibe drove the green Sebring which had been rebuilt after the accident in which Joe Cooper lost his life at Des Moines in August. Ira Vail turned five laps in his white Mulford. Eddie O'Donnell experienced considerable trouble with the engine of his Duesenberg and had to stop frequently. At times the Due-senberg was almost enveloped in the flames which shot up from its engine.

A few cars were already housed in the garages at the plant: Barney Oldfield's 4.5-liter Delage, a pair of red Mercers for Guy Ruckstell and Eddie Pullen, Resta's 4.5-liter Peugeot, Bob Burman's special, Jack LeCain's Pugh special, and the Bugatti owned by Charles Fuller. Oldfield explained that "although the racer he drove was his own, it was practically a gift from David G. Joyce, a Minnesota lumberman. Mr. Joyce bought the racer and turned it over to Oldfield for a one-dollar bill. Barney said that the money he had won by racing the car had been offered to Mr. Joyce, but the Western lumberman told Barney the money he won was his own. Joyce always turns up a few days before every race that Barney enters, and gives what assistance he can."[11] The gear ratios of the Delage were too short for Sheepshead, and Oldfield intended to change the ratio from 3 to 2.5:1. On 24 September, the 4.5-liter Peugeots of Aitken and Wilcox were out for the first time. Eddie Rickenbacher sent his Maxwell around in 1 min 6.20 sec or 108.86 mph. Rickenbacher and Resta sent their racers high up on the curves, along the top edge, and came bounding down into the stretches at great speed. The qualifying trials started on Saturday, 25 September 1915, at 3 o'clock in the afternoon. Each car had three chances to circle the track at more than 85 mph. Resta made the best time in the trials, 1 min 8.20 sec. Harry Grant qualified his Maxwell in 1 min 13 sec: "Grant is bigger than ever, but the extra weight doesn't seem to retard his speed any."[12] Oldfield in the Delage achived 1 min 10.07 sec, Gil Anderson in the Stutz 1 min 10.84 sec, his teammate Tom Rooney 1 min 11.45 sec, Burman in his Peugeot special 1 min 10.85 sec, and Ora Haibe in the Sebring 1 min 19.29 sec.

On Monday, 27 September, Grant was mounting the high bank at the Sheepshead Bay end, when flames started to shoot from the back of his Maxwell. Grant steered the racer down the embankment. The Maxwell was on fire in a few seconds, the flames leaping several feet in the air. Riding mechanic Red Stafford jumped off, but Grant was pinned in behind the steering wheel. "The floor of the car was burning through and Grant was unable to extricate his legs from the blaze. As the car plunged down to the foot of the embankment a dozen workmen went to his aid and after getting Grant out of the burning car they put the fire out with sand."[13] Teammate Rickenbacher in the other Maxwell raced to Grant's aid. Engineer Bell of the Maxwell camp jumped on the rear of Rickenbacher's car but was thrown off and sustained a fractured ankle. Finally, Earl Cooper carried Grant to the Coney Island hospital in his Stutz racer. Grant's legs were severely burned to the hips. His recovery was expected until Wednesday when his condition suddenly changed and he failed to rally. Harry Grant died on 7 October 1915, aged 40.

Harry Harkness entered two racers, a 4.5-liter Delage and a 3-liter Peugeot. On 29 September he was on the track, and "made several rounds at a high rate of speed.... Mr. Harkness has had a varied experience at automobile racing, and as far back as 1895 he drove a car in the Paris-Bordeaux race."[14] This was Sheepshead promotion. Carl Limberg qualified the Delage. Jack Peacock was not fast enough on the 3-liter Peugeot and was replaced by Hughie Hughes. Grant's Maxwell could not be repaired and was replaced by another car which was tested by Tom Orr, Ralph Mulford, and Bob Moore, a former mechanic for Grant. DePalma was unable to put his Mercedes in racing condition and switched to a Stutz. The Hugo Ogren Motor Car Co. entered an Ogren, a renamed Duesenberg, for Tom Alley. The Mercers were slowed by lubrication problems. Thursday, 30 September, was the last qualifying day. Because of Saturday's rainy weather the Astor Cup was postponed to 9 October 1915, while the races at Trenton were advanced to Wednesday, 6 October. On the same Wednesday, Alphonse Kaufmann entered an additional 4.5-liter Peugeot for Mulford. But five cars of one make were not allowed to compete, so the Hughes 3-liter Peugeot was out. During the night of 8 to 9 October, Burman's Peugeot special burned in its garage, due to a leak in the fuel tank. George Farrah and Eric Schroeder, the mechanics who were working on the car, were severely burned.

Twenty cars started in the Astor Cup:

Race no.	Make	Driver	Riding mechanic
1	Peugeot	Dario Resta	Fred McCarthy
2	Peugeot	Johnny Aitken	Maurice Becker
3	Delage	Barney Oldfield	Ray Dasbach
4	Peugeot	Bob Burman	Jack Gable
5	Stutz	Gil Anderson	C.W. Scott
6	Peugeot	Howdy Wilcox	Ben Rout
7	Stutz	Tom Rooney	Maurice Rocco
8	Stutz	Earl Cooper	Reeves Dutton
9	Duesenberg	Eddie O'Donnell	Jim Henderson
10	Maxwell	Eddie Rickenbacher	Harry Goetz
11	Mulford	Ira Vail	Harold Wright
12	Pugh	Jack LeCain	Frank Hickey
14	Sebring	Ora Haibe	Robert Guion
15	Duesenberg	Willie Haupt	Jim Alexander
16	Duesenberg	Pete Henderson	Arthur Johnson
17	Maxwell	Eddie Pullen	Reuben Stafford
18	Peugeot	Ralph Mulford	Paul Stevens
19	Delage	Carl Limberg	Roxie Palotti
20	Stutz	Ralph DePalma	Louis Fountaine
22	Ogren	Tom Alley	Harold Smith

Numbers 13 and 21 did not compete.

Sixty thousand people saw the race. Anderson in the Stutz won in 3 h 24 min 42 sec, averaging 102.60 mph, ahead of his teammate Rooney and the Duesenbergs of O'Donnell, Alley and Henderson. Limberg in the Harkness Delage finished sixth, 45 minutes back. Anderson suffered from temporary deafness after the race, "as a result of the noises of his machine during the 350-mile run."[15]

Prince Paul Troubetzkoy, the famous sculptor, had agreed to a match race with Harry Harkness for $10,000. Troubetzkoy was born in 1866 in Italy, the son of the Russian prince Peter Troubetzkoy and Ada Winans, an American lyric singer. His older brother Pierre was married to the novelist Amelie Rives. Paul Troubetzkoy's masterpiece was a bronze equestrian statue of Tsar Alexander III at St. Petersburg. Bernard Shaw, Henri de Rothschild, Anatole France and the William K. Vanderbilts sat as models for his sculptures. On 26 October 1915, Troubetzkoy had to qualify with a speed of 85 mph. He circled the track in an old-fashioned five-passenger Mercedes, first alone, then with his wife and Frank Coffyn, the aviator. Then Troubetzkoy posed for pictures. The cameras snapped like a battery of machine guns. In fact, Troubetzkoy had intended to make a real trip around the course in a real racing car, at the wheel of Harkness's 3-liter Peugeot. But the tiny Peugeot was not built to hold such a big man, and after he had tried and tried to squeeze his huge body into the small racer without success he was compelled to postpone his flight over the wooden course. On 28 October, Troubetzkoy and his wife were back at the track. The Princess went around at "102 miles an hour," with Johnny Aitken in the 4.5-liter Peugeot.

When the Princess was climbing into Aitken's racer, Johnny asked:

> "How fast do you want to go?"
> "I don't care," answered the wife of the royal Russian sculptor and Aitken took her at her word and circled the track at terrific speed.
> "Very exhilarating," was the way the Princess spoke of her speedy trip.[16]

On Election Day, Tuesday, 2 November 1915, Dario Resta in the 4.5-liter Peugeot won the Harkness Gold Trophy, a 100-mile invitation race "in which Resta, De Palma, Mulford, Aitken, 'Wild Bill' Burman and Rickenbacker were drivers,"[17] in 56 min 55.71 sec, with Bob Burman second in his Peugeot special. No Stutz? When Harry Stutz carried off the Astor Cup and the big money, he told everyone that he was through, at least for the year. Stutz was sticking to his word and had his cars locked up at the factory. The closing event of the afternoon was a match race between Ralph DePalma in a V-12 Sunbeam and Burman in Harkness's Blitzen Benz. Harkness had just bought the old 21-liter Benz from Stoughton Fletcher. In the spring of 1913, Moross and Burman had sold the Blitzen to Fletcher, an Indianapolis banker and businessman, owner of the Remy Electric Co., of several oil fields, and of Laurel Hall, a large estate and farm that bred famous racehorses including Peter the Great and Senator. When Burman examined the old Blitzen he was surprised to find that the engine and running gear were in good condition. The only things needed to put the car in racing condition were a new body and two new wheels, and larger sprockets for the Sheepshead course. DePalma won the first 4-mile heat of the Sheepshead Bay match race in 2 min 8 sec or 111.97 mph, defeating Burman by the length of his car. The second 6-mile heat was also won by DePalma, in 3 min 3.78 sec, with Burman 0.07 back.

The first 1916 meeting was run on Saturday, 13 May. The day opened with the 20-mile Coney Island Cup. It was won by Aitken in a Peugeot in 11 min 15 sec at an average speed of 106.72 mph, a new record for the distance. Christiaens in a Sunbeam finished second 11 seconds back, then Limberg in a 4.5-liter Delage owned by Harry Harkness. The 50-mile Queens Cup was won by Mulford in a Peugeot. Ten cars started in the 150-mile Metropolitan Cup, including two of the Harkness Delages for Limberg and Devigne. Limberg immediately went in front, his 10-mile mark being 5 min 56 sec. Then Resta in his Peugeot and Devigne took the lead. In lap 14, Limberg in the orange Delage no. 6 passed his teammate Devigne and Resta on the outside of the track. He was forced to run high up on the steep embankment of the north turn, within a couple of feet of the guard rail. Then, one of the front tires blew out. The Delage smashed into the guard rail. The impact threw both Limberg and his riding mechanic Roxy Pallotti high into the air, off the top of the track to the ground 40 feet below. The Delage bounded back, caught fire, and tumbled down to the inside of the track.

Pallotti died instantly, Limberg in the ambulance on the way to the hospital. Limberg, who lived in Brooklyn and was 34 years old, had always been known as a careful driver. Rickenbacker[18] in a Maxwell won the 150-miler in 1 h 33 min 31 sec, with Devigne second and Ira Vail in a Hudson third. Resta's Peugeot withdrew with a broken valve and smashed cylinder casting.

On Saturday, 30 September 1916, 31 cars lined up for the second Astor Cup, to be run over 250 miles or 125 laps as in the previous year. Ralph DePalma had entered a 4.5-liter Peugeot but was unable to get the engine working right and did not start. "The stiff breeze from the west made heavy wraps indispensable and furs were largely in evidence. Sports coats of varied colors were worn, and the predominating colors in feminine garb seemed to be gray, yellow, red and purple."[19] The thin nickeled body of Christiaens' Sunbeam was "as clean as a hound's tooth."[20] In spite of the great care, the Sunbeam did not stand the initial pace and had to stop because of a burned bearing. Resta's Peugeot also broke down. Johnny "Jack" Aitken in another 4.5-liter Peugeot won in 2 h 23 min 4.2 sec, averaging 104.8 mph and beating the record for the 250-mile distance by 3 min 20 sec. Rickenbacker in a Maxwell took second, more than three minutes back, then Ira Vail in a Hudson, Ralph Mulford and Tommy Milton in Duesenbergs, Art Klein in a Crawford-Duesenberg and the Harkness Delages handled by Jack LeCain and Jules Devigne on seventh and eighth. Grover Ruckstell and his riding mechanic Clarence Zuckall were slightly bruised when their Mercer rolled to the bottom of the incline.

Four weeks later, on Saturday, 28 October 1916, Aitken also won the 100-mile Harkness Gold Trophy. His time was 56 min 37 sec, equaling to 105.86 mph. Frank Galvin, a former six-day bicycle rider, finished second in a Premier, 8 seconds back. Again Resta's Peugeot was out, because of a broken crankshaft. A 50-mile consolation race was won by Jules Devigne in one of the 4.5-liter Harkness Delages. A late entrant for the Harkness Trophy was William Weightman III of Casanova, Virginia. His grandfather, William Weightman (I), was "popularly known as the richest man in Pennsylvania." He was "the head of the great drug firm of Powers & Weightman," and was "often called the 'Quinine King,' as he was the first man to introduce that drug into this country."[21] Quinine sulfate was the first effective treatment for malaria. The young Weightman was 26 and had "been a cowboy on a Western ranch. On the Pacific Coast he was interested in automobile racing and rode as mechanician with Barney Oldfield in several events. He has entered two cars in the Harkness race, a Duesenberg, which he plans to drive himself, and a Weightman Special to be piloted by D. Braily Gish of Washington, D.C., the former Olympic quarter miler."[22]

On 18 August 1917, DePalma took the wheel of his creamy V-12 Packard in a match race of three heats, 30, 20 and 50 miles. Louis Chevrolet drove a Frontenac. Barney Oldfield ran his Golden Submarine in the first two heats and "his less showey green Delage"[23] in the 50-miler. DePalma won all three heats, in 16 min 35⅗ sec, 10 min 53⅘ sec, and 27 min 32⅕ sec.

Louis Chevrolet in his Frontenac won the Harkness Trophy on 22 September 1917. DePalma in the V-12 Packard met his hard luck after 40 miles, when he had to replace two front tires, and finished second. Dario Resta, who ran his Resta Motors, Inc. at 17 West 50th Street, "Manufacturers and Dealers in Automobiles and Accessories,"[24] took two cars to the course, his old 4.5-liter Peugeot and a Frontenac painted maroon and bought from Chevrolet a few days before the race. He started in the Frontenac and withdrew after lap 8 with a broken crankcase.

Racing at Sheepshead resulted in a heavy loss. The expense of operating the speedway exceeded the receipts by $336,065 in 1916–1917, and by $279,869 between 1 June and 31 December 1917.

Despite the war, two meetings took place in 1918. On 1 June, Louis Chevrolet in his Frontenac won the 10-mile final of the Futurity Handicap, with Ralph Mulford in another Frontenac taking the first heat, and Dario Resta in his Resta Special taking the second heat. Resta's special was a combination of his older 4.5-liter Peugeot frame with a 3¾ × 6¾-inch twin-cam engine, his "own especially built aero motor."[25] Upon re-examination of the score sheets, DePalma in the Packard won the 100-mile Harkness Handicap, ahead of Tommy Milton in a silver-tinted Duesenberg and "that picturesque patriarch of the motor game,"[26] Barney Oldfield, in the Golden Submarine. "Dario Resta came to grief when he had covered forty miles. In his Resta Special the Italian-English driver was going great guns and burning up distance at a rate which brought gasps of admiration from the spectators. After forty miles Resta's car, while on the back stretch, burst into flames. The driver and his mechanician were in great danger, but drove on around the back turn, and it was then a race with the fire until they reached the pit."[27] On 17 August, DePalma and the Packard also won the 5-heat 112-mile race named International Sweepstakes, with a best lap in 1 min 2.20 sec. "The entire difficulty, so far as competition is concerned, is that De Palma's Packard '12,' with its sweet running aero motor, has been tuned up to such an exquisite pitch that there isn't anything in America that can touch it, particularly now when all automobile manufacturers are engaged in war time production. Next year the motor which Dario Resta has laboriously built may reach that pitch of fine perfection that De Palma has attained now."[28] Arthur Duray, the winner of the 1906 Circuit des Ardennes, was in America to drive a Frontenac in the Sweepstakes: "The famous Belgian driver was a picturesque figure, clad in tight jersey of Belgian colors. His car, a Frontenac special, was camouflaged with gray and blue splashes of paint and looked like one of the cruisers which lurk in the North River."[29]

Harry Harkness died of influenza on 23 January 1919, at his home, 270 Park Avenue. The last race on the Sheepshead boards was held on 20 September 1919, a 150-miler won by Gaston Chevrolet in a Frontenac, with Joe Boyer in a Duesenberg second. The Sheepshead Bay property was sold in the spring of 1920 for building lots.

16

Farewell Performance

In 1913, the name Ballot stood for reliable L-head engines. Delage and a lot of lesser known French manufacturers, including Barré, SCAP, Pierron, Philos, Sigma, Ponette, Ryjan and Terrot, used Ballot engines in some of their production chassis. Ballot engined cars even won their class at Gaillon and other typical French hillclimbs and sprints. Ballot also stood for a nice factory in the south of Paris. "MM. Ballot frères,"[1] the Ballot brothers, Ernest and Albert, were subtle observers during the *pesage* of the 1913 Grand Prix de France at Le Mans, and a rumor was going around that Ballot was on the point of building engines for racing cars. The sportsmen had to wait until the end of the Great War, until the late autumn of 1918, when it was announced that Ballot would enter a batch of racers in the Victory Sweepstakes, the 1919 Indianapolis 500.

Ernest Ballot was born on 11 January 1870 in Angoulême, between Poitiers and Bordeaux, the son of a tailor. At 17 he joined the Marine Nationale, the French Navy, qualifying two years later for its engineering school. In 1894 he left the Navy in the rank of *second maître mécanicien*. In 1904 he suddenly emerged in the deep south of Paris. With partner Julien Faivre he formed the Ballot et Cie. at 103–105 Boulevard Brune in the 14th Arrondissement. Ballot et Cie. took over a factory for mechanical constructions, "exploitation d'une usine de construction mécanique."[2] Ballot produced L-head engines, singles and fours, to be used for stationary purposes, in ships and motorcars. On 4 October 1908, Paul Bablot drove a Ballot engined Pierron to victory in the Gaillon hillclimb, not overall but in the seventh category, meaning a bore between 101 and 106 mm. Bablot and the Pierron covered the 1-km climb in 41.1 sec, ahead of two Belgian Imperias. A second Ballot engined Pierron, driven by Mass, won the eighth category for 110 mm-bore cars, with a Guillemin-Le Gui second. Two weeks later, on 18 October 1908, at Château-Thierry, Ernest Ballot himself took the wheel of a Barré powered by one of his engines and won the class for 85 mm-bore cars. A proof for the quality of Ballot's engines? Not really, for the number of classes in these sprints enabled nearly every starter to win something.

On 4 July 1911 the limited liability corporation Ballot & Cie. was converted into a stock company and hence renamed "Établissements Ballot, Société Anonyme, au capital de 1.800.000 Francs, divisé en 18.000 Actions de 100 Francs chacune, siège social à Paris, 103–105 Boulevard Brune."[3] There were twelve shareholders. "Ernest Ballot and, above all, a mysterious company called Omnium Central were the main shareholders. To his new company Ernest Ballot contributed the land he owned, all the plant and equipment of the old Ballot & Cie. and the patents he had registered.... Omnium Central were an investment holding company whose shareholders were ... Jacques Sée, head of the Hutchinson Tyre Co., ... Charles Pathé, Viscount d'Autroche, Victor Continsouza and a vast array of bankers and landowners."[4] The principal financial backer was Pierre-Victor Continsouza. He was partner and main owner at Pathé Frères, then the most completely integrated film company in the international marketplace, and manufacturer of film projectors and miscellaneous *appareils cinématographiques*. Ernest and Albert Ballot were allotted 2000 shares and a sum of money equalling two million francs, so that the Ballot brothers remained the major owners. The directing figure was Ernest Ballot. On 12 July 1911, he was named managing director with an annual salary of 24,000 francs and a bonus of up to 12 percent of the net earnings exceeding one million Francs. And the role of Omnium Central? In the 1960s a few historians described it as an obscure network of competitors having taken control of Ballot. But Omnium Central simply had the objective to assist the formation of Établissements Ballot. On 3 October 1912, Omnium Central was dismantled. On 19 January 1912, Ballot applied for a building permit at no. 37–39, Boulevard Brune. For the design of the new factory he chose the famous architect Raoul Brandon, who was responsible for the Orosdi-Back department store and the Villa Hug in Cairo, and in 1919 for the *nouvel hôtel de la poste*, the new post office in Chartres. Over the winter of 1912–1913 Ballot began to move into the new complex.

During the Great War the Boulevard Brune factory continued to manufacture its well-established range of engines for *Automobiles, Aviation, Marine, Agriculture, Industrie et Applications diverses*. Ballot delivered thousands of L-head engines for army trucks, mostly in the dimensions of 90 × 150 mm and 100 × 170 mm, and added the production of 75-mm shells and of the famous Hispano V-8, the 8A aero-engine built under license. Due to the war boom, by the end of 1918 the Boulevard Brune was better equipped than ever. Ernest Ballot was in the same situation as André Citroën. How could they profit from a fully paid up and perfectly tooled up plant? Citroën adopted Henry Ford's course, deciding to mass-produce automobiles using a moving assembly line. Ballot took a slightly different view and decided to add luxury automobiles to the existent engine production. In view of a decent launch he was thinking of a victory or at least a successful participation in the Indianapolis 500-mile race which was scheduled for the end of May 1919. During the war, Ballot's old connection to Delage did not break away. Ernest Ballot continued to be in touch with René Thomas, a member of the 1912 Peugeot team, winner of the 1914 Indianapolis 500 for Delage, and leader of the Ballot engined Barré team in the 1914 Tour de France. Hence Ballot had close contact with Peugeot designer Ernest Henry and Delage designer Arthur Michelat, the most capable specialists for high performance cars in Paris.

In the 1950s, in his book *The Grand Prix Car*, Laurence Pomeroy wrote that Henry "severed his connection with Peugeot and was working for a company called Bara at Levallois,"[5] describing Bara as a license manufacturer of the 16-cylinder Bugatti aero-engine, hence Henry's idea of a straight-eight. "H. Bara et Cie., Automobiles,"[6] was formed on 20 May 1911, and was the Hispano agency in Paris, the *Agence Centrale* or *Agents Exclusifs*, at 93 Avenue Malakoff. In the 1960s, a few French historians, in particular Paul Yvelin, observed that a company called Bara did not exist and replaced the name Bara with Bariquand et Marre: "Where Henry went was to the Société Barriquand et Marre, in Paris; 'BARA' may have been its nickname. At B et M Henry redesigned his V-8 aero engine. It never went into production."[7] But it was long ago that Bariquand & Marre had been in the limelight. The "Société des Ateliers Bariquand et Marre, Mécanique de Précision,"[8] had been formed before the turn of the century and was located at 127 Rue Oberkampf, Paris, in the 11th Arrondissement. On 6 November 1907, the Wright brothers had unloaded their weak aero-engine in the Rue Oberkampf. In a first step Bariquand & Marre adapted a Lavalette high

Summer 1914. Victor Rigal and Georges Boillot spent the first months of the war as military motorists (Library of Congress).

tension magneto raising the output from 16 to 22 hp and then, within three months, completely rebuilt the engine which finally delivered 30 hp and made possible the flights at Le Mans. On 15 March 1908, the Wright brothers signed a contract for seven engines. But until the war began in 1914, Bariquand & Marre was more or less forgotten in aero-engine circles and concentrated on the production of guns. In the 1960s, it was also claimed that Louis Pilleverdier, the former Hispano driver who, in 1912, switched over to the Peugeot racing department, became director of the Peugeot aero-engine factory at Levallois in the summer of 1914, at the beginning of the war: "Henry followed him there,"[9] and began to design a twin-cam V-8 aero-engine.

According to contemporary magazines the Peugeot and Delage racing car departments were immediately shut down in August 1914 and the staffs engaged by the French army. Georges Boillot and Victor Rigal drove for French generals, Boillot for General Joffre. Many accounts were given of his dashes from one end of the line to the other in the critical days before the battle of the Marne. He broke all records in carrying Joffre to points where his presence was needed and in delivering messages and dispatches of the utmost importance. His hairs-breadth escapes and his performances were as frequently discussed in the Paris newspapers as were those of Joffre himself. In January 1915 Joffre selected a new chauffeur, a reservist named Edmond Théodore from Niort, who passed his conscript service as a naval mechanic. Now Joffre could sleep peacefully through his hundred-mile rushes along the battlefront. Georges Boillot moved to the aviation fighting service. On 3 February 1911 he had received license no. 395, his friend Jules Goux no. 398. On 13 October 1915 Boillot received military license no. 1759. Between 4 February 1916 and 4 April 1916 he served as *sous-lieutenant* in the escadrile N.49, then in the escadrille N.65. Boillot was killed in action on 19 May 1916 near Vadelaincourt, Meuse. His friend Jean Navarre, the first *As des As*, the first French pilot with ten victories, described the circumstances: "His death was a great loss. We had just been flying for an hour together, as was our custom, when my machine gun jammed, and I descended in order to repair it. He followed me down. On the ground Boillot saw that the repairs would require too much time and he said: 'I am off again. I shall see you above.' Less than an hour later he fell in with a squadron of six German fighting machines and heroically accepted battle. He was surrounded and passed into a spray of projectiles and was struck down with a bullet between the eyes."[10]

Jules Goux's "indicated post was in a fort at Belfort, practically within a stone's throw of German territory."[11] In the autumn of 1914 he was tranferred "to the motor section, driving officers in a Peugeot."[12] Albert Guyot drove an officer of the Orléans corps. René Thomas "volunteered for aeroplane service and has been accepted in this branch of the army,"[13] and Delage's star engineer Michelat as "military motorist."[14] Charles Faroux, chief editor of *La Vie Automobile*, Hispano director Jean Lacoste, Joseph de Crawhez, Jean Chassagne, Louis Wagner, Gustave Caillois, Arthur Duray, Henri Rougier, Fernand Gabriel, René de Knyff, Robert Laly and Henry Matthys were all in the same position of military motorists. There was no exception and until 1916 there was no Peugeot aero-engine department at Levallois. Ernest Henry was in an unusual situation in that he was Swiss. He was not engaged by the French army. At the outbreak of the war he more or less ended up on the street. Was it René Thomas who placed his friend Henry with Automobiles Gaston Barré? Automobiles Barré supplied dozens of Ballot engined trucks for the French forces, the *Défense Nationale*. The way for a switch-over to the Boulevard Brune would have been paved. Or did Henry work for H. Bara & Cie.? Where and how Ernest Henry spent the war years remains a mystery. For Henry's son his father "left Peugeot to get away from the engineers there. He designed the cars, made all the calculations and sent the results to the engineering center at Sochaux. They resented that. They were fully capable of making the same calculations, if not of really realizing a racing machine. Robert Peugeot would not invest a centime until every detail had been verified by the entire engineering staff. My father did all that work in his little drafting room at home. I can still hear him say, 'Oh, how they hunger to find errors in my work!'"[15]

Was Ballot rather inclined towards Henry or towards Michelat? The question did not really come up. In 1917 Michelat was still hoping that Louis Delage would accept his proposition of a luxury car powered by an overhead-cam six. It was not until the end of the war that Michelat fell out with his patron Delage and went looking for a new job. Now, Ballot was forced to decide in favor of Henry. In a first step, the former Peugeot engineer proposed an updated 4.5-liter as used in the 1914 Grand Prix at Lyon, a four-cylinder with twin-cam four-valve head, with dimensions of 95 × 172 mm to conform to the American 300-inch formula which held between 1915 and 1919. But in the meantime, twin-cam fours could be found all over the place, in England from Sunbeam and Humber, in Belgium from Nagant, and in America from Premier and Maxwell. Ballot asked for something exceptional. Did Henry keep in mind the V-12 Packard? He came up with a straight-eight, with a duplication of his last Peugeot design. Henry's last Peugeot was a 2.5-liter (73 × 146 mm) intended for the 1914 Coupe de l'Auto which was to be run in the Auvergne and was cancelled because of the war. A straight-eight was lower than a four of the same displacement, thus providing an opportunity to reduce the frontal area. The pistons and connecting rods of an eight were smaller and hence lighter. At 3500 rpm, the load transmitted by each piston was reduced by 30 percent, the inertia forces by 50 percent. Engine speed could be raised, even with an obsolete lubrication system. And Ernest Ballot was convinced that a straight-eight racer was the right crowd puller for his future production cars. The contract between the Ballot company, designer Ernest Henry and team manager René Thomas was signed between Christmas 1918 and New Year's day. It implied the condition that four cars would be ready by the end of April 1919 and that the whole affair would be kept secret. The drawing office of Ballot's new racing car department was located at Rue Cormeilles, Levallois. The different components were manufactured by the old Peugeot suppliers, and just the final assembling took place at the Boulevard Brune factory. And Michelat? By the end of the war, he moved to Marseille where Léon Paulet immediately approved of the 3.5-liter overhead-cam six which had been rejected by Delage. The Paulet was introduced at the 1921 Paris Salon.

The cylinders of the Ballot straight-eight were iron castings made in two blocks of four. The two overhead camshafts were driven by a train of gears at the front end, each camshaft running in five ball bearings. The two 42 mm intake and the two 37 mm exhaust valves were inclined at 30 degrees to the cylinder axis, operated via cup type tappets. The Ballot displaced 4.9 liters or 300 cubic inches with cylinder dimensions of 74 × 140 mm. The four-piece crankshaft ran in five ball bearings, within a barrel type crankcase. Henry retained his one-pump dry sump lubrication initiated in the 1913 Peugeot: A plunger pump scavenged oil from the sump, delivered it under pressure to a remote tank and pumped it back to the main bearings. These main ball bearings were fed with oil by means of jets. Then the oil was collected in catcher rings placed on the webs and fed by centrifugal force into the floating bush plain bearings of the big ends. At engine speeds above 3000 rpm the big ends were underlubricated and overheated so that Pomeroy wrote: "Henry sowed but did not reap so far as the eight-cylinder in-line engine was concerned."[16] Henry did not take full advantage of the straight-eight but he realized that the concept was trend-setting. As a result of the outdated big end lubrication, his straight-eight had more or less the same specific output as a corresponding four, but brought into play the additional complexity of eight cylinders. The 4.9-liter Ballot delivered 125 hp at 3000 rpm or 140 at 3500 for a short time with peaks of 150 hp at 4000 rpm. The power was transmitted via a Ferodo lined cone clutch to a separate four-speed gearbox. The engine-gearbox complex was carried in a U-shaped sub-frame having a three-point mounting within the main side members, in combination with a Hotchkiss type rear axle. Since the Ballot was intended to race on the Indianapolis speedway and not on a classical road course comprising a twisty part and a long straight, the front brakes and the streamline tail seen on the 1914 Peugeot were dropped. At 275 cm, the wheelbase was 5 cm longer than on the 4.5-liter Peugeot ancestor; front track was 143 cm and rear, 138 cm. Tires were 875 × 105 front, 880 × 120 rear. Dry weight was 980 kg, all-up starting line weight 1250 kg, and maximum speed was 190 km/h. In comparison to the Peugeot, the Ballot was much lower, with the advantage of a smaller frontal area and a lower center of gravity. Did Henry really appreciate that the big step forward was the smaller frontal area? Certainly, since it was Henry who had used Eiffel's laboratoire d'Auteuil to polish the bodies of the Peugeots.

In America, the 1919 season opened on Saturday, 15 March, with a 250-miler at Santa Monica, California. Two 300-inch Stutzes took first and second. The racers started as Chevrolets, driven by Cliff Durant, the son of the in-and-out head of General Motors, and Eddie Hearne. One week later, Roscoe Sarles in a Duesenberg engined Roamer won a 150-miler on the 1-mile dirt oval at Ascot, with Hearne in the Stutz Chevrolet second. On 19 May, Tommy Milton drove a Duesenberg to victory in a 100-lap race on the 1.125-mile board track at Union Town, Pennsylvania, ahead of Louis Chevrolet and Ralph Mulford in aluminum Frontenacs.

Meanwhile, on 26 April 1919, a batch of four Ballots was shipped from Le Havre to New York and then to Indianapolis, to be driven by René Thomas (with mechanic Robert Laly), Albert Guyot (with Flohot), Louis Wagner (with Jules Moriceau), Paul Bablot, and Jean Chassagne as relief. Thomas set the best qualifying time at 104.7 mph. Then he decided to replace the Michelin 880 × 120 rear tires with smaller Goodrich straight-side 32 × 4½ units, against Henry's advice. Bablot refused to start with the smaller tires so that he was replaced by Chassagne. Throughout the race the Ballots were plagued by tire and magneto trouble. Guyot finished fourth, Thomas eighth, Bablot and Wagner retired. The winner was an older 4.5-liter Peugeot driven by Howdy Wilcox, with Eddie Hearne second in a Stutz which started as Durant Special, Jules Goux in a Premier engined Peugeot third, and DePalma in the V-12 Packard sixth. *Motor Age* wrote:

> From a viewpoint of interest and attendance it was a big success, but these were the only two particulars in which it was even partly so. For aside from the satisfaction Americans might take in the fact that the race was won by an American, Howdy Wilcox, the race was a complete failure.... Several reasons contributed to this failure. First, with the exception of one team, the cars entered were of a vintage of several years previous — in fact the wonder was not that some of these cars were extremely slow, but rather that a great many of them were able to run at all, in view of the hard knocks they had received in their long careers. Second, an inconceivable blunder kept the only new cars in the race from figuring seriously in the result. Ballot, a French manufacturer, was the only one who had a team of new cars in the race. Considerable interest attached to these machines, for they embodied a new idea in racing cars with eight cylinders in a row. They had shown extreme speed in practice and gave every indication of having the race "sewed up." At the last minute, however,

René Thomas, captain of the Ballot team, changed the wheels on the cars and the resultant change in gear ratios caused so much wheel trouble to the cars in the race that they never were serious contenders.[17]

The assembling of three Duesenberg straight-eights was completed so late that there was no time for practice. Somehow Tommy Milton managed to qualify one of them, but was out in lap 49. The block and the detachable head of the Duesenberg eight were made of cast iron, supplied by a patternmaker and foundry in Chicago. Cylinder dimensions were $3 \times 5\frac{1}{4}$ inches. The overhead camshaft, driven by a vertical shaft via bevel gears at the front of the engine, operated a large intake and, via a forked rocker, two smaller exhaust valves per cylinder, with the valves inclined 30 degrees to the cylinder axis. Low percentage tungsten was used for the intake valves, cobalt-chrome for the exhaust. The two-piece crankshaft ran in three main bearings, ball bearings rear and center, a plain bearing at the front. For the big ends the brothers relied on splash lubrication as in the older fours. The connecting rods, which always had been of H-section in the fours, were replaced by hand-forged tubular rods. The tubular section was not better but less expensive. A Delco battery system from the Dayton Engineering Laboratories Co., a compact aero-engine unit, fed two plugs per cylinder. Two rotary-valve Miller carburetors supplied the mixture. Output was 125 hp at 3000 rpm. The first straight-eights were mounted in older 106-inch frames, offset by one inch to the left, whereby the huge cone clutch and the separated three-speed gearbox of the four were retained. Milton's eight approached 4000 rpm on the straights of the Indianapolis speedway. At this speed, the splash lubricated big ends overheated so that a connecting broke. In the future, Duesenberg drilled out the crankshaft in order to push through the lubricant from one end to the other.

On 23 November 1919, René Thomas and his 4.9-liter Ballot started in the Targa Florio on Sicily, over four laps of the 108-km Madonie circuit, but went out during the last lap because of a broken differential. Again the winner was an old Peugeot, this time a 2.5-liter driven by André Boillot, the younger brother of Georges. The season ended with a small consolation when Thomas, on 17 October 1919, achieved fastest time of the day in the Gaillon hillclimb. In September 1920, Jean Chassagne took a 4.9-liter Ballot, made a detour to Brooklands and lapped the track at 112.17 mph, nearly 180 km/h, confirming a maximum speed of 190 km/h for the 4.9-liter Ballot in original form. Later the racer was handled in a few Brooklands meetings by Louis Zborowski while, in October 1924, Douglas Hawkes drove it to third place in the Grand Prix de l'Ouverture at Montlhéry. In March 1925, Harold Cooper drove the Ballot in a 1-km sprint at Nice, in the hillclimb to La Turbie, and in the Mont Angel hillclimb, always finishing second behind Robert Benoist's Delage. The 4.9-liter used by Thomas in the Targa remained in Italy, in the hands of Francesco Conelli who, in May 1922, won the hillclimb between Parma and Poggio di Berceto, and in October 1924, was second in the Gran Premio d'Autunno at Monza. In May 1925, the 4.9-liter was driven by Conte Gastone Brilli-Peri to victory in the Coppa della Perugina. The 4.9-liter Ballots and DePalma's V-12 Packard were the fastest cars of the 300-inch formula. Although, by the irony of fate, older warhorses from Peugeot and Stutz took first and second in the 1919 Indianapolis 500, the era of the four-cylinder was running out.

In the autumn of 1919, Fernand Vadier began to work for Ballot and quickly became Ernest Henry's right-hand man. Born on 18 September 1894 in Poitiers, Vadier was an engineer of the Arts-et-Métiers school of Angers. In 1917 he began his career as *dessinateur*, or draftsman, at Panhard. In 1919 he switched over to Ballot, to the diesel engine department. The Ballot racing car for the 1920 and 1921 seasons was simply a scaled down 4.9-liter.

2 October 1921— Gaillon hill-climb. Bac and his 1914 Peugeot, a 2.5-liter Coupe de l'Auto racer, took second in the 3-liter class in 29²⁄₅ sec, averaging 122.45 km/h (Mercedes-Benz Classic).

2 April 1922 — Targa Florio, Sicily. Jules Goux and his 2-liter 4-cylinder Ballot finished second, covering 4 laps of 108 km in 6 h 52 min 37 sec (Mercedes-Benz Classic).

"These Ballots are a redevelopment of the four Ballot jobs that were here last year, except of course, that they are smaller as regards piston displacement. They are very light in weight, with the majority of the weight carried at an exceptionally low center of gravity. The three cars are representative of European practice in that the driver's seat was placed rather high. Ralph De Palma has rebuilt the seating arrangement in his car, lowering it, which gives the car a smarter appearance."[18] According to the new capacity limit, the straight-eight now displaced three liters, 183 cubic inches, with a bore of 65 mm and a stroke of 112 mm, and produced 107 hp at 3800 rpm. *La Vie Automobile* quoted the output as 105–108 hp at 3500 rpm while *Motor Age* wrote: "It is understood that the Ballot engines develop 108 hp at rather more than 3000 revolutions."[19] Overall the chassis was smaller: wheelbase 265 cm, track 133 cm, tires 820 × 120 front, 835 × 135 rear. For the 1920 Indianapolis 500, Ballot mounted 32 × 4½ Goodyear Cord straight side tires with wheels specially built in France, "owing to the unsatisfactory results obtained last year."[20] The maximum speed was 180 km/h at 3550 rpm thanks to a long-tailed, barrel-shaped body containing a vertically mounted spare wheel. "The cars are built very low and are perfectly streamlined. The under-pan extends from the base of the radiator to the bulbous tail, and thus envelopes the rear axle. The front springs are underslung. Both the front axle and the tie rod uniting the spring horns are profiled to reduce head resistance. Double Hartford shock absorbers are employed front and rear. Front wheel brakes are provided for in the design but as they are not essential for track work, they will only be fitted when the car takes part in road races."[21]

By the beginning of May 1920 Ernest Ballot declared: "Last September, when I announced my intention of building racing cars, the French Syndicate of Automobile Manufacturers informed me that they did not wish any of their members to take part in racing during the year 1920. As I am not a member of this Syndicate, for I only manufacture engines and not complete cars, I informed them that I did not attach any importance to their decision. Immediately I was informed that if I built racing cars I should be shut out of every show, exhibition or race held in France. That's why I held back my programme until December, when the Syndicale informed me that the decision against racing applied to French events and not to contests abroad. I got to work with the loss of three months owing to this jealous attitude of the official body."[22] Was Peugeot behind it? Peugeot engineer Marcel Grémillon had designed a new 3-liter four for the Indianapolis 500: "The engine is an entirely new production having four block cast cylinders measuring 80 × 149 mm bore and stroke. There are three camshafts and 20 valves for the four cylinders."[23]

On 30 May 1920, in the Indianapolis 500, the 3-liter Ballots driven by René Thomas, Ralph DePalma and Jean Chassagne finished second, fifth and seventh. "When the cars wheeled across the wire at the end of the pacing lap, it was seen that De Palma's right rear tire was flat and he was forced to drive into the pits for a change, even before he had made his first lap. This mischance threw him into seventeenth place and forced him to go out and beat it from the start to catch up with his competitors."[24] DePalma and his white Ballot led until only 35 miles remained when his car caught fire and then ran out of fuel: "Ralph De Palma had more than his share of bad luck, but a trifle more care probably would have won the race for him, despite all his misfortunes. He twice had tire trouble in the first 200 miles of the race, both coming at crucial times, but was remarkably fortunate in escaping trouble for the last 300 miles, and had he stopped and made assurance doubly sure by taking on fuel when he had an advantage of more than two laps over his closest competitor, he probably would have flashed over the wire in first place."[25] After the race it was discovered that a cork gasket had disintegrated and had blocked the fuel system. The three-cam Peugeots

Cresswell drawing of the 3-liter Ballot: straight-eight, 65 × 112 mm, 107 hp at 3800 rpm (Mercedes-Benz Classic).

driven by André Boillot, Jules Goux and Howdy Wilcox failed because of "designing defects, defects which were admitted even before the race by the Peugeot drivers, but which they had not the time to remedy."[26]

Gaston Chevrolet won the 1920 Indianapolis 500 in a Frontenac-Monroe. Frontenacs had finished the 1919 season with victories at Uniontown, Sheepshead Bay, and Cincinnati. For William Small this was reason enough to engage Louis Chevrolet as consulting engineer. Small was the Monroe distributor in Indianapolis and, in the fall of 1918, had purchased the Monroe assets. Louis Chevrolet quickly hired Cornelius Van Ranst, the former Duesenberg engineer. Chevrolet moved to Indianapolis, where Small provided a well-equipped shop, and began to build a batch of 183-inch racers for the 1920 season. Chevrolet and Van Ranst came up with their own interpretation of the 3-liter Peugeot. The block of the four-cylinder Frontenac-Monroe, the twin-camshaft head and the upper part of the crankcase were a single cast iron casting. Cylinder dimensions were 3⅛ × 5¹⁵⁄₁₆ inches. Two intake and two exhaust valves measuring 1⁷⁄₁₆ inch were opened by finger-type cam followers to a lift of ⁷⁄₁₆ inch and were inclined at 20 degrees to the cylinder axis. The valves were closed by a pair of concentric coil springs which were exposed to the fresh air. The two camshafts were enclosed in a pair of aluminum housings and driven by a train of spur gears running in ball bearings. The two-piece crankshaft ran in three ball bearings within a barrel-type aluminum crankcase, lubricated via dry sump. The big ends ran in plain bearings 2.1 inches in diameter. Other features were aluminum pistons, tubular connecting rods, Delco ignition and a 2-inch Miller carburetor. The Frontenac delivered 100 hp at 3300 rpm. Power was transmitted via a multiple-disk clutch to a three-speed gearbox. The rear axle was of the Hotchkiss type. Wheelbase was 98 inches, track 56 inches. Tires were Firestone-built Oldfields, 32 × 4 front, 32 × 4½ rear. Four green Monroes were built and, since Chevrolet was free to assemble duplicates, three burgundy-red Frontenacs.

Despite the Frontenac-Monroe victory, the car to beat was the Duesenberg eight. Cylinder dimensions were 2½ × 4⅝ inches, 63.5 × 117.5 mm. The four-four crankshaft was made in one piece now. It continued to run in three main bearings, a ball bearing at the rear, plain bearings front and center. As before three valves per cylinder were operated by a single overhead camshaft, the intake having a diameter of 1⅜ inch with a lift of ⅜ inch, the two exhausts ¹⁵⁄₁₆ inch with a lift of ⁵⁄₁₆ inch. There was a single spark plug on the intake side. In 1920 the 183-inch eight delivered 100 hp at 3500 rpm. A multiple-disc clutch replaced the cone, and the three-speed gearbox was mounted in unit with the engine. The rear axle was of the torque tube type. Two engines were mounted in older 106-inch frames for Hearne and O'Donnell. The two cars to be driven by Milton and Murphy were completely new, with the offset mounting of the engine increased to 1½ inch. The rear cross-member of the frame was of box section and filled with wood. Wheelbase was 106 inches, track 51 inches, tires 32 × 4½ or 33 × 5 all around. The yellow factory cars ran well. Milton, Murphy and Hearne finished third, fourth and sixth.

The first great Ballot victory followed on 28 August 1920: DePalma won the Elgin National Trophy, a distance of 30 laps of 8.55 miles, or 256 miles, "in the remarkable time of 3:09:54, an average speed of 79.5 mph. In addition to winning the race, De Palma set a new record for the course and broke the lap record. In his 11th lap DePalma equalled the track record of 6:17, which he cut down to 6:10 in his last lap."[27] This was the last race at

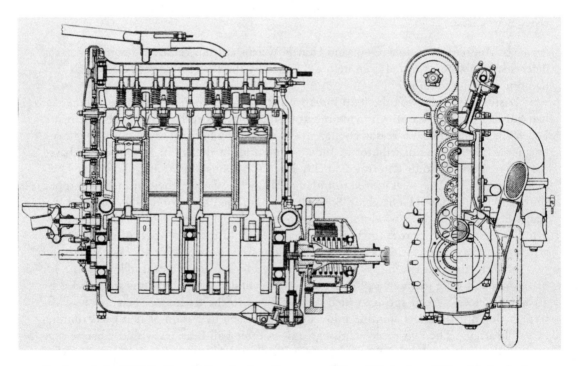

Engine of the 1920 Indianapolis-winning Frontenac (3⅛ × 5¹⁵⁄₁₆ inches, 183 cubic inches), an American interpretation of the 3-liter Peugeot (*La Vie Automobile*, 1920).

Elgin and the last great American road race since Willie Vanderbilt had decided in 1916 to withdraw his Cup from competition, involving the cancellation of the Grand Prize. America was to concentrate on oval-track racing.

In May 1921 DePalma was the only Ballot driver at Indianapolis. The fastest qualifier at 100.75 mph, he set a flying pace and led for all but two of the first 112 laps, only to withdraw because of a broken connecting rod. Tommy Milton won the race in a new Frontenac, a straight-eight with the same features as the four: twin-camshaft head and four valves per cylinder. The block, head and upper part of the crankcase were a single iron casting. Bore and stroke dimensions were 2.625 × 4.219 inches. The followers of the four were replaced by cup-type tappets, Ballot fashion. The crankshaft ran in five plain bearings, pressure lubricated via dry-sump. The straight-eight was mounted in a double-drop frame with a wheelbase of 102 inches, dry weight 1850 pounds. In France, the flower-petal radiator shells of the Frontenacs became so popular that they were copied by Louis Delage for his 6- and 12-cylinder record cars.

On 25 July 1921 the first post-war Grand Prix de l'ACF was run at Le Mans over 30 laps of 17.262 km. The Ballots started with Scintilla magnetos, KLG plugs, Pirelli tires (820 × 120 front, 835 × 135 rear), and Claudel carburetors. The trouble with the Claudels was sticking throttle barrels, occasioned by road dust. Chassagne foresaw this and fitted a very heavy recall spring. Wagner and DePalma had to fit extra springs during the race. DePalma finished second, behind Jimmy Murphy's Duesenberg, and ahead of Goux's 2-liter four-

25 July 1921— Grand Prix de l'ACF, Le Mans. Jimmy Murphy, mechanic Ernie Olson and the 3-liter Duesenberg: the first American victory in the French Grand Prix (Mercedes-Benz Classic).

25 July 1921—Grand Prix de l'ACF, Le Mans. Jean Chassagne, riding mechanic Robert Laly and the 3-liter Ballot took the lead for a few laps but did not finish because of a broken rear axle (Mercedes-Benz Classic).

2 October 1921—Gaillon hill-climb. Jules Goux and his 3-liter Ballot, with smaller rear wheels for better acceleration, achieved the fastest time of the day and won the 3-liter class in 25⅖ sec, averaging 141.7 km/h (Mercedes-Benz Classic).

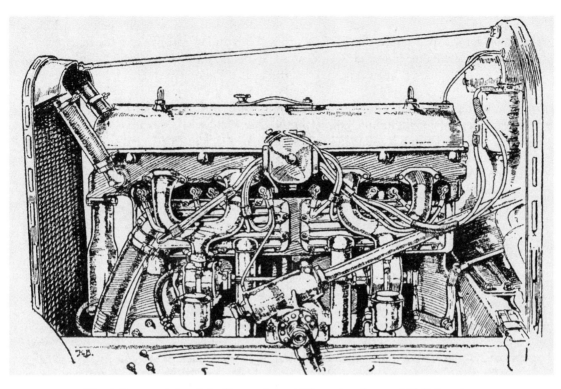

The 3-liter straight-eight Duesenberg (*Allgemeine Automobil-Zeitung*).

cylinder Ballot which completed the distance at an average of 115 km/h and a fuel consumption of 14.2 liters per 100 km. "De Palma did not have on his car the servo-brake that Chassagne had so that he lost time when braking and was unable to harass Murphy."[28] Wagner finished seventh. Chassagne retired when leading the race, pulling into the pits with fuel streaming from his tank caused by the breaking of the rear axle when the Ballot skidded in an effort to avoid Dubonnet's Duesenberg. On 4 September 1921, in a race near Brescia over 30 laps of 17.3 km via Montichiari and Ghedi, which was appointed first Gran Premio d'Italia, the team of Ernest Ballot turned up with three cars: DePalma with mechanic Pete DePaolo, Jules Goux assisted by the former Sizaire et Naudin voiturette driver Jules Leboucq, and Jean Chassagne with Robert Laly. There were entries from Fiat, Duesenberg and Sunbeam, but only the Italians turned up. DePalma's Ballot went out in lap 21 because of magneto problems. Goux won in 3 h 35 min 9 sec, averaging 144.75 km/h, ahead of Chassagne and the Fiat of Wagner, who was not in top form because of his brother's death a day before the race.

It was also during the summer of 1921 that another straight-eight celebrated its first victories at Tacoma and Beverly Hills. It came from the Miller Mfg. Co. which had just moved to to 2652 Long Beach Avenue, Los Angeles. Tommy Milton was not happy with the engine of his Duesenberg and asked Miller for a replacement, and Barney Oldfield for the money. Barney borrowed the money from his bank. The Miller was a mixture of Ballot and Duesenberg, with two overhead camshafts, four valves per cylinder, and a crankshaft running in three main bearings. Cylinder dimensions were $2\frac{11}{16} \times 4$ inches, for displacement of 181.5 cubic inches. The first two engines had detachable heads. Later engines adopted integral heads. The valves were inclined at 30 degrees to the cylinder axis. They were opened via cup-type tappets and closed by three concentric springs. The Miller delivered 125 hp at 4000 rpm, with compression of 7.5:1, using a mixture of gasoline and benzene.

Originally Ballot intended to enter a four in the 1920 Indianapolis 500. But it was not yet *au point*. William Bradley reported that the smaller Ballot was entered in the 1921 French Grand Prix, however, only because of the wrecking of the 8-cylinder used by Renard, who was killed in practice in July 1921. Driven by Renard, the 2-liter four had made its initial appearance in the Gaillon hillclimb on 10 October 1920, where Renard achieved a time of 31 seconds for the uphill kilometer, while Chassagne at the wheel of the 3-liter straight-eight Ballot crossed the line after 22.6 sec. Fastest time of the day went to René Thomas and a big V-12 aero-engined Sunbeam: 20.6 sec, one second faster than his previous year's time at the wheel of the 4.9-liter Ballot. In addition Renard took the *classement au rendement*, the efficiency classification, whereby the Ballot weighed 948 kg. Henry had designed a four-cylinder interpretation of the 3-liter racer, an interpretation suitable for production at the Boulevard Brune. The four was to be offered under the designation 2LS, *Deux Litres Sport*: a Grand Tourisme in the classical sense, a racer for the weekend and at the same time a sportscar for fast road runs. Henry was assisted by Fernand Vadier. Cylinder dimensions of the 2LS were 69.9 × 130 mm. The general layout followed the eight, with a crankshaft in three ball bearings and a twin-cam four-valve head, although the camshafts were driven by a vertical shaft instead of the spur gears. The 2-liter developed 80 hp at 3900 rpm, could reach 4200 rpm. In view of the future production, the chassis was rather long, with a wheelbase of 280 cm (15 cm longer than the 3-liter eight) and track of 130 cm. Tires were 815 × 105 or 820 × 120. In the autumn of 1921 the Deux Litres Sport was displayed at the Paris Salon in the Grand Palais as a two-seater and a spectacular and very highly finished three-seater which was designed and built in the shops of Felber et Fils at 33 Avenue de la Défense, Puteaux. It weighed 1250 kg *en ordre de marche*, in running order. The chassis was priced at 80,000 Francs, just 9000 under the magnificent 6.6-liter Farman which was the most exclusive car at the salon. Ballot declared that just 100 of the 2LS would be built. The Felber three-seater was on the market as a second-hand car in August 1924, for sale by John Sartini, 2 Rue Greuze, Paris, at a price of 50,000 Francs.[29]

At the time of the 1921 Paris Salon, Henry had already left Ballot and the Boulevard Brune. In the late summer of 1921, Henry moved to Suresnes, to an office within the Darracq factory which was part of the STD group, Sunbeam-Talbot-Darracq. Jean Chassagne followed in November 1921. In 1912, the Basque Alexandre Darracq had withdrawn from his company, the A. Darracq & Co. (1905) Ltd. Owen Clegg had become the new director. In October 1919, Darracq & Co. bought Clement-Talbot Ltd. of Kensington. In June 1920, they in turn merged with Sunbeam of Wolverhampton. The London based commercial vehicle manufacturer W. & G. du Cros was thrown in and the international grouping that resulted was known as Sunbeam-Talbot-Darracq.

By the end of 1915, the former Excelsior driver Josef Christiaens had suggested to Sunbeam director Louis Coatalen to build a 300-inch six based on the cylinder dimensions of the 3.3-liter four (81 × 160 mm) which won the 1914 Tourist Trophy on the Isle of Man. Coatalen agreed. Dimensions of the twin-cam six were 81.5 × 157 mm. As in one of the 3.3-liter Tourist Trophy engines and in the subsequent 4.5-liter Grand Prix engines, finger-type cam followers were used to operate the four valves per cylinder. Output was 152 hp at 3200 rpm. Two sixes were mounted into 280-cm frames borrowed from 1914 Grand Prix racers. With Christiaens at the wheel the Sunbeam made its début in the 20-mile Coney Island Cup at Sheepshead Bay on 13 May 1916 and finished second behind Aitken's Peugeot.

Then, Christiaens took fourth in the Indianapolis 300, third in the Chicago 300, and third in the Minneapolis 150. Frank Galvin drove the second Sunbeam to third in the Cincinnati 300. During the spring of 1919, the sixes were mounted into shorter and lighter 270-cm Tourist Trophy frames. On 23 February 1919, Christiaens was killed when his new racer turned over during a demonstration run near the Sunbeam factory. Two sixes were shipped to Indianapolis for Resta and Chassagne but did not start, allegedly because of engine vibrations.

On 3 November 1920, Coatalen ordered four chassis and seven engines for a new 3-liter Sunbeam racer. On 14 December 1920 and 20 April 1921, he ordered two additional engines. At the same time, at Suresnes, the original location of the Darracq factory, three identical cars were assembled as Talbot-Darracqs. Total costs were estimated at £50,000. The STD straight-eight was designed by the former Fiat engineer Edmondo Moglia. It had the same dimensions as Henry's 3-liter Ballot, 65 × 112 mm, and was composed of two 4-cylinder aluminum blocks with steel liners. Two overhead camshafts operated four valves per cylinder, inclined at 30 degrees to the cylinder axis as in the Peugeots and the Ballots. The camshafts were driven by a train of spur gears. But the conditions within the crankcase had nothing in common with Peugeot, Ballot or Henry custom. The crankshaft was completely counterbalanced so that a flywheel was superfluous and cancelled. It ran in five plain bearings, lubricated under pressure via dry sump. The Delco ignition showed American influence. Four Zenith carburetors supplied the mixture. The STD delivered 108 hp at 4000 rpm, with compression of 5.7:1. The engine, the Hele Shaw clutch and the four-speed gearbox were mounted in a subframe as in the Peugeots or Ballots. Wheelbase was 270 cm, track 135 cm. The engine was lighter than the Duesenberg and Ballot engines, while the frame members and the rear axle were heavier.

"There is reason to believe that the lightest engines were the Talbot and the Darracqs, yet these cars swere the heaviest of the group. In the frame members alone there was very much more weight than in the Duesenberg frames and less strength. The rear axle, too, was considerably heavier, and the very fine work done in the engine had not been carried out in all the details of the chassis, with the result that total weight was unnecessarily high."[30] Dry weight was around 950 kg. Before the Grand Prix de l'ACF at Le Mans, the Duesenbergs weighed in between 909 and 925 kg, the Ballots between 930 and 938 kg, the Talbots and the Darracqs between 930 and 993 kg. In May 1921, three cars were shipped to Indianapolis to be handled by René Thomas, André Boillot and Ora Haibe. Haibe, born in Guilford, Indiana, on 27 September 1887, had worked with Joe Cooper until Cooper's death in 1915. In the 1916 Indianapolis 500, Haibe had driven a Wisconsin engined Ostewig to tenth; in 1919 he had finished fourteenth in a Hudson six. In the Sunbeam he finished fifth, while Thomas went out in lap 144 because of a broken water hose and Boillot in lap 41 because of a burned out connecting rod bearing. In the French Grand Prix at Le Mans, Boillot finished fifth.

In the autumn of 1921, in his new office at Suresnes, Ernest Henry designed a four-cylinder racer for Sunbeam, a 2-liter according to the new displacement limit which was to remain in force in Europe between 1922 and 1925. Jean Chassagne was responsible for the data flow towards Wolverhampton where Louis Coatalen supervised the assembly of the car. In contrast to the 2-liter Ballot, the Sunbeam was a pure racer and much smaller, having a wheelbase of 250 cm, front track of 120 cm, rear track of 118 cm. Rolling on either 765 × 105 clincher bead or 30 × 4 straight side tires, the Sunbeam weighed 700 kg, 120 kg lighter than the Ballot. The Sunbeam engine was a refined Ballot four, with slightly reduced bore and longer stroke: 68 × 136 mm instead of the Ballot's 69.9 × 130 mm. The intake valves were inclined at 20 degrees to the cylinder axis, the exhaust valves at 40 degrees so that the included valve angle of 60 degrees, which was typical for all Henry designs, was retained. The six-piece crankshaft ran in three ball bearings. The big ends continued to run in plain bearings whereby big ends one-two and three-four were connected by circular tubings in order to increase the oil flow. Further features were a dry sump using two oil pumps, two Solex carburetors and two Scintilla magnetos feeding eight plugs, one in the center of the head and the second between the two intake ports. Output was 83 hp at 4250 rpm, with a compression ratio of 6.5:1. Engine and gearbox were in one unit, three-point mounted on the frame without the traditional U-shape subframe. The frame was upswept over both front and rear axles, the springs being underslung. The front axle was made in three parts, an H-section in the center with tubular outer ends to resist the torsional stress of the front wheel brakes. A spare wheel was carried longitudinally in the tail, as on the 1914 Peugeot and the 1921 Ballot. The Grand Prix de l'ACF was run on 16 July 1922, near Strasbourg. Three Sunbeams were driven by Chassagne, Kenelm Lee Guinness and Henry Segrave: "The three Sunbeams had shown themselves to be the fastest in practice until the Fiats appeared on the scene, when the English engineers decided to drop their gear ratio from 3.6:3.8. Made on the eve of the race, there was no time to try out the effect of this change, and the contest showed that the engines were running beyond the safety limit, for in each case a valve stem broke and caused withdrawal of the car."[31] The entries for the Gran Premio d'Italia were cancelled.

15 July 1922 — Grand Prix de l'ACF, Strasbourg. Jules Goux and the cigar-shaped Ballot did not finish (Mercedes-Benz Classic).

Another car built up according to Henry's ideas appeared in the 1922 French Grand Prix: the 1.5-liter Aston Martin. It was financed by Louis Zborowski of Chitty Bang Bang fame, Margaret's and William Elliot Morris Zborowski's son. Allegedly based on a design by Peugeot engineer Marcel Grémillon, the Aston was built and assembled in Feltham, England, under the direction of Zborowski's friend Clive Gallop. In principle it was a 1.5-liter voiturette racer, a four with dimensions of 65 × 112 mm, with twin-cam head and four valves per cylinder. The wheelbase was 245 cm, track 120 cm, weight 660 kg. The two cars driven by Zborowski and Gallop did not finish because of engine trouble.

While Henry moved from Ballot to STD, his counterpart Moglia moved from STD to Ballot. It was Moglia who gave the 2-liter Ballot the famous cigar-shaped streamline bodies for the 1922 Grand Prix de l'ACF. The Ballots weighed 816, 810 and 840 kg, and were driven by Goux, Foresti and Masetti. Giulio Masetti started with Pete DePaolo as riding mechanic. All the Ballots retired. This was the last appearance of a Ballot factory team, since the entries for Goux and Foresti in the 1922 Gran Premio d'Italia in Monza were cancelled. After the French Grand Prix, Moglia left Ballot. In the autumn of 1922 and in 1923 he worked on the enigmatic Djelmo. Originally the Djelmo was a record car project from Sunbeam, powered by a 10-liter straight-eight (107 × 140 mm) of 350 hp. The project was sold to Paris based Egyptian Prince Djellalledin and Edmondo Moglia, hence the new name: Djelmo. The record racer was to be driven by Giulio Foresti, who was an Itala and Ballot agent in London with workshops at Bryanston Square near Edgeware Road and at

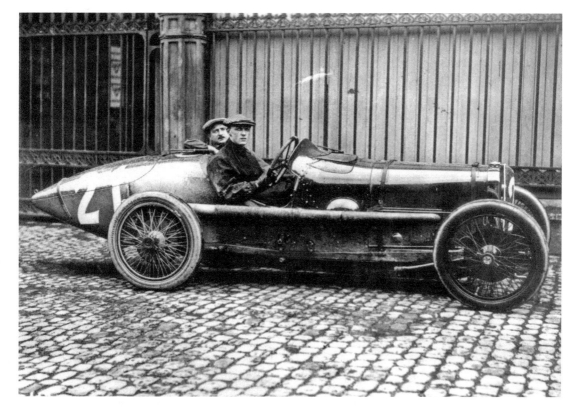

15 July 1922 — Grand Prix de l'ACF, Strasbourg. Henry Segrave and mechanic Jules Moriceau in the 2-liter Sunbeam, Ernest Henry's last racing car design (Mercedes-Benz Classic).

Brooklands. The Djelmo was not finished before 1927, and Foresti crashed it at Pendine Sands, Wales.

The 1922 French Grand Prix marked not only the end of Ernest Henry's career with Sunbeam but with racing cars in general. Henry's son remembered: "Nelson-Bohnalite in America had patented a type of aluminum piston and took out the European patents for it in Zurich. Some investors there came to Paris to set up a factory for the manufacture of these pistons. The factory was named Nova. My father put his money into the project and created the factory and ran it. But the money people in Zurich wanted all the control, and the stronger fraction won. I think that it was this affair which finally broke my father's health and spirit. That was in about 1932."[32] Ernest Henry died in Paris on 12 December 1950, in poverty.

After designing a blower for Bugatti, Edmondo Moglia worked for Nacional Pescara in Barcelona and for Hotchkiss in Paris. Henry's assistant Fernand Vadier stayed at Ballot until 1926, developing (with the former Panhard engineer Louis Germain) the Ballot 2 LT, the Deux Litres Tourisme, before switching to the servo-brake manufacturer Albert Dewandre. André Boillot was killed on 9 June 1932 in the Ars hillclimb near Chateauroux.

17

Fiat School

In Europe, the first race after the Great War was held on 24 August 1919, a sprint on a beach of Fanø island, on Denmark's west coast. Nando Minoia and his 4.9-liter Fiat achieved the best time of the day over the flying kilometer. The Fiat was a tipo S57A. The S57 was the last Fiat racer designed by Giuseppe Coda, a 4.5-liter for the 1914 French Grand Prix with cylinder dimensions of 100 × 143 mm, with one overhead camshaft operating two 60-mm valves per cylinder. The S57A was a rebored evolution of the 4.5-liter intended to conform to the American 300-inch formula and compete in the 1917 Indianapolis race. Cylinder dimensions of the S57A were 104 × 143 mm, and the valves were operated via roller tappets and inclined at 18 instead of 30 degrees to the cylinder axis. The S57A did not cross the Atlantic:

> After the announcement of the 500 mile race for May 30, 1917, the Fiat factory at Turin, Italy, cabled its entries for two cars to be driven by Jack Scales, an engineer in the Fiat factory and an Italian driver named Fagnano, who participated in a number of European events with marked success. On account of difficulties in shipping from Italian ports because of the submarine menace the Fiat officials were sending their race cars by trucks to Bordeaux, and were half way between Turin and Bordeaux when they were notified by cable of the cancellation of the Indianapolis event on account of America's entry into the hostilities. The cars were immediately recalled, shipping arrangements for the cars and reservations for the drivers cancelled, and it is believed that these cars have been held in the factory.[1]

On 5 October 1919, Antonio Ascari drove his 4.5-liter S57 to victory in the 50.9-km hillclimb between Parma and Poggio di Berceto in 38 min 11 sec, averaging 83.2 km/h. This was also the first race of 21-year-old Enzo Ferrari, who finished fifth in his class in 50 min 13 sec. Ferrari drove a CMN, Costruzioni Meccaniche Nazionali, an L-head 2.3-liter, 75 × 130 mm, built in the former factory of Giuseppe De Vecchi, Milan. Three weeks later, on 26 October, Ascari and the 4.5-liter Fiat won the Coppa della Consuma, a 16-km hillclimb a few kilometers east of Florence. On 23 November, in the Targa Florio on Sicily, over 4 laps of 108 km, Ascari and his red 4.5-liter Fiat were in the lead after 31 kilometers, at Caltavuturo. But after 58 kilometers, at Polizzi, he went too fast into a corner, overturned and landed in the ditch. André Boillot won in a 2.5-liter Coupe de l'Auto Peugeot. The turn of the 4.9-liter S57A came on 29 May 1921, when Giulio Masetti won the Targa, ahead of Max Sailer's Mercedes, a 7.2-liter six.

In the same 1921 Targa, Fiat entered a pair of new 3-liter Grand Prix racers, the tipo 801/401, for Nando Minoia and Pietro Bordino. Minoia finished eighth; Bordino was out in lap 1. Three weeks before, the 801/401 had won its class in the Parma-Poggio hillclimb.

In addition to the 801/401 four, an 801/402 eight was in the making. The new Fiats were designed by Carlo Cavalli and Giulio Cesare Cappa. Cavalli was known as the *Avvocato* since, according to his father's wishes, he became a lawyer. But, in 1905, he entered Fiat as an engineer, and was appointed technical director in 1919. Cappa had been co-founder and technical director of Aquila Italiana. He was responsible for the six-cylinder which started in the 1914 French Grand Prix. He switched over to Fiat in 1914 where he worked on the aero-engine A15R, then on the Superfiat 520, the tipo 519 and the 509. Cavalli and Cappa were assisted by Vincenzo Bertarione and Vittorio Jano, who both joined Fiat in 1911 as *disegnatori*, or designers. From the outset, the tipo 801 chassis was conceived to receive two different 3-liter engines, the low weight four-cylinder tipo 401 for Targa Florio type courses and hillclimbs, and the powerful straight-eight tipo 402 for fast triangle courses or speedways.

Both engines were composed of steel cylinders, with welded-up ports. The cylinders were enclosed by sheet steel jackets. The four-cylinder 401 had dimensions of 85 × 131 mm. The counterbalanced crankshaft ran in four double-row ball bearings and a normal ball bearing at the front. The big ends ran in two-piece roller bearings. There were four 54-mm valves per cylinder inclined at 35 degrees to the cylinder axis, operated by a desmo system via a vertical shaft and eccentrics. Output was 112 hp at 4000 rpm. The cylinder dimensions of the straight-eight tipo 402 were 65 × 112 mm. Its crankshaft ran in ten roller bearings, with the big ends in two-piece rollers. A two-pump dry sump system was responsible for the lubrication, as in the four-cylinder 401. There were two 39-mm valves per cylinder inclined at 51 degrees, operated by two overhead camshafts via finger type followers. Output was 120 hp at 4400 rpm. Despite a crankshaft running in ten main bearings, the length of the straight-eight could be restricted to 92 cm. But the eight was much heavier than the four.

Power in both cases was transmitted through a multiplate clutch and a four-speed gearbox to a torque-tube rear axle: There was only one universal joint at the rear of the gearbox and the rear springs were free to perform with no extraneous loading. Laurence Pomeroy wrote: "The breakaway from Henry design in the Fiat transmission was as marked as in the engine layout."[2] Wheelbase was 275 cm, track 140 cm, tires 820 × 120 front and 835 × 120 or 835 × 135 rear, dry weight of the four 810 kg, of the eight 920 kg. The straight-eight heralded the end for the Henry school of thought, and the beginning of an Italian domination which was to prevail, with brief interruptions, for many years. The shape of the body was evolved through extensive wind tunnel research by the Fiat *Aviazione* department and its chief engineer Celestino Rosatelli. It departed from usual practice in carrying a clean underside from front to rear, and a flat-sided, wedge-shaped tapering tail, ending in a vertical knife-edge, setting a fashion soon to oust the narrowing cigar style.

Fiat entered a team of straight-eights in the 1921 French Grand Prix but the cars did not start. Their preparation suffered from the difficult political and social conditions during the famous *Biennio Rosso*.[3] The Fiat 801/402 appeared in the late summer of 1921, in the speed week called *Gran Premio d'Italia Automobilistico* which took place on a 17.3-km course near Brescia. The meeting opened with the main event, the 30-lap *Gran Premio* for 3-liter racers, on Sunday, 4 September. A flying kilometer race followed on Wednesday 7 September, then the 20-lap voiturette race limited to 1.5 liters on Thursday, and the 25-lap Gran Premio

Opposite: 2 April 1922 — Targa Florio, Sicily. Biagio Nazzaro's Fiat, a 3-liter eight Tipo 801/402. He left the road in lap 2 (Mercedes-Benz Classic).

Gentlemen on Sunday, 11 September. Ballot, STD, Duesenberg, Fiat, Scat and Itala had the intention to start in the Gran Premio, but only six cars turned up, three Fiats and three Ballots. The straight-eight Fiats were driven by Pietro Bordino, Ugo Sivocci and Louis Wagner, with Ambrogio Bruno, Morganti and Evasio Lampiano acting as riding mechanics. Ballot shipped a trio of straight-eights for Goux, Chassagne and DePalma. In lap 12, Bordino and his Fiat set a new lap record in 6 min 54 sec. But the engine failed in lap 16. Sivocci's Fiat went out in lap 18. Wagner finished third, nearly ten minutes behind Goux on the Ballot.

On 21 February 1922, Pietro Bordino and the eight-cylinder Fiat appeared on the Beverly Hills speedway: "The Italian speed hero, Pietro Bordino, continued to shine forth on the boards of the Beverly speed bowl yesterday afternoon, doing many laps of the course at 40 seconds, without any effort."[4] On 5 March, Bordino started in the 250-miler, but withdrew in lap 139 with engine trouble, after whirling around the speedway in 38⅘ sec, averaging 117 mph, the fastest time ever made on a 1.25-mile track by a 183-inch car. On 2 April, again at Beverly Hills, Bordino finished fourth in a 50-miler and won a 25-miler in 13 min 4 sec, ahead of Milton in a Miller. On 27 April, Bordino took fifth in a 150-miler on the 1-mile board speedway at Fresno, California. On 7 May, in the 100-miler on the 1.25-mile board speedway at Cotati, California, he retired in lap 72 because of engine trouble, but won the 50-miler in 23 min 13 sec, ahead of Harry Hartz in a Duesenberg. It was surprising that Bordino and the Fiat did not start in the 1922 Indianapolis 500.

The next Grand Prix racer built by the Fiat racing department was ready in time for the French Grand Prix. The new Grand Prix formula for the 1922 Grand Prix de l'ACF specified a maximum displacement of two liters, a minimum weight of 650 kg whereby the driver and his riding mechanic had to weigh at least 120 kg, and a maximum rear overhang of 1.5 meters. Chassis tipo 803 and engine tipo 403 were the designations for a 1.5-liter voiturette racer with dimensions of 65 × 112 mm, in principle a straight-eight cut in half. Thus the 2-liter Grand Prix racer which came next was called 804/404. The 2-liter was a six, based on the preceding straight-eight. The cylinders were still welded up, and were grouped in two blocks of three. The bore remained unchanged at 65 mm, and the stroke was reduced from 112 to 100 mm. The crankshaft ran in eight roller bearings, the diameter of the journals being 40 mm, with a roller diameter of 10 mm and a roller width of 18.5 mm. While the main bearings were lubricated directly by the two-pump dry sump, the big ends had to be content with the oil trapped in circular grooves in the crank cheeks and supplied by centrifugal pressure. The big ends had rollers of 8 mm diameter and 18 mm width. Initially the split cages of the roller bearings were made of bronze, later of duralumin. The connecting rods were 223 mm long. The two overhead camshafts were driven by a combination of vertical shaft and two inclined shafts, a Y formation. Each camshaft ran in seven roller bearings. There were two 39-mm valves per cylinder, inclined at 51 degrees to the cylinder axis, opened via cam followers and closed by three springs. The intake opened at TDC and closed 50 degrees after BDC, giving a total opening of 230 degress; the exhaust opened 50 degrees before BDC and closed 10 degrees after TDC; overlap was 10 degrees. For the French Grand Prix the 2-liter Fiat delivered 92 hp at 4500 rpm with a compression ratio of 7:1. In the French Grand Prix the Fiat started with one carburetor: "Originally it had been intended to use two carbureters, one for each group of three cylinders, but in the race a single Fiat carbureter was employed, with an unusual type of cast aluminum intake manifold of small section forming a double 'Y.'"[5] Later in the season the output was increased to 112 hp at 5000 rpm. Cappa subjected one engine to a 5-hour full-throttle bench test at 5000 rpm.

Power was transmitted by a multi-disc clutch to a four-speed gearbox mounted in unit with the engine. A sphere at the back of the gearbox took the drive of the torque tube rear axle: "For the first time in racing Fiat used an enclosed propeller shaft. Drive was transmitted through the spherical head, just back of the gearbox."[6] Since the front brakes imposed considerable stresses on the axle beam, Cappa fixed upon a tubular front axle. The dimensions of the car were kept as small as possible: wheelbase 250 cm, track 120 cm, tires from Pirelli, either clincher bead 760 × 90 front and 765 × 105 rear, or straight side cord 30 × 3½ front and 31 × 4 rear. Dry weight was 660 kg, nearly matching the prescribed minimum. The Fiat aviation department "produced a body of exceptional lightness and perfect lines. To get the best shape, the main frame members gradually swept in from the center to the rear, so as to follow the outline of the tail. The mechanician's seat was staggered about 8 in., and the space back of the driver's seat was used for the mechanician to obtain a grip. The fire extinguisher and a thermos bottle were carried in this compartment.... The Fiat arrangement of riveting the exhaust collector to the body, thus making use of it to stiffen this latter, was very good."[7]

The 1922 Grand Prix de l'ACF was run on Saturday, 15 July, near Strasbourg, over 60 laps of a 13.38-km triangle course through Entzheim, Innenheim and Duttlenheim, a total of 802.8 km. Fiat entered three cars for Pietro Bordino, Felice Nazzaro and Biagio Nazzaro, Felice's nephew. The race began at 8 A.M. with a rolling start, a mass start for the first time in Europe. At the halfway point the Fiats were in the first three places, the others far behind. Then, in lap 52, Biagio Nazzaro ran off the road when the rear axle failed, and was killed.

15 July 1922 — Grand Prix de l'ACF, Strasbourg. Felice Nazzaro at the wheel of the winning Fiat, a 2-liter six Tipo 804/404 (Mercedes-Benz Classic).

2 July 1923 — Grand Prix de l'ACF, Tours. *La Squadra Fiat* in the village of Semblançay: no. 4, Pietro Bordino with mechanic Bruno; no. 9, Enrico Giaccone with Carignano; and no. 14, Carlo Salamano with Ferretti (Mercedes-Benz Classic).

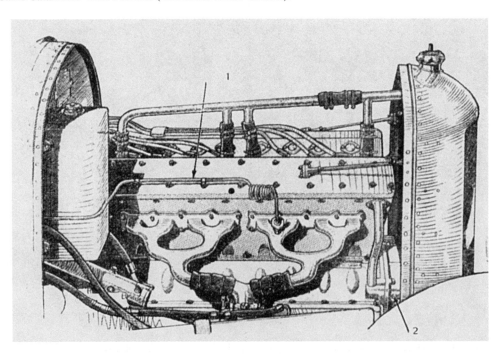

1923 Fiat Tipo 405 engine, a supercharged 2-liter straight-eight (*Allgemeine Automobil-Zeitung*).

Shortly afterwards Bordino also went off the course with a broken rear axle. Felice Nazzaro, ignorant of his nephew's death, won in 6 h 17 min 17 sec, nearly one hour ahead of Pierre de Vizcaya in a Bugatti. The rear axle of the Fiat was made from thin gauge pressings welded together. At Strasbourg, the flange at the wheel end was not strong enough and broke away, so that Biagio Nazzaro's and Bordino's cars lost a rear wheel. The winning Fiat changed two rear tires as a precaution.

In September 1922 the Gran Premio d'Italia was held for the first time on the new *autodromo* at Monza near Milan, in the park of the Villa Reale. The autodrome combined a fast road course with a banked speedway, a 4.5-km *pista stradale* with a 5.5-km *anello*. The autodromo, which had been completed within 110 days between May and August 1922, was opened on 3 September with the Gran Premio Vetturette. The Grand Premio delle Nazioni for motorcycles followed on 8 September, the Gran Premio dell'Automobile Club d'Italia for Grand Prix cars on 10 September, and the formula free Gran Premio d'Autunno on 1 October. Three improved 2-liter Fiats rolled to the start of the Gran Premio d'Italia driven by Bordino, Nazzaro and Enrico Giaccone, whose car did not leave the lineup. Pietro Bordino completed 80 laps or 800 km in 5 h 43 min 13 sec, averaging 139.848 km/h. Nazzaro finished second, 8 min 22 sec back, then Pierre de Vizcaya in a Bugatti far behind.

Fiat's 1923 racer was a supercharged 2-liter straight-eight, chassis tipo 805 and engine tipo 405. Of course, the block was still composed of steel cylinders, grouped in two blocks of four, 60 × 87.5 mm. The two-piece crankshaft ran in nine roller bearings. The diameter of both the main journals and the crank pins was increased from 40 mm in the tipo 404 to 44 mm in the tipo 405. The connecting rods were still made of chrome nickel steel and shortened both absolutely and relatively, to a length of 165 mm. A Wittig vane type blower coupled to the nose of the crankshaft ran at engine speed and pumped air into the Memini carburetor. The new straight-eight delivered 130 hp at 5500 rpm. Surprisingly, the weight of the engine was reduced from 180 kg for the older six to 170 kg. Wheelbase was 262 cm, track 120 cm, tires Pirelli straight side cord 29 × 4 front, 29 × 4½ rear, dry weight 700 kg. The 1923 French Grand Prix took place on Monday, 2 July, on a triangle course near Tours, covering 35 laps of 22.83 km, a total of 799 km. Fiat entered three tipi 805 for Pietro Bordino, Carlo Salamano and Enrico Giaccone, with their riding mechanics Bruno, Ferretti and Carignano. In April, Bordino had used one of the older 2-liter sixes to turn a few laps at Tours. The new eight-cylinder Fiats arrived on Wednesday, 20 June, by road from Turin over the Alps. Bordino did the fastest practice lap in 9 min 56 sec, so there was no surprise when he took the lead in the first lap of the race and, after five laps, was 2 min 20 sec ahead of Kenelm Lee Guinness in the Sunbeam, and 4 minutes ahead of his teammate Giaccone. But the road surface broke up and in lap 8 a stone wrecked the crankcase of Bordino's Fiat. After lap 11, when Guinness came to the pits for fuel, oil and water, Giaccone and Salamano took first and second places. In lap 17 Giaccone was in the pits to fill up with fuel and get new plugs and rear tires. In the next lap he stopped again to work on the carburetor. The Fiat refused to restart and withdrew because of a broken exhaust valve. In lap 33 Salamano and the remaining Fiat came to a standstill nearly a kilometer away from the pits. Mechanic Ferretti ran to the pits for a can of fuel. But the engine of the Fiat did not restart. Henry Segrave and Albert Divo took the first two places for Sunbeam.

Looking ahead to the Gran Premio d'Italia e d'Europa to be held at Monza on 9 September 1923, the Wittig vane type blower was replaced by a Roots type. In a practice session on 27 August, both Bordino and Giaccone had serious accidents. Bordino escaped with a broken arm, but Giaccone was killed. Three Fiats started in the Gran Premio: Nazzaro,

Salamano, and Bordino with a bandaged arm. With the Roots blower the Fiat was good for 220 km/h on the straights. Carlo Salamano completed 80 laps of 10 km in 5 h 27 min 38 sec, 24 seconds ahead of his teammate Nazzaro who burst a front tire two laps from the end, and 5 min 13 sec ahead of Jimmy Murphy in a Miller. *La Stampa* praised: "La magnifica vittoria torinese a Monza."[8]

For the 1924 season the Fiat 805/405 was refined and its output increased to 145 hp at 5500 rpm. In practice for the French Grand Prix at Lyon, Bordino crashed his Fiat which had to be sent back to Turin on a lorry to be completely rebuilt. Four cars started in Lyon on 3 August 1924, with Nazzaro and riding mechanic Carignano, Bordino and Bruno, Pastore and Mauro, and Marchisio and Lorenzo. Bordino led the race between lap 4 and lap 10, being forced to retire with defective brakes. Nazzaro went out for the same reason, Onesimo Marchisio dropped out with engine trouble, and Cesare Pastore left the road. The 805/405 finished its career in America. On 1 March 1925, Bordino finished sixth in a 250-miler at Culver City. On 11 May, in a 250-miler at Charlotte, North Carolina, the Fiat broke its rear axle in lap 182. And at Indianapolis, on 30 May, Bordino finished tenth, 20 minutes behind DePaolo's yellow Duesenberg, the *Banana Wagon*.

When the 1.5-liter formula was announced in 1925, Fiat planned to use a two-stroke engine. With Cappa, Bertarione and Jano employed elsewhere, the design came into being under the direction of Tranquilo Zerbi, assisted by Giuseppe Sola and Scipione Treves. The engine was designated tipo 451. It was an opposed piston six-cylinder, with a bore of 52 mm and two geared crankshafts with a stroke of 58.5 mm. Bench tests gave 152 hp at 5200

3 August 1924 — Grand Prix de l'ACF, Lyon. Pietro Bordino and his Fiat coming down the *Esses* (Mercedes-Benz Classic).

Top: 3 August 1924 — Grand Prix de l'ACF, Lyon. Onesimo Marchisio's Fiat ahead of Segrave's Sunbeam on the start-finish straight. *Bottom*: 28 June 1925 — Grand Prix de Belgique, Spa. Antonio Ascari at the wheel of the winning Alfa P2. Opening the hood mechanic Giulio Ramponi, and behind him in the pit, with cap and bow tie, is Vittorio Jano (Mercedes-Benz Classic).

rpm, 170 at 6000, with the Roots blower delivering a boost of 1.37 bar. But the engine was unreliable, generating too much heat on the exhaust side. During 1927, Zerbi designed an alternative four-stroke engine, the tipo 406 — a double-six composed of two vertical banks of six steel cylinders with dimensions of 50 × 63 mm, with two crankshafts geared together and three overhead camshafts for both cylinder blocks. The central camshaft was mounted between the banks and was responsible for the 30-mm intake valves of both sides. The two outer camshafts operated the exhaust valves. It was surprising that Zerbi and his team did not rely on roller bearings anymore. The built-up crankshafts each ran in four plain bearings, with one-piece connecting rods. A Roots blower was mounted at the front of the engine and delivered to two intake pipes between the banks. There were two exhaust pipes of oval section, on the outer side of each bank. With compression of 7.25:1 and a boost of 1.88 bar, the 406 delivered 175 hp at 8500 rpm; with a compression of 7.5:1 the output was 187 at 8500. The double-six weighed 170 kg. With a four-speed gearbox it was mounted in a frame designated tipo 806, with a wheelbase of 240 cm and track of 130 cm; tires were 29 × 4½ front, 29 × 5.00 rear. The front semi-elliptic springs slid between rollers instead of shackles at their rear ends. The Fiat was extremely low. Dry weight was 700 kg. On paper, the Fiat 806/406 was the most powerful and the fastest car built under the European 1.5-liter formula.

On 4 September 1927, at Monza, Bordino drove the 806/406 to victory in the Gran Premio di Milano, winning the first heat over 10 laps of 5 km in 20 min 4 sec, and the final over the same distance in 19 min 43 sec. Three 806/406s were entered for the last race of the 1927 season, the European finale of the 1.5-liter formula, the British Grand Prix to be held at Brooklands on 1 October 1927. But the Fiat entries were scratched since the racing department was too preoccupied with the Schneider Trophy seaplane race. In any case, only one car was assembled. It was rumored that Fiat president Giovanni Agnelli was furious at the work put into the new racer at a time when the economic depression began to reach Turin, and ordered the cars to be scrapped. And, of course, Agnelli was furious at the successes of Sunbeam and Alfa Romeo which had won the French Grand Prix in 1923 and 1924.

Ernest Henry's last racing car design, the 1922 Sunbeam, was no match for the Fiat 804/404, although the Sunbeam was much better and faster than its result at Strasbourg suggested. After the defeat in the French Grand Prix, Sunbeam director Louis Coatalen immediately tried to hire Fiat engineer Vincenzo Bertarione with the objective to design a copy of the 1922 Grand Prix winner. Bertarione agreed since Fiat refused a pay rise, and persuaded his confrère Walter Becchia to come along. Working at Wolverhampton in England as well as in the Parisian suburb Suresnes, Bertarione and Becchia designed a green-painted Fiat, an improved tipo 804/404. For the Sunbeam, the cylinder dimensions were changed from 65 × 100 mm to 67 × 94 mm while the block was still composed by two blocks of three. The crankshaft was carried on eight roller bearings, with the big ends in two-piece rollers. The Y-formation to drive the camshaft was replaced by a train of spur gears, and the valve angle was reduced from 102 to 96 degrees, with valve diameter at 39 mm. Output was 108 hp at 5000 rpm, with compression of 7.3:1, and using a single Solex carburetor. Bertarione's engine was combined with a new cone clutch, three-speed gearbox and Hotchkiss rear axle. In comparison to Henry's 1922 chassis, the wheelbase was unchanged at 250 cm, but the track was larger, 130 cm front and 120 cm rear. The tires were 765 × 105 Michelins, and dry weight was 660 kg. Sunbeam entered three cars in the 1923 French Grand Prix for Henry Segrave, Kenelm Lee Guinness and Frenchman Albert Divo, with their riding mechanics Dutoit, Perkins and Hivernat.

Divo tested an unpainted prototype at Brooklands by the middle of May 1923, and on the Grand Prix course near Tours early in June. Before driving down to Tours for the official practice, which opened on Sunday, 17 June, and ended on Friday, 22 June, Guinness and Segrave stopped at the Darracq factory in Suresnes for some adjustments. Segrave turned a practice lap in 10 min 30 sec, 14 seconds slower than Bordino in the supercharged Fiat. The *pesage*, or scrutineering, was held on Friday, 29 June, at Semblançay. The Sunbeam team lodged in the *Boeuf Couronné*, the village inn at Neuvy le Roi, a few kilometers to the north. On Monday, 2 July, the 17 starters were led toward the starting line by champion motorcyclist Meunier riding an Alcyon. He drew to the side and René de Knyff dropped the flag. Segrave fell back because of a slipping clutch. Divo's mechanic, Hivernat, was knocked out by a flying stone, and replaced by Jules Moriceau. When Bordino in the Fiat fell out in lap 8, Guinness took the lead for two laps. Then it was the turn of the two remaining Fiats, with the Sunbeams behind in third, fourth and fifth. When Divo stopped for fuel, he was unable to unscrew the tank cap but continued by filling the reserve tank on each lap. By the end of the race, Segrave's clutch trouble vanished and since the Sunbeam had not been highly stressed in the early stages, it was now running well. But Salamano was so far ahead that there was no chance of catching him. Segrave did not believe his eyes when he saw the Fiat by the roadside: "Salamano stopped two kilometers from the grandstand!"[9] Segrave won in 6 h 35 min 19 sec, with Divo second, Friderich in a Bugatti third, and Guinness fourth because of gearbox troubles. Segrave drove his Sunbeam back to London where it was displayed in the Hanover Square showroom. On 28 October, Divo and Sunbeam won the Spanish Grand Prix at Sitges.

For the 1924 season, the Sunbeam retained its 2-liter six with dimensions of 67 × 94 mm, and was upgraded by a Roots blower. The application of the blower was directed by Captain J.S. Irving, head of the Sunbeam Experimental Department at Wolverhampton. In a first step, Irving followed Fiat and Mercedes practice by placing the carburetor on the pressurized side of the blower, between the supercharger and the engine. The output was increased by a few percent to 115 hp. In a second step, the carburetor was placed on the atmospheric side of the blower. As a consequence the blower ran cooler and the latent heat of the fuel lowered the temperature of the mixture in the induction pipe. Using the same boost of 6 psi, the power increased to 138 hp. In addition, the output throughout the range was improved. A large Solex barrel throttle carburetor supplied the mixture, whereby a small addition of oil to the fuel lubricated the Roots compressor. The power transmission was completely new, with Hele-Shaw clutch, four-speed gearbox and torque tube rear axle. The frame, too, was new, with the wheelbase of 260 cm, though the track remained unchanged at 130 cm front, 120 cm rear. The center section of the front axle was tubular now, instead of H-section. The Rudge-Whitworth wheels were fitted with 765 × 105 Rapson beaded-edge tires.

The supercharged Sunbeam made its first appearance on 17 May 1924 in the Aston Clinton hillclimb, with Dario Resta putting up the fastest time of the day. In the French Grand Prix on 3 August, the Sunbeams were the only cars with the carburetor on the atmospheric side of the blower. The three cars were driven by Segrave, Guinness and Resta, with the riding mechanics Marocchi, Perkins and Ledu. When one engine broke up during practice, Louis Coatalen imposed a limit of 5200 rpm. The day before the race, a Bosch representative persuaded Coatalen to replace the magnetos. Segrave took the lead during the first three laps, then stopped at the pits to replace the plugs. His Sunbeam misfired. Guinness took the lead in lap 16, suffered a puncture, and retired because of a defective drive shaft ball bearing. Resta went out in lap 33 with engine trouble. Segrave finished fifth. The night after the race, Captain Irving got up, went down to the garage and replaced Segrave's magneto with the original one. The Sunbeam started immediately and ran without any trace of a misfire. The new Bosch magnetos had faulty wiring between their primary and secondary circuits.

A few weeks after the French Grand Prix, on 2 September 1924, at Brooklands, Dario Resta took the wheel of one of the Sunbeams and achieved new 2-liter class E records: the standing kilometer at 71.49 mph, the standing mile at 83.04 mph, the flying kilometer at 121.18 mph, the flying mile at 114.56 mph, and the flying 5-miles at 114.23 mph. Next day, on 3 September, Resta attempted to attack longer distance records. In the fourth lap a rear tire left the rim. The Sunbeam hit the iron fence tail first. The fuel tank was split and caught fire. Dario Resta was killed. A broken duralumin security bolt was found on the track. On 27 September, in lap 11 of the San Sebastian Grand Prix, Guinness and his Sunbeam left the road. Mechanic Perkins was killed, Guinness seriously injured. Teammate Segrave won the race, covering 35 laps of the 17.745-km Lasarte Circuit in 6 h 1 min 19 sec. For the 1925 season, the Sunbeam was just polished and had a hard time against the Alfa Romeos and Delages. Giulio Masetti finished third in the 1925 French Grand Prix at Montlhéry.

The 1925 season was the last for the 2-liter formula. The 1926 formula restricted the displacement to 1.5 liter. The new car representing the STD group started under the name Talbot since it was built at Suresnes and not at Wolverhampton, although the engine was bench tested by the "Experimental Dept., Sunbeam Motor Car Co. Ltd., Wolverhampton."[10] Like the Sunbeam, the Talbot was designed by Vincenzo Bertarione and his assistant Walter Becchia. It was a straight-eight composed of steel cylinders, 56 × 75.5 mm (the French magazine *Omnia* quoted 56 × 75.7 mm), in four blocks of two, with welded-on water jackets. The two-piece crankshaft ran in ten roller bearings, with a bearing on each side of the camshaft drive. The big ends ran in two-piece rollers. Lubrication was via a two-pump dry sump including a large finned cooler outside the body, on the left-hand side. The two overhead camshafts each ran in five two-piece roller bearings, operated two valves per cylinder via cam followers, and were driven by a train of gears at the rear of the engine. The Roots blower was mounted at the front of the engine. Bertarione and Becchia took the boost pressure up to 1.92 bar (1.92 ata): With a "BP Special"[11] gasoline-benzene mixture, a 49-mm choke and a 55-mm intake pipe, the 1.5-liter Talbot delivered 137 hp at 6500 rpm and 140 hp at 6800 rpm. Compression was 6.5:1 and the manifold temperature 87° C. With another fuel, a mixture of 40 percent methanol, 40 percent benzene and 20 percent gasoline, a 55-mm choke and 59-mm intake pipe resulting in a rise in fuel consumption, the output was 144 hp at 6500 rpm. Compression in this case was 7:1 and the manifold temperature 50° C, and the boost pressure dropped by 0.2 bar.

Power was transmitted by a multiplate clutch to a four-speed gearbox. The whole engine-transmission line was mounted offset across the chassis center line, with the front end of the engine slightly to the right-hand side and the drive shaft to the left-hand side of the center line, resulting in a low position for the driver, whose seat cushion rested in the underpan, eight inches from the ground. The frame itself differed from the conventional channel-section type looping over the axles. It was made up of ladder-section side members, 2-mm pressings similar to the Lancia Lambda frame, braced laterally by steel tubes and girder cross members. The front and rear axles passed through the side members. The front axle was formed from two tapering tubular halves flanged together. The half-elliptic springs passed through forged eyes. The rear half-elliptics were underslung. Wheelbase was 262 cm, track was 127 cm front and 124 cm rear, dry weight was 720 kg, and tires were 765 × 120 Michelins, or sometimes 29 × 5 or 30 × 4.75 Dunlops. In contrast to the competitor from Delage, the Talbot was pure Fiat school. Depending on the point of view it was either an extrapolation of the Sunbeam six or a development of the 805/405 Fiat eight. Three cars were built, including a large amount of spares.

The Talbot turned up in the British Grand Prix, the first formula Grand Prix staged on English soil, at Brooklands, on Saturday, 7 August 1926, a 110-lap race on a 4.21-km or 2.616-mile circuit, for a total distance of 463.1 km. The course featured the finishing straight which diagonally bisected the Brooklands oval and cut the home banking, the main Railway straight, the long sweep round the Byfleet banking, and two chicanes built from large piles of sand on the finishing straight. It was run counterclockwise. Three Talbots were entered as British and painted in British green. The drivers were Henry Segrave, Albert Divo and Jules Moriceau, their erstwhile mechanic. Moriceau, who was born on 2 January 1887 in Nantes, served an apprenticeship at Mors and Darracq, finished fourth in the 1919 Indianapolis 500 as riding mechanic for Louis Wagner in the 4.9-liter Ballot, then joined Talbot as *chef des essais*, or head of the test department. At the first turn of the first lap of this first British Grand Prix, the front axle of Moriceau's Talbot broke under braking. Segrave's Talbot emitted long yellow flames from its exhaust when braking for the corners, but was good for the fastest lap at 85.99 mph. The Talbots left the Delages on acceleration, but cut-out much earlier for the bends. Segrave as well as Divo withdrew because of supercharger trouble.

The next important race for Talbot was the 1927 French Grand Prix at Montlhéry, on 3 July. Three racers were entered for Albert Divo, Louis Wagner and "Williams." Williams' real name was William Charles Frederic Grover-Williams. He was born on 16 January 1903 in the Paris suburb of Montrouge. His English father worked as a groom to a Russian diplomat in London, then moved to Paris, married a French woman and founded a car rental business. The young Williams worked as a chauffeur for the portrait painter William Orpen, began his racing career riding a Harley-Davidson motorcycle, and drove a Bugatti to second in the 1926 Provence Grand Prix. Later, in November 1929, he married Orpen's mistress, Yvonne Aubicq. Obviously Orpen was feeling generous since he gave the bride not only his chauffeur but also a house in the Rue Weber and his Rolls-Royce. In any case Orpen drank too much and, in 1931, died in a nursing home, aged only 53.

The day before the Grand Prix, Divo won the 125-km formula free race at Montlhéry in 1 h 2 min 20 sec, averaging 120.3 km/h, ahead of a young Louis Chiron in a 2.3-liter Bugatti. Divo also set the best lap in 6 min 7 sec, a speed of 122.6 km/h. In the Grand Prix, Divo immediately took the lead, but only for three laps. He withdrew in lap 23 because of a broken blower, Wagner following in lap 42 because of a leaking cooling system. Despite being forced to stop several times to change his Talbot's spark plugs, Williams, who shared the car with Moriceau, finished fourth behind three Delages. Montlhéry was the last appearance of the Talbots as works cars. Financial straits prevented their full development.

The three straight-eight Talbots along with spare parts and two older 1.5-liter fours were sold to Emilio Materassi, who founded his own scuderia, or stable. Materassi was born in Borgo San Lorenzo near Florence, on 1 November 1894. It was there that in 1923 he opened the Autogarage Nazionale in the via dei Poggi, representing Itala. His first racing car was an Itala special, the "Italona," which was powered by one bank of an older Hispano V-8 aero-engine. During the 1928 season, Materassi drove a straight-eight Talbot to fourth at Alessandria, first in the Circuito di Mugello, third in the Premio Reale di Roma, and first in the Circuito di Montenero, while his teammate Luigi Arcangeli won the Circuito di Cremona and took second in the Coppa Acerbo. Thus the Talbots were far more successful under private ownership than they had been as works cars. On 9 September 1928, Materassi was at the wheel of one of his Talbots in the Italian Grand Prix at Monza. In lap 17 he was passing Giulio Foresti's Bugatti on the start-finish straight when the Talbot suddenly shot off course and dashed into the crowd. Materassi and 27 spectators were killed.

There was another racer which followed the features of the six-cylinder Fiat 804/404, but not as closely as the Sunbeam. It was built in Italy, by Alfa Romeo in Milan, and designed by Alfa's technical director Giuseppe Merosi and his assistant Antonio Santoni. Merosi was born in Piacenza on 17 December 1872. He had worked for Fiat between 1904 and 1906, then for Bianchi until October 1909 before entering the A.L.F.A., the Societa Anonima Lombarda Fabbrica Automobili. In 1915 the A.L.F.A. was taken over by Nicola Romeo, a manufacturer of railway and mining equipment. After the war the A.L.F.A. cars were offered under the name Alfa Romeo. The 1923 Alfa racer was named GPR, Gran Premio Romeo, or P1. The six-cylinder was composed of two blocks of three, 65 × 100 mm. The crankshaft was not counterbalanced and ran in seven main bearings, four roller bearings and three combined roller and ball bearings in the middle and at the ends. Two overhead camshafts were driven by a train of spur gears at the rear of the engine, and operated two valves per cylinder inclined at 45 degrees to the cylinder axis. The GPR delivered 80 hp at 4800 rpm and was mounted in a rather sturdy and heavy frame: wheelbase 265 cm, track 124 cm, tires 28 × 4½ front, 28 × 5 rear. Dry weight was 850 kg, 200 kg above the minimum, nearly 200 kg more than the Fiat. The GPR was tested for the first time on 16 August 1923, at Monza, with Antonio Ascari, Giuseppe Campari and Ugo Sivocci at the wheel. But on 8 September, the day before the Italian Grand Prix, Sivocci left the track, crashed into a tree and was killed on the spot. Mechanic Guatta survived, seriously injured. Nicola Romeo withdrew the Alfa entries.

In Milan, Giorgio Rimini was responsible for Alfa's racing department. He was Alfa's commercial director, the *deus ex machina*, and Nicola Romeo's right hand man. Like Romeo, he came from Naples, the son of a director of the then famous Magazzini Mele. According to Enzo Ferrari he was "a young Catanian engineer, olive skinned, with enormously dilated eyes and a cigarette always glued to his lips."[12] Meanwhile Ferrari worked for Alfa too. After his Targa Florio experience in a CMN in 1919, Ferrari drove an older Isotta-Fraschini in 1920, before taking the wheel of a works Alfa Romeo in the 1920 Targa. The 22-year-old Ferrari promptly finished second behind Guido Meregalli in a Nazzaro, catapulting him to the top level in a flash. In 1922 and 1923 Ferrari was an Alfa works driver beside Campari, Ascari and Sivocci. It was Rimini who gave Ferrari the specific assignment to find a good engineer for the racing department. Ferrari's friend Guglielmo Carraroli, who served as his mechanic in the Isotta-Fraschini in 1920, made contact with Luigi Bazzi, who worked in the Fiat racing department. Following a dispute with Guido Fornaca during the 1923 French Grand Prix at Tours, Bazzi switched over to Alfa.

Bazzi proposed hiring one of his former coworkers, Vittorio Jano: "There is a man of great worth at Fiat, who is being treated a bit as a subordinate. Go talk to him."[13] Ferrari contacted Jano and in September 1923 went to Turin, to the Via San Massimo. The door was opened by Jano's wife Rosina. Jano recalled: "The first one to come to me about leaving Fiat was Ferrari. But he was not in final authority and I was not happy about leaving Turin. I did not leave until Romeo sent his vice-president to me."[14] Alfa's vice-president Fucito offered him 3600 lire per month, plus lodging and other inducements. At Fiat, Jano was earning 1800. It was not hard for him to accept. Secondo Molino, a young draftsman, came along with him. Jano was born in Turin on 22 April 1891. His father was the technical head of one of Turin's two arsenals. At age 18, in 1909, Vittorio completed his technical studies at the Istituto Professionale Operaio di Torino. He worked as a draftsman at Rapid, and after two years moved on to Fiat where, by 1923, he headed a design group. Jano left Fiat by the end of September 1923 and in October took up his duties at Alfa in Milan. Romeo told him: "I don't pretend that you should build a world-beater for me, but I want you to build me a Grand Prix car that will give this company a competitive image."[15]

Jano designed an improved Fiat 805/405: "When my engine was born, people said, 'Hah! It's a Fiat-Alfa Romeo!' But when the Fiat people saw it they said, 'It's not ours.' After all, my school had been Fiat, but after observing what others had done, I added something from my own."[16] The Alfa was named P2. Jano assembled the cylinders in blocks of two instead of four, to avoid thermal distortions. Cylinder dimensions were 61 × 85 mm. The two-piece crankshaft ran in ten bronze caged roller bearings, big ends in two-piece rollers, with lubrication via a two-pump dry sump. The two overhead camshafts were driven by a train of spur gears at the rear of the engine. Each camshaft ran in ten roller bearings and operated two 35.5-mm valves per cylinder. The valves were inclined at 52 degrees to the cylinder axis. There were three concentric springs per valve, a weak point in the Fiat, which could not exceed 5500 rpm and used to break a lot of them within a race distance of 800 km. The valve springs in the Alfa were higher and of larger section wire, resulting in lighter spring loading. The Alfa was able to reach 6500 rpm. A smaller Roots blower was driven at 1.235 times crankshaft speed, producing a pressure of 0.75 bar. The first engine was assembled in March 1924 and delivered 85 hp at 3000 rpm, 115 at 4000, and 134 hp at 5200 rpm, with a compression ratio of 6:1 and a single Memini carburetor. The first, still unpainted car left the shop at Il Portello on 2 June. The four-speed gearbox had ratios of 2.88, 1.91, 1.27 and 1:1. Fuel capacity was 145 liters and oil capacity 45 liters. Wheelbase was 263 cm, front track 130 cm, rear track 120 cm. Pirelli supplied the low pressure balloon tires, 29 × 5.25 front, 29 or 30 × 6.00 rear. Dry weight was 750 kg.

On 4 June the first prototype of the P2 was painted red. It was shipped to Monza for trials, and then to the hillclimb between Parma and Poggio di Berceto. A second P2 was unpainted when it started in the Circuito di Cremona on 9 June 1924, a race of five laps of 64.3 km. Antonio Ascari, with Luigi Bazzi as riding mechanic, won in 2 h 2 min 4 sec and covered 10 kilometers in 3 min 4.6 sec at an average of 195 km/h. On 13 July, Giuseppe Campari started in the Coppa Acerbo at Pescara, but did not finish.

Alfa entered four cars in the Grand Prix de l'ACF et d'Europe which was held near Lyon on Sunday, 3 August 1924, and consisted of 35 laps of 23.145 km, a total of 810 km. Three drivers were confirmed, Ascari, Campari and Louis Wagner, with the riding mechanics Giulio Ramponi, Marinoni and Sozzi. The driver of the fourth car was to be either Giulio Masetti, Gastone Brilli-Peri, or Enzo Ferrari, who was *pilota di riserva* (reserve driver). Ferrari was confirmed in the first week of July. On 18 July he turned a few laps at the wheel of a P2: "I did more than one lap of practice, with the faithful Bazzi beside me. I was struck by a powerful nervous exhaustion. I went to do the trials, had to return home. I had the courage to telegraph and to say, 'I don't feel up to it,' and I didn't go."[17] Four days later, on 22 July, when Ferrari was already back in his hometown Modena, the P2 intended for him arrived at Lyon. Ferrari's P2, starting no. 19, appeared for the *pesage*, the scrutineering, with Boninsegna, Ferrari's riding mechanic, at the wheel. But Ferrari stayed at Modena. The comment of the Italian press was brief and dry: "Ferrari dell'Alfa-Romeo è l'unico iscritto alla gara che non prendera il via" (Ferrari of Alfa Romeo is the only entry of the race who does not start).[18]

Twenty racers lined up at 9 o'clock, nine French, seven Italian, three British and one American. As in 1923, it was a rolling start led by two motorcyclists who drew to the side as the cars reached the timekeeper's box. Segrave's green Sunbeam was the first to reappear over the famous hill leading to the hairpin at Les Sept Chemins, then Ascari, Guinness, Campari and Bordino. The Alfas of Ascari and Campari took the lead in lap 20. Ascari went out in lap 34 with a broken magneto drive. Campari won in 7 h 5 min 35 sec, averaging 114.2 km/h, followed by the Delages of Divo and Benoist, and Louis Wagner in the second Alfa, 20 minutes back.

On 19 October 1924, Alfa P2s took the first four places in the Gran Premio d'Italia at Monza, with Ascari, Wagner, the P2 shared by Campari and Pastore, and Minoia. Ascari's car was equipped with two Memini carburetors. Ascari completed the 800-km distance in 5 h 2 min 5 sec, with a fastest lap in 3 min 34 sec, 12 seconds faster than Salamano and the Fiat 805/405 in 1923, 24 seconds faster than Ascari's practice time in the Alfa GPR. The latest Mercedes which started in this 1924 Gran Premio did not have the speed of the Alfas. It was a straight-eight, 62×82.8 mm, largely designed by Ferdinand Porsche, with the usual Mercedes separate steel cylinders, full roller bearing crankshaft, two overhead camshafts, four valves per cylinder and Roots blower sucking through the carburetor. The output was quoted optimistically as 170 hp at 7000 rpm. Wheelbase was 260 cm, track 136 cm. At Monza four cars were driven by Giulio Masetti, Christian Werner, Alfred Neubauer and Louis Zborowski. In lap 44 Zborowski was killed when he left the track in the Lesmo bend. Director Max Sailer retired the other cars.

During the winter of 1924–1925, the P2 was improved in detail. Ascari had called Jano's attention to a fuel offered by the Werner brothers and called "Elcosina."[19] With the new fuel, the blower of the P2 could be run at 1.35 times engine speed and the engine delivered 154 hp at 5500 rpm. Ascari opened the 1925 Grand Prix season by winning the Belgian and European Grand Prix which was held at Spa-Francorchamps on 28 June 1925. "Ascari started as fast as an arrow and within a few meters had distanced the others."[20] Ascari completed 54 laps of 14.98 km in 6 h 42 min 57 sec. Campari finished second, 22 minutes back. Brilli-Peri in the third Alfa was out in lap 18 with a broken leaf spring. There were only seven starters and the four Delages did not finish.

The next race was the Grand Prix de l'ACF on 26 July, on the new autodrome of Linas-Montlhéry in the south of Paris, consisting of 80 laps of 12.5 km, a total of 1000 km. The dry weights of the Alfa trio were 786, 793 and 818 kg, while the Sunbeams weighed 810, 822 and 876 kg, the Delages 918, 940 and 967 kg, and each of the Bugattis 735 kg.[21] Ascari completed the first 20 laps in 2 h 1 min 14 sec, with a best lap in 5 min 50.2 sec. He was 3 min 40 sec ahead of Benoist in the V-12 Delage, 4 minutes ahead of his teammate Campari. André Boillot, who had driven a Peugeot to victory in the *Grand Prix de Tourisme* the week before, was a spectator at the high-speed left-hander at kilometer 9 near the *Hôtellerie de Saint Eutrope* where, in lap 23, Ascari "touched a fencing post of the wooded palisades. The car which was running at 190 kilometers per hour skidded, then turned over and, after ejecting Ascari, fell down on his left leg."[22] Ascari died in the ambulance. Before the race, he had suggested removing the palisades, which had been erected to prevent the drivers from cutting the corners and using parts of the ditch. Alfa Romeo retired the cars of Brilli-Peri and Campari, who was leading after 40 laps. Benoist in the Delage won. On 6 September 1925, Brilli-Peri and Campari took the first two places in the 800-km Gran Premio d'Italia at Monza. Alfa did not built a racer for the new 1.5-liter formula but decided to abstain from Grand Prix racing and concentrate on sports cars. Giuseppe Merosi and Giorgio Rimini left Alfa at the beginning of 1926. Brilli-Peri, Campari, the Swiss hillclimber Hans Kessler, and Varzi drove the P2 privately until 1929. And in 1930 Varzi won the Targa Florio in a modified P2.

Giulio Cesare Cappa left Fiat in 1924 and opened a consulting office in Turin, Via Pier Carlo Boggio. First of all he worked for Itala, designing a 2-liter production car powered by an overhead-valve six, and a *vetture speciale da corsa*. Originally, in 1924, the small 1.1-liter racer was intended for the Conelli brothers, Franz and Caberto. In 1925 Itala took over the project. The engine was a 60-degree V-12, cast in aluminum with steel liners and detachable heads, 46 × 55 mm. The crankshaft ran in seven two-piece roller bearings. Connecting rods were tubular, with the big ends of the main rods running in rollers and the big ends of the secondary rods in bronze bearings. Borgo supplied the pistons. A single camshaft was mounted centrally on cylinder head level. It operated two valves per cylinder via rockers. The valves were arranged in one file and nearly horizontal. With the help of a Roots blower the V-12 delivered 60 hp at 7000 rpm. Power was transmitted via a four-speed gearbox to the front wheels, with independent suspension front and rear via transverse leaf springs. The single-seat frame had a 249 cm wheelbase and track of 120 cm, and rolled on 27 × 4.40 tires. Dry weight was 550 kg. A second version, rebored to 53.5 mm, displaced 1.5 liters, but the Itala voiturette was never fully developed and never raced.

All the racers built according to the Fiat school were pure factory cars requiring highly trained craftsmen and mechanics for the supply of spare parts and for maintenance. Especially the making of the steel cylinders and the mounting of the roller-bearing cranks were not everyone's cup of tea. The Fiats never ended up in private hands. But the Sunbeams, Alfas and Talbots did, with a lot of success, thanks to direct assistance from the factories or support from former factory engineers and mechanics. While the adherents of the Fiat school promoted high-tech engineering, an Italian manufacturer living in Alsace focused on a rather conventional racer and turned it into a big seller: Bugatti.

18

Bugatti's Way Up

At the turn of the century, the huge starter fields of the town-to-town races had created a distinctive market for racing cars. Panhard, Mors and Mercedes were able to sell entire batches of racing cars. The last Bennett and the first Grand Prix races with their restricted starter fields changed the situation, although there were still enough sportsmen who wanted a racing car for the numerous sprints and hillclimbs. During the 1920s, there was a new trend towards production racing cars which were customer-friendly, easy to maintain, standardized, and could be bought off-the-shelf. In America the road races disappeared completely. There were more races now, beside the essential Indianapolis. Two specialists moved into the foreground, Duesenberg and Miller. In 1920 and in 1921, the 183-inch straight-eight Duesenberg was the car of the year. The Duesy not only won the Indy 500, but took the 1921 French Grand Prix. Harry Miller followed suit and offered a production racer which could be used as promotion platform by any sponsored driver or production car manufacturer. In Europe, Bugatti was the first to capitalize on this niche by delivering a Grand Prix racer from stock.

Ettore Arco Isidoro Bugatti was born on 15 September 1881 in Milan, Italy. His father Carlo was an artist and designer of furniture and jewelry. Ettore was not formerly trained in engineering. He worked for De Dietrich at Niederbronn, Alsace, in 1902, for Emil Mathis at Strasbourg in 1905, then for Deutz at Cologne, Germany, in 1907. In the fall of 1909 he launched his own shop at Molsheim, Alsace. Molsheim was German between 1871 and the Great War and French thereafter. In 1910, Bugatti began production of a tiny vehicle closely resembling two 4-cylinder voiturettes which started in the 1908 Grand Prix des Voiturettes at Dieppe, the Swiss Martini and in particular the Italian Isotta. The first Bugatti displaced 1.3 liter with cylinder dimensions of 65 × 100 mm. A single overhead camshaft operated two vertical valves per cylinder, via curved tappets. The crankshaft ran in two ball bearings, the big ends in plain bearings. Bugatti offered the little car as type 13 with a wheelbase of 200 cm, as type 15 with 240 cm, and as type 17 with 255 cm. In all cases the track was 115 cm. In 1913 the engine was modified, receiving a crankshaft running in three white-metal plain bearings. At the same time the half elliptic rear springs of the long types 15 and 17 were replaced by quarter elliptics and the cars renamed types 22 and 23. In 1914 the short chassis type 13 also received the quarter elliptics. In January 1914, the Bugatti appeared in New York, at the Importers' Automobile Salon in the Hotel Astor: "The first appearance in America of this light car, built in Germany. Three complete cars with three passenger 'boat' bodies by Wiederkehr, coachmaker to the Imperial family of Germany."[1]

In addition to the voiturette range, Bugatti mounted a 5-liter (100 × 160 mm) engine, a copy of a Prince Henry Deutz, into reinforced 255-cm frames, with wider 125-cm axles

Early Bugatti type 13 voiturette engine: 65 × 100 mm, 1.3 liter, OHC-head (*Allgemeine Automobil-Zeitung*).

and chain or shaft drive at the customer's choice. The 5-liter became known as type "Garros." Two small intake valves and a large exhaust valve were operated by a single overhead camshaft. Ernest Friderich drove a Garros in the 1914 Indianapolis 500. The Indy engine was restroked to 180 mm, 5.65 liters. The Bugatti was shaft driven. Friderich, born in Paris on 23 October 1886, was a former mechanic at Mathis and Bugatti's right-hand man. Another 5-liter Bugatti was shipped to America in 1915, bought by Charles Fuller, and restroked to 150 mm to comply with the 300-inch formula. It had a wheelbase of 280 cm and was chain driven. It was handled by George Hill in the 1915 Indianapolis race and by Johnny Marquis in Pacific Coast events. Only a handful of 5-liters were built. The 5-liter for the famous French aviator Roland Garros was delivered on 18 September 1913, hence the name. Garros was born on 6 October 1888 in Saint-Denis de La Réunion, on the French island in the East of Madagascar. In 1908 he graduated at the renowned HEC (Hautes Études Commerciales) business school in Paris and opened a Grégoire agency at 6 Avenue de la Grande Armée. On 19 July 1910, Garros got his flying license, no. 147. In October of the same year he sailed for New York, and until the spring of 1911 was one of the attractions at the aviation tournaments at Belmont Park, at Richmond, Virginia, at El Paso, Texas, and Havana. On 23 September 1913, at 5:55 A.M., Garros and his Gnôme engined Morane-Saulnier monoplane left Saint-Raphaël on the French Riviera, flew over Corsica and Sardinia, and landed at Bizerta in Tunisia, the first non-stop crossing of the Mediterranean. Garros was shot down and killed on 5 October 1918 while flying a SPAD near Vouziers. Garros' 5-liter Bugatti was bought by Sunbeam director Louis Coatalen.

In view of the voiturette race to be held in the Auvergne in August 1914, Bugatti produced a batch of 1.4-liter racers with cylinder dimensions of 65.64 × 100 mm. The crankshaft ran in three main bearings, a plain bearing front, ball bearings in the middle and rear. The single overhead camshaft operated four vertical valves per cylinder, still via curved tappets.

11 August 1912 — Mont Ventoux hill-climb. Ettore Bugatti and his 5-liter Bugatti won the "third category" of the racing car class, in 19 min 16⅖ sec. Georges Boillot in the 7.6-liter Grand Prix Peugeot achieved the fastest time of the day in 17 min 46 sec (Mercedes-Benz Classic).

29 August 1920— Coupe des Voiturettes, Le Mans. Ernest Friderich, mechanic Étienne and the winning 1.4-liter Bugatti (Mercedes-Benz Classic).

Output was 29.5 hp at 2750 rpm. Wheelbase was 200 cm, dry weight 420 kg. Of the five racers built, three were left at Molsheim during the war. Their camshafts were buried and recovered in January 1919. On 29 August 1920, Friderich drove one of the 1914 racers to victory in the Coupe des Voiturettes at Le Mans, covering 24 laps of 17.10 km, a total of 410.40 km, in 4 h 27 min 46 sec, averaging 91.965 km/h. In the spring of 1921 the bore was increased to 68 mm, the big ends received rollers, the combustion chambers gained a second spark plug, and two Zenith carburetors were installed. On 8 September 1921, four Bugattis took the first four places in the 346-km Gran Premio delle Vetturette near Brescia. Hence the tiny voiturette racer became known as the "Brescia." In 1922 and 1923 a "Brescia modifié" was part of the production program, with dimensions of 68 × 100 or 69 × 100 mm, with ball bearing mains but plain bearing big ends. The Brescia modifié was available in the 200-, 240- or 255-cm frame. At the same time, the crankshaft of the normal production engine continued to run in three white-metal bearings.

In 1921 Bugatti also produced a 3-liter straight-eight touring car which was displayed at the Paris and London shows. The car was called "14 CV" with the factory designation type 28. Cylinder dimensions were 69 × 100 mm, wheelbase 335 cm, track 135 cm. It was offered for 45,000 Francs, while the 1.5-liter four was priced at 22,000.[2] The 3-liter remained a prototype. After 28 came type 29, the straight-eight racer designed for the 1922 Grand Prix de l'ACF. Since the Grand Prix was to take place just 10 kilometers from the Bugatti factory, it was evident that Ettore Bugatti would enter a complete team. Early type 29 drawings were dated April 1921 and depicted a 1.6-liter straight-eight, 55 × 85 mm with the crankshaft running in nine main bearings.

The 1922 Grand Prix Bugatti was powered by a straight-eight composed of two blocks of four cylinders, 60 × 88 mm, mounted on a one-piece crankcase. The two-piece crankshaft

29 July 1922 — Grand Prix des Voiturettes, Boulogne, a race of 12 laps of 37.375 km. Eugène Van der Bossche, mechanic Raymond Tycokzinski and the 1.5-liter Bugatti finished fourth in 5 h 30 min 25 sec. The Bugatti was a Brescia modifié type 22 with stripped body from Lavocat & Marsaud (Mercedes-Benz Classic).

ran in three large twin-row ball bearings, with a fourth ball race for the end thrust at the rear. The big ends ran in plain bronze bearings. Oil jets squirted into grooves in the crank webs so that the big ends were lubricated through drilled holes by centrifugal pressure only, according to Peugeot, Ballot, or Henry practice. The blocks had integral heads. A single overhead camshaft was driven by a vertical shaft at the nose of the engine, and ran in bronze bearings in a cast aluminum box. It operated three vertical valves per cylinder via fingers, "the single exhaust valve measuring 32 mm. and the pair of intake vales each having a diameter of 23 mm. The overhead camshaft drive is at the front, the water and oil pump drive is by means of a cross shaft at the foot of the vertical shaft and the two magnetos are at the rear, driven directly off the camshaft."[3] Valve clearance was adjusted by fitting hardened caps of different lengths on the valve stems. The intake opened 3 degrees before TDC and closed 30 degress after BDC; the exhaust opened 55 degrees before BDC and closed 25 degrees after TDC. The timing accounted for the great flexibility and good top-gear performance of these straight eights. With two Zenith carburetors, dual ignition and a 7:1 compression ratio, the 2-liter Bugatti delivered 80 hp at 4000 rpm. William Bradley wrote: "Bugatti declares that one of his 122 cu. in. engines has held 99.78 hp. at 4825 r.P.M. This is more than anybody else claims to have obtained and is a vast improvement on what was secured in the race."[4]

The engine and the 4-speed gearbox, which came from the Brescia, were rigidly bolted to the frame. In principle it was a type 22 frame, with a 240 cm wheelbase, 120 cm track, and 765 × 105 tires. Drive torque was taken via a rod parallel to the drive shaft and located by a leather link at the front. Leather was also used in the steering mechanism: "Among the peculiarities is the use of compressed leather for most of the steering connections."[5] Semi-

15 July 1922 — Grand Prix de l'ACF, Strasbourg. Pierre de Vizcaya at the wheel of his 2-liter Bugatti. He finished second, nearly one hour behind Felice Nazzaro's Fiat (Mercedes-Benz Classic).

elliptic front springs and reversed quarter-elliptic rears were typical Bugatti. Front brakes were hydraulic with a mixture of glycerine and water as fluid. Originally Bugatti intended to run with a bolster tank body, but Pierre de Vizcaya persuaded him at the last minute to let a local sheet metal worker knock up a streamlined body, similar to the Ballots designed by Edmond Moglia. The tail was long and finished in a funnel through which the exhaust escaped. "Bugatti had a big circular cowl around the radiator, with a large hole for the passage of the air. A long circular section tapering tail, having the exhaust going through it, was employed. Ballot had a somewhat similar general arrangement in front, with a much narrower pointed tail and external exhaust pipe."[6]

Bugatti entered four cars for Ernest Friderich, Pierre de Vizcaya, Pierre Mones-Maury and Pierre Marco. The bank of de Vizcaya's father had backed Bugatti when founding the company. Mones-Maury's exact name was Don Pedro José Monés y Maury; later he became the first Marquess de Casa Maury and married Paula Gellibrand, who was Cecil Beaton's childhood vision and became one of his favorite models. The Bugattis did not have the speed of the Fiats. Friderich "succeeded in getting the lead for a few minutes on the third lap. On the 12th lap he went out by reason of the breakage of the gears in one of his two magnetos. These magnetos were mounted side by side on the dash and driven from the overhead camshaft by a universal joint shaft. When the magneto gears went they broke the intermediaries."[7] Mones-Maury was flagged after 57 of the 60 laps. But the other two cars finished, with de Vizcaya second, one hour behind Nazzaro in the winning Fiat, and Marco third. The Bugattis "were very liberally lubricated and smoked freely throughout the race."[8] After the race, chassis no. 4001 was sold to Vincenz Junek of Prague, no. 4002 to Prince de Cystria, no. 4003 to Marcel Vidal, and no. 4004, on 26 March 1923, to Louis Zborowski. On 5 April 1923, Zborowski's car was registered "FN 5615" at Canterbury.

De Cystria's exact name was Bertrand de Faucigny, Prince de Lucigne, Prince de Cystria. He was married to Princess Paule Murat, a descendant of Joachim Murat, one of Napoleon's marshalls. Five Bugattis were entered in the 1923 Indianapolis 500: de Cystria's no. 4002, Zborowski's no. 4004, and three brand-new cars carrying nos. 4014, 4015 and 4016 which had been bought in early 1923 by Martin de Alzaga for himself, for Raoul Riganti and Pierre de Vizcaya. The three new cars were ordered on 18 January 1923 and invoiced on 23 January. The crankshafts of the three new engines relied on the 1922 three-ball-bearing solution. They did not run in five main bearings as originally announced and promised, although there were drawings of the five-bearing crank dated April 1923. Output was quoted as 104 hp at 5000 rpm, with compression of 7.5:1 and a benzene mixture as fuel. The single-seat bodies were designed by Louis Béchereau and manufactured by Lavocat & Marsaud at 16bis Rue Édouard Vaillant, Boulogne-sur-Seine. Béchereau was a famous aircraft designer who had been responsible for the Déperdussin and SPAD aeroplanes, and was a good friend of the French ace Charles Guynemer. The single-seat body was flush with the frame on the right side, the offset being the wrong way for the Indianapolis speedway. The Bugattis started on Firestone tires, 29 × 4½, and had a rear axle ratio of 14 to 54. George Robertson acted as team manager. Martin "Macoco" de Alzaga Unzué was an Argentinian cattle millionaire,[9] and was also described as the second husband of Kathleen Williams Capps, later the fifth Mrs. Clark Gable. Riganti was a star in national racing in Argentina, a well-known motorcycle rider before and after the Great War. Alzaga's Bugatti was the first to drop out in the Indianapolis race, in lap 6, with an overheated big end bearing. In lap 20, Riganti went out with a broken gas tank. Zborowski retired in lap 41 with a broken connecting rod, and de Vizcaya in lap 165 because of the same defect. De Cystria finished ninth. In the

15 July 1922 — Grand Prix de l'ACF, Strasbourg. Start of the Grand Prix: no. 5 Ernest Friderich's Bugatti, no. 6 Albert Guyot's Rolland-Pilain, no. 7 Jules Goux's Ballot (Mercedes-Benz Classic).

spring of 1924, Zborowski sold his Bugatti to the famous jockey and fellow Brooklands racing driver George Duller. In 1925 the car finished up in the hands of Woolf Barnato, who achieved a best Brooklands lap at 106.19 mph.

Indianapolis was dominated by the local single-seaters, Duesenberg and Miller. The 122-inch Duesenberg had two overhead camshafts, driven by a train of spur gears. The block of the straight-eight was made of aluminum, with wet steel liners. Cylinder dimensions were 2.375 × 3.422 inches. The head was detachable. The crankshaft continued to run in three main bearings, a plain bearing in the center and ball bearings front and rear. Four valves per cylinder were operated via cup-type tappets. Four dual-throat 1½-inch Miller carburetors fed the engine. The 122-inch straight-eight Miller had dimensions of 2.3425 × 3.5 inches. The crankshaft of the Miller ran in five main bearings, four plain bearings and a large ball bearing at the rear. Two overhead camshafts operated only two valves per cylinder inclined at 49 degrees to the cylinder axis, meaning two large valves per cylinder instead of four smaller ones and a hemispherical combustion chamber instead of a pent roof, according to the trend set by Fiat. Both the Duesenberg and the Miller delivered 120 hp at 5000 rpm, with a compression ratio of 7.5:1. And both engines were mounted into 100-inch wheelbase frames, rolling on 29 × 4½ or 29 × 5 tires all around.

The next evolution of Bugatti's 2-liter straight-eight racer started in the 1923 Grand Prix de l'ACF, on 2 July, near Tours. The factory designation of the car was type 32, while for the press it was the *tank* since its body resembled a battle of the Marne tank. In principle, the engine was unchanged, although the big ends were fitted with roller bearings now, to avoid the connecting rod problems of the Indianapolis race. But the frame and the body were completely new. The car was extremely small for an eight, having only a 200 cm wheelbase, as used before on the short chassis four-cylinder Brescia, and a narrow track of 105 cm. The frame carried reversed quarter-elliptics at both ends, with the springs mounted

2 July 1923 — Grand Prix de l'ACF, Tours. Ernest Friderich, mechanic Rohfritsch and the Bugatti *Tank* finished third (Mercedes-Benz Classic).

at the end of the frame pointing inwards and above the frame member so that the axles were underslung. Dunlop supplied the straight-side 28 × 4 tires. The three-speed gearbox was mounted in unit with the rear axle. Again the brakes were hydraulic. Four cars were entered for Friderich, Pierre de Vizcaya, Marco and de Cystria. As in the previous year the Bugattis were too slow and unable to follow the fastest competitors, the Fiats and the Sunbeams. De Vizcaya left the road in the first lap. Marco was out in lap 3, de Cystria in lap 12. But Friderich finished third, 25 minutes behind the winner, Segrave in the Sunbeam. On 6 October 1923, one of the tanks, chassis no. 4059, was sold to Vincenz Junek. In 1924, de Vizcaya took his car, no. 4057, to the Arpajon speed trials and achieved 189 km/h over the flying kilometer.

Originally, Bugatti's racer for the 1924 French Grand Prix at Lyon was designated type 30A, a derivation of the type 30, the 2-liter straight-eight touring car. But it became famous as the type 35, a Grand Prix racer which could be purchased by the wealthy sportsman and which sold as fast as it could be produced. The factory used the designation type 30 for the first 200 cars, until chassis no. 4802. Basically the straight-eight remained unchanged. Bugatti took over the type 30 cylinders, two blocks of four, with unaltered dimensions of 60 × 88 mm. The crankcase was new, split on the center line. The built-up crankshaft ran in five main bearings now: three twin-row ball bearings at the ends and in the center, and two additional roller bearings in between. The one-piece big ends of the connecting rods ran on rollers too. Lubrication was by means of jets receiving oil from a gear-type pump and squirting it into annular groves around the webs, and from there to the big ends under centrifugal force. There was no dry sump. The deep wet sump was cooled by 13 copper

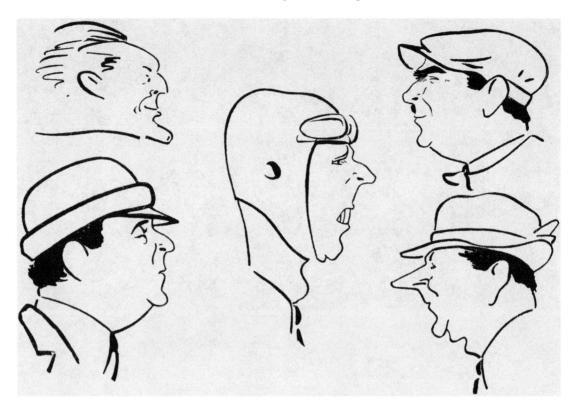

Caricatures of Robert Benoist and Giulio Masetti (left); Henry Segrave (center); and Giuseppe Campari and Ettore Bugatti (right) (*Allgemeine Automobil-Zeitung*).

tubes running fore and aft to carry cooling air right through the oil. The single overhead camshaft continued to run in pressure lubricated plain bearings. It operated three vertical valves per cylinder through rocking fingers; the two intake valves were increased from 23 to 23.5 mm, and the exhaust valve from 32 to 35 mm. In later type 35 engines, the intake valves were enlarged to 25.5 mm. Streicher and Kortz, two engineers in the design office of the Molsheim factory, were responsible for detail work. The intake opened 10 degrees before TDC and closed 35 degrees after BDC; the exhaust opened 50 degrees before BDC and closed 20 degrees after TDC. The valve timing remained unchanged in the supercharged type 35 models. As a consequence of the vertical valve stems and Bugatti's interest in exhaust scavenging, the cooling of the head was indifferent. Laurence Pomeroy wrote: "In point of fact, there can be few successful racing engines which have run with so little water in contact with so many hot spots.... There is only cast iron cooling for the important bridge which forms the adjoining sides of the intake and of the exhaust valve seats.... Bugatti, in this engine clearly expressed his choice of simple machining operations backed up by highly skilled handwork in fitting and assembly, as against a type that requires a great deal of expensive tooling and jigging, but can be easily put together by ordinary labour."[10] Ignition was by a single magneto driven from the back end of the camshaft. Output was between 100 and 105 hp at 5000 rpm.

Power was transmitted via a small diameter multi-disc clutch to a four-speed gearbox derived from the Brescia unit. The frame was new, with the front part tied up by the engine which was rigidly anchored at four points, and the back part stiffened by the cross tube mounting of the gearbox and transverse tubular members. The frame was waisted at the rear to support splayed out quarter-elliptic springs which were connected to the rear axle by shackle bolts. Two external arms were necessary to deal with the driving torque. The front axle was bored hollow and turned round in the straight, eyes punched through for the half-elliptic springs. Wheelbase was 240 cm, track was 124 cm front and 120 cm rear, and dry weight was 650 kg. Wheels were made of light alloy, with integral brake drums, and clad in straight side 28 × 4 cord tires from Dunlop, made in England. Later production cars were delivered with 710 × 90 or 710 × 105 clincher bead tires. In 1925 a handful of cars were delivered with smaller diameter aluminum wheels and the latest 730 × 130 low pressure tires, Michelin Cablé Confort or Dunlop Cord Balloon. The body, with the new horseshoe radiator, was aesthetically highly satisfactory. The type 35 was small, light and easy to handle, a jewel of a car.

The first type 35 was chassis no. 4323, factory designation "type 30A, 11 CV, 650 kg," registered 6963 J 1 on 12 July 1924, to the name of Automobiles Ettore Bugatti, Molsheim. It was used as spare car in the 1924 French Grand Prix at Lyon. Bugatti entered five cars in the Grand Prix, chassis nos. 4324 to 4328, the drivers being Ernest Friderich, Bartolomeo "Meo" Costantini, Pierre de Vizcaya, Jean Chassagne and Léonce "Leonico" Garnier, with the riding mechanics Rohfritsch, Soderini, Étienne, Epting and Zirn. Friderich had moved to Nice in January 1924, and opened his famous Bugatti agency at 40 Rue de la Buffa. Garnier was a famous early aviator and the owner of the Garage Garnier at 9 Calle Miracruz,

13 July 1924 — Coupe de l'Autodrome, Miramas, Marseille. Mambouk at the wheel of his 2-liter 8-cylinder Bugatti. He finished fourth covering 150 km in 1 h 12 min 25 sec, behind de Alzaga's 4.9-liter Sunbeam, Arthur Duray's Hispano-engined D'Aoust and Guyot's Duesenberg-engined Rolland-Pilain (Mercedes-Benz Classic).

San Sebastian. During the 1920s, Garage Garnier was the Spanish importer of Piccard-Pictet, Rochet-Schneider, Zedel and Buick touring cars, of Ariès and Pierce-Arrow trucks, and an agency for Hispano, Mercedes and Talbot. Bugatti came to Lyon with a trainload of spares and a large tent for his *équipe*. The Bugattis suffered badly from tire trouble. De Vizcaya was out in lap 11, Costantini in lap 16. Garnier was flagged with 33 laps. Chassagne and Friderich finished seventh and eighth.

On 24 September 1924, chassis no. 4324 was sold to Carlo Masetti of Rome, a brother of the better known Giulio Masetti. On 22 February 1925, Carlo Masetti drove the Bugatti to victory in the Premio Reale di Roma. Vincenz Junek purchased no. 4329 after it had been displayed at the Paris Salon. Chassis no. 4332 was the first one to be designated type Grand Prix Lyon; it was sold on 21 November 1924 to Étienne Bunau-Varilla, director and co-owner of the Bugatti agency in Paris, with showrooms at 116 Avenue des Champs-Élysées and repair shops at 32–34 Rue Marboeuf. Bunau-Varilla's father, Philippe, was known as the "Inventor of the Straits of Panama,"[11] having promoted the construction of the Panama canal. Étienne, born on 10 May 1890 in Paris, was an aviation pioneer with the early license no. 16, and was in the limelight in 1913 because of the records made with his *vélo torpille*, his streamlined bicycle.

There was also a Miller in the Grand Prix at Lyon, driven by Zborowski. In the summer of 1923, de Alzaga and Zborowski had purchased two 122-inch Millers. By the end of August, Zborowski tested his car in a private session at Brooklands. Miller mechanic Riley Brett sorted the suspensions and the coil distributor cam out. However, the axle ratio was

3 August 1924 — Grand Prix de l'ACF, Lyon. Meo Costantini, mechanic Soderini and their Bugatti during the *pesage* (Mercedes-Benz Classic).

too long for Brooklands so that the Miller pulled only 4000 rpm and a lap speed of 102 mph. Zborowski had hoped for at least 120 mph. While in England, Brett paid a visit to his uncle: "Brett's father had emigrated from the Canterbury area and he found his uncle running a shop near Higham, Zborowki's home."[12] The Miller was shipped on Zborowski's Mercedes truck to Monza for the Gran Premio d'Italia e d'Europa which was run on Sunday, 9 September 1923. A third Miller started with Jimmy Murphy at the wheel. Murphy's and Zborowski's engines had four twin-choke 1½-inch carburetors, whereas de Alzaga's had eight single-choke instruments. In practice, de Alzaga turned over in the Lesmo curve, without damage to himself or the car. In the race, he had to change the oil pump, and was flagged after 70 laps. Zborowski was out after 15 laps. Murphy finished third, behind two supercharged Fiats driven by Carlo Salamano and Felice Nazzaro, ahead of Nando Minoia's mid-engined Benz. The Murphy and de Alzaga racers were shipped back to America, converted to single-seaters, and ended up in the hands of Pete DePaolo and Leon Duray. The Zborowski Miller remained in Europe. On 28 October 1923, Zborowski started in the Spanish Grand Prix on the new 2-km speed bowl at Sitges. He finished second behind Albert Divo's Sunbeam. Next year, on 3 August 1924, Zborowski and his Miller started in the French Grand Prix at Lyon. Sammy Davis acted as riding mechanic. Davis was a reporter for *The Autocar* but became better known as a Bentley driver. The brakes and the steering of the Miller were too frail for the rough road course. In lap 16, after 350 km of the 810-km race, the front axle broke and the Miller was out. Zborowski sold it to Dan Higgins, who used it for sand racing at Southport, England.

3 August 1924 — Grand Prix de l'ACF, Lyon. L'équipe Bugatti: no 7, Jean Chassagne with riding mechanic Epting; no. 13, Ernest Friderich with Rohfritsch; no. 18, Pierre de Vizcaya with Étienne; no. 21, Leonico Garnier with Ernest Zirn; no. 22, Meo Costantini with Soderini (Mercedes-Benz Classic).

On 3 May 1925, Costantini, mechanic Soderini and the type 35 Bugatti won the 540-km Targa Florio in 7 h 32 min 27 sec, 5 minutes ahead of Louis Wagner in a sleeve-valve Peugeot. Wagner might have won, but he was delayed when he helped his teammate Dauvergne, who had turned over and was in danger of burning to death. Molsheim entered five new cars in the 1925 French Grand Prix which was held on 26 July at Montlhéry, chassis nos. 4571 to 4575, for Giulio Foresti, Pierre de Vizcaya, Meo Costantini, Fernand de Vizcaya, and Jules Goux. The cars were unchanged from the previous year. Bugatti did not fit a supercharger and mounted clincher bead Michelin tires. The Bugattis finished fourth to ninth, with Costantini fourth, 13 minutes behind the winner, Benoist in the Delage. The Delage was described as iridescent blue with royal blue wheels and the Bugatti as pastel blue. In the same meeting, Costantini won the 1.5-liter class of the touring car Grand Prix at the wheel of a small-bore version of the type 35 with dimensions of 52 × 88 mm, with additional mudguards and folding top. In preparation for the Italian Grand Prix in September 1925, five 1.5-liters were equipped with normal Grand Prix bodies. Costantini finished third behind Brilli Peri's and Campari's Alfas, ahead of Milton's Duesenberg. Two weeks later, on 19 September, Pierre and Fernand de Vizcaya took fourth and fifth at San Sebastian. The season ended on 18 October when Aymo Maggi drove a type 35 to victory in the 244-km Circuito di Garda.

After 1925, when the French Grand Prix lost its status and when a vast number of new races became open to private entrants, Bugatti's type 35 turned into a runner. Race organizers cancelled the entry fees and offered starting and prize money. Suddenly a catalogue racer

3 August 1924 — Grand Prix de l'ACF, Lyon. Louis Zborowski, mechanic Sammy Davis and the Miller were forced to retire in lap 16 (Mercedes-Benz Classic).

could be a profitable investment. It was in May 1925, after around 40 of the genuine racers had been produced, that Molsheim delivered the first *Imitation Course* model, the type 35A. In principle the 35A was a combination of the 240-cm type 35 frame with the three-main-bearing type 30 engine. The 35A crankshaft ran in three ball bearings with plain bearing big ends. There were small valves, Delco ignition, 70 hp at 4000 rpm, and wire wheels with 710 × 90 or 27 × 4.40 tires. The aluminum wheels could be supplied to special order. Externally, the 35A was virtually indistinguishable from the true racer and around 130 were sold for 65,000 francs. In addition, Bugatti designed a new 1.5-liter four as replacement for the outdated Brescia, retaining the old Brescia cylinder dimensions of 69 × 100 mm, but otherwise new in all respects. The crankshaft ran in five plain bearings with the lubrication for the big ends from jets squirting into grooves in the crank webs, as usual. In 1929 a full pressure crank was introduced. The cylinder head followed type 35 practice, a single overhead camshaft operating three valves per cylinder, two 26-mm intake valves and one 38-mm exhaust. Ouput was 60 hp at 4500 rpm. Beginning in 1926, this 1.5-liter four was mounted in the 35A frame, creating the type 37. A blown 37A was added in April 1927.

Bugatti's type 36 was a 1.1-liter racer. It turned up in practice for the Grand Prix de l'Ouverture which celebrated the opening of the new road track at Montlhéry on 17 May 1925 with 200 laps of the 2.5-km *anneau de vitesse*, the speed oval. The single-seat type 36

25 July 1926 — Formule libre Gran Premio de Espana, Lasarte, San Sebastian. Segrave's 4-liter V-12 Sunbeam leading Morel's 2-liter V-12 Delage and Costantini's Bugatti. The big Sunbeam was powered by a 60-degree V-12, built up from two blocks of the Grand Prix engine (67 × 94 mm), and had a 270 cm wheelbase. Its front axle broke in lap six. Costantini and his Bugatti won in 5 h 35 min 17 sec (Mercedes-Benz Classic).

was an oddity: The front axle was a straight tube sliding in guides on the frame, some restricted vertical movement being allowed by forward facing quarter elliptic springs. At the rear there were no springs at all. The engine was the 1.5-liter, 52 × 88 mm straight-eight which was to reappear in the Grand Prix de Tourisme in July. Ettore Bugatti himself drove one of the single seaters to Montlhéry, but the cars were rejected by the drivers as unmanageable and did not start. The Grand Prix de l'Ouverture was won by a trio of French 1.5-liter four-cylinder Talbots driven by George Duller, Caberto Conelli and Henry Segrave.

Early in 1926 Bugatti produced cylinder blocks with bores of 52 and 60 mm and crankshafts with strokes of 66, 88 and 100 mm. The biggest bore and the longest stroke were combined in the 2.3-liter type 35T which made its first appearance on Sicily. Meo Costantini drove it to victory in the Targa. In order to cope with the larger cylinder capacity, the front width of the famous horseshoe radiator was increased from 270 to 310 mm, the rear width of 350 mm remaining unchanged. Many 1926 cars were fitted with 715 × 115 tires, the new dimension replacing 710 × 90 and 710 × 105.

In the second half of 1925, Bugatti had enlisted the help of Edmondo Moglia, the former Fiat, STD and Djelmo engineer, to design a supercharger. Factory drawings of the blower rotor were dated August 1925, drive details February 1926. It was a three-lobed Roots blower. For the Grand Prix d'Alsace which was run over 35 laps of the 13.2-km Entzheim course near Strasbourg on 30 May 1926, the new Roots blower was fitted to three 1.1-liter straight eights, 51.3 × 66 mm. Two engines were mounted in improved type 36 sin-

25 April 1926 — Targa Florio, Sicily. Jules Goux and the 2.3-liter Bugatti 35T finished third, behind teammates Costantini and Minoia (Mercedes-Benz Classic).

gle-seat chassis with quarter elliptics at the rear, chassis nos. 4752 and 4790, for Aymo Maggi and Pierre de Vizcaya. The third 1.1-liter powered a normal two seater, for André Dubonnet. The conventional car with Dubonnet won the race in 4 h 22 min 52 sec, 9 minutes ahead of Maggi. Chassis no. 4790 was sold to Malcolm Campbell, who drove the car at Brooklands but found the 1.1-liter too small and sent the engine back to the factory to be converted to 2.3 liter. No. 4752 went to Switzerland, to Josef Karrer. Maggi was born on 30 July 1903 in Brescia. In 1925 he managed the Bugatti agency at 5 Via Ludovico Muratori, Milan. Later, with Carlo Bianchi as partner, he opened additional agencies at Turin, Teramo, Naples, Verona and Palermo. Maggi died on 23 October 1961.

The 1926 Grand Prix de l'ACF was run for 1.5-liter 600-kg cars on Sunday, 27 June, on the Autodrome at Miramas, 50 kilometers northwest of Marseille. The new track was initiated in 1923 by Paul Bablot, the former Delage and Ballot driver. It was a 5-km oval, more or less similar to the Indianapolis speedway, having two one-kilometer straights joined by two semi-circles, to be run clockwise. For the Grand Prix two chicanes, two tight loops

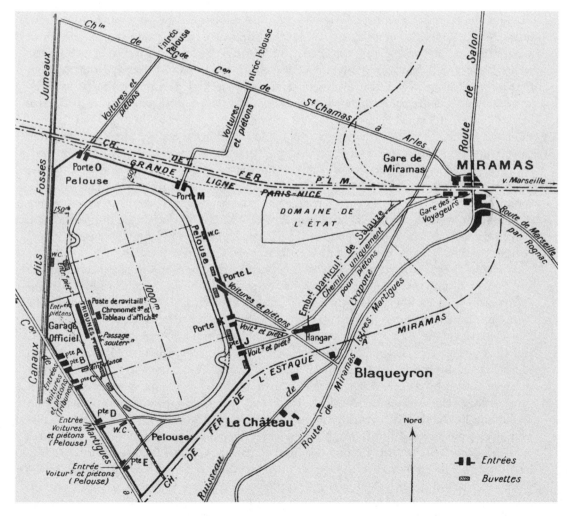

L'Autodrome de Miramas, the Miramas track near Marseille, was opened on 13 July 1924 (*La Vie Automobile*).

at the ends of the straights, were added increasing the lap length to 5.0956 km. Distance of the Grand Prix was 100 laps, 509.56 km. Talbot on behalf of Sunbeam, Sima-Violet, Delage and Bugatti each entered three-car teams. Bugatti could realize the 1.5-liter displacement with dimensions of 52 × 88 and 60 × 66 mm. In fact both options were bench tested at Molsheim. On 22 May 1926, the short-stroke engine, fitted with a carburetor and a vane-type blower supplied by the specialist René Cozette, delivered 99 hp at 4000 rpm and 111 at 5000, with the Cozette blower providing a pressure of 1.25 bar (1.25 ata). The long-stroke version used smaller valves and a three-lobed Roots-type blower. It delivered 103.5 hp at 4600 rpm, 110 at 5000, 114.4 at 5200 and 120 at 5500. But the long-stoke engine tended to overheat and to misfire. Molsheim tested different compression ratios using 44- and 45-mm pistons. The long-stroke 1.5-liter continued to overheat and refused to run properly. The short stroke in combination with the Roots blower gave the best results. With 45-mm pistons, the 60 × 66-mm engine delivered 114 hp at 5200 rpm, 117.5 at 5500, 119.5 at 5700 and 125 at 6250. With 44-mm pistons, the output was 107.5 hp at 5000 rpm and 113.4 at 5400.[13] The 44-mm pistons avoided self-ignition during test drives on the long straights between Molsheim and Strasbourg. The dimensions of 60 × 66 mm, 44-mm pistons and a Roots blower were adopted for the Miramas Grand Prix, in combination with a rear axle ratio of 13:54, giving top speed at 5700 rpm. The radiator was enlarged for the second time to 345 mm front and rear width, and moved forward slightly to make room for the blower drive. The Bugatti was not supercharged at high pressures owing to the well-known allergy between the single-cam vertical-valved head and the coolant. A distinctive mark of all supercharged Bugattis was now the small round hole in the right-hand side of the hood for the blow-off valve of the Roots blower. Bugatti entered three cars for Meo Costantini, Jules Goux and Pierre de Vizcaya. Later the 1.5-liter eight-cylinder Bugattis were designated type 39, or 39A in supercharged form. Talbot, Delage and Sima-Violet did not start in the Grand Prix at Miramas. Bugatti alone was ready, started, and secured a complete walk-over. Jules Goux completed the 100-lap distance in 4 h 38 min 43 sec, averaging 109.76 km/h, with the fastest lap at 2 min 23 sec or 127.39 km/h. Costantini was second, flagged after 85 laps and 4 h 43 min 13 sec. De Vizcaya withdrew in lap 45 because of supercharger trouble. It was a fiasco of a race — three starters and two finishers.

The 1.1-liter voiturette and cyclecar race, run in the afternoon over a distance of 50 laps or 254.78 km, was won by Georges Casse and his Salmson in 2 h 25 min 56 sec, at an average speed of 104.752 km/h, just 5 km/h slower than Goux in the Bugatti! The Salmson was manufactured in the Paris suburb of Billancourt, designed by Émile Petit. Its four-cylinder engine, 62.2 × 90 mm, with twin-cam head, crankshaft in three roller bearings, and Cozette blower, was good for 80 hp at 6000 rpm and a top speed of 160 km/h, which was stabilized by the rather long wheelbase of 252 cm. The fastest 1.1-liter racers, three Amilcars driven by André Morel, Charles Martin and Arthur Duray, retired with broken valve springs. The six-cylinder Amilcar, designated type CO, appeared in the hillclimb at Gaillon on 18 October 1925, and promptly won its class. Cylinder dimensions of the cast iron block were 55 × 77 mm. Two 33.5-mm valves per cylinder were inclined at 56 degrees to the cylinder axis, opened by two overhead camshafts via cam followers and closed by four springs. The crankshaft ran in seven main bearings, two ball bearings and five two-piece roller bearings, with the big ends in rollers and dry sump lubrication. With the aid of a Roots blower the Amilcar delivered 90 hp at 6500 rpm. Two chassis had a wheelbase of 223.5 cm, while that of a third was 216 cm; track was 109 cm; tires were 700 × 90; and dry weight was 500 kg. On 9 May 1926, on the famous dead-straight *chaussée* at Arpajon south of Paris, the Amilcar covered a flying kilometer at 197 km/h. In principle the Amilcar was a 2-liter V-12 Delage cut in half. This was no surprise since André Morel, Amilcar's star driver and director of the racing department, was at times also a Delage driver. Whether Delage engineer Albert Lory was involved in the design of the Amilcar was kept in the dark. Later the Amilcar six was available as a production racer, the C6, with cylinder dimensions of 56 × 74 mm, and the crankshaft in seven plain bearings, with a 219.5 cm wheelbase.

For the first British Grand Prix to be held at Brooklands on 7 August 1926, a solitary but brand-new Bugatti, chassis no. 4810, was shipped to England for Malcolm Campbell. Campbell worried about the strength of the delicate aluminum wheels on the rough Brooklands track. Roland Bugatti, Ettore's younger son, recalled: "Those wheels were absolute junk. They had to be thrown away after every race. At every pit stop the mechanics would swarm over them, tapping them with hammers like the tenders of a locomotive, to see if they still rang true or had already cracked. Any time you would nick a curb at any speed at all they were finished. The great thing about them was that they were so wonderfully cheap. There was nothing to making them. You just tossed a ladle of metal into a mould, gave the casting a few cuts on a lathe, a little polishing, and there was your wheel. They were laughably cheaper than the wire wheels that everybody used."[14] Campbell changed the alloy wheels to wire and finished second, ten minutes behind the 1.5-liter Delage shared by Sénéchal and Wagner.

Two 1.5-liter Bugattis driven by Sabipa and Costantini took the first two places in the 60-lap, 600-km Italian Grand Prix at Monza, on 5 September 1926. Goux's Bugatti, Serboli's Chiribiri and a Maserati duo with Materassi and Maserati did not finish. Sabipa won in 4 h 20 min 29 sec. Sabipa was the *nom de course* of Louis Charavel; he was born in Clermont-Ferrand in 1890 and started racing after the war, driving a Weler cyclecar. The Milan Grand Prix, held one week later on September 12, over a distance of 40 laps, saw the first appearance of the supercharged 2-liter Bugatti, the type 35C, which retained the cylinder dimensions of 60 × 88 mm. Costantini won in 2 h 36 min 18 sec, averaging 153.5 km/h. It was Costantini's last race. He retired from racing and acted as manager at Molsheim. Giovanni Canestrini, the Italian counterpart to Charles Faroux, described him as one of the most noble characters of the racing community. Costantini was born in 1909, in Vittorio Veneto, Italy. He was a good friend of Giovanni Marsaglia, the son of the owner of Aquila-Italiana, and thus began his career at the wheel of an Aquila before the Great War. During the war he was a member of the 78th *Squadriglia Aeroplani*. In 1917 he was appointed a captain in Baracca's squadron. Costantini died on 19 July 1941.

In 1927, the 2.3-liter 35T also received its supercharger, initially the 135-mm blower of the 1.5-liter, but later a larger 155- or 185-mm unit. The result was named type 35TC, for Targa Compresseur, or 35B. Engine no. 157TC, used by Albert Divo to win the 1928 Targa Florio, was tested on 21 February 1928 and developed 68 hp at 2350, 82 at 2800, 89 at 3000, 99 at 3400, 105 at 3700, 117 at 4200, and 130 hp at 5100 rpm, with a blower boost of 1.38 bar.[15] Early supercharged cars started on 715 × 115 tires, later 28 × 4.75 or 28 × 4.95 tires were adopted.

Between October 1927 and March 1929, Molsheim offered the 2-liter type 35 for 120,000 francs, the 2.3-liter 35T for 135,000, the 35A Imitation Course for 70,000, the 1.5-liter 39 for 135,000, the supercharged 2-liter 35C for 150,000, and the 35B and the 39A for 165,000 francs. The 35B price of 165,000 francs was also valid for the type 43, which was introduced in the spring of 1927 as the 35B's sports car version with a 297.2 cm wheelbase, 125 cm track, 28 × 4.95 tires, and 13:54 rear axle ratio.

The 1929 Gran Premio di Monza, held on 15 September, was of special interest for Bugatti. Leon Duray brought two purple-painted front-drive Millers to Europe, his Packard Cable Specials, a 1.5- and a 2-liter. Jean Marcenac, the Frenchman who had gone to America in 1920 to fit front brakes to DePalma's Ballot for the Elgin road race, and had decided to settle there, was in Monza to look after the racers. Duray's first act in Europe was to set a new record on the Montlhéry track. On 8 and 10 August 1929, he broke several records up to a distance of 10 miles, covering 5 kilometers at 220.85 km/h: "The 'Black Devil' Leon Duray has attacked the speed records on the Linas-Montlhéry track with one of his famous 1,500-cc. 8-cylinder cars."[16] At Monza in September, Duray broke the 1.5-liter lap record in practice, led the voiturette heat, but was forced to retire because of bearing trouble. He took his 2-liter Miller for the 3-liter heat and climbed to third, before going out again with an overheated bearing. Bugatti offered Duray a substantial amount of cash and three sports Bugattis in exhange for the two Packard Cable Specials. Duray accepted, selling the Bugattis in California. Was the original thinker Bugatti in need of inspiration? In any case the master of Molsheim copied the Miller head. In the future, the Bugattis had two overhead camshafts.

Was Ettore Bugatti a mechanical genius or a lunatic inventor? In 1953 the French front-drive pioneer Jean Albert Grégoire wrote: "Bugatti was a pure artist. His only scientific knowledge resulted from experience which increased with the years, and a natural mechanical ability aided by a gift of observation. He joked about pages of mathematical figures and about integration signs which he called violin holes. He had happily the wisdom to surround himself with talented engineers whom he paid generously, but demanded from them total anonymity."[17] Ettore Bugatti died in Paris on 21 August 1947.

New Generation

Just after the Great War, the Delage factory at Courbevoie launched two new production models, the 4.5-liter CO six and the 3-liter DO four, both with L-head and dimensions of 80 × 150 mm. The CO six was also available as Grand Sport or GS with OHV-head and 85 hp at 2500 rpm instead of 72 for the pure touring model. Louis Delage was living in the lap of luxury. He had a city apartment at no. 42, Avenue du Bois, a château at Le Pecq, Rue Victor Hugo, a mansion at Saint-Briac near Saint Malo, and his yacht *Oasis*, a refurbished submarine chaser. Arthur Michelat, Delage's technical director who was responsible for the 1914 Indianapolis winning 6.2-liter, had left Courbevoie in 1919 and was working for Léon Paulet in Marseille. Michelat's place was taken by Delage's cousin, Charles Planchon, an engineer who graduated at the Arts-et-Métiers school of Angers in 1895. Planchon worked for Peugeot at Levallois between 1902 and 1904, then for Charron, Clément-Bayard, Panhard and the aero-engine specialist Gnome-Rhône. At Delage, Planchon designed a 2.1-

Ernest Ballot, Louis Delage and Alfieri Maserati (*Allgemeine Automobil-Zeitung*).

liter production car, assisted by Frégal Escure. The result was displayed at the Paris Salon in the autumn of 1921, the type DE (72 × 130 mm, L-head). In 1922 the former Chenard & Walcker engineer Henri Toutée was engaged to design a racing version of the DE. The block was updated with an OHV-head, and the bore reduced to 69.9 mm. The result was the 2 LS, 2 Litres Sport. On 15 July 1923, Belben, a mechanic of the Delage racing car department, drove the 2 LS prototype to second in the touring car race at San Sebastian. After that the project was cancelled.

In 1922, Courbevoie came up with a hillclimb special. A CO/GS six engine from the production line was rebored from 80 to 85 × 150 mm. The crankshaft continued to run in four plain bearings. Henri Toutée adjusted the valve dimension and timing so that the 5-liter delivered 120 hp at 3500 rpm. The engine was mounted in a 270-cm frame similar to the chassis of the 1914 4.5-liter Grand Prix car and the new special was called Sprint I. Later, the sprint racer was sold to England and became known as Delage II. A second sprint car was assembled in 1923, using a longer 280-cm frame and a new 5.7-liter six with dimensions of 95 × 140 mm, with the crankshaft running in seven ball bearings, tubular connecting rods, twin-cam head and four valves per cylinder. It delivered 150 hp at 3500 rpm and was based on the block of the GL, the car that was Delage's response to the Hispano H6. This second sprint racer also ended up in England where it was called Delage I. René Thomas used both cars for hillclimbs and kilometer sprints, sometimes with a radiator cowl à la Frontenac-Monroe. The 5-liter OHV racer was successful, but its twin-cam counterpart proved to be unreliable and did not meet expectations.

A third sprint racer appeared in the autumn of 1923, the DH or *Torpille*, a 10.7-liter, 90 × 140 mm V-12 with OHV-head. The twelve cylinders were iron singles with welded-

7 October 1923 — nineteenth Gaillon hill-climb. René Thomas and the 10-liter V-12 Delage scored the fastest time of the day, covering one kilometer from a standing start on a 9 percent gradient in 31 seconds, averaging 116.129 km/h (Mercedes-Benz Classic).

2 July 1923 — Grand Prix de l'ACF, Tours. René Thomas at the wheel of the first 2-liter V-12 Delage (Mercedes-Benz Classic).

on water jackets made of steel. Fed by four Zenith carburetors, the V-12 delivered 280 hp at 3200 rpm. It was mounted in a 280-cm wheelbase frame with front and rear track of 142 and 138 cm, on 835 × 135 tires. On 6 July 1924, during the "Journée des Records,"[1] the speed trials organized by the Motocycle Club de France on the Route Nationale no. 20 at Arpajon, Thomas covered the flying kilometer in 15.615 sec (230.548 km/h), the flying mile in 25.012 sec (230.634 km/h), the standing kilometer in 28.17 sec, and the standing mile in 37.67 sec. But "the Frenchman Thomas and his Delage did not hold the speed scepter for long."[2] In the early morning of 12 July Ernest Eldridge and his Fiat Mephisto were faster, covering the kilometer in 15.320 sec (234.986 km/h). In 1929, the Torpille was sold to England. At Brooklands it was very successful in the hands of John Cobb, Oliver Bertram and Kay Petre.

Meanwhile, in the spring of 1923, Charles Planchon finished the design of a new Grand Prix racer, the 2 LCV, the 2 Litres Courses de Vitesse. Planchon's Delage was designed and built within four months. It was a combination of old Peugeot and new Fiat ideas. The cast iron block and the three-point mounting of the engine-gearbox complex in combination with a Hotchkiss axle were typical for the prewar Peugeots, for Ballot and Ernest Henry. The two-valve head and the roller bearing crankshaft reflected the latest Fiat school. The Delage was the first V-12 built for European Grand Prix racing. Cylinder dimensions of the 60-degree V-12 were 51.3 × 80 mm. "These blocks were extraordinarily fine examples of the foundrymen's art, and showed a very careful arrangement of water passages together with ample means for eliminating sand from the casting."[3] The exhaust pipes were mounted on the inside of the vee. The crankshaft ran in roller bearings throughout, the seven mains

15 July 1922 — Grand Prix de l'ACF, Strasbourg. The Rolland-Pilain team during the pesage at Strasbourg: no. 6 Albert Guyot, no. 13 Victor Hémery and no. 19 Louis Wagner. Guyot withdrew in lap 3 when the crankshaft broke near the Entzheim hairpin. Wagner was out in lap 2 because of a broken connecting rod, with Hémery's car eliminated by a fire in lap 7 (Mercedes-Benz Classic).

and the big ends, with lubrication by a single-pump wet-sump system. Two overhead camshafts per cylinder bank were driven by a train of spur gears. Each camshaft ran in seven roller bearings. The 30-mm intake and the 28-mm exhaust valve were inclined at 30 degrees to the cylinder axis and were opened via finger type followers and closed by three springs. The V-12 did not contain any plain bearings, just ball and roller bearings. Fed by four Zenith carburetors, the 2-liter Delage delivered 110 hp at 5500 rpm, with a compression ratio of 7:1. The multiplate clutch and the four-speed gearbox were in unit with the engine, and the whole complex three-point mounted in a conventional ladder frame in combination with a Hotchkiss-type rear axle. Wheelbase was 260 cm, track 125 cm, tires 765 × 105, dry weight 690 kg.

Only one car was assembled for the 1923 Grand Prix de l'ACF at Tours, for René Thomas and riding mechanic Lhermitte. Thomas took the lead after the start. But after a few laps the oil of the V-12 began to overheat and the new Delage went out in lap 6 with a broken connecting rod. Thomas commented: "*On faisait des frites avec le moulin*" (We made French fries with the mill).[4] Obviously the lubricating system was not au point. For the press it was not an engine problem: "By the end of the sixth lap and after a beautiful start Thomas was forced to withdraw because of a leaky fuel tank."[5]

The French sportsmen were bitterly disappointed since not only the Delage but also the Rolland-Pilains, which came from Tours, were unable to finish. The 2-liter Rolland-Pilain Grand Prix racer appeared in 1922. It was designed by an engineer named Grillot, and Albert Guyot added his experience gained with the 3-liter Duesenberg. The 2-liter straight-eight (59.7 × 90 mm) of the Rolland-Pilain was composed of an aluminum block with steel liners and a detachable cast iron head with two overhead camshafts and two valves per cylinder. In 1922 a desmo system was tested: "Rolland-Pilain had expected to run the race with a positive valve closing mechanism, but so many difficulties were encountered during the preparatory period that it was decided to change the cylinder head and use spring controlled valves."[6] The engines were "of the two-valve type, with the valves at an angle of 160 deg. and the spark plug in the head."[7] The 13-piece crankshaft ran in five large ball bearings from SRO, the big ends in rollers: "Rolland-Pilain made use of roller bearings in the connecting rods, but instead of the single row type adopted by Fiat, made use of a double row staggered, each roller measuring 8 mm. diameter × 10 mm. long.... While the Fiat construction gave satisfactory results defects which led to the breakage of connecting rods were developed on the Rolland-Pilain."[8] Pistons were made of magnesium and were claimed to weigh 100 grams each instead of 210 grams for aluminum equivalents. Output was 85 hp at 4500 rpm. Power was transmitted by a four-speed gearbox to a torque tube rear axle. The frame was underslung at the rear. The wheelbase was 250 cm, track was 125 cm front and 115 cm rear, and the tires were 765 × 105. The left-hand steering, the shape of the body and the hydraulic front-wheel brakes showed direct Duesenberg influence: "The Rolland-Pilains have hydraulic brakes on the front wheels; the rear wheel brakes are separately operated by hand."[9]

Messieurs Rolland et Pilain entered three cars in the 1922 Strasbourg Grand Prix, for the French veterans Albert Guyot, Victor Hémery and Louis Wagner. "The eight cylinder Rolland-Pilains proved to be green. Guyot went out on the third lap, when holding third place, with a broken crankshaft. Louis Wagner's car broke a connecting rod on the second lap. A fire started on Hemery's car on the seventh lap, and it was finally abandoned after the flames had been extinguished."[10] In 1923 two Rolland-Pilains appeared with a modified straight-eight, with the exhaust on the left and 95 hp at 5200 rpm. In lap 8 of the 1923 French Grand Prix at Tours, Hémery retired with a broken oil pump. Guyot held fourth until lap 28 of the 35-lap race when he was also forced to retire because of the oil pump. A third car which had been entered for Jules Goux did not start. It was powered by a sleeve-valve six of 64.8 × 100 mm designed by Ernest Schmid, the director of the French SRO ball bearing factory at Annecy (Usines de Roulements à Billes Jakob Schmid-Roost S.A.). On 28 July 1923, the Rolland-Pilains driven by Albert Guyot and Gaston Delalande took first and second in the 716-km Gran Premio do San Sebastian, ahead of Jean Haimovici in a 2-liter Ballot.

After the disaster in the 1923 Grand Prix at Tours, Louis Delage fired his cousin Planchon. Thomas proposed Ernest Henry as new director of the racing car department, while production director Augustin Legros suggested bringing back Arthur Michelat. But Louis Delage decided in favor of Albert Lory, Planchon's assistant. Lory was born on 19 June 1894, in Vibraye, a village near Le Mans, which was part of the 1906 Grand Prix circuit. And of course, he had graduated at the École des Arts-et-Métiers, in 1911 at Angers. Before he switched over to Delage, he worked for SCAP and Salmson. Lory took Planchon's V-12 as a basis and transformed it into the best unblown 2-liter racer. Three oil pumps took care of the lubrication and ensured a reasonable oil temperature. The revised V-12 delivered 120 hp at 6000 rpm. The frame was refined, with an unchanged 260-cm wheelbase but new axles, changing the track measurements to 130 and 120 cm, front and rear. Ernest Eimer was director of the racing car department and mechanic Achille Secuws supervised the

3 August 1924 — Grand Prix de l'ACF, Lyon. Albert Divo, mechanic Frétet and the 2-liter Delage during the pesage. They finished second (Mercedes-Benz Classic).

assembling of the racers. Three cars started on 3 August 1924 in the French Grand Prix at Lyon, driven by René Thomas, Albert Divo and the former Salmson voiturette star Robert Benoist. Divo finished second, just one minute behind Campari's Alfa, with Benoist third and Thomas sixth. On 23 September, at San Sebastian, André Morel drove the Delage to third, with Divo fourth.

For the 1925 season, the 2LCV was upgraded with a couple of Roots blowers, one per cylinder bank. Ouput was 170 hp at 6000 rpm, with a pressure of 1.5 bar (1.5 ata). The 260-cm frame got new axles increasing the front track to 133 cm and the rear track to 134 cm. Michelin supplied the tires, which were either clincher bead 820 × 120, or straight side 31 × 4.75 front and 31 × 5.25 rear. Four cars started in the 800-km Belgian and European Grand Prix at Spa on 28 June 1925, driven by Thomas, Divo, Benoist and Paul Torchy. By the halfway point all four cars were out with broken connecting rods. Of course, Louis Delage went through the roof. The V-12 had to be polished within four weeks. When, on 26 July, the Delages of Divo, Benoist and Wagner rolled to the start of the French Grand Prix at Montlhéry, their engines were good for 190 hp at 6500 rpm. The *poids à vide*, the dry weights of the trio, were 918, 940 and 967 kg, around 150 kg more than the Alfa Romeos. "The French Grand Prix represented a notable change with tradition. Since its inception it had always been run on closed road circuits, but this year it was staged on the Montlhéry circuit, one having all the features of a road, but artificially built and without the hazards of the Route Nationale."[11] The 12.5-km *circuit routier* was a combination of artificial road circuit with a part of the *anneau de vitesse*. It had to be covered 80 times, a total of 1000 km. "Montlhéry is more than a track on which world's records are broken. It has attached to it a road circuit, artificial roads, it is true, but offering difficulties in the way of gradients, unbanked corners, changes from macadam to concrete, which are not to be found on the

3 August 1924 — Grand Prix de l'ACF, Lyon. Robert Benoist, mechanic Carra and the 2-liter Delage finished third (Mercedes-Benz Classic).

26 July 1925 — Grand Prix de l'ACF, Montlhéry. Louis Wagner and his 2-liter Delage finished second (Mercedes-Benz Classic).

well-engineered highways of the Republic. By linking this road circuit up to the track proper, a course nearly eight miles round is obtained."[12] After Ascari's accident and Alfa's retirement, Benoist, who was relieved by Divo, won in 8 h 54 min 41 sec, while Wagner and Torchy finished second, 8 minutes back. Delage did not start at Monza, but on 19 September, in the absence of the Alfas, Divo, Benoist and Thomas took the first three places in the 710-km San Sebastian Grand Prix. Paul Torchy was killed when his Delage crashed into a tree in lap five. Torchy was an impetuous driver. A few minutes before the start he said to Thomas: "*Je gagne ou je me tue*" (I'll win or I'll kill myself!).[13] On 25 April 1926, four 2-liter Delages started in the Targa Florio, driven by Thomas, Divo, Benoist and Giulio Masetti, "the gentleman from Florence, one of the most friendly and distinctive figures of the Italian automobilism."[14] Masetti left the road near Sclafani and was killed. Both Torchy and Masetti had driven Delages carrying race number 13.

In the fall of 1923, Rolland-Pilain's racing car department was shut down. Albert Guyot, who shared a workshop with Ernest Eldridge at Levallois-Perret, bought one of the 250-cm frames and mounted a 3-liter Duesenberg engine. This was his first Guyot Spéciale. Guyot drove it in the Miramas meeting on 13 July 1924, and finished third in the Coupe de l'Autodrome behind Martin de Alzaga's 4.9-liter Sunbeam six and Arthur Duray's Hispano engined D'Aoust. During the winter of 1924–1925, Guyot assembled a completely new special. The frame had a wheelbase of 245 cm and a track of 120 cm. It was powered by a two-liter sleeve valve six (70 × 86 mm) designed by the carburetor and blower specialist René Cozette according to the Burt-McCollum single-sleeve system used by Argyll, of Alexandria near Glasgow. The crankshaft ran in seven roller bearings, with the big ends in rollers too. Assisted by a chain driven Cozette no. 9 vane-type blower, the Guyot six delivered 125 hp at 5000 rpm. The 2-liter Guyot was entered in the 1925 Belgian Grand Prix, but did not appear. In August 1925 it finished fourth behind three Bugattis in a short race at Montlhéry. In September, Guyot started in the Italian Grand Prix at Monza but retired in lap 7 with engine trouble.

In the autumn of 1925, at the Paris salon, Albert Schmidt, a director and development engineer of the Continental Motor Co., took to Guyot's sleeve valve engine, and decided to order three 1.5-liter racers for the 1926 Indianapolis 500 and to assist Guyot in the preparation. Three light blue cars were entered by Albert Schmidt as Schmidt Specials, while Albert Guyot entered a fourth car for himself as Guyot. The track of the 245-cm frame was increased from 120 to 125 cm, and tires were 29 × 4.40. The bore of the sleeve valve six was reduced from 70 to 60.7 mm, while the stroke of 86 mm remained unchanged. The Cozette vane type blower was replaced by a Roots compressor. Output was 100 hp at 5500 rpm. Only three cars qualified, Slim Corum and Steve Nemish in the Schmidts and Guyot in the Guyot. Guyot went out in lap 8 with a broken steering linkage, Nemish in lap 41 with a broken transmission, and Corum in lap 44 with a broken shock absorber. During the summer of 1926, Guyot assembled a fifth 1.5-liter, a two-seater. On 17 October 1926, Guyot started in the 200-km Grand Prix du Salon at Montlhéry. After 13 of 16 laps he was flagged, behind the Talbots of Divo, Segrave and Moriceau. A sixth 1.5-liter, the second two-seater, was finished in March 1927 and driven by Jean de Maleplane in the Grand Prix de Provence at Miramas. Later, it was sold to the Bucciali brothers and received a Bucciali badge.

In the autumn of 1925 the frame of the first 2-liter Delage driven by Thomas at Tours was sold to Maurice Béquet and Roland Coty.[15] Roland was the son of François Coty who had just bought Bennett's Villa Namouna. Parfums Coty were the world's largest perfume makers with factories at Suresnes, Puteaux, Neuilly and Pantin. Maurice Béquet received pilot's license no. 1294 just before the Great War, and had worked for Louis Blériot preparing the SPAD fighters before they were sent to the front. After the war, he became the technical director at Repusseau & Cie., the *carrossier* and supplier of the *silentbloc*. Béquet was active in sprints and hillclimbs at the wheel of a 1914 Grand Prix Alda. When the Alda engine was worn out, he replaced the 4.5-liter four with a V-8 from Hispano. In the 1922 Coppa Florio he finished third at the wheel of a Peugeot. By the spring of 1926, Béquet and Coty had a 12-liter Hispano V-8 mounted into the Delage frame and the car was called the Béquet Spéciale. The Spéciale was entered in the Grand Prix de Provence which was held on 28 March 1926 at Miramas, but did not appear. On 26 July the Béquet took part in the practice for the Spanish Grand Prix at San Sebastian, but did not start in the race. On 28 August, the Béquet appeared in the Grand Prix de La Baule, under another name, Coty Spéciale. Roland Coty drove the Spéciale to third behind Wagner's V-12 Delage and Montier's Montier. In the flying kilometer sprint at La Baule, Coty took the wheel of his Bugatti and finished second behind Benoist's Delage. On 17 October 1926, Christian Dauvergne was to drive the Coty Spéciale in a match race as part-event of the Grand Prix du Salon at Montlhéry, two heats of three laps and a final heat of three laps, altogether 22.5 km. But the match was cancelled because of heavy rain and replaced by a demonstration run: Dauvergne in the Coty, Ernest Eldridge in a 2-liter Miller, Albert Divo in a V-12 Sunbeam, and Guérin in the Sadi Lecointe Spéciale, a Hispano engined special. In November 1926, Coty finished second in the over-8-liter class of the Gometz-le-Châtel hillclimb near Paris, behind Guérin on the Lecointe. In the thirties, the Hispano V-8 of the Béquet-Coty was used to rebuilt an old SPAD aeroplane.

Three of the 1925 V-12 Delages finished their career in Italy, in the hands of Federico Valpreda, Giulio Aymini and Roberto Serboli. One of them was driven by the young Achille Varzi in the 1928 Premio Reale di Roma. The Delage for the new 1.5-liter Grand Prix formula of 1926 and 1927 was a straight-eight interpretation of the V-12. Designer Albert Lory was assisted by Maurice Gaultier, who was back at Delage after a short stint with Georges Irat. Gaultier had designed a beautiful 2-liter production car for Irat, which was built by Filtz & Grivolas in the former Pathé Phonographe factory at Chatou, a western suburb of Paris. During the 1927 season the 1.5-liter Delage experienced no difficulty in keeping far ahead of its rivals, Robert Benoist winning all the impotant races. By the end of 1927 Louis Delage announced that he was giving up racing, after having spent seven million francs on his *département course* during the 1927 season, the equivalent of 40 Grand Prix Bugattis. Benoist began to work as *directeur des ventes*, or sales director, for the Garage de Banville, rue de Courcelles, Paris, then for the French Lancia agency and in 1929 for Bugatti. Albert Lory designed an aero-engine. Louis Delage continued to build luxury cars but soon had to sell his factory to Delahaye. He died on 14 December 1947.

Pure factory racers of the 2- and 1.5-liter formula were simply too expensive in relation to the influence on sales. The old manufacturers were forced one after another to withdraw from racing. At the same time the sporting and commercial success of the Grand Prix Bugatti made a small workshop in Bologna wonder. Within a few years this workshop was to turn into one of the most successful racing car manufacturers: Officine Alfieri Maserati.

It was on Monday, 6 July 1908, at 6:40 in the morning, that Alfieri Maserati was about to start in his first great race. He was the driver of the Isotta no. 41 in the Grand Prix des Voiturettes at Dieppe. In the French press he was called "Mazerati."[16] The Isotta was built in Milan. The *veturetta* was powered by a 1.2-liter (62 × 100 mm) overhead cam engine producing 22 hp at 2500 rpm.[17] The frame was short, with a wheelbase of 210 cm, track of 120 cm, with Michelin 710 × 90 tires on wood wheels, and a dry weight of 610 kg. Maserati and his riding mechanic Pontiroli finished 14th. A few weeks later, in September 1908, Alfieri Maserati played the role of riding mechanic, in the Coppa Florio at Bologna, alongside Vincenzo Trucco in a big 13.5-liter Lorraine-Dietrich. Isotta and Lorraine were connected by license agreements. Trucco and Maserati finished second, behind Nazzaro in a Fiat.

Alfieri Maserati was born on 23 September 1887, in Voghera, 50 km south of Milan. His father Rodolfo was born in 1852 in Sant'Antonio di Piacenza, and married Carolina Losi in 1879. Rodolfo worked as a mechanic for the Regie Ferrovie, the Italian railway, first at Piacenza, then at Voghera. The Maseratis had seven sons, Carlo (born in 1881), Bindo (1883), Alfieri (1885) who died when a few months old, so that the next son was again called Alfieri (1887), Mario (1890), Ettore (1894) and Ernesto (1898). In the middle of the 1890s the eldest brother Carlo began to work in a bicycle factory at Affori, a northern suburb of Milan. In 1898, with Cesare Carcano, he assembled a small single-cylinder engine to be used in a motorcycle. The single featured the usual turn-of-the-century valve layout, with an automatic intake in the head and a mechanically operated exhaust in a pocket on the side. The output was quoted as ¾ hp. Of course, it resembled the ubiquitous French De Dion. Carlo was backed by Cesare's father, the Marchese Michele Carcano, so the single-cylinder was quickly mounted into a bicycle frame. In 1899 Carlo drove his motorcycle in the Brescia meeting and started in the 30-km race between Brescia and Orzinuovi and a 5-km sprint. In 1900, the single was mounted in a quadricycle. After leaving the patronage of the Carcano family, Carlo worked for Fiat in Turin. In 1903 he went back to Milan, working for Isotta-Fraschini and in 1907 for Bianchi where he acted as *pilota ufficiale*, or

18 May 1908 — Targa Florio, Sicily. Vincenzo Trucco, mechanic Alfieri Maserati and the winning Isotta-Fraschini (Mercedes-Benz Classic).

works driver. He drove an 8-liter Bianchi in the 1907 Kaiserpreis near Frankfurt and the Coppa Florio at Brescia. In 1909 he worked as technical director for the Officine Turkheimer per Automobile e Velocipedi, the OTAV Junior, at Milan (no connection with the Junior of the Ceirano brothers). He also made a side trip into the aeroplane business, adapting an inline-four and a five-cylinder radial engine to a monoplane of the Blériot type. But Carlo fell ill, and despite renting a villa near the Lago Maggiore to cure his tuberculosis, he died in 1911.

In Carlo's tow, Alfieri began to work for Isotta in 1903 as *aiutante motorista* (motorist assistant), then in 1905 in the test department, and in 1906 in the racing department. His first start in a race was in the 1906 Coppa d'Oro as mechanic for Trucco. His brothers Ettore and Bindo followed him and worked for Isotta. Soon after Carlo's death, Alfieri went to Buenos Aires where he spent one year working for the Isotta agency. From Argentina he travelled to London, and in 1912 moved back to Italy, to Bologna, where Isotta put him in charge of organizing an *agenzia* and a service shop. Two years later, he went into business for himself: On 1 December 1914, the Societa Anonima Officine Alfieri Maserati was registered at the Bologna chamber of commerce and industry, the idea being the preparation of Isottas for road racing. Two weeks later, on 14 December, Officine Maserati was opened at 11 Via de' Pepoli. Alfieri was joined by Ettore, 16-year-old Ernesto, and five mechanics.

When Italy entered the war on 24 May 1915, Alfieri and Ettore were called up. In 1916, Alfieri was sent to Florence, Via Milognano, to assemble Hispano aero-engines for the former De Dion agent Ettore Nagliatti. Ettore did the same job in Legnano near Milan,

2 April 1922 — Targa Florio, Sicily. Massola at the wheel of his 2-liter Diatto Tipo 20. The brand new Diatto did not finish (Mercedes-Benz Classic).

assembling Isotta aero-engines for the Meccanica Franco Tosi. Meanwhile young Ernesto kept running the Officine at Bologna, and Bindo continued to work for Isotta. When working for Nagliatti, Alfieri designed a mica-insulated spark plug, filed a patent for it, and founded a business in Milan to produce his Candele Maserati, his Maserati spark plugs. When Gabriele D'Annunzio flew to Vienna in 1918, his aero-engine used Maserati plugs. In 1919, Alfieri and Ettore went back to Bologna, including the spark plug production as additional support, and took a larger shop, an old demijohn factory at Frazione Alemanni 179, zona Ponte Vecchio, in the southeastern end of Bologna.

On 13 June 1920 Alfieri Maserati started in the Circuito di Mugello at the wheel of a special powered by a 2.5-liter from a Nesselsdorf truck (built by Nesselsdorfer Wagenbau in Nesselsdorf, Moravia). He withdrew in lap 3. A second Nesselsdorf driven by Giulio Ansaldi was out in lap 2. In the fall of 1920, Maserati began to assemble a special, an Isotta frame powered by a four-cylinder Hispano, a 6.3-liter OHC-block with dimensions of 120 × 140 mm, one bank of a V-8 aero-engine. The gearbox came from a SCAT, the rear axle from an Itala, the wheels from Rudge. In 1921 he drove his special to victory in the hillclimb from Susa to the Moncenisio and finished fourth in the Circuito di Mugello and in the Gentleman Grand Prix at Brescia. In 1922 he won the Circuito di Mugello, one of the "piu quotate prove,"[18] one of the most prestigious events in Italy; the Moncenisio again; and the hillclimb between Aosta and the Gran San Bernardo.

In the same year, 1922, Alfieri Maserati and Giuseppe Coda developed a 2-liter Grand Prix racer based on the Diatto tipo 20. Giuseppe Coda was born on 8 July 1883 in Biella Cossila, 50 kilometers to the northeast of Turin. He worked for Isotta, Züst, Fiat, Rapid and SCAT. During the war, at SCAT, the Società Ceirano Automobili Torino, he directed the licensed production of Hispano engined SPAD aeroplanes. In 1920, Coda worked on his own account in a small shop at 33 Via Salerno, Turin. He designed and built the prototype of a 2-liter production car. The engine featured a single overhead camshaft, and was

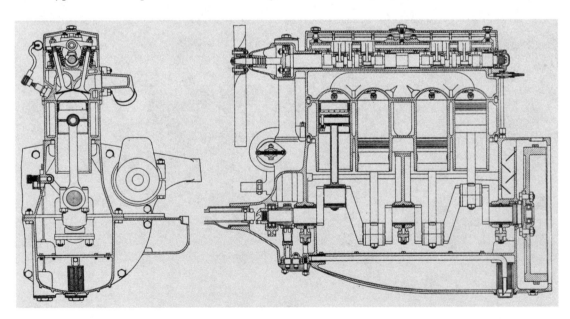

Diatto Tipo 20 engine: 79.7 × 100 mm, 2 liters, one overhead camshaft, two valves per cylinder, design by Giuseppe Coda (*Automobile Engineer*).

a little brother of Coda's 1914 Grand Prix Fiat. The SAA Diatto was interested in the project, bought the prototype and offered Coda a job as technical director. The Società Anonima Autocostruzioni Diatto was founded at Turin in 1919, as successor of the different previous companies building Diatto cars. In 1915 Diatto had purchased the Caesar factory at Chivasso and Newton at Turin, and in 1916 the majority of the Italian Gnome et Rhône factory at Turin which built a few Bugatti aero-engines under license. In 1919 Diatto was taken over by the Banca Italiana di Sconto and was located at 21 Via Fréjus, Turin. The 2-liter Diatto was displayed for the first time in April 1922 at the Salone di Milano, as tipo 20.

The sportsmen immediately realized that the tipo 20 was a disguised racer and the SAA Diatto decided to assemble a batch of short wheelbase frames. Moreover, a member of the Diatto board named Pozzi suggested handing the preparation of two pure racers over to Alfieri Maserati's Officine. Of course, Maserati worked in his shops at Bologna but also, during a few weeks, in the Diatto factory at Turin. In August 1922, the press described the 2-liter Grand Prix car, the "due litri da corsa" or "tipo Gran Premio."[19] Cylinder dimensions of the 2-liter were 79.7 × 100 mm. The crankshaft ran in three plain bearings, 40 mm in diameter, 55 mm wide. The big end diameter of the tubular connecting rods was also 40 mm, their width 40 mm. The single overhead camshaft was driven by a vertical shaft via helical gears. Two 40-mm valves per cylinder were inclined at 12 degrees to the cylinder axis and were operated via bell-crank rockers. Valve lift was 9 mm. Output was 75 hp at 4500 rpm, while the production engine delivered 40 hp at 2500 rpm, 48 at 3000 and 55 hp at 3500 rpm. The power was transmitted via a Ferodo lined single-disc clutch and the four-speed gearbox to a torque tube rear axle. All shafts were made of chrome nickel steel from the Bismarck Steel Works. Wheelbase was 250 cm, track 130 cm, and tires 810 × 90 front and 815 × 105 rear. The cars' dry weights at the *pesaruta*, the scrutineering at Monza, were 666 and 670 kg. The bodies of the racers were designed and built by a friend of Giuseppe Coda, Augusto Schieppati, who had shops in Milan, in the Via Lazzaro Papi and the Via Colletta, and who took over the Diatto agency for the Lombardy.

On 10 September 1922, two Grand Prix Diattos started in the Gran Premio d'Italia at Monza, no. 9 Guido Meregalli with *meccanico* Giacchino, and no. 22 Alfieri Maserati with his younger brother Ernesto. Maserati left the road in lap 27, while Guido Meregalli was forced to retire in lap 52 because of a broken connecting rod. On 15 October, the Diatto Gran Premio scored its first victory when Meregalli won the Circuito di Garda at Salo, covering 247.2 km in 3 h 1 min 38 sec. During the following weeks, enlarged engines displacing three liters with dimensions of 90 × 116 mm were mounted in two 250-cm frames. On 22 October, in the Gran Premio d'Autunno, Meregalli retired in the first lap but Alfieri Maserati finished third, covering 40 laps or 400 km in 3 h 11 min 19.6 sec, averaging 125.439 km/h, nine minutes behind André Dubonnet's 6.6-liter Hispano and Francesco "Franz" Conelli's 4.9-liter ex–Indianapolis Ballot. Maserati won the 3-liter class and set the fastest lap in 4 min 15.8 sec, averaging 140.784 km/h, good for a prize of 10,000 Lire. On 2 November 1922, Alfieri Maserati drove the same 3-liter Diatto in the Coppa Florio on Sicily, a distance of four laps of 108 km. He completed the first two laps in 3 h 34 min 40 sec, lying third, eight minutes behind André Boillot in a Peugeot. Then the oil tank broke. Alfieri refilled the tank with olive oil but the crankshaft bearings did not agree and overheated.

During the winter of 1922–1923, Maserati assembled a second Hispano special, this time a 265-cm Diatto frame powered by a 6-liter Hispano four, again one V-8 bank, and drove it to victory in the Moncenisio and San Bernardo hillclimbs. Later the Marchese Diego de Sterlich bought the Hispano-engined Diatto and fitted a new Schieppati body.

15 April 1923 — Targa Florio, Sicily. Alfieri Maserati and his 3-liter Diatto withdrew in lap 3 (Mercedes-Benz Classic).

During the summer of 1923, Maserati and Coda combined two tipo 20 blocks forming a 4-liter straight-eight. Coda tested different types of head gaskets, Feroldi aero-engine carburetors and 36-mm Zeniths. Finally two engines were mounted in 310-cm stock frames. Coda, Maserati and Diego de Sterlich tested a car fitted with a light body, a *carrozzeria spartana*, up to the Moncenisio. In 1924 the two 4-liter eights were mounted in shorter 265-cm frames, but the project was cancelled since Alfieri and Coda were working on a 2-liter straight-eight Grand Prix racer. When, on 6 July 1924, at the Colline Pistoiesi, Ernesto Maserati drove his first race, he was still at the wheel of an older 3-liter four.

The 2-liter eight was designed and built in the Officine at Bologna. A first engine was tested in February 1924. Elektron pistons were quickly replaced by more conventional aluminum ones. By May, the new engine was mounted in a 265-cm frame and entered in the hillclimb from Parma to Poggio di Berceto. Alfieri Maserati won the 3-liter class. The 2-liter eight reappeared on 9 November 1924, when Ernesto Maserati drove it in the Circuito del Garda, finishing tenth, 25 minutes behind Meregalli's older 2-liter four. Obviously the French Grand Prix winning Duesenberg and its twin-cam evolution of 1923 had left a heavy mark, without forgetting the three Millers driven by Murphy, de Alzaga and Zborowski in the 1923 Gran Premio at Monza. Had Coda and Maserati disassembled a 122-inch Duesenberg or a Miller for a detailed scrutineering, or both? While the 2-liter four completely reflected Coda's earlier designs for Fiat, the layout of the new 2-liter eight had nothing in common with the previous single-overhead-cam fours. The new Diatto was clearly an Italian interpretation of a typical American special coming directly from the board speedways.

The block of the 2-liter straight-eight Diatto was made of aluminum with steel liners, with dimensions of 65.5 × 74 mm. The detachable twin-cam head was also made of aluminum, and reflected Duesenberg influence. The two camshafts were driven by a train of spur gears and operated two valves per cylinder. The crankshaft ran in five plain bearings. The engine of the prototype was unblown, using four Zenith carburetors, but the second 2-liter eight received a supercharger. It appeared on 14 June 1925, for a few demonstration laps on the occasion of the Coppa del Re at Monza, and achieved 180 km/h. The Roots blower was manufactured by Maserati. Two Memini carburetors were mounted on the pressurized side. Output was raised from the unblown 105 hp at 5000 rpm to 120 at 4800 and 137 at 5200. Wheelbase was 265 cm, and tires were "Pirelli Milano Cord," 29 × 5 front, 29 × 5.50 rear. Again the bodies were made by Augusto Schieppati and closely followed Miller fashion. The former Fiat driver Onesimo Marchisio drove the unblown Diatto on 5 July 1925 in the hillclimb from Susa to the Moncenisio, finishing third in the 2-liter class, and on 9 August from Cuneo to the Colle della Maddalena where the Diatto turned over. Marchisio was so severely injured that he died the next day. On 6 September 1925, Emilio Materassi took the wheel of the blown Diatto in the 800-km Gran Premio d'Italia. He retired in lap 39 because of engine problems. Two Diattos were entered in the San Sebastian race but did not appear.

By the end of 1924, Alfieri Maserati and Diatto were banned by the RAC de Espana from Spanish events, Maserati for two years, Diatto for five years, allegedly because Maserati started with a 3-liter engine in the 2-liter class of the Rabassada hillclimb, Barcelona. The Diatto disqualification was cancelled in May 1925, Maserati's in January 1926. Maserati had informed the Rabassada race organizers about the replacement of a defective 2-liter by a 3-liter engine, but the organizers had forgotten to reclass the car. In any case, during the winter of 1925–1926, Diatto's Grand Prix program was cancelled due to financial problems. Alfieri Maserati took over the design of the Diatto Grand Prix racer and turned it into the first Maserati.

The first Maserati was called *Gran Premio 26* and became known as the tipo 26 according to its year of birth. The first chassis number was no. 11. The financial power of the Maserati shop was still limited, essentially based on Maserati's spark plug business. In addition, the Maserati shop continued to repair and service the Diattos raced by customers, and Diego de Sterlich was a generous backer. Maserati could still rely on the skills of Giuseppe Coda. Alfieri called him "il mio maestro."[20] Although in 1925 Coda had moved to Paris where he worked for Citroën, he remained in close contact with Alfieri regarding development of the Diatto straight-eight and thus the first Maserati. The Diatto badge was replaced by the Tridente, the new marque's badge, Neptune's trident recalling Bologna's *Il Gigante*, the famous Fontana dell Nettuno. Neptune's fountain had been executed by the Flemish sculptor Jean Boulogne, also known as Giovanni da Bologna or Giambologna, between 1563 and 1567. The marque's badge was shaped by Mario Maserati, the only one of the Maserati brothers who was not interested in racing cars but in fine arts. Alfieri reduced the cylinder dimensions to 60 × 66 mm so that the first Maserati displaced 1.5 liter, complying with the 1926 Grand Prix formula. The Maserati's first race was the Targa Florio on Sicily, on 25 April 1926, over a distance of five laps of 108 km. In March, the Italian press still quoted Alfieri Maserati's Targa entry as a Diatto. But by April, the Diatto had turned into a Maserati so that Alfieri started in a Maserati. He finished ninth overall and won the 1.5-liter class in 8 h 37 min 11 sec, ahead of two Bugattis driven by Croce and Caliri. A 19-year-old Guerino Bertocchi acted as riding mechanic since Luigi Parenti, Alfieri's regular attendant, was completing his military service. Two weeks later, on 2 May, Emilio Materassi took the wheel of the first Maserati in the Coppa Vinci at Messina but did not finish. On 13 June, Ernesto Maserati drove the car in a sprint meeting on the Via Emilia near Bologna, between Borgo Panigale and Lavino di Mezzo, and achieved 167.441 km/h over a flying kilometer.

During the summer of 1926, Maserati assembled two additional 1.5-liter racers, chassis nos. 12 and 13. The final drawings were dated June 1926 and were based on the experience gained earlier in the year. Engine no. 12 had a "blocco cilindri in ghisa,"[21] a cast iron block, while no. 13 had an aluminum block with steel liners. Cylinder dimensions were taken over from the Targa car, 60 × 66 mm, with aluminum pistons supplied by Borgo. Both no. 12 and no. 13 had a detachable twin-cam head made of cast iron. The camshafts each ran in five plain bearings and were driven by a train of gears at the front. There were two valves per cylinder. Intake and exhaust had the same diameter, 42 mm, and were inclined at 45 degrees to the cylinder axis. The valves were opened via cup-type tappets, and closed by two springs. The crankshaft ran in five main bearings, roller bearings for nos. 1, 3 and 5, plain bearings for 2 and 4, with plain big ends, and lubrication under pressure via a two-pump dry sump. The tubular connecting rods were supplied by Piccinini, Bologna. A Roots blower with two-lobed 115-mm rotors was mounted at the front and blew through two Memini carburetors. Output was 120 hp at 5300 rpm, with a compression ratio of 5.75:1, and using Elcosina SG fuel. The gearbox had three speeds, with a separate lever for reverse. The engine-gearbox complex was three-point mounted in combination with a torque tube rear axle. Wheelbase was 265 cm, track 134 cm front and 136 cm rear, tires 27 × 4.40 front and 28 × 4.95 rear, and dry weight 720 kg. In September, the first three Maseratis turned up at Monza, chassis nos. 11, 12 and 13, to be driven by Emilio Materassi and Alfieri Maserati, the third mount being a spare car for Guido Meregalli. Materassi was out in lap 3, Maserati in lap 5, both with engine problems.

Officine Maserati produced four cars in 1927, two 1.5-liters and two 2-liters with dimensions of 62 × 82 mm. In 1928 the number rose to ten; in 1929 it was back to eight. The next development step of the original tipo 26 was a 2.5-liter (65 × 94 mm) which became the most succesful racing car of the 1930 season. At the same time Alfieri Maserati began the development of a front-driven 2.5-liter single-seater. It was inspired by Leon Duray's Millers, the Packard Cable Specials, and by Carlo Pedrazzini's new Cord. Pedrazzini was a Swiss customer from Lugano who had just bought the last tipo 26B, chassis no. 2010. The body had a width of just 63 cm, a wheelbase of 258 cm, and track of 130 cm. The front wheels were independently suspended via short transverse quarter-elliptic springs and Lancia-type vertical pillar guides. Brake operation was hydraulic. After Ettore Maserati had an accident when testing the *trazione anteriore* on the Via Emilia, the project was put on ice. Alfieri Maserati suddenly died on 3 March 1932, the long-term consequence of a kidney removal after an accident in the 1927 Coppa Messina.

Ernesto Maserati took over the leadership of the Officine, backed by Ettore and Bindo who switched over from Isotta. Ernesto, Ettore and Bindo carried on to finance their Officine by building racing cars for sale to a wealthy sporty clientele. The engines and the frames were assembled in Bologna, with the engines first tested on the bench, then on the road, and finally tuned on the car. Of course the brothers continued to work in their factory, in overalls among the 50 specialized mechanics who were the whole staff of the little marque. By the beginning of 1938, the three brothers sold the shares in the Officine and the spark plug factory to the Orsi family, Modenese industrialists with diverse interests in machine production. The brothers continued in a consulting role until 1947. Giuseppe Coda worked for Citroën in Paris until the end of 1936. Then, in 1937, he was active as general manager of Citroën Italiana in Milan. It was also in 1937 that he accepted a job as consultant for the aero-engine division of Alfa Romeo at Portello. In 1938 he went back to Turin, working for the Officine Viberti and the Officine di Savigliano. Coda died in Biella Cossila on 30 October 1977.

The Italian episode of the transatlantic interaction came full circle in 1939 when Wilbur Shaw won the Indianapolis 500 at the wheel of a 3-liter Maserati. The 3-liter 8CTF was a distant development step of the initial tipo 26. Shaw and the Maserati won again in 1940. The original Duesenberg and Miller influences had found their way back to the Brickyard.

Appendix A: Biographical Data

Aitken, Johnny. *born* 3 May 1885 — Indianapolis, Indiana; *died* 15 October 1918

Alley, Tom. 21 May 1889 — Metamora, Indiana; 26 March 1953 — Indianapolis, Indiana

Alzaga, Martin de. 25 January 1901 — Buenos Aires, Argentina; 15 November 1982 — Buenos Aires, Argentina

Anderson, Gil. 27 November 1879 — Horten, Vestfold, Norway; 26 July 1935 — Logansport, Indiana

Ascari, Antonio. 15 September 1888 — Casteldari, Italy; 26 July 1925 — Montlhéry, France

Avanzo, Maria Antonietta. 5 February 1889 — Contarina Veneta, Italy; 17 January 1977 — Rome, Italy

Aymini, Giulio. 3 August 1891 — Turin, Italy; 29 November 1967 — Turin, Italy

Bablot, Paul. 20 November 1873; 23 December 1932

Ballot, Ernest. 11 January 1870 — Angoulême, France; 1937

Basle, Charles. 8 January 1885; 4 February 1962 — Los Angeles, California

Bazzi, Luigi. 13 October 1892; 1986

Béchereau, Louis. 25 July 1880 — Plou, Cher, France; 18 March 1970 — Paris, France

Bennett, James Gordon, Jr.. 10 May 1841 — New York City; 14 May 1918 — Beaulieu, France

Benoist, Robert. 20 March 1895 — Rambouillet, France; 12 September 1944 — Buchenwald, Germany

Béquet, Maurice Joseph Jules. 10 May 1889 — Sainte Adresse, Le Havre, France; 1 February 1943 — Deauville, France

Bergdoll, Erwin. 24 June 1890 — Philadelphia, Pennsylvania; 21 March 1965 — Camden, New Jersey

Bergdoll, Grover Cleveland. 18 October 1893 — Philadelphia, Pennsylvania; 15 January 1966 — Richmond, Virginia

Bertarione, Vincenzo. 1892 — Italy; 1962 — Suresnes, France

Boillot, André. 8 August 1891 — Beaulieu-Valentigney, France; 8 June 1932 — Châteauroux, France

Boillot, Georges. 3 August 1884 — Beaulieu-Valentigney, France; 20 May 1916 — Vadelain-court, France

Bordino, Pietro. 22 November 1887 — Turin, Italy; 15 April 1928 — Allesandria, Italy

Borzacchini, Baconin. 28 September 1898 — Terni, Italy; 10 September 1933 — Monza, Italy

Bradley, William Fletcher. 8 March 1876 — Scarborough, England; 6 October 1971 — Condom-en-Armagnac, France

Bragg, Caleb Smith. 1888 — Cincinnati, Ohio; 24 October 1943 — New York City

Branger, Maurice-Louis. 25 August 1874 — Fontainebleau, France; 1950 — Mantes-la-Jolie, France

Brilli-Peri, Gastone. 24 March 1893 — Montevarchi, Italy; 22 March 1930 — Tripoli, Tunesia

Brown, William Wayne. 27 February 1886 — Dodge City, Kansas; 14 June 1958 — Kansas City, Missouri

Bruce-Brown, David L.. 13 August 1887 — New York City; 1 October 1912 — Milwaukee, Wisconsin

Burman, Robert "Bob." 23 April 1884 — Imlay City, Michigan; 18 April 1916 — Corona, California

Cagno, Alessandro. 2 May 1883 — Turin, Italy; 23 December 1971 — Turin, Italy

Campari, Giuseppe. 8 June 1892 — Lodi, Italy; 10 September 1933 — Monza, Italy

Cappa, Giulio Cesare. 1880; 1955 — Voghera, Italy

Carlson, William "Billy." 17 October 1889 — San Diego, California; 4 July 1915 — Tacoma, Washington

Cavalli, Carlo. 7 July 1878 — Vigezzo nel Novarese, Italy; 1 October 1947 — Domodossola, Italy

Cedrino, Emanuele. 7 April 1879; 29 May 1908 — Baltimore, Maryland

Charron, Fernand. 1866 — Angers, France; August 13, 1928 — Maisons-Laffitte, France

Chassagne, Jean. 26 July 1881— La Croisille-sur-Briance, France; 13 April 1947 — La Croisille-sur-Briance, France

Chevrolet, Arthur. 25 April 1884 — La Chaux de Fond, Switzerland; 16 April 1946 — Slidell, Louisiana

Chevrolet, Gaston. 4 October 1892 — Beaune, France; 25 November 1920 — Beverly Hills, California

Chevrolet, Louis. 25 December 1878 — La Chaux de Fond; 6 June 1941 — Detroit, Michigan

Chiron, Louis. 3 August 1899 — Monte Carlo; 22 June 1979 — Monte Carlo

Christiaens, Joseph. 1880; 23 February 1919

Christie, Walter. 6 May 1865 — River Edge, New Jersey; 11 January 1944 — Falls Church, Virginia

Coda, Giuseppe. 8 July 1883 — Biella Cossila, Italy; 30 October 1977 — Biella Cossila, Italy

Cooper, Earl. 2 December 1886 — Broken Bow, Nebraska; 22 October 1965 — Atwater, California

Cooper, Joe. Indianapolis; 7 August 1915 — Valley Junction, Iowa

Costantini, Bartolomeo. 14 February 1889 — Vittorio Veneto, Italy; 19 July 1941— Milan, Italy

Cystria, Bertrand de. 3 December 1898 — Paris, France; 22 February 1943 — Paris, France

Daimler, Paul. 13 September 1869 — Karlsruhe, Germany; 15 December 1945 — Berlin, Germany

Dawson, Joe. 19 April 1889 — Odon, Indiana; 17 June 1946 — Langhorne, Pennsylvania

Delage, Louis. 22 March 1874 — Cognac, France; 14 December 1947 — Le Pecq, Paris, France

Delling, Erich Hermann. 7 July 1884 — Germany

DePalma, John. 16 February 1885 — Biccari, Italy; 18 January 1951

DePalma, Ralph. 19 December 1882 — Biccari, Italy; 31 March 1956 — Pasadena, California

DePaolo, Peter. 15 April 1898 — Roseland, New Jersey; 26 November 1980

Dingley, Bert. 21 August 1885 — Oakdale, California; 7 April 1966 — Indianapolis

Disbrow, Louis. 24 March 1888 — Indianapolis; 9 July 1939

Divo, Albert. 24 January 1895 — Paris, France; 19 September 1966 — Morsang-sur-Orge, France

Duesenberg, Augie. 11 December 1879 — Kirchheide, Germany; 18 January 1955 — Indianapolis

Duesenberg, Fred. 6 December 1877 — Kirchheide, Germany; July 26, 1932 — Indianapolis

Duray, Arthur. 9 February 1882 — Brussels, Belgium; 11 February 1954

Duray, Leon. 30 April 1894 — Cleveland, Ohio; 12 May 1956 — San Bernadino, California

Eldridge, Ernest Arthur. 18 July 1897 — Willesden, London, England; 27 October 1935 — Kensington, London, England

Faroux, Charles. 20 December 1873 — Noyon, France; 9 February 1957 — Neuilly-sur-Seine, France

Ferrari, Enzo. 18 February 1898 — Modena, Italy; 14 August 1988 — Maranello, Italy

Fisher, Carl Graham. 12 January 1874 — Greensburg, Indiana; 15 July 1939 — Miami, Florida

Fountaine, Louis. December 20, 1882 — Cato, Michigan

Fournier, Achille. 6 February 1868 — Le Mans, France

Fournier, Henry. 13 April 1871 — Le Mans, France

Fournier, Maurice. 30 December 1880 — Le Mans, France

Friderich, Ernest. 23 October 1886 — Paris, France; 22 January 1954 — Nice, France

Girardot, Léonce. 30 April 1864 — Paris, France

Giraud, Étienne-Édouard. 10 November 1865 — Rochefort-sur-Mer, France

Goossen, Leo William. 7 June 1892 — Kalamazoo, Michigan; 4 December 1974

Gordon, Huntley. 5 September 1883; 15 December 1967

Goux, Jules. 6 April 1885 — Beaulieu-Valentigney, France; 6 March 1965 — Mirmande, France

Grant, Harry. 10 July 1877 — Cambridge, Massachusetts; 7 October 1915 — New York

Greiner, Arthur. 1884 — Chicago, Illinois; 15 December 1916 — Chicago, Illinois

Guyot, Albert. 25 December 1881 — Orléans, France; 24 March 1947 — Neuilly, France

Harroun, Ray. 12 January 1879 — Spartansburg, Pennsylvania; 19 January 1968 — Anderson, Indiana

Haupt, Willie. 10 July 1885 — East Cameron, Pennsylvania; 16 April 1966 — Elkins Park, Pennsylvania

Hearne, Eddie. 1 March 1887 — Kansas City, Kansas; 9 February 1955 — Los Angeles, California

Hémery, Victor. 18 November 1876 — Sillé-le-Guillaume, Sarthe, France; 8 September 1950 — Le Mans, France

Henry, Ernest. 12 January 1885 — Geneva, Switzerland; 12 December 1950 — Paris, France

Hughes, Hugh. 1886 — London, England; 2 December 1916 — Uniontown, Pennsylvania

Huillier, Georges. 12 May 1870 — Bagneux, France

Jano, Vittorio. 22 April 1891 — San Giorgio Canavese, Italy; 13 March 1965 — Turin, Italy

Jenatzy, Camille. 4 November 1868 — Schaerbeek, Belgium; 8 December 1913 — Habay-la-Neuve, Belgium

Klein, Arthur. 9 October 1889 — Cleveland, Ohio; 6 June 1955

Lamberjack, Émile. 17 July 1869 — Paris

Lancia, Vincenzo. 24 August 1881 — Fobello, Italy; 15 February 1937 — Turin, Italy

Lautenschlager, Christian. 13 April 1877 — Magstadt, Germany; 3 January 1954 — Untertürkheim, Germany

LeCain, Jack. 28 June 1887 — Roxbury, Massachusetts; 13 February 1939 — Charleston, West Virginia

Lewis, Dave. 11 May 1881 — Syracuse, New York; 13 May 1928 — La Jolla, San Francisquito Canyon, CA

Limberg, Carl. 1878 — Pennsylvania; 13 May 1916 — Sheepshead Bay, New York

Lory, Albert. 19 June 1894 — Vibraye, France; 20 February 1963

Marmon, Howard. 24 May 1876 — Richmond, Indiana; 4 April 1943

Maserati, Alfieri. 23 September 1887 — Voghera, Italy; 3 March 1932 — Bologna, Italy

Maserati, Bindo. 1883 — Voghera, Italy

Maserati, Ernesto. 4 August 1898 — Voghera, Italy; 24 November 1975 — Bologna, Italy

Maserati, Ettore. 1894 — Voghera, Italy; 4 August 1990 — Bologna, Italy

Mason, George. 12 March 1891 — Valley City, North Dakota; 8 October 1954 — Detroit, Michigan

Materassi, Emilio. 1 November 1889 — Porga San Lorenzo, Italy; 9 September 1928 — Monza, Italy

Mégevet, Charles-Jules. 10 August 1874 — Geneva, Switzerland

Merosi, Giuseppe. 8 December 1872; 27 March 1956

Merz, Charlie. 6 July 1888 — Indianapolis, Indiana; 8 July 1952 — Indianapolis, Indiana

Miller, Harry Armenius. 9 December 1875 — Menomonie, Wisconsin ; 3 May 1943 — Detroit, Michigan

Milton, Tommy. 14 November 1893 — St. Paul, Minnesota; 11 July 1962 — Mount Clemens, Missouri

Minoia, Ferdinando. 2 June 1884; 28 June 1940

Morel, André. 3 August 1884; 5 October 1961

Moriceau, Jules. 2 January 1887 — Nantes, France; 1977

Mulford, Ralph. 28 December 1884 — Brooklyn, New York; 23 October 1973 — Asbury Park, New Jersey

Nazzaro, Biagio. 3 July 1890 — Turin, Italy; 15 July 1922 — Entzheim near Strasbourg, France

Nazzaro, Felice. 4 December 1881 — Turin, Italy; 21 March 1940 — Turin, Italy

O'Donnell, Eddie. 20 December 1886 — Minnesota; 26 November 1920 — Beverly Hills, California

Offenhauser, Fred. 11 February 1888; 17 August 1973

Oldfield, Barney. 3 June 1878 — Wauseon, Ohio; 2 October 1946 — Beverly Hills, California

Oldfield, Lee. 6 June 1889 — Lone Tree, Kansas; 1 November 1978 — Cathedral City, California

Patschke, Cyrus. 6 July 1889 — Lebanon, Pennsylvania; 6 May 1951 — Lebanon, Pennsylvania

Pilette, Théodore. 8 September 1883 — St. Gillis, Belgium; 13 May 1921 — Capellen, Luxembourg

Planchon, Charles. 20 June 1880 — Paris, France

Porter, Finley Robertson. 28 December 1872 — Lowell, Ohio; 8 February 1964 — Manorville, Long Island

Pullen, Eddie. 16 August 1890 — Trenton, New Jersey; 6 October 1940 — Hightstown, New Jersey

Resta, Dario. 19 August 1882 — Faenza, Italy; 3 September 1924 — Brooklands, England

Rickenbacher, Eddie. 8 October 1890 — Columbus, Ohio; 23 July 1973 — Zürich, Switzerland

Riganti, Raoul. 2 February 1893 — Buenos Aires, Argentina; 1 October 1970 — Buenos Aires, Argentina

Rooney, Tom. 30 November 1881 — Wolburn, Massachusetts; 1939

Ruckstell, Grover. 5 May 1891 — San Francisco, California; 28 May 1963 — Riverside, California

Segrave, Henry. 22 September 1896; 13 June 1930

Sivocci, Ugo. 29 August 1885; 8 September 1923

Sterlich, Diego de. 13 August 1898 — Pescara, Italy; 30 August 1976 — Teramo, Italy

Stutz, Harry Clayton. 12 September 1876 — Ansonia, Ohio; 26 June 1930 — Indianapolis

Tetzlaff, Teddy. 5 February 1883 — Los Angeles, California; 8 December 1929 — Artesia, California

Thomas, René. 7 March 1886 — Périgueux, France; 23 September 1975 — Bois-Colombes, France

Vadier, Fernand. 28 September 1894 — Poitier, France

van Raalte, Noel. 22 December 1888 — Paddington/London, England; 5 May 1940 — Kensington/London, England

van Ranst, Cornelius Willett. 7 December 1892 — New York; 11 October 1972

Vizcaya, Pierre de. 5 July 1894; 15 July 1933

Wagner, Louis. 5 February 1882 — Pré-Saint-Gervais, France; 13 March 1960 — Montlhéry, France

Wilcox, Howard. 24 June 1889 — Crawfordsville, Indiana; 4 September 1923 — Tipton, Pennsylvania

Winton, Alexander. 20 June 1860 — Grangemouth, Scotland; 21 June 1932

Wishart, Spencer. December 3, 1889 — Philadelphia, Pennsylvania; August 22, 1914 — Elgin, Illinois

Zengle, Len. 15 March 1887 — Philadelphia, Pennsylvania; 24 September 1963 — Bryn Mawr, Pennsylvania

Zerbi, Tranquillo. 2 January 1891 — Saronno, Italy; 1939

Zuccarelli, Paolo. 24 August 1886 — Milan, Italy; 19 June 1913 — Nonancourt, France

Appendix B: Technical Data

	Bore × Stroke (mm; inches = ")	Head/ valves	Wheelbase (cm; inches = ")	Tires front / rear (mm or inches)
Alco— *Providence, Rhode Island*				
1910 585 ci six	4.75" × 5.5"	T	126"	36 × 4 / 35 × 4.75
Alfa Romeo— *Milan, Italy— design by Giuseppe Merosi (1923) and Vittorio Jano (1924)*				
1923 2 ltr six	65 × 100	DOHC	265	28 × 4.5 / 28 × 5
1924/25 2 ltr eight	61 × 85	DOHC	263	29 × 5.25 / 29 × 6
Ballot— *Paris, France— design by Ernest Henry*				
1919 4.9 ltr eight	74 × 140	DOHC/4	275	875 × 105 / 880 × 120
1920/21 3 ltr eight	65 × 112	DOHC/4	265	820 × 120 / 835 × 135
1922 2 ltr four	69.9 × 130	DOHC/4	280	815 × 105 / 820 × 120
Benz— *Mannheim, Germany— design by Hans Niebel, Georg Diehl and Louis de Groulart*				
1908 12 ltr four	155 × 160	OHV	275	875 × 105 / 895 × 135
1908/1912 15 ltr four	155 × 200	OHV	275	875 × 105 / 895 × 135
1910 21 ltr four	185 × 200	OHV	275	35 × 4.5 / 35 × 5
Bugatti— *Molsheim, Alsace, France (Germany between 1871 and 1918)*				
1914 5 ltr four	100 × 180	OHC/3	255	33 × 5
1914/20 1.4 ltr four	65.64 × 100	OHC/4	200	700 × 85
1922 2 ltr eight	60 × 88	OHC/3	240	765 × 105
1923 2 ltr eight	60 × 88	OHC/3	200	28 × 4
1924 2 ltr eight	60 × 88	OHC/3	240	710 × 90
1926 1.5 ltr eight	60 × 66	OHC/3	240	710 × 90
1927/30 2.3 ltr eight	60 × 100	OHC/3	240	28 × 4.75
1931/33 2.3 ltr eight	60 × 100	DOHC	240	29 × 5
Burman's specials				
1913 Keeton 450 ci four	5.1" × 5.5"	T	108.3"	33 × 4.5 / 34 × 4.5
1914 Burman 450 ci four	5.1" × 5.5"	OHV/4	109.25"	35 × 5
1915 Peugeot 300 ci four	3.66" × 7.1"	DOHC/4	106"	34 × 4.5
1916 Premier 280 ci four	3.66" × 6.656"	DOHC/4	106"	32 × 4 / 34 × 4.5
Delage— *Courbevoie, Paris, France— design by Arthur Michelat (1913/14), Charles Planchon (1923) and Albert Lory (1924/27)*				
1913 6.2 ltr four	105 × 180	OHV/horiz./4	275	875 × 105 / 880 × 120
1914 4.5 ltr four	94 × 160	DOHC/4-desmo	270	875 × 105 / 895 × 135
1923/25 2 ltr V-12	51.3 × 80	DOHC	260	31 × 4.75 / 31 × 5.25
1926/27 1.5 ltr eight	55.8 × 76	DOHC	250	30 × 4.75
Deltal— *Connecticut— design by Eric Delling and P. F. Hackethal*				
1913 300 ci four	4" × 5.945"	L	109"	34 × 4.5

	Bore × Stroke (mm; inches = ")	Head/ valves	Wheelbase (cm; inches = ")	Tires front / rear (mm or inches)
Diatto—*Turin, Italy—design by Giuseppe Coda and Alfieri Maserati*				
1922 2 ltr four	79.7 × 100	OHC	250	810 × 90 / 815 × 105
1923 3 ltr four	90 × 116	OHC	250	810 × 90 / 815 × 105
1924/25 2 ltr eight	65.5 × 74	DOHC	265	29 × 5 / 29 × 5.5
Mason-Duesenberg, Duesenberg—*Marshalltown, Iowa; St. Paul, Minnesota; Indianapolis, Indiana*				
1912 235 ci four	3.875" × 5"	OHV/horiz.	104"	32 × 3.5
1913/14 350 ci four	4.316" × 6"	OHV/horiz.	106.5"	32 × 4 / 34 × 4.5
1915/19 300 ci four	3.985" × 6"	OHV/horiz.	106"	32 × 4 / 34 × 4.5
1919 300 ci eight	3" × 5.25"	OHC/3	106"	32 × 4 / 33 × 5
1920/22 183 ci eight	2.5" × 4.625"	OHC/3	106"	32 × 4.5
1923/25 122 ci eight	2,375" × 3.422"	DOHC/4 (2)	100"	29 × 4.5
1926/29 91 ci eight	2.286" × 2.75"	DOHC	100"	29 × 5 or 29 × 5.25
Fiat—*Turin, Italy—design by Giuseppe Coda (1910/14), Giulio Cesare Cappa (1921/24) and Tranquillo Zerbi (1927)*				
1910 10 ltr four	130 × 190	OHC/4	275	875 × 105 / 895 × 135
1911 14 ltr four	150 × 200	OHC/4	272	875 × 105 / 895 × 135
1914 4.5 ltr four	100 × 143	OHC	275	875 × 105 / 880 × 120
1921 3 ltr four	85 × 131	DOHC/4-desmo	275	820 × 120 / 835 × 120
1921 3 ltr eight	65 × 112	DOHC	275	820 × 120 / 835 × 120
1922 2 ltr six	65 × 100	DOHC	250	760 × 90 / 765 × 105
1923/25 2 ltr eight	60 × 87.5	DOHC	262	29 × 4 / 29 × 4.5
1927 1.5 ltr V-12	50 × 63	3×OHC	240	29 × 4.5 / 29 × 5
Frontenac—*Indianapolis, Indiana—design by Louis Chevrolet (1917) and Cornelius Van Ranst (1920/21)*				
1917 300 ci four	3.87" × 6.375"	OHC/4	104"	33 × 5
1920 183 ci four	3.125" × 5.9375"	DOHC/4	98"	32 × 4 / 32 × 4.5
1921 183 ci eight	2.625" × 4.219"	DOHC/4	102"	32 × 4.5
Marmon—*Indianapolis, Indiana*				
1910/11 477 ci six	4.5" × 5"	T	116"	34 × 4.5 / 35 × 5
1910/11 445 ci four	4.5" × 7"	F	120"	34 × 4.5 / 35 × 5
Maserati—*Bologna, Italy*				
1926/30 1.5 ltr eight	60 × 66	DOHC	258/265	27 × 4.4 / 28 × 4.95
1927/30 2 ltr eight	62 × 82	DOHC	258/265	28 × 4.75 / 28 × 4.95
1929/31 4 ltr U-16	62 × 82	2×DOHC	267	29 × 5.25 / 31 × 5.5
1930/32 2.5 ltr eight	64 × 95	DOHC	258/265/275	29 × 5.25 / 29 × 5.5
Maxwell—*Detroit, Michigan—design by Ray Harroun*				
1914 450 ci four	4.2" × 8"	OHC	104"	32 × 4.5 / 33 × 5
1915 300 ci four	3.75" × 6.75"	OHC/4-DOHC/4	110"	33 × 5
Mercedes—*Untertürkheim, Stuttgart, Germany—design by Paul Daimler, Eugen Link, Karl Schnaitmann and Ferdinand Porsch (1924)*				
1912/14 9.5 ltr four	130 × 180	OHV/3	270	880 × 120 / 895 × 135
1914 4.5 ltr four	93 × 165	OHC/4	285	815 × 105 / 835 × 135
1923 2 ltr four	70 × 129	DOHC/4	273	29 × 4.5
1924 2 ltr eight	62 × 82.6	DOHC/4	260	29 × 4.5 / 29 × 5
Mercer—*Trenton, New Jersey—design by Finley R. Porter (1911/14) and Eric Delling (1914/15)*				
1911/14 300 ci four	4.375" × 5"	T	108"	32 × 4
1913/14 450 ci four	4.8" × 6.189"	T	112"	34 × 4.5 / 35 × 5
1914/15 300 ci four	3.75 × 6.75	L	109"	35 × 5
Miller—*Los Angeles, California—design by Leo Goossen (from 1920)*				
1917 300 ci four	3.625" × 7"	OHC/4	104"	33 × 5

	Bore × Stroke (mm; inches = ")	Head/ valves	Wheelbase (cm; inches = ")	Tires front / rear (mm or inches)
1922 183 ci eight	2.6875" × 4"	DOHC/4	104"	32 × 4.5
1923/25 122 ci eight	2.3125" × 3"	DOHC	100"	29 × 4.5
1926/29 91 ci eight	2.1875" × 3.091"	DOHC	100"	29 × 5 or 29 × 5.25

National—*Indianapolis, Indiana*

1911 590 ci four	5" × 7.5"	F	115"	34 × 4 / 34 × 5
1912 490 ci four	5" × 6.25"	T	108"	34 × 4 / 34 × 5

Peugeot—*Levallois-Perret, Paris, France*—*design by Ernest Henry*

1912 7.6 ltr four	110 × 200	DOHC/4	275	875 × 105 / 880 × 120
1913 5.6 ltr four	100 × 180	DOHC/4	270	875 × 105 / 895 × 135
1913 3 ltr four	78 × 156	DOHC/4	256	32 × 5 (1914 Indy)
1914 4.5 ltr four	92 × 169	DOHC/4	270	34 × 4.5 (1915 Indy)

Stutz—*Indianapolis, Indiana*

1911/12 390 ci four	4.75" × 5.5"	T	110"	34 × 4 / 34 × 4.5
1913/14 435 ci four	4.813" × 6"	T	112"	34 × 4.5 / 34 × 4.5
1915 300 ci four	3.816" × 6.484"	OHC/4	104"	33 × 5

Sunbeam-Talbot-Darracq—*Wolverhampton, England and Suresnes, Paris, France*—*design by Edmondo Moglia (1920/21), Ernest Henry (1922), Vincenzo Bertarione and Walter Becchia (1923/27)*

1914 4.5 ltr six (Indianapolis)	80 × 150	L	211	34 × 4.5
1920/21 3 ltr eight	65 × 112	DOHC/4	270	820 × 120 / 835 × 135
1922 2 ltr four	68 × 136	DOHC/4	250	30 × 4
1923/25 2 ltr six	67 × 94	DOHC	250/260	765 × 105
1926/27 1.5 ltr eight	56 × 75.5	DOHC	262	30 × 4.75

Appendix C: Riding Mechanics

Names of the forgotten heroes of early auto racing, the riding mechanics, as reported in contemporary magazines and newspapers:

14 October 1905 — Vanderbilt Cup, Long Island

Car	Driver	Riding mechanic
no. 1 Mercedes	Camille Jenatzy	Bariz
no. 2 De Dietrich	Arthur Duray	Franville
no. 3 Pope-Toledo	Bert Dingley	Nichols
no. 4 Fiat	Vincenzo Lancia	Aissa
no. 5 Mercedes	Foxhall Keene	Willy Lüttgen
no. 6 Darracq	Louis Wagner	Ruillet
no. 7 Locomobile	Joe Tracy	Al Poole
no. 8 Fiat	Felice Nazzaro	Antonio Fagnano
no. 9 Mercedes	John B. Warden	Oestreicher
no. 10 Renault	Ferenc Szisz	Dimitriévitch
no. 11 Christie	Walter Christie	Selvar
no. 12 Fiat	Emanuele Cedrino	Siefest
no. X Mercedes	Al Campbell	?
no. 14 Panhard	George Heath	Gaubert
no. 15 Pope-Toledo	Herb Lyttle	Tattersall
no. 16 Fiat	Louis Chevrolet	Schettling
no. 18 Darracq	Victor Hémery	?
no. 19 White	Rollin T. White	Hantak
no. 10 Fiat	Paul Sartori	Letrini

24 October 1908 — Vanderbilt Cup, Long Island

no. 1 Locomobile	Joe Florida	L. Travis
no. 2 Knox	A. Denison	J. Crane
no. 3 Mercedes	Emil Stricker	H. Conners
no. 4 Chadwick	Willie Haupt	E. A. Lindquist
no. 5 Mercedes	Willy Lüttgen	William Pfeiffer
no. 6 Isotta-Fraschini	Herb Lytle	William Fehr
no. 7 Matheson	J. B. Ryall	Roy Hook
no. 9 Hotchkiss	E. J. Kilpatrick	Gustav Kiehn
no. 10 Brasier	Léon Pouget	Fred Stone
no. 11 Acme	Cyrus Patchke	F. Dearborn
no. 12 Thomas	George Salzman	A. Blanchard
no. 15 Matheson	Louis Chevrolet	Joe Nelson
no. 16 Locomobile	George Robertson	Glenn Ethridge
no. 17 Renault	Lewis Strang	Leo Anderson

Car	*Driver*	*Riding mechanic*
no. 18 Mercedes	Foxhall Keene	R. Ahrweiler
no. 19 Thomas	Howard Gill	J. Gerhardt
no. 20 Knox	W. A. Bourque	Jerre Lynch

30 May 1911— First Indianapolis 500

no. 1 Case	Lewis Strang	Everett
no. 2 Simplex	Ralph DePalma	Charles Bury
no. 3 Inter-State	Harry Endicott	C. E. Sprague
no. 4 National	Johnny Aitken	W. F. Kepner
no. 5 Pope-Hartford	Louis Disbrow	Richard Ulbrecht
no. 6 Pope-Hartford	Frank Fox	Jap Clemens
no. 7 Westcott	Harry Knight	John Fuller
no. 8 Case	Joseph Jaegersberger	C. L. Anderson
no. 9 Case	Will Jones	Russel Smith
no. 10 Stutz	Gil Anderson	Frank Agan
no. 11 Mercedes	Spencer Wishart	William Pfeiffer
no. 12 Amplex	W. H. Turner	?
no. 15 Knox	Fred Belcher	William Jahn
no. 16 Buick	Arthur Chevrolet	Albert Seraye
no. 17 Buick	Charlie Basle	Joseph Demand
no. 18 Fiat	Eddie Hearne	Louis Lindenstruth
no. 19 Alco	Harry Grant	Frank Lee
no. 20 National	Charlie Merz	L. E. Banks
no. 21 National	Howard Wilcox	J. P. Walker
no. 22 McFarlan	Fred Clemens	?
no. 23 McFarlan	Melvin Marquette	Henry Richardt
no. 24 Jackson	Fred Ellis	E. F. Scheifler
no. 25 Jackson	Harry Cobe	Miller
no. 26 Jackson	Jack Tower	Bob Evans
no. 27 Cutting	Ernest J. Delaney	J. D. McNay
no. 28 Fiat	David Bruce-Brown	Anthony Schudelare/Scudelari
no. 29 Lozier	Harold Van Gorder	George Ainslee
no. 30 Firestone-Columbus	Lee Frayer	Eddie Rickenbacker
no. 31 Marmon	Joe Dawson	Bruce Keene
no. 32 Marmon	Ray Harroun	
no. 33 Lozier	Ralph Mulford	Billy Chandler
no. 34 Lozier	Teddy Tetzlaff	Dave Lewis
no. 35 Apperson	Herb Lytle	W. W. Cliffton
no. 36 Mercer	Hughie Hughes	L. P. Firmin
no. 37 Mercer	Charles H. Bigelow	Charles Illingworth
no. 38 Simplex	Ralph Beardsley	George Scott
no. 39 Fiat	Caleb Bragg	Edward H. Parker
no. 40 Velie	Rupert Jeffkins	J. J. McCoy
no. 41 Velie	Howard Hall	Gus Overbeck
no. 42 Cole	Bill Endicott	Johnny Jenkins
no. 43 Cole	Louis J. Edmunds	Herb Wilson
no. 44 Amplex	Arthur Greiner	Samuel P. Dickson
no. 45 Benz	Bob Burman	?
no. 46 Benz	Billy Knipper	?

25 and 26 June 1912 — Grand Prix de l'ACF
and Coupe de l'Auto, Dieppe

no. 11 Lorraine-Dietrich	Victor Hémery	Michael Gilli
no. 12 Mathis	Willy Esser	Bauer
no. 13 Peugeot	Jules Goux	Émile Bégin

Car	Driver	Riding mechanic
no. 22 Peugeot	Georges Boillot	Prévost
no. 23 Fiat	Louis Wagner	Ferro
no. 30 Rolland-Pilain	Albert Guyot	Arnault
no. 31 Lorraine-Dietrich	Paul Bablot	Lausson
no. 34 Lorraine-Dietrich	René Hanriot	Vauthier
no. 37 Fiat	David Bruce-Brown	Anthony Schudelare/Scudelari
no. 42 Fiat	Ralph DePalma	Antonio Fagnano
no. 45 Peugeot	Paolo Zuccarelli	Ernesto Fanelli
no. 49 Rolland-Pilain	Fauquet (Anford)	Bertrand
no. 50 Excelsior	Joseph Christiaens	?
no. 57 Lorraine-Dietrich	Franz Heim	?
no. 3 Sunbeam	Victor Rigal	Jean Chassagne
no. 4 Alcyon	Philippe Barriaux	Gilbert
no. 7 Sizaire-Naudin	Georges Sizaire	Voignier
no. 8 Vinot-Deguingand	Léon Molon	Bajan
no. 9 Th. Schneider	Champoiseau	Daclin
no. 10 Grégoire	Philippe de Marne	Dubos
no. 14 Calthorpe	Garcet	Dogson
no. 16 Sunbeam	Gustave Caillois	Vivet
no. 17 Sunbeam	Dario Resta	Harrison
no. 18 Grégoire	Collinet	Bassagnana
no. 19 Sizaire-Naudin	Louis Naudin	Champion
no. 20 Th. Schneider	Croquet	?
no. 21 Grégoire	Romano	?
no. 24 Grégoire	Eugène Renaux	Pouliguem
no. 25 Singer	Rollason	Clarke
no. 26 Calthorpe	Hornsted	Alsopp
no. 27 Alcyon	Page	Gauthier
no. 28 Arrol-Johnston	Reid	Nelville
no. 29 Côte	Fernand Gabriel	Badier
no. 32 Vinot-Deguingand	Vonlatum	Carteau
no. 33 Vauxhall	Percy Lambert	Gibbs
no. 36 Arrol-Johnston	Crossman	Barré
no. 38 Sizaire-Naudin	Schweitzer	Royer
no. 39 Singer	Haywood	Janod
no. 40 Alcyon	Arthur Duray	Albin
no. 41 Côte	Cyril de Vère	Paupert
no. 43 Calthorpe	F. Burgess	I. Burgess
no. 47 Lion-Peugeot	René Thomas	Robert Laly
no. 51 Vauxhall	A. J. Hancock	Fraser
no. 52 Sunbeam	Ernst Medinger	Strothers
no. 54 Vauxhall	Watson	Sivain
no. 55 Arroll-Johnston	Wyse	Renfrew
no. 56 Vinot-Deguingand	Lucien Molon	Le Bris

12 July 1913 — Grand Prix de l'ACF, Amiens

Car	Driver	Riding mechanic
no. 1 Sunbeam	Gustave Caillois	Smith
no. 2 Delage	Paul Bablot	Lausson
no. 3 Opel	Carl Joerns	Breckheimer
no. 4 Mathis	Willy Esser	Henrard
no. 5 Excelsior	Joseph Christiaens	Dills
no. 6 Th. Schneider	Croquet	Didier
no. 7 Itala	Felice Nazzaro	Cosso
no. 8 Peugeot	Georges Boillot	Prévost
no. 9 Sunbeam	Dario Resta	Harrison
no. 10 Delage	Albert Guyot	Achille Secuws

Car	*Driver*	*Riding mechanic*
no. 11 Excelsior	Hornsted	Caerells
no. 12 Th. Schneider	Fernand Gabriel	Mongeot
no. 13 Itala	Pope	Aldertella
no. 14 Peugeot	Jules Goux	Émile Bégin
no. 15 Sunbeam	Jean Chassagne	Mitchell
no. 16 Th. Schneider	Champoiseau	Didier
no. 17 Itala	Antonio Moriondo	Giulio Foresti
no. 18 Peugeot	Jean Delpierre	Marronet
no. 19 Sunbeam	Kenelm Lee Guinness	Cook
no. 10 Th. Schneider	René Thomas	Benblant

28 February 1914 — American Grand Prize, Santa Monica

no. 1 Fiat	Teddy Tetzlaff	F. L. Radford
no. 2 Mercer	Spencer Wishart	Johnny Jenter
no. 3 Stutz	Gil Anderson	Tom Rooney
no. 4 Mercer	Eddie Pullen	Andy Vollman
no. 5 Mason-Duesenberg	Billy Carlson	F. E. Allen
no. 6 Alco	Billy Taylor	J. F. Smith
no. 7 Mercer	Barney Oldfield	George Hill
no. 8 Stutz	Earl Cooper	Bob Aulert
no. 9 Mercer	Huntley Gordon	George Puterbaugh
no. 11 Apperson	Frank Goode	George Storck
no. 14 Sunbeam	Johnny Marquis	Harry Haugh
no. 15 Marmon	Charles Muth	B. H. Jones
no. 16 Fiat	Dave Lewis	August Duesenberg
no. 17 Marmon	Guy Ball	Harry Sohner
no. 18 Fiat	Frank Verbeck	Henry Miller
no. 19 Alco	Tony Janette	Bert Hooper
no. 20 Mason-Duesenberg	Eddie Rickenbacker	Lou Sorrell
no. 22 Mercedes	Ralph DePalma	Tom Alley

9 January 1915 — San Diego Exposition Road Race, Point Loma

no. 2 Duesenberg	Tom Alley	L. R. Shipley
no. 3 Tahis	Jack Gable	W. H. Carlton
no. 4 Mercer	Grover Ruckstell	John Jepson
no. 5 Gordon-Mercer	Huntley Gordon	W. W. Gordon
no. 6 Peugeot	Bob Burman	Eric Schroeder
no. 7 Peugeot	Eddie Rickenbacker	M. T. Diebolt
no. 8 Stutz	Earl Cooper	Reeves Dutton
no. 9 Peugeot	Fred McCarthy	O. C. Linthwaite
no. 10 Duesenberg	Jesse Callaghan	Louis LeCocq
no. 11 Marmon	Arthur Cadwell	Jack Williams
no. 12 Mercer	Louis Nikrent	Kenneth Nikrent
no. 14 Maxwell	Barney Oldfield	George Hill
no. 15 King	Art Klein	Fred Comer
no. 16 Carling	A. T. Dickey	A. K. Lambra
no. 17 Maxwell	Billy Carlson	Paul Franzen
no. 18 Shields	L. B. Shields	Grover Young
no. 19 Duesenberg	Eddie O'Donnell	Pete Henderson
no. 20 Alco	Billy Taylor	C. P. Johnson

26 June 1915 — 500-Mile Race, Chicago, Maywood Speedway

Car	*Driver*	*Riding mechanic*
no. 1 Peugeot	Dario Resta	Fred McCarthy
no. 2 Stutz	Howdy Wilcox	C. W. Scott
no. 3 Stutz	Gil Anderson	Tom Rooney
no. 4 Stutz	Earl Cooper	Reeves Dutton
no. 5 Maxwell	Billy Carlson	Paul Franzen
no. 7 Maxwell	Eddie Rickenbacker	Eric Schroeder
no. 10 Sunbeam	Noel van Raalte	Copple
no. 11 Sunbeam	Jean Porporato	Rocco
no. 12 Delage	Louis Chevrolet	Phillips
no. 15 Duesenberg	Eddie O'Donnell	Pete Henderson
no. 17 Sunbeam	Harry Grant	Bob Moore
no. 20 Mercer	Otto Henning	Caris
no. 21 Duesenberg	Willie Haupt	C. P. Johnson
no. 22 Peugeot	George Babcock	Roxie Palotti
no. 23 Sebring	Joe Cooper	Louis Peio
no. 24 Ogren	Billy Chandler	Liphardt
no. 27 Maxwell	Tom Orr	Reuben Stafford
no. 30 Mulford (Duesenb.)	Ralph Mulford	Paul Stevens
no. 31 Sunbeam	Carl Limberg	Longchamp

9 October 1915 — Astor Cup, Sheepshead Bay

no. 1 Peugeot	Dario Resta	Fred McCarthy
no. 2 Peugeot	Johnny Aitken	Maurice Becker
no. 3 Delage	Barney Oldfield	Ray Dasbach
no. 4 Peugeot	Bob Burman	Jack Gable
no. 5 Stutz	Gil Anderson	C. W. Scott
no. 6 Peugeot	Howdy Wilcox	Ben Rout
no. 7 Stutz	Tom Rooney	Maurice Rocco
no. 8 Stutz	Earl Cooper	Reeves Dutton
no. 9 Duesenberg	Eddie O'Donnell	Jim Henderson
no. 10 Maxwell	Eddie Rickenbacher	Harry Goetz
no. 11 Mulford	Ira Vail	Harold Wright
no. 12 Pugh	Jack LeCain	Frank Hickey
no. 14 Sebring	Ora Haibe	Robert Guion
no. 15 Duesenberg	Willie Haupt	Jim Alexander
no. 16 Duesenberg	Pete Henderson	Arthur Johnson
no. 17 Maxwell	Eddie Pullen	Reuben Stafford
no. 18 Peugeot	Ralph Mulford	Paul Stevens
no. 19 Delage	Carl Limberg	Roxie Palotti
no. 20 Stutz	Ralph DePalma	Louis Fountaine
no. 22 Ogren	Tom Alley	Harold Smith

4 September 1921 — Gran Premio d'Italia, Brescia

no. 2 Fiat	Louis Wagner	Evasio Lampiano
no. 4 Ballot	Ralph DePalma	Peter DePaolo
no. 6 Fiat	Pietro Bordino	Bruno
no. 8 Ballot	Jean Chassagne	Rober Laly
no. 10 Fiat	Ugo Sivocci	Morganti
no. 11 Ballot	Jules Goux	Jules Leboucq

2 July 1923 — Grand Prix de l'ACF, Tours

Car	Driver	Riding mechanic
no. 1 Delage	René Thomas	Lhermitte
no. 2 Sunbeam	Kenelm Lee Guinness	Perkins
no. 3 Rolland-Pilain	Albert Guyot	Létigny
no. 4 Fiat	Pietro Bordino	Bruno
no. 5 Voisin	Arthur Duray	Blanc
no. 6 Bugatti	Ernest Friderich	Rohfritsch
no. 7 Sunbeam	Albert Divo	Hivernat
no. 9 Fiat	Enrico Giaccone	Carignano
no. 10 Voisin	André Lefebvre	Fortin
no. 11 Bugatti	Pierre de Vizcaya	Étienne
no. 12 Sunbeam	Henry Segrave	Paul Dutoit
no. 13 Rolland-Pilain	Victor Hémery	Gaston Delalande
no. 14 Fiat	Carlo Salamano	Ferretti
no. 15 Voisin	Henri Rougier	Lalaurie
no. 16 Bugatti	Pierre Marco	Ernest Zirn
no. 17 Voisin	André Morel	Chanut
no. 18 Bugatti	Bertrand de Cystria	Georges Lutz

3 August 1924 — Grand Prix de l'ACF, Lyon-Givors

Car	Driver	Riding mechanic
no. 1 Sunbeam	Henry Segrave	Marocchi
no. 2 Delage	Albert Divo	Frétet
no. 3 Alfa Romeo	Antonio Ascari	Giulio Ramponi
no. 4 Schmid	Giulio Foresti	Janin
no. 5 Fiat	Felice Nazzaro	Carignano
no. 6 Miller	Louis Zborowski	Sammy Davis
no. 7 Bugatti	Jean Chassagne	Epting
no. 8 Sunbeam	Kenelm Lee Guinness	Perkins
no. 9 Delage	Robert Benoist	Carra
no. 10 Alfa Romeo	Giuseppe Campari	Attilio Marinoni
no. 11 Schmid	Jules Goux	Schoenenberger
no. 12 Fiat	Pietro Bordino	Bruno
no. 13 Bugatti	Ernest Friderich	Rohfritsch
no. 14 Sunbeam	Dario Resta	Ledu
no. 15 Delage	René Thomas	Lhermitte
no. 16 Alfa Romeo	Louis Wagner	Sozzi
no. 17 Fiat	Cesare Pastore	Mauro
no. 18 Bugatti	Pierre de Vizcaya	Étienne
no. 20 Fiat	Onesimo Marchisio	Lorenzo
no. 21 Bugatti	Leonico Garnier	Ernest Zirn
no. 22 Bugatti	Barlolomeo Costantini	Soderini

Notes

Chapter 1

1. "Annecdotes about J. Gordon Bennett," *New York Times*, 19 May 1918.
2. "Obituary — James Gordon Bennett," *New York Times*, 2 June 1872.
3. "The Late James Gordon Bennett," *New York Times*, 25 June 1872.
4. "Bennett a Figure in Many Annecdotes," *New York Times*, 15 May 1918.
5. "A Street Encouter — James Gordon Bennett Attacked," *New York Times*, 4 January 1877.
6. "The Bennett-May Affair — The Truth at Last," *New York Times*, 13 January 1877.
7. David Rains Wallace, *The Bonehunters' Revenge: Dinosaurs, Greed, and the Greatest Scientific Feud of the Gilded Age* (New York, 1999).
8. "To Buy the Yacht Namouna," *New York Times*, 28 March 1901.
9. *The Bonehunters' Revenge.*
10. The ACF was a society for encouraging the development of the automobile industry in France. The club was managed by a committee of 50 members elected for five years by the annual general assembly. JGB was elected member in 1896, Willie Vanderbilt and Albert Bostwick in 1900.
11. *The Horseless Age,* 28 June 1899, page 12.
12. The *New York Times* published the original Bennett rules on 23 February 1903: "In view of the fact that a team of American automobilists will compete in the annual race for the Bennett International Automobile Cup, representing the automobile racing championship of the world, next Summer, the rules under which the contest will be held are of interest."
13. *The Automobile* (New York), 20 July 1905, page 73.
14. *The Horseless Age,* 4 July 1900, page 14.
15. Charles Jarrott, *Ten Years of Motors and Motor Racing* (London: Dutton, 1906), page 209.
16. *Ibid.*
17. *Archives Commerciales de la France, 15ème Année,* Paris, 1888, page 363.
18. *The Horseless Age,* 22 October 1902, page 452.
19. *New York Times*, 12 November 1905.
20. "Fournier Winner of Automobile Race," *New York Times*, 30 June 1901.
21. "World's Auto Records Made by Oldfield," *New York Times*, 30 October 1904.
22. *The Automobile* (New York), 13 July 1905, page 36.
23. *Ibid.*
24. "J.G. Bennett Weds Baroness De Reuter," *New York Times*, 11 September 1914.

Chapter 2

1. Jerry F. Patterson, *The Vanderbilts* (New York: Abrams, 1989), page 236.
2. "Mr. Vanderbilt's New Locomobile," *New York Times*, 2 June 1900.
3. "May Arrest Mr. Vanderbilt," *New York Times*, 8 June 1900.
4. "Newport's Automobile Races," *New York Times*, 7 September 1900.
5. "New Automobile Records," *New York Times*, 19 September 1900.
6. *The Horseless Age,* 9 May 1900, page 22.
7. *The Horseless Age,* 20 June 1900, page 27.
8. *Automobile Magazine* (New York), October 1901.
9. Edward L. Bowen, *Legacies of the Turf: A Century of Great Thoroughbred Breeders* (Lexington, KY: Eclipse Press, 2003).

10. "New Automobile Records," *New York Times*, 17 November 1901.

11. "Vanderbilt's New Record," *New York Times*, 4 May 1902.

12. "Americans and Others in Paris," *New York Times*, 8 June 1902.

13. "Race of Automobiles," *New York Times*, 27 June 1902.

14. "Vanderbilt Quits Automobile Race," *New York Times*, 28 June 1902.

15. "Count Zborowski's Career," *New York Times*, 2 April 1903.

16. "Free and Married Again," *New York Times*, 8 March 1892.

17. Charles Jarrott, *Ten Years of Motors and Motor Racing* (London: Dutton, 1906), page 218.

18. "Count Zborowski Killed," *New York Times*, 2 April 1903.

19. The identity of Zborowski's riding mechanic remains mysterious. Hans Willem van Pallandt (1866–1929) was related to the Astor family, and his name appears in the Jellinek correspondence. In the contemporary press the mechanic was described as Baron de Pallange or de Pallande. The French newspaper *L'Auto* claimed after the accident that he was not a titled nobleman, just M. Pallange.

20. "Count Zborowski Killed," *New York Times*, 2 April 1903.

21. "Paris Automobilists Off," *New York Times*, 24 May 1903.

22. "Six Persons Killed in Automobile Race," *New York Times*, 25 May 1903.

23. *Ibid.*

24. "New Automobile Record," *New York Times*, 28 January 1904.

25. "Vanderbilt Breaks More Records," *New York Times*, 31 January 1904.

26. "Vanderbilt Trick Rider," *New York Times*, 31 January 1904.

27. "Shanley Sells Racing Automobile," *New York Times*, 2 April 1905.

28. "Automobile Topics of Interest," *New York Times*, 28 September 1902.

29. "Contest for Vanderbilt Cup Will Be America's Greatest Automobile Event," *New York Times*, 2 October 1904.

30. "Race for Vanderbilt Cup," *New York Times*, 8 June 1904.

31. "Heath Auto Wins — One Man Killed," *New York Times*, 9 October 1904.

32. *Ibid.*

33. "Automobile Racers Observe Speed Laws," *New York Times*, 6 October 1904.

34. *The Automobile* (New York), 6 July 1905.

35. "Personal and Otherwise," *New York Times*, 19 January 1908.

36. *Power Boat News*, 2 September 1905, page 422.

37. *Motor Age*, 11 May 1905, page 1.

38. "World's Auto Record in Ten-Mile Race," *New York Times*, 29 January 1905.

39. "New Auto Records Made by Wridgway," *New York Times*, 7 May 1905.

40. *The Automobile* (New York), 22 April 1905, page 502.

41. *Ibid.*

42. *Ibid.*

43. "Rival Auto Shows Vie for Patronage," *New York Times*, 14 January 1906.

44. "Daredevil Tracy Wins Auto Race," *New York Times*, 23 September 1906.

45. "Vanderbilt Auto Breaks," *New York Times*, 23 January 1906.

46. "Auto Builder Sues A.G. Vanderbilt," *New York Times*, 10 January 1908.

47. *Ibid.*

48. "Vanderbilt Buys Car and Will Race for Cup," *New York Times*, 19 September 1906.

49. "Foreign Autoists Out on Cup Racing Course," *New York Times*, 27 September 1906.

50. "Luttgen Tells How to Equip Car," *New York Times*, 15 December 1907.

51. "H.B. Plant's Widow a Bride," *New York Times*, 20 January 1904.

52. "Auto Cup Race Won by Wagner," *New York Times*, 7 October 1906.

53. "'I Have Fastest Car,' Says E.F. Shepard," *New York Times*, 9 September 1906.

54. "Foreign Autoists Out on Cup Racing Course," *New York Times*, 27 September 1906

55. "'I Have Fastest Car,' Says E.F. Shepard," *New York Times*, 9 September 1906.

56. "Shepard Sells Auto," *New York Times*, 26 October 1906.

57. "E.R. Thomas Injured in an Auto Smash," *New York Times*, 15 August 1908.

58. "Recent Achievements of Men Who Will Handle Cars Make Record Breaking Probable," *New York Times*, 21 March 1909.

59. *Motor Age*, 5 March 1914, page 12.

Chapter 3

1. "Auto Club Formed for Track Racing," *New York Times*, 20 October 1904.

2. "Wide Open All the Way by Barney Oldfield — Reported by William F. Sturm," *The Saturday Evening Post*, 19 and 26 September 1925.

3. *Ibid.*

4. *Ibid.*

5. *Ibid.*

6. *Ibid.*

7. *Ibid.*

8. *Ibid.*

9. *Ibid.*

10. *Ibid.*

11. *Ibid.*

12. "Carl Fisher, Speedway Builder," *Motor Age*, 28 May 1914, page 29.

13. "Wide Open All the Way by Barney Oldfield — Reported by William F. Sturm," *The Saturday Evening Post*, 19 and 26 September 1925.

14. *Ibid.*

15. *Ibid.*

16. *Ibid.*

17. "Motors in Close Races," *New York Times*, 26 October 1902.

18. "New Automobile Records," *New York Times*, 2 December 1902.

19. "Wide Open All the Way by Barney Oldfield — Reported by William F. Sturm," *The Saturday Evening Post*, 19 and 26 September 1925.

20. *New York Times*, 2 December 1902.

21. *The Automobile* (New York), 11 July 1903, page 34.

22. *Ibid.*

23. *The Automobile* (New York), 25 July 1903, page 87.

24. *Ibid.*

25. *The Automobile* (New York), 1 August 1903, page 97.

26. "Wide Open All the Way by Barney Oldfield — Reported by William F. Sturm," *The Saturday Evening Post*, 19 and 26 September 1925.

27. *Ibid.*

28. "Winton's Automobile Record Trial," *New York Times*, 11 October 1901.

29. *The Automobile* (New York), 10 October 1903, page 363.

30. *Los Angeles Times*, 21 November 1903.

31. "Wide Open All the Way by Barney Oldfield — Reported by William F. Sturm," *The Saturday Evening Post*, 19 and 26 September 1925.

32. *Ibid.*

33. "World's Auto Records Made by Oldfield," *New York Times*, 30 October 1904.

34. "Wide Open All the Way by Barney Oldfield — Reported by William F. Sturm," *The Saturday Evening Post*, 19 and 26 September 1925.

Chapter 4

1. *Cycle and Automobile Trade Journal* (Philadelphia and New York), 1 April 1906, page 32.

2. "Heath Auto Wins — One Man Killed," *New York Times*, 9 October 1904.

3. "Frank Croker May Die; Auto Plunged into Sea," *New York Times*, 22 January 1905.

4. "Auto Briefs from Clambakes to Government Doings," *New York Times*, 28 June 1908.

5. *The Automobile* (New York), 13 July 1905, page 34.

6. Fiat factory drawing no. 1543, dated April 1905.

7. *Motor Age*, 6 July 1905, page 22.

8. "Autos at Cape May Attract Big Crowd," *New York Times*, 26 August 1905.

9. "Cedrino's Auto Records," *New York Times*, 31 May 1907.

10. "New Auto Record on Ormond Beach," *New York Times*, 6 March 1908.

11. "100-Mile Record Broken at Ormond," *New York Times*, 7 March 1908.

12. "Cedrino Killed in Racing Auto Test," *New York Times*, 30 May 1908.

13. Welsh, Charles, ed., *Chauffeur Chaff, or, Automobilia: Anecdotes, Stories Bon-mots: Also a History of the Evolution of the Automobile* (Boston: H.M. Caldwell Co., 1905).

14. "F.A. La Roche Dead," *New York Times*, 5 March 1905.

15. "Racing Cars Removed from Foreign Exhibit," *New York Times*, 19 January 1907.

16. "Cycles and Cycle Makers," *New York Times*, 16 February 1896.

17. "Heath Auto Wins — One Man Killed," *New York Times*, 9 October 1904.

18. "Garage Fire Off Broadway," *New York Times*, 25 November 1911.

19. "Free Rides Popular at Automobile Show," *New York Times*, 6 December 1906.

20. "Racing Cars Removed from Foreign Exhibit," *New York Times*, 19 January 1907.

21. "Buys Grand Prix Car," *New York Times*, 19 April 1908.

22. Floyd Clymer, *Treasury of Early American Automobiles* (New York: McGraw-Hill,, 1950), Bergdoll advertisement, page 133.

23. "Berdoll as an Aviator," *New York Times*, 12 December 1909.

24. "Heiress Weds Chauffeur," *New York Times*, 15 May 1909.

25. "On Road and in Shop," *New York Times*, 13 December 1908.

26. "After More Benz Cars," *New York Times*, 7 February 1909.

27. " Recent Achievements of Men Who Will Handle Cars Make Record Breaking Probable," *New York Times*, 21 March 1909.

28. "Brown Makes New Record at 10 Miles," *New York Times*, 25 March 1909.

29. "George Robertson New Houpt Driver," *New York Times*, 25 April 1909.

30. "Benz Car Wins Fort George Hill Climb," *New York Times*, 27 April 1909.

31. *Ibid.*

32. "Oldfield After New Records: Purchases Champion Benz Car," *New York Times*, 8 August 1909.

33. "Motor Speedway Opening," *New York Times*, 19 August 1909.

34. "Oldfield Breaks World's Records," *New York Times*, 22 August 1909.

35. "News Notes of the Automobile Trade," *New York Times*, 12 September 1909.

36. "Manager of Buick Racing Team Quits," *New York Times*, 6 October 1909.

37. "Oldfield Breaks Record," *New York Times*, 22 November 1909.

38. "New Record for Oldfield," *New York Times*, 9 December 1909.

39. *Ibid.*

40. When Oldfield bought the 21-liter Benz, he christened the car "Lightning Benz." Legend has it that Emperor Wilhelm cabled after the records at Daytona: "All Germany congratulates the daring Yankee for his achievement with the Blitzen Benz. It was a triumph of American skill and German construction." Since then it has been called the "Blitzen" Benz and so "Emperor Wilhelm named the world's greatest racing car."

41. "Johnson Wins in 15 Rounds; Jeffries Weak," *New York Times*, 5 July 1910.

42. "Barney Oldfield Is Disqualified," *New York Times*, 12 October 1910.

43. Fred J. Wagner, "Some Superlatives of the Speed Game," *Motor Age*, 11 December 1913, page 22.

44. "Wide Open All the Way by Barney Oldfield — Reported by William F. Sturm," *The Saturday Evening Post*, 19 and 26 September 1925.

45. "140 Miles an Hour in an Automobile," *New York Times*, 24 April 1911.

46. *Ibid.*

47. Fred J. Wagner, "Some Superlatives of the Speed Game," *Motor Age*, 11 December 1913, page 22.

48. "Froehlich Leaves Benz Company," *New York Times*, 28 April 1912.

49. "Barney Oldfield," *New York Times*, 9 October 1946.

Chapter 5

1. "Petites Nouvelles," *La Presse* (Paris), 21 April 1907, page 2.

2. Sports of the Times, *Story of the Automobile from the First Toy Car to the Present Perfect Self Propelled Vehicle* (New York, 1905), page 169.

3. *Ibid.*

4. J.A. Hammerton, *Mr. Punch Awheel: The Humours of Motoring and Cycling* (London: The Educational Book Co. Ltd., 1903), page 154.

5. "Personal," *The Motor* (London), 21 June 1910, page 766.

6. "Personal," *The Motor* (London), 14 June 1910, page 729.

7. "Aeroplane Drops into Sea," *New York Times*, 19 April 1910.

8. "Details of the Race," *New York Times*, 8 July 1908.

9. "Un 200 HP," *El Mundo Deportivo* (Barcelona), 7 March 1912.

10. Enrique Traumann was "director general" of the Benz agency in Madrid. Paul Anderssen was Traumann's partner and "*gerente de la Sociedad General de Automóviles*." Juan Ratés died on 13 July 1920.

11. *L'Aéro* (Paris), 1 December 1912, page 6.

12. *International Motor Cyclopaedia: Year Book, March 1908 to March 1909* (New York: E.E. Schwarzkopf, 1909).

13. "Le Grand Prix des Voiturettes," *Le Petit Parisien* (Paris), 7 July 1908, page 1.

14. "Le Président de la République au Grand Palais," *Le Figaro* (Paris), 29 November 1908, page 3.

Chapter 6

1. "Speedway Racing at Atlanta Keen Sport," *Motor Age*, 12 May 1910, page 2.

2. "Fast Time on Coast," *Motor Age*, 23 March 1910, page 11.

3. "Speedway Racing at Atlanta Keen Sport," *Motor Age*, 12 May 1910, page 3.

4. "Harroun and Marmon First Names to Be Inscribed on Wheeler & Schebler Trophy," *Motor Age*, 2 June 1910, page 7.

5. *Ibid.*, page 8.

6. "Marmon Six Wins on Latonia Track," *New York Times*, 11 July 1910.

7. Fred J. Wagner, "Some Superlatives of the Speed Game," *Motor Age*, 11 December 1913, page 22.

8. "Vanderbilt Cup Race at Daybreak," *New York Times*, 30 September 1910.

9. "Vanderbilt Entries Number Seventeen," *Motor Age*, 15 September 1910, page 16.

10. "Harry F. Grant's Career," *New York Times*, 2 October 1910.

11. "Auto Driver Killed," *El Paso Herald*, 14 November 1910, page 3.

12. "Big Cars Ready for the Grand Prix Race," *Motor Age*, 10 November 1910, page 11.

13. Fred J. Wagner, "Some Superlatives of the Speed Game," *Motor Age*, 11 December 1913, page 21.

14. "Analysis of the Mechanical Mishaps During Race," *Motor Age*, 1 June 1911, page 10.

15. *Ibid.*, page 11.

16. *Ibid.*

17. "Lozier's Name Goes on Vanderbilt Cup," *Motor Age*, 30 November 1911, page 1.

18. E.C. Alft, *Elgin: An American History*, published online at ElginHistory.com, 7 — Whirling Twenties

19. "Mechanical Features of the Racing Cars," *Motor Age*, 30 May 1912, page 15.

20. "Five-Century Race to Dawson, National," *Motor Age*, 6 June 1912, page 7.

21. "Contest Board Rejects de Palma's Marks," *Motor Age*, 4 July 1912, page 28.

22. In a letter to Floyd Clymer dated 2 April 1948, National engineer A.J. Paige wrote that the F-head engine "developed 138 hp at 1900 rpm on first block test." In 1912 the engine was picked to win the Speedway Race, but it was sabotaged. "The hose connection to the crankcase was found to be stopped by a piece of cloth which had been rammed in tight. Ironically, the mechanic who favored another make of car was killed shortly after while riding in a car of the make he preferred." Obviously the man accused by Paige was Anthony Schudelare, Bruce-Brown's riding mechanic. Letter published online at chuckstoyland.com/national/racing.

23. J.C. Burton, "Prepping the Car for the 500 Mile Race," *Motor Age*, 27 May 1915, page 10.

24. "National Quits Competition," *Motor Age*, 20 June 1912, page 18.

Chapter 7

1. "Newcomer Makes Hit," *New York Times*, 2 January 1910.

2. "Mercer Car After Record," *New York Times*, 16 May 1910.

3. "World's Fastest Auto," *New York Times*, 16 October 1908.

4. "Two New Four-Cylinder Models in the Mercer Line," *Motor Age*, 11 December 1913, page 34.

5. "Vanderbilt Aid Inspects Race Course," *Motor Age*, 22 August 1912, page 12.

6. "Speed Merchants Gather at Milwaukee," *Motor Age*, 12 September 1912, page 9.

7. "Bruce-Brown Meets Death at Milwaukee," *Motor Age*, 3 October 1912, page 13.

8. "Bruce-Brown's Mechanician Dead," *New York Times*, 9 October 1912. Correct spelling of the name unclear: Anthony Schudelare in *Motor Age*; Antonio "Tony" Scudelari in the *New York Times*.

9. "De Palma Proves His Sportsmanship," *Motor Age*, 5 June 1913, page 11

10. "De Palma Mending Rapidly," *Motor Age*, 24 October 1912, page 17.

11. "Accident Unavoidable," *New York Times*, 6 October 1912

12. Fred J. Wagner, quoted in J.C. Burton, "Some Superlatives of the Speed Game," *Motor Age*, 11 December 1913, page 22.

13. "Engineers Learn Much from Racing," *Motor Age*, 7 May 1914, page 12.

14. *Ibid.*

15. "Fragments from Mercury's Note-Book," *Motor Age*, 4 September 1913, page 13.

16. *Ibid.*

17. "Tuning Up the Cars for the Memorial Day Motor Marathon," *Motor Age*, 29 May 1913, page 11.

18. "Mechanical Features of Cars at Elgin," *Motor Age*, 4 September 1913, page 16.

19. Birthdates provided by Doug Wick, Bismarck, North Dakota.

20. "Mechanical Features of Cars at Elgin," *Motor Age*, 4 September 1913, page 16.

21. "Wide Open All the Way by Barney Oldfield — Reported by William F. Sturm," *The Saturday Evening Post*, 19 and 26 September 1925.

22. "De Palma and Pullen Are Victors at Santa Monica," *Motor Age*, 5 March 1914, page 6.

23. "Wide Open All the Way by Barney Oldfield — Reported by William F. Sturm," *The Saturday Evening Post*, 19 and 26 September 1925.

24. Jon Blackwell, "1914: That Marvelous Mercer Motor Car," published online at www.capitalcentury.com/1914.html.

25. "Speedway Race Brings Out Novel Engine Designs," *Motor Age*, 28 May 1914, page 27.

26. "Spencer Wishart," *Motor Age*, 27 August 1914, page 23.

27. *Ibid.*

28. "World's Road Racing Record Smashed by Pullen," *Motor Age*, 3 December 1914, page 6.

29. *Ibid.*

30. *Ibid.*

31. "Oldfield Suggests Rule Change," *Motor Age*, 22 April 1915, page 16.

32. "Mercer Docks 300-Inch Cars," *Motor Age*, 3 June 1915, page 27.

Chapter 8

1. Fred J. Wagner, "Some Superlatives of the Speed Game," *Motor Age*, 11 December 1913, page 23.

2. In the contemporary press Gil Anderson's name was always spelled Anderson. The oldracingcars.com website run by Richard Jenkins has Gil Andersen, born on 27 November 1879 in Horten, Norway. He became a U.S. citizen, worked for Stutz and Revere, and died on 29 July 1935 in Logansport, Indiana.

3. Bert C. Smith, "Santa Monica Road Race May Never Been Held Again — Los Angeles Grand Prize Next." *Los Angeles Times*, 8 May 1912.

4. "Inside History of Maier Bowling Experts," *Los Angeles Times*, 14 April 1912.

5. "West End House Italian in Type," *Los Angeles Times*, 29 December 1912. Edwin Janss died on 19 August 1959, aged 77.

6. "Teddy Tetzlaff Again King of the Road," *Motor Age*, 9 May 1912, page 8.

7. "Aftermath of Elgin Road Races," *Motor Age*, 5 September 1912, page 17.

8. "Grand Prix Honors Captured by Bragg," *Motor Age*, 10 October 1912, page 9.

9. "Speedway Honors Go to French Car," *Motor Age*, 5 June 1913, page 6.

10. "Fragments from Mercury's Note-Book," *Motor Age*, 4 September 1913, page 13.

11. *Ibid.*

12. In the contemporary press the name was spelled Kramer, Kraemer or Craemer. Craemer was correct.

13. "Mechanical Features of Cars at Elgin," *Motor Age*, 4 September 1913, page 16.

14. "Fragments from Mercury's Note-Book," *Motor Age*, 4 September 1913, page 13.

15. *Ibid.*

16. "Anderson and De Palma Divide Elgin Honors," *Motor Age*, 4 September 1913, page 5.

17. Fred J. Wagner, "Some Superlatives of the Speed Game," *Motor Age*, 11 December 1913, page 22.

18. "Tires a Determining Factor," *Motor Age*, 4 June 1914, page 21.

19. "Dick Wallen Books Caption Corrections," *Nostalgia Forum*, at forums.autosport.com, 18 November 2006.

20. "Floods Cause Postponment of Santa Monica Races," *Motor Age*, 26 February 1914, page 15.

21. Darwin S. Hatch, "The 500-Mile Race as Seen from the Repair Pits," *Motor Age*, 4 June 1914, page 19.

22. "Interesting Facts About the Rayfield, Beaver Bullet and Burman Special Entered in the Indianapolis Race," *Motor Age*, 14 May 1914, page 17.

23. "Speedway Race Brings Out Novel Engine Designs," *Motor Age*, 28 May 1914, page 24.

24. "Interesting Facts About the Rayfield, Beaver Bullet and Burman Special Entered in the Indianapolis Race," *Motor Age*, 14 May 1914, page 17.

25. *Ibid.*

26. "Speedway Race Brings Out Novel Engine Designs," *Motor Age*, 28 May 1914, page 33.
27. *Ibid.*

Chapter 9

1. "Duesenberg Shares in Mason Honors," *Motor Age*, 24 October 1912, page 40.
2. Father Konrad with "K," mother Luise Conradine with "C," and son Conrad with "C."
3. "Duesenberg Shares in Mason Honors," *Motor Age*, 24 October 1912, page 40.
4. *Ibid.*
5. "The Under-Over Car Feature of Mason Line for 1914," *Motor Age*, 10 July 1913, page 28.
6. "Wide Open All the Way by Barney Oldfield — Reported by William F. Sturm," *The Saturday Evening Post*, 19 and 26 September 1925.
7. "Speedway Race Brings Out Novel Engine Designs," *Motor Age*, 28 May 1914, page 27.
8. "Race Echoes from the Resonant Bowl of Speed," *Motor Age*, 4 June 1914, page 11.
9. "Speedway Race Brings Out Novel Engine Designs," *Motor Age*, 28 May 1914, page 27.
10. "The 500-Mile Race as Seen from the Repair Pits," *Motor Age*, 4 June 1914, page 20.
11. *Ibid.*, page 18.
12. "Troubles that Made the Cars Stop at Pits at Sioux City," *Motor Age*, 9 July 1914, page 11.
13. *Ibid.*
14. "Rickenbacher in Duesenberg Wins Sioux City 300-Mile Race," *Motor Age*, 9 July 1914, page 6.
15. "Racing Results on the Fourth," *Motor Age*, 9 July 1914, page 5.
16. "Lautenschlager und Rickenbacher," *Motor Age*, 9 July 1914, page 23.
17. "The Elgin National Trophy Race," *Motor Age*, 27 August 1914, page 12.
18. "Tom Alley," *Motor Age*, 29 October 1914, page 14.
19. "Mulford Will Race at Speedway Saturday," *Des Moines Capital*, 27 July 1915.
20. "Sketches of the Racers," *Burlington Gazettel*, 9 July 1915.

Chapter 10

1. During the 1920s, Lucien Picker had a Métallurgique and Fiat agency at 1ter Rue Voltaire, Geneva. In 1930 he sold Johnson outboard engines at 38 Rue du Môle.
2. "El Garage de los Hispanos," *El Mundo Deportivo* (Barcelona), 20 May 1909, page 2.
3. "Interesting New Light Engine," *The Motor* (London), 24 May 1910, page 623.
4. "The Gaillon Hillclimb," *The Motor* (London), 4 October 1910, page 322.
5. "Le Moteur Bignan-Picker," *L'Aéro* (Paris), 24 October 1913, page 3.
6. "La 15 HP Despagna," *L'Aéro* (Paris), 23 September 1913, page 1.
7. "La Course de Côte de Gaillon," *L'Aéro* (Paris), 6 October 1913, page 2.
8. "How Giuppone's Accident Occurred," *The Motor* (London), 20 September 1910, page 252.
9. Henri Petit, "Les voitures Peugeot gagnantes du Grand Prix de l'ACF," *La Vie Automobile*, 9 August 1913, page 491.
10. "Interesting New Light Engine," *The Motor* (London), 24 May 1910, page 623.
11. "Mechanical Points of Little Cars," *Motor Age*, 13 October 1910, page 19.
12. "Constructional Features of the Peugeot," *Motor Age*, 26 September 1912, page 34.
13. "Peugeot Sending Race Team to America," *Motor Age*, 22 August 1912, page 13.
14. Charles Ernest Faroux was born in Noyon, Picardie, on 20 December 1873, and lived at 16 Rue Bachaumont, Paris.
15. "The Foreigners," *Motor Age*, 29 May 1913, page 12.
16. "Tuning Up the Cars for the Memorial Day Motor Marathon," *Motor Age*, 29 May 1913, page 10.
17. "The Foreigners," *Motor Age*, 29 May 1913, page 13.
18. "Practice Starts for the International Motor Sweepstakes," *Motor Age*, 22 May 1913, page 10.
19. "France Rejoices in Its Indianapolis Speedway Victory," *Motor Age*, 2 July 1913, page 16.
20. "New Race Driver Enters the Field," *New York Times*, 27 April 1913.
21. "Simplex and Peugeot Battle on Beach," *Motor Age*, 31 July 1913, page 11.
22. "Mercer Wins All Five Races at Brighton Beach Meet," *Motor Age*, 14 August 1913, page 16.
23. "La Belle France Wins the Grand Prix," *Motor Age*, 17 July 1913, page 6.
24. "Guyot Promises Delage Entry for Indianapolis," *Motor Age*, 29 January 1914, page 32.
25. "Foreign Cars in 500-Mile Race," *Motor Age*, 19 February 1914, page 10.
26. "Foreign Racing Cars Now on the Atlantic Ocean," *Motor Age*, 30 April 1914, page 15.

27. *Ibid.*

28. For the victory in the 1913 Coupe de l'Auto, Ernest Henry was awarded the Émile Croupy prize, a gold medal.

29. "The Foreigners," *Motor Age*, 28 May 1914, page 20.

30. "French Cars Early Favorites for Indianapolis Race," *Motor Age*, 21 May 1914, page 14.

31. "Trials Reduce Indianapolis Field to Thirty Cars," *Motor Age*, 28 May 1914, page 18.

32. *Ibid.*

33. "The Foreigners," *Motor Age*, 28 May 1914, page 20.

34. "Rickenbacher in Duesenberg Wins Sioux City 300-Mile Race," *Motor Age*, 9 July 1914, page 9.

Chapter 11

1. "Wagner Tells of Santa Monica Prospects," *Motor Age*, 29 January 1914, page 32.

2. "Woman in Auto Race," *New York Times*, 27 January 1914.

3. "Floods Cause Postponement of Santa Monica Races," *Motor Age*, 26 February 1914, page 14.

4. "Guyot Promises Delage Entry for Indianapolis," *Motor Age*, 29 January 1914, page 32.

5. "France Clears Up Mystery," *Motor Age*, 2 April 1914, page 29.

6. "Speedy Delages as Tuned Up for the Indianapolis Race," *Motor Age*, 16 April 1914, page 28.

7. *Ibid.*

8. "Foreign Racing Cars Now on the Atlantic Ocean," *Motor Age*, 30 April 1914, page 15.

9. "Sunbeam Builds Car for Indianapolis," *Motor Age*, 12 March 1914, page 22.

10. "William Ziegler, Jr., Heir to $30,000,000, to Wed," *New York Times*, 27 January 1914.

11. "The Foreigners," *Motor Age*, 28 May 1914, page 21.

12. "French Cars Early Favorites for Indianapolis Race," *Motor Age*, 21 May 1914, page 15.

13. "How the Race Was Run," *Motor Age*, 4 June 1914, page 12.

14. "Race Echoes from the Resonant Bowl of Speed," *Motor Age*, 4 June 1914, page 11.

15. "Tires a Determing Factor," *Motor Age*, 4 June 1914, page 21.

16. "The Small Car Victory," *Motor Age*, 4 June 1914, page 22.

17. "Paris Greets Winning Drivers from Indianapolis," *Motor Age*, 2 July 1914, page 19.

18. "Mechanical Lessons Taught in Record-Breaking Contest," *Motor Age*, 3 June 1915, page 19.

19. "World's Best Race Won by Peugeot," *New York Times*, 8 August 1915.

Chapter 12

1. "Resta's Peugeot Car Wins in Cup Race," *New York Times*, 7 March 1915.

2. J.C. Burton, "Racing's Latest Sensation — The Man from Over the Sea," *Motor Age*, 1 April 1915, page 23.

3. Resta was born in Faenza, 175 Via Fadina. His Father was Federico Resta, his mother Adelaide née Niccodemi. Published online at onli.it.

4. "Looking at 500-Mile Race from Under Hoods of the Cars," *Motor Age*, 27 May 1915, page 22.

5. J.C. Burton, "Prepping the Car for the 500 Mile Race," *Motor Age*, 27 May 1915, page 9.

6. "Burman's Reconstructed Peugeot," *Motor Age*, 13 May 1915, page 22.

7. *Ibid.*.

8. "A New Light Alloy," *Motor Age*, 13 May 1915, page 22.

9. "Looking at 500-Mile Race from Under Hoods of the Cars," *Motor Age*, 27 May 1915, page 23.

10. "Bob Burman, in Peugeot, Takes Oklahoma City Road Race," *Motor Age*, 6 May 1915, page 14.

11. "Chicago Speedway Will Be Ready for Race on June 19," *Motor Age*, 29 April 1915, page 10.

12. "Resta in Peugeot Makes New Record," *New York Times*, 27 June 1915.

13. "'Bob' Burman Killed in California Race," *New York Times*, 9 April 1916.

14. "Resta Favorite at Indianapolis," *New York Times*, 28 May 1916.

15. "'Wonder Who'll Take Bob Burman's Place," *Washington Times*, 22 April 1916, page 5.

16. "Resta's Peugeot Wins Sweepstakes," *New York Times*, 31 May 1916.

Chapter 13

1. "Mercedes for 500-Mile Race," *Motor Age*, 26 February 1914, page 16.

2. "Aftermath of the Road Race Meet at Santa Monica," *Motor Age*, 12 March 1914, page 25.

3. "Indianapolis Adds Three to Entry List," *Motor Age*, 26 March 1914, page 16.

4. "Patterson to Race a Mercedes," *Motor Age*, 19 March 1914, page 16.

5. *Ibid.*

6. "Speedway Race Brings Out Novel Engine Designs," *Motor Age*, 28 May 1914, page 25.

7. *Ibid.*

8. *Ibid.*

9. "A Last Look Round," *The Motor* (London), 7 July 1914, page 1088.

10. "Germans Run One, Two, Three in French Grand Prix," *Motor Age*, 9 July 1914, page 18.

11. "Six Nations Represented in French Grand Prix," *Motor Age*, 2 July 1914, page 16.

12. "The Magic Mercédès," *The Motor* (London), 14 July 1914, page 1153.

13. "The Winning Mercédès Cars," *The Motor* (London), 7 July 1914, page 1108A.

14. "The Race from Various Points," *The Motor* (London), 7 July 1914, page 1103.

15. William F. Bradley, "Aftermath of the French Grand Prix," *Motor Age*, 23 July 1914, page 5.

16. J.C. Burton, "Mercedes Fritz, the Gypsy of the Gasoline Circuit," *Motor Age*, 30 July 1914, page 20.

17. *Ibid.*

18. *Ibid.*

19. *Ibid.*

20. *Ibid.*

21. *Ibid.*

22. "Motor Age's Review of 1914 Road Racing," *Motor Age*, 10 December 1914, page 5.

23. "Drivers Burn Up Brick Oval in Practice for Hoosier Race," *Motor Age*, 20 May 1915, page 21.

24. *Ibid.*

25. "Looking at 500-Mile Race from Under Hoods of the Cars," *Motor Age*, 27 May 1915, page 22.

26. *Ibid.*

27. "Twenty-three Cars Will Face Starter in Hoosier Classic," *Motor Age*, 27 May 1915, page 13.

28. "Mechanical Lessons Taught in Record-Breaking Contest," *Motor Age*, 3 June 1915, page 17.

29. "Enemy Aircraft Engines — Part X — The 300 h.p. Maybach Engine," *The Automobile Engineer* (London), September 1918, page 255.

30. Glenn D. Angle, *Airplane Engine Encyclopedia* (Dayton, Ohio: The Otherbein Press, 1921), page 305.

31. "Roosevelt Tries 'Liberty Motor,'" *New York Times*, 14 September 1917.

32. "La significante vittoria delle Diatto nella corsa in salita Vermicino-Frascati-Rocca di Papa," *La Stampa* (Turin), 26 January 1921, page 3.

Chapter 14

1. "Speedway Race Brings Out Novel Engine Designs," *Motor Age*, 28 May 1914, page 23.

2. "Ray Harroun's Maxwell Racers Are in Completed State," *Motor Age*, 7 May 1914, page 26.

3. *Ibid.*

4. *Ibid.*

5. *Ibid.*

6. "Indianapolis Entry List Now Totals Twenty-Seven," *Motor Age*, 23 April 1914, page 18.

7. "Speedway Race Brings Out Novel Engine Designs," *Motor Age*, 28 May 1914, page 25.

8. "Superstitions of the Speed Mercants," *Motor Age*, 1 April 1915, page 25.

9. *Ibid.*

10. "San Diego's Road Race Promises to Eclipse Corona," *Motor Age*, 24 December 1914, page 11.

11. "Maxwell Auto Wins Venice Race," *New York Times*, 18 March 1915.

12. "Drivers Burn Up Brick Oval in Practice for Hoosier Race," *Motor Age*, 20 May 1915, page 22.

13. "Looking at 500-Mile Race from Under Hoods of the Cars," *Motor Age*, 27 May 1915, page 21.

14. "*Ibid.*

15. "500-Mile Race Echoes from the Resonant Saucer of Speed," *Motor Age*, 3 June 1915, page 11.

16. "Sectional Views of Wisconsin-Stutz Racing Motor 3 13/16-in. Bore and 6 1/2-in. Stroke," *The Automobile*, 14 October 1915, page 699.

17. "Looking at 500-Mile Race from Under Hoods of the Cars," *Motor Age*, 27 May 1915, page 21.

18. In the 1915 Chicago 500, two Stutzes had a wheelbase of 104 inches, the third car a wheelbase of 102 inches; their weights were 2340, 2385 and 2404 pounds.

19. "Bob Burman Breaks the 100-Mile Dirt Track Record," *Motor Age*, 1 October 1914, page 14.

20. "Looking at 500-Mile Race from Under Hoods of the Cars," *Motor Age*, 27 May 1915, page 22.

21. "Lap-by-Lap Story of Ralph de Palma's Spectacular Victory," *Motor Age*, 3 June 1915, page 12.

22. "Mechanical Lessons Taught in Record-Breaking Contest," *Motor Age*, 3 June 1915, page 20.
23. "Porter-Knights First American Sleeve-Valve Racers," *Motor Age*, 6 May 1915, page 22.
24. "If the Emden Wins, Kaiser Wilhelm Will Rejoice," *Motor Age*, 20 May 1915, page 22.
25. "Race Drivers on Their Way to the Top," *Motor Age*, 13 May 1915, page 16.
26. "Wide Open All the Way by Barney Oldfield — Reported by William F. Sturm," *The Saturday Evening Post*, 19 and 26 September 1925.
27. "Oldfield to Race Here," *New York Times*, 5 August 1917.

Chapter 15

1. "Sheepshead Bay to Be Auto Course," *New York Times*, 9 March 1915.
2. "Fisher Out of Speedway," *New York Times*, 20 August 1915.
3. "New Automobile Records," *New York Times*, 24 August 1902.
4. "Automobiles Race To-day," *New York Times*, 14 April 1903.
5. "Automobilists Selected," *New York Times*, 21 April 1903.
6. Léon Levavasseur (1863–1922), Ingénieur-Constructeur, 10 Rue des Bas-Rogers, Puteaux.
7. "Antoinette Monoplane Tried," *New York Times*, 25 August 1910.
8. "27 Miles of Seats for New Speedway," *New York Times*, 25 April 1915.
9. "Rush Work on New York Speedway," *Motor Age*, 22 April 1915, page 16.
10. "World's Record at Speedway Opening," *New York Times*, 19 September 1915.
11. "Resta's Fast Spin Around Speedway," *New York Times*, 25 September 1915.
12. "Cars Qualify in Astor Cup Trials," *New York Times*, 26 September 1915.
13. "Autodriver Grant Severely Burnt," *New York Times*, 28 September 1915.
14. "Another Day for Speedway Trials," *New York Times*, 30 September 1915.
15. "Prizes for Drivers Today," *New York Times*, 12 October 1915.
16. "De Palma's Car Tried on Speedway," *New York Times*, 29 October 1915.
17. "Resta's Auto First in Speedway Race," *New York Times*, 3 November 1915.
18. Sometime in the fall of 1915, Rickenbacher changed the spelling of his name to Rickenbacker.
19. "Aitken the Victor in Astor Cup Race," *New York Times*, 1 October 1916.
20. *Ibid.*
21. "William Weightman Dead," *New York Times*, 26 August 1904.
22. "Weightman Enters Race," *New York Times*, 26 October 1916.
23. "Speedway Triumph Won by De Palma," *New York Times*, 19 August 1917.
24. "Business Records," *New York Times*, 12 February 1922.
25. "Flaming Car Adds to Speedway Thrills," *New York Tribune*, 2 June 1918.
26. *Ibid.*
27. "Milton Pilots Car to Victory in Race," *New York Times*, 2 June 1918.
28. "De Palma Hangs Up New Records in Auto Races," *New York Tribune*, 18 August 1918.
29. "Four Auto Records Made by De Palma," *New York Times*, 18 August 1918.

Chapter 16

1. "Le Grand Prix de France Automobile," *L'Aéro* (Paris), 5 August 1913, page 1.
2. *Archives Commerciales de la France, 31ème Année*, Paris, 1904, page 5.
3. 100-Francs share certificate, 1911.
4. "Ballot's Bread & Butter: Marc Douezy and Nicolas Boissier recall Ballot's days as a maker of proprietary engines," *The Automobile Magazine*, March and April 2002.
5. Laurence Pomeroy, *The Grand Prix Car* (London: Motor Racing Publications, 1956), page 168.
6. *Archives Commerciales de la France, 38ème Année*, Paris, 1911, page 823.
7. Griffith Borgeson, "The Charlatan Mystery," *Automobile Quarterly*, 11, no. 3 (1973).
8. *Archives Commerciales de la France, 24ème Année*, Paris, 1897, page 930.
9. Griffith Borgeson, "The Charlatan Mystery," *Automobile Quarterly*, 11, no. 3 (1973). The Peugeot V-8 aero-engine followed closely the design of the successful racing car engines. Bore was 100 mm, stroke 180 mm, displacement 11.3 liters or 691 cubic inches, with four 44-mm valves per cylinder; output was 200 hp at 2,000 rpm, weight 400 kg or 882 pounds.
10. "Navarre Winged 19 German Aircraft," *New York Times*, 18 June 1916.
11. "France in War Time," *Motor Age*, 3 September 1914, page 7.
12. "Boillot Ditched Driving Officers," *Motor Age*, 15 October 1914, page 17.
13. "France in War Time," *Motor Age*, 3 September 1914, page 7.

14. "More Than 70,000 Motor Vehicles in French Service," *Motor Age*, 10 September 1914, page 14.

15. Griffith Borgeson, "The Charlatan Mystery," *Automobile Quarterly*, 11, no. 3 (1973).

16. Laurence Pomeroy, *The Grand Prix Car* (London: Motor Racing Publications, 1956), page 171.

17. "Decade Brings Great Races at Indianapolis," *Motor Age*, 27 May 1920.

18. "New Designing Gets Test at Indianapolis," *Motor Age*, 27 May 1920.

19. "Details Are Given of French Cars in Indianapolis Race," *Motor Age*, 6 May 1920.

20. "New Designing Gets Test at Indianapolis," *Motor Age*, 27 May 1920.

21. "Details Are Given of French Cars in Indianapolis Race," *Motor Age*, 6 May 1920.

22. "Boillot Predicts New Record at Indianapolis This Year," *Motor Age*, 6 May 1920.

23. *Ibid.*

24. "The Small Engine Has Made Good!" *Motor Age*, 3 June 1920.

25. *Ibid.*

26. *Ibid.*

27. "De Palma Wins Elgin Race," *Motor Age*, 2 September 1920.

28. "Le Grand Prix de l'ACF," *La Vie Automobile* (Paris), 10 August 1921, page 275.

29. "Annonces Classées," *Le Figaro* (Paris), 21 August 1924, page 6.

30. William Bradley, "Design Features Brought Into Relief by Grand Prix," *Automotive Industries — The Automobile*, 18 August 1921, page 303.

31. William Bradley, "Engineering Lessons of the Grand Prix," *Automotive Industries — The Automobile*, 17 August 1922, page 319.

32. Griffith Borgeson, "The Charlatan Mystery," *Automobile Quarterly*, 11, no. 3 (1973).

Chapter 17

1. "Allies in Speedway Race," *New York Times*, 22 December 1918.

2. The "Two Red Years" of 1919 and 1920, a period of social movements, strikes and factory occupations, in particular at Fiat, which was not only an automobile factory but the biggest industrial complex in Italy.

3. Laurence Pomeroy, *The Grand Prix Car* (London: Motor Racing Publications, 1956), page 179.

4. "Bordino Burns Up Big Bowl," *Los Angeles Times*, 22 February 1922.

5. William Bradley, "Some Mechanical Details of French Grand Prix Racing Cars," *Automotive Industries — The Automobile*, 3 August 1922, page 210.

6. *Ibid.*

7. *Ibid.*

8. "La magnifica vittoria torinese a Monza," *La Stampa* (Turin), 10 September 1923.

9. "L'aspra corsa," *La Stampa* (Turin), 3 July 1923.

10. Laurence Pomeroy, *The Grand Prix Car* (London: Motor Racing Publications, 1956), page 197.

11. *Ibid.*

12. Enzo Ferrari, *My Terrible Joys: The Enzo Ferrari Memoirs* (London: Motoraces Book Club, 1965).

13. Griffith Borgeson, *The Alfa Romeo Tradition* (Sparkford, Somerset, UK: Haynes Publishing Group, 1990), page 68.

14. *Ibid.*, page 45.

15. *Ibid.*, page 71.

16. *Ibid.*

17. Enzo Ferrari, *My Terrible Joys: The Enzo Ferrari Memoirs* (London: Motoraces Book Club, 1965).

18. "Folla enorme e febbriel attesa a Lione," *La Stampa* (Turin), 3 August 1924.

19. Elcosina was available in different mixtures. A first group contained between 43 and 75 percent benzene, between 18 and 50 percent 95-degree ethanol, and between 2 and 7 percent sulfur ether. A second group contained gasoline in addition. Sometimes ethanol was replaced by methanol. The most used racing fuel on the Brooklands track was Discol, a mixture of benzene and methanol. In Germany there was Rennmetalin and Rennmonopolin.

20. "L'Italia vince per la terza volta i Gran Premio Automobilistico d'Europa," *La Stampa* (Turin), 29 June 1925.

21. "Le Grand Prix de Vitesse," *La Vie Automobile* (Paris), 10 August 1925, page 291.

22. "La Vérité sur la Mort d'Ascari," *Très Sport* (Paris), 1 September 1925, page 11.

Chapter 18

1. "Beauty and Luxury Mark Auto Salon," *New York Times*, 3 January 1914.

2. "Tableau des Caractéristiques & des Prix des Automobiles et des Cyclecars exposés au Salon de 1921," *Omnia* (Paris), November 1921.

3. William Bradley, "Races and Cars Compared," *Automotive Industries—The Automobile*, 20 July 1922, page 110.

4. William Bradley, "Engineering Lessons of the Grand Prix," *Automotive Industries—The Automobile*, 17 August 1922, page 319.

5. William Bradley, "Races and Cars Compared," *Automotive Industries—The Automobile*, 20 July 1922, page 110.

6. William Bradley, "Some Mechanical Details of French Grand Prix Racing Cars," *Automotive Industries—The Automobile*, 3 August 1922, page 210.

7. *Ibid.*

8. *Ibid.*

9. During the 1920s and 1930s, de Alzaga purchased 26 cars with bodies by Fernandez & Darrin.

10. Laurence Pomeroy, *The Grand Prix Car* (London: Motor Racing Publications, 1956), page 184.

11. Editorial article, *New York Times*, 24 May 1906.

12. "The Story of a Miller," *Thoroughbred & Classic Cars* (London), August 1978, page 28.

13. Antoine Raffaelli, *Archives d'une Passion* (Paris, 1997), factory test sheet page 155.

14. Griffith Borgeson, "The Dawn of the Light-Alloy Wheel," *Thoroughbred & Classic Cars* (London), May 1979, page 48.

15. Antoine Raffaelli, *Archives d'une Passion* (Paris, 1997), factory test sheet page 180.

16. G. Fraichard, "Le Duel Duray-Marchand," *Match* (Paris), 13 August 1929, page 11.

17. Jean-Albert Grégoire, *L'Aventure Automobile* (Flammarion, Paris, 1953).

Chapter 19

1. "Le Dimanche Sportif," *Le Petit Parisien* (Paris), 7 July 1924, page 4.

2. "Toujours Plus Vite," *Le Petit Parisien* (Paris), 13 July 1924, page 3.

3. Laurence Pomeroy, *The Grand Prix Car* (London: Motor Racing Publications, 1956), page 210.

4. Paul Yvelin, *Delage, Levallois-Courbevoie, Notes et Souvenir* (Paris, 1971), page 39.

5. "Toujours Plus Vite," *La Vie Automobile* (Paris), 10 July 1923, page 228.

6. William Bradley, "Engineering Lessons of the Grand Prix," *Automotive Industries—The Automobile*, 17 August 1922, page 319.

7. William Bradley, "Races and Cars Compared," *Automotive Industries—The Automobile*, 20 July 1922, page 110.

8. William Bradley, "Engineering Lessons of the Grand Prix," *Automotive Industries—The Automobile*, 17 August 1922, page 319.

9. William Bradley, "Races and Cars Compared," *Automotive Industries—The Automobile*, 20 July 1922, page 110.

10. William Bradley, "Some Mechanical Details of French Grand Prix Racing Cars," *Automotive Industries—The Automobile*, 3 August 1922, page 210.

11. Laurence Pomeroy, *The Grand Prix Car* (London: Motor Racing Publications, 1956), page 55.

12. "Grand Prix," *The Autocar* (London), 26 June 1931, page 1164.

13. Paul Yvelin, *Delage, Levallois-Courbevoie, Notes et Souvenir* (Paris, 1971), page 43.

14. "La morte del conte Giulio Masetti funesta la uta della Targa Florio," *La Stampa* (Turin), 26 April 1926.

15. "Béquet-Delage," *Auto-Passion* (Paris), no. 76, January 1993.

16. *L'Automobile — Revue des Locomotions Nouvelles* (Paris), July 1908, pages 428, 441 and 442.

17. It remains unclear whether the 1908 Isotta voiturette was designed by Giustino Cattaneo, Giuseppe Coda, Ernesto Stefanini or all three of them. According to Cattaneo, Stefanini played a principal role.

18. "Il Mugello," *Auto-Moto-Ciclo* (Milan), 1 July 1922, page 460.

19. "La Diatto al Gran Premio d'Italia," *Motori Aero Cicli e Sporst* (Milan and Turin), 22 August 1922, page 19.

20. Daniele Neri, "Un'automobile nella storia: un 'puzzle' in composizione," *Incontri,* no. 64, 2000, published online at www.carispaq.it

21. "Vettura no. 12," Maserati factory sheet.

Bibliography

Newspapers and Magazines

L' Aéro (Paris)
Allgemeine Automobil-Zeitung (Wien)
Archives Commerciales de la France (Paris)
Auto Passion (Paris)
Automotive Industries—The Automobile (New York and Chicago)
The Autocar (London)
The Automobile Engineer (London)
The Automobile Magazine (Cranleigh, Surrey, UK)
Automobile Quarterly (New Albany, Indiana)
Thoroughbred & Classic Cars (London)
L' Automobile, Revue des Locomotions nouvelles (Paris)
Le Chauffeur (Paris)
La Côte d'Azur Sportive (Nice)
La France Automobile (Paris)
Le Figaro (Paris)
Le Petit Parisien (Paris)
Match (Paris)
The Horseless Age (New York)
Il Littoriale (Rome)
Los Angeles Times
The Motor (London)
Motor Age (Chicago)
Motori, Aero, Cicli e Sport (Milano and Torino)
El Mundo Deportivo (Barcelona)
New York Herald
New York Times
Omnia—La Locomotion (Paris)
La Presse (Paris)
The Saturday Evening Post (Philadelphia)
Lo Sport Fascista (Milano)
La Stampa (Torino)
La Stampa Sportiva (Torino)
Très Sport (Paris)
La Vie Automobile (Paris)

Books

Angle, Glenn D. *Airplane Engine Encyclopedia*. Dayton, Ohio: The Otterbein Press, 1921.
Anselmi, Angelo Tito. *Automobili Fiat*. 2 vols. Milano: Libreria dell'Automobile, 1986.
Association of Licensed Automobile Manufacturers. *Handbook of Gasoline Automobiles*. New York: Association of Licensed Automobile Manufacturers, 1906.
_____. *Handbook of Gasoline Automobiles*. New York: Association of Licensed Automobile Manufacturers, 1907.

Borgeson, Griffith. *The Alfa Romeo Tradition*. Sparkford, Somerset, UK: Haynes Publishing Group, 1990.
_____. *The Golden Age of the American Racing Car*. New York: Bonanza Books, 1966.
Conway, Hugh G. *Bugatti, le Pur Sang des Automobiles*. London: G.T. Foulis, 1974.
_____. *Grand Prix Bugatti*. London: G.T. Foulis, 1968.
Ferrari, Enzo. *My Terrible Joys: The Enzo Ferrari Memoirs*. London: Motoraces Book Club, 1965.
Fusi, Luigi. *Alfa Romeo, tutte le Vetture dal 1910*. Milano: Emmetigrafica s.a.s., 1978.
Heal, Anthony S. *Sunbeam Racing Cars, 1910–1930*. Sparkford, Somerset, UK: Haynes, 1989.
International Motor Cyclopaedia: Year Book, March 1908 to March 1909. New York: E.E. Schwarzkopf, 1909.
Jarrott, Charles. *Ten Years of Motors and Motor Racing*. London: Dutton, 1906.
Kimes, Beverly Rae, and Henry Austin Clark, Jr. *Standard Catalog of American Cars, 1805–1942*. Iola, WI: Krause, 1996.
Ludvigsen, Karl. *The Incredible Blitzen Benz*. Deerfield, IL: Dalton Watson Fine Books, 2006.
_____. *The Mercedes-Benz Racing Cars*. Newport Beach, CA: Bond/Parkhurst Books, 1971.
Mathieson, T.A.S.O. *Grand Prix Racing 1906–1914. A History of the Grand Prix de l'Automobile Club de France*. Stockholm: Connaisseur Automobile A.B., 1965.
Mr. Punch Awheel: The Humours of Motoring and Cycling. London: The Educational Book Co. Ltd., 1903.
MoToR, The National Monthly Magazine of Motoring. *An Illustrated Directory of the Specifications of All Domestic and Foreign Motor-Cars and Motor Business Wagons— Gasoline, Steam and Electric— Sold in This Country*. New York: MoToR, 1907.
Orsini, Luigi, and Franco Zagari. *Maserati, una Storia nella Storia, dalle Origini al 1945*. Milano: Emmetigrafica s.a.s., 1980.
Pomeroy, Laurence. *The Grand Prix Car*. 2 vols. London: Motor Racing Publications Ltd., 1956.
Pray, Isaac Clarke. *Memoirs of James Gordon Bennett and His Times*. New York: Stringer & Townsend, 1855.
Raffaëlli, Antoine. *Archives d'une Passion*. Paris: Maeght Éditeur, 1997.
Rousseau, Jacques. *Les Automobiles Delage*. Paris: Éditions Larivière–Fanauto, 1978.
Schmidt, Giulio. *Le Corse Ruggenti. La vera storia di Enzo Ferrari pilota*. Milan: Libreria dell'Automobile, 1988.
Welsh, Charles, ed. *Chauffeur Chaff, or, Automobilia : Anecdotes, Stories, Bon-Mots : Also a History of the Evolution of the Automobile*. Boston: H.M. Caldwell Co., 1905.
Yvelin, Paul. *Delage, Levallois-Courbevoie, Notes et Souvenirs*. Paris: published privately and for limited distribution, 1971.

Index

ACF 6–7
Aitken, Johnny 72, 77, 80, 156, 160, 179, 193–194
Alco "Bête Noire" 1910 73
Alfa Romeo 2-liter 1923 228
Alfa Romeo 2-liter 1924 229
Alley, Tom 87, 91, 115–118, 162
Alloyanum 152
Alzaga, Martin de 237, 242
Amilcar 1.1-liter 1926 248
Anasagasti 125
Anderson, Gil 97–106, 149, 156, 168, 178–179, 181, 183, 191–192
Antoinette Monoplane 189
Antony see Debray, Henry "Antony"
Arpajon 1924 239, 248, 253
Ascari, Antonio 215, 230
Aston Martin 1922 213
Astor Cup 1915 191–192
Astor Cup 1916 194
Atlanta 1910 69
Auger, Georges "Augières" 10
Avanzo, Maria Antonietta 172
Avaray, Antoine d' 66, 125

Babcock, George 94, 152–153
Bablot, Paul 139, 147, 196, 201, 247
Ballot, Ernest 196–197, 204
Ballot 2-liter 1921 210, 213
Ballot 3-liter 1920 204
Ballot 4.9-liter 1919 200
Bariquand & Marre 198
Barriaux, Philippe 65
Bazzi, Luigi 228–229
Beaver Bullet 1914 107
Becchia, Walter 224, 226
Béchereau, Louis 237
Benoist, Robert 230, 256–259
Bentel, George 94–95
Benz Auto Import 49
Benz Blitzen 51, 64, 193
Béquet, Maurice 258–259
Béquet Spéciale 258–259
Bergdoll, Erwin 48, 76, 99, 101–103, 181
Bergdoll, Louis 47–49

Bernin, Maurice 20, 39, 46
Bertarione, Vincenzo 217, 224
Beverly Hills 1922 218
Bigelow, Charles 82–83
Birkigt, Marc 122
BLM 1906 46
Boillot, André 202, 205, 211, 214
Boillot, Georges 126, 128, 136, 143–145, 151, 164, 198–199
Bolide 7, 9
Bordino, Pietro 215, 218, 224
Bostwick, Albert 14
Boudreaux-Verdet 65, 126
Bowden, Herbert 20, 22
Bowman, Sidney B. 45
Boyer, Joe 180, 195
Bradley, William 134, 140
Braender Bulldog 1914 115
Bragg, Caleb 86–88, 92, 98
Branger, Maurice 65
Brescia 1921 209, 217–218
Brett, Riley 242
Brooklands 1926 227, 249
Brown, Walter 104–105
Bruce-Brown, David 26, 43, 50, 76–81, 85, 94, 98
Bugatti, Ettore 232, 250
Bugatti 1.5-liter 1926 248
Bugatti 2-liter 1922 235–237
Bugatti 2-liter 1923 238
Bugatti 2-liter 1924 239
Bugatti 5.6-liter 1914 142, 232
Bugatti Brescia 1921 234–235
Bugatti Garros 1914 232
Buick 1910 70
Bunau-Varilla, Étienne 242
Burman, Bob 50, 52–53, 70, 76–79, 102, 106–107, 118, 137, 152–157, 167, 191–193
Burman Special 1914 106–107
Burman Special 1915 152–153
Busson, Guillaume 121

Callaghan, Jesse 106, 117
Campari, Giuseppe 230
Campbell, Malcolm 247, 249
Cappa, Giulio Cesare 217, 231

Carlson, Billy 101, 113–114, 175–178, 181–182
Caters, Pierre de 8, 10, 18, 60
Cavalli, Carlo 217
Cedrino, Emanuele 43–44
CGV 8–9, 55
Chandler, Billy 113–116, 120
Charavel, Louis "Sabipa" 249
Charley see Lehmann, C.L. "Charley"
Charron, Fernand 8–10, 55–56
Chassagne, Jean 125, 141, 201–202, 208–211, 241–243
Chevrolet, Gaston 183, 195, 205
Chevrolet, Louis 69–70, 179–180, 184, 194–195, 205
Chicago 1915 118, 154–155
Christiaens, Joseph 143–145, 156, 210–211
Cincinatti 1911 97
Clément, Adolphe 56
Clément, Albert 45
Clément, Jeanne, 56
Clément-Bayard 1908 123
Coatalen, Louis 141, 210–211, 224–225
Coda, Giuseppe 262, 265, 267
Collomb, Joseph 64
Cooper, Earl 83, 90, 94, 98, 101–104, 154, 177–179, 181–183, 191
Cooper, Joe 118, 155, 191, 211
Cooper, Tom 32, 36
Copa Catalunya 122, 125
Cornelian 1915 179
Corona 1913 90
Corona 1914 94, 105
Corona 1916 155
Costantini, Meo 241–246, 248–249
Coty, Roland 259
Craemer, Fritz 101–102
Croker, Frank 41
Cystria, Bertrand de 237, 239

Dahnke, Bob 157
Daimler, Paul 78, 161, 164
Daimler White Ghost 14

D'Alene, Wilbur 80, 120, 156–157, 176
Davis, Sammy 243
Dawson, Joe 70–71, 75–81, 89, 135–136
Daytona 1904 18
Daytona 1905 22
Debray, Henry "Antony" 7
de Hymel, Tobin 76
Delage, Louis 145, 200, 251, 255, 259
Delage 2-liter 1923 253
Delage 2-liter 1924 255
Delage 2-liter 1925 256
Delage 4.5-liter 1914 147
Delage 5-liter 1922 252
Delage 6.2-liter 1913 139
Delage Torpille 252–253
Delalande, Gaston 255
Delling, Eric 90, 92, 95, 185
Delpierre, Jean 132
Deltal 1913 89–90
DePalma, John 146, 165
DePalma, Ralph 50, 69, 77, 79, 81, 84–85, 87–93, 101, 105, 118, 161, 163, 165–167, 172, 193–194, 204, 206
Derny, Louis 122
Desjoyeaux, Léon 67–68
Despagna 1913 125
Devigne, Jules 193–194
Diatto 1922 262–263
Diatto 1925 264–265
Dickson, George 81, 144–145
Dingley, Bert 105
Divo, Albert 221, 225, 227, 243, 249, 256, 258
Dixie 21–22, 41–42
Djelmo 213
Duesenberg, Augie 110
Duesenberg, Fred 110, 117
Duesenberg 1912 110
Duesenberg 1913 111, 113
Duesenberg 1914 114
Duesenberg 1915 117
Duesenberg 122 c.i. 1923 238
Duesenberg 183 c.i. 1920 206
Duesenberg 300 c.i. 1919 202
Duray, Arthur 61, 134, 136, 144, 147, 195
Duray, Leon 243, 250

Eiffel Wind Tunnel 132, 151
Elcosina 230, 266
Eldridge, Ernest 253, 258–259
Elgin 1912 99–100, 109
Elgin 1913 89, 102, 113
Elgin 1914 93, 105, 117, 165
Elgin 1915 182–183
Elgin 1920 206
Emden 1915 182
Empire City Track 1903 38
Endicott, Bill 103
Endicott, Harry 109
Erbes, Louis C. 137

Erbstein, Charles 79
Erwin Special 102, 181
Evans, Bob 111–113
Excelsior 1913 142

Fairmount Park 1910 74
Fanelli, Ernesto 125, 129–130, 132
Farman, Henry 59–60
Faroux, Charles 129, 199
Faure, Paul 62
Ferguson, Armour 132
Ferrari, Enzo 172, 215, 228–229
Fiat 1.5-liter 1927 224
Fiat 2-liter 1922 218–219
Fiat 2-liter 1923 221–222
Fiat 3-liter 1921 215–217
Fiat "Cyclone" 43
Fiat "Junior" 42
Fiat "Mephisto" 72
Fisher, Carl 33, 40, 77, 143, 168, 183, 187
Fletcher, Harry 22, 25
Fletcher, Stoughton 193
Ford, Henry 32
Ford "999" 33, 36
Foresti, Giulio 213, 244
Fournier, Henry 8–9, 16, 18, 56, 60
Franquist, Gustave 41
Friderich, Ernest 142–144, 233–235, 237–239, 241–242
Froehlich, Jesse 49–51, 54
Frontenac 183 c.i. 1920 205
Frontenac 183 c.i. 1921 207
Frontenac 300 c.i. 1916 184
FRP 180
Fuller, Charles W. 177, 191, 233

Gable, Jack 167
Gabriel, Fernand 17, 20–21, 55–56, 199
Gaillon Hillclimb 124–125, 196, 210
Gallaher, Edward 46
Galvin, Frank 152, 160, 194, 211
Garnier, Léonce 240
Garros, Roland 232
Gast, Camille du 18, 56–57
Gaubert, Louis 60
Giaccone, Enrico 221
Girardot, Léonce 8–9, 56
Giraud, Étienne 9, 56
Giuppone, Giosue 125
Goetz, Harry 77, 89, 111, 175
Gordon, Huntley 84, 107, 184
Gordon Bennett, James 3–6, 13
Gordon Bennett, James, Sr. 3
Gordon Bennett Cup 7
Gordon Bennett Cup 1900 8
Gordon Bennett Cup 1901 10
Gould Brokaw, William 12, 20, 22, 39, 41, 47
Goux, Jules 122, 129, 131, 135–136, 151, 199, 201, 209, 244, 248, 255

GP de l'ACF 1909–1910 67
GP de l'ACF Le Mans 1921 207
GP de l'ACF Lyon 1914 151, 163
GP de l'ACF Lyon 1924 229–230, 241–242, 256
GP de l'ACF Miramas 1926 247–248
GP de l'ACF Montlhéry 1925 230, 244, 256–258
GP de l'ACF Montlhéry 1927 227
GP de l'ACF Strasbourg 1922 212, 219, 237, 255
GP de l'ACF Tours 1923 221, 225, 239, 254
GP Milwaukee 1912 85, 109
GP San Francisco 1915 149
GP Santa Monica 1914 91, 114
GP Savannah 1910 76
GP Savannah 1911 78–79
Grant, Harry 73–74, 102, 142, 155, 177, 191
Graves, Robert 27
Gray Dinsmore, Clarence 11, 17
Great Western 1914 176
Grémillon, Marcel 204, 213
Grosse Pointe 1902 33–34
Guinness, Kenelm Lee 212, 221, 225–226
Guyot, Albert 66, 124, 130, 138, 140–143, 147, 199, 201, 255, 258
Guyot Spéciale 258

Haardt, Georges-Marie 60
Hackethal, Paul 90
Haibe, Ora 14c, 15b, 211
Harkness, Harry 17, 34, 148, 187–189, 193, 195
Harroun, Ray 69–78, 175, 177
Harroun Special 1915 178
Haupt, Willie 111, 113–115, 181–183
Hearne, Eddie 72, 79, 97, 107, 153, 201, 206
Heath, George 19–23
Hémery, Victor 49–51, 62, 64, 76, 165, 254–255
Henderson-Duesenberg 1912 111
Henning, Otto 93, 155
Henry, Ernest 121, 125, 132, 197, 199–200, 211, 213–214, 255
Herr, Don 101
Hewlett, Eugene 86, 98
Hill, George 91, 101, 233
Hispano-Suiza 1910 125
Hispano-Suiza V-8 Aero-Engine 170
Hollander, Elmer 42
Hol-Tan 42
Horan, Joe 176
Hourgières, Gilles 7
Huff, Edward 33
Hughes, Hughie 83–85, 104, 109, 149, 160, 180
Huillier, Georges 7

Indianapolis 1910 70
Indianapolis 1911 77, 80, 84
Indianapolis 1912 80, 84, 98
Indianapolis 1913 88, 101, 111,
  129–131
Indianapolis 1914 92, 104, 114,
  134–136, 143–145, 175–176
Indianapolis 1915 95, 117, 146,
  152, 167, 179–181
Indianapolis 1916 156
Indianapolis 1919 201
Indianapolis 1920 204
Indianapolis 1923 237
Irving, J.S. 225
Isotta-Fraschini 1908 260
Itala 1.1-liter 1925 231

Jano, Vittorio 217, 228–229
Janss, Edwin 98
Jay, Webb 39
Jenatzy, Camille 7–11, 19, 26–27,
  29
Jenkins, Johnny 97
Jenter, Johnny 88, 93
Johnson, Jack 51–52
Josephs, Joseph S. 42
Joyce, David 147, 191
Junek, Vincenz 237, 239, 242

Kalamazoo 1914 167
Katzenstein, Robert 11
Kaufmann, Alphonse 137, 151–
  152, 187
Keene, Bruce 76, 79
Keene, Foxhall Parker 15–17, 27,
  165
Keeton 106
King 1914 107
Kiser, Earl 33, 38
Klein, Arthur 105, 107, 118, 177
Knipper, Billy 98, 106, 111, 146
Knyff, René de 7–8

Labor-Picker 1910 123
Lacroix, Paul 46, 128, 161
Laly, Robert 141, 199, 201, 209
Lamberjack, Émile 67
La Roche, F.A. 44
Lautenschlager, Christian 116,
  151, 161, 163–164
Lazarnick, Nathan 65, 187
LeCain, Jack 152, 191, 194
Lehman, Charles "Baby" 29
Lehmann, C.L. "Charley" 18,
  47, 63, 68
Levegh *see* Velghe, Alfred "Lev-
  egh"
Lewis, Dave 97–99, 102, 105,
  114, 160, 176–177
Liberty Aero-Engine 171
Limberg, Carl 148, 192–194
Link, Eugen 78, 161, 170
Locomobile 1905 22
Locomobile 1908 25
Lory, Albert 255, 259

Lozier 1911 78
Lucia 121
Lüttgen, Willy 26–28

Maggi, Aymo 244, 247
Magnalium 102, 152, 175, 178
Maier, Eddie 98
Marchisio, Onesimo 222–223,
  265
Marco, Pierre 237
Marmon "Wasp" 69, 77
Marquis, Johnny 91, 142, 177,
  233
Martin, Harry 102
Martini Voiturette 1908 66
Maserati, Alfieri 259–266
Maserati, Bindo 260–262, 266
Maserati, Carlo 260–261
Maserati, Ernesto 260–264, 266
Maserati, Ettore 260
Maserati 1.5-liter 1926 265–266
Masetti, Carlo 242
Masetti, Giulio 213, 215, 226,
  230, 258
Mason, Georges 110, 113, 115
Mason-Duesenberg 1912 110
Mason-Duesenberg 1913 111, 113
Massenat, André 46
Materassi, Emilio 227–228,
  249, 266
Matthys, Henry 135, 199
Maxwell 300 c.i. 1915 178
Maxwell 450 c.i. 1914 174–175
Maywood Speedway 154
McCarthy, Fred 191
McKesson Brown, George 26
Mégevet, Charles J. 121
Ménard, Paul 67
Menier Family 134–135
Mercedes 2-liter 1924 230
Mercedes 4.5-liter 1914 164, 167
Mercedes 7.2-liter 1913 162
Mercedes Aero-Engine 1915 170
Mercedes "Flying Dutchman"
  22
Mercedes "Grey Ghost" 78–79,
  91, 101, 162–163
Mercedes-Peugeot 1914 163
Mercer 300 c.i. 1912 84
Mercer 300 c.i. 1914 92, 95
Mercer 450 c.i. 1913 88, 90
Mercer "Monk" 84, 107
Mercer 1910 82–84
Meregalli, Guido 228, 263
Merosi, Giuseppe 228
Merz, Charlie 98, 101, 156
Metropol 1914 176
Meurisse, Louis 65
Michaux, Gratien 126, 183
Michelat, Arthur 139–140, 145,
  147, 197, 199–200, 251
Milbrath, Arthur F. 97, 106, 178
Miller, Harry 152, 184
Miller 122 c.i. 1923 238
Miller 183 c.i. 1921 209–210

Miller 300 c.i. 1916 184
Miller Golden Submarine 185,
  195
Milton, Tommy 120, 194–195,
  201–202, 207, 209
Milwaukee 1912 85, 109
Minoia, Nando 215, 243
Moccand, Charles 121
Moglia, Edmondo 211, 213, 246
Mones-Maury, Pierre 237
Mont Ventoux 65, 125
Monza 1922 221, 263
Monza 1923 221–222, 243
Monza 1924 230
Mooers, Louis 37–39, 42
Morel, André 249, 256
Moriceau, Jules 201, 225, 227,
  258
Moross, Ernie 52, 80, 107, 175
Mulford, Ralph 76–79, 99, 101,
  113–116, 118, 132, 137, 156–157,
  162, 192, 194–195, 201
Murphy, Jimmy 120, 206–207,
  209, 222, 243

National 1911 80
Navarre, Jean 199
Nazzaro, Biagio 219
Nazzaro, Felice 64, 72, 141, 219,
  221, 243
Newhouse, Claude 146
Nikrent, Louis 94–95, 176–177
Northam, Leotia 138

O'Donnell, Eddie 117–118, 146,
  182–183, 191–192, 206
Offenhauser, Fred 152
Oklahoma City 1915 153
Oldfield, Barney 31–40, 50–51,
  54, 86, 90–91, 94–95, 98,
  102, 104, 114, 147, 153–154,
  177, 184, 191–192, 194–195,
  209
Oldfield, Lee 111, 113
Ono 105, 149
Orr, Tom 176–178, 192
Oury, Victor 10
Ouzou, Émile 62
Owen, Percy 46

Packard "Gray Wolf" 40
Packard V-12 172, 195
Paris-Berlin 1901 10–11
Paris-Vienna 1902 10, 17
Paris-Madrid 1903 18, 56
Pastore, Cesare 222, 230
Patschke, Cyrus 77–79
Patterson, Ellmore 128, 161–162
Peerless "Green Dragon" 38
Petit, Émile 248
Peugeot 3-liter 1913 135
Peugeot 3-liter 1920 204
Peugeot 4.5-liter 1914 151
Peugeot 5.6-liter 1913 132–133
Peugeot 7.6-liter 1912 127–129

Peugeot Auto Import 137, 149, 151–152, 160
Pickens, Bill 36, 51, 54
Picker, Charles 121
Picker, Lucien 121
Pilleverdier, Louis 122, 132
Planchon, Charles 251, 253, 255
Poole, Alfred 22–23
Porporato, Jean 155
Porter, Finley Robertson 84, 88, 92, 180, 185
Premier 1916 156–157
Pullen, Eddie 91–95, 109, 149, 167, 176, 182, 191

Ramponi, Giulio 229
Ratés, Juan 64
Rayfield 1914 176
Resta, Dario 149–151, 156–158, 168, 191–195, 225–226
Resta Special 195
Richard, François 25
Rickenbacher, Eddie 94, 113–118, 120, 146, 152, 156, 177–178, 182, 191–192
Rigal, Victor 62, 199
Riganti, Raoul 237
Riker, Andrew Lawrence, 22–23
Rimini, Giorgio 228, 230
Roberts, Mortimer 101, 109, 176
Robertson, George 25, 27, 50, 237
Roch-Brault, René 62
Roebling, Washington 83
Roebling-Planche 83
Rogers, Charles 107
Rol, Marcel 65
Rolland-Pilain 2-liter 1922 254–255
Romeo, Nicola 228
Rooney, Tom 103, 109, 156, 183, 191–192
Rosatelli, Celestino 217
Rougier, Henri 60–62, 65, 199
Ruckstell, Grover 94–95, 104, 117, 177, 182, 191, 194

Salamano, Carlo 222, 225
Salmson 1.1-liter 1926 18d
San Diego 1915 117
Santa Monica 1912 97–98
Santa Monica 1913 102
Santa Monica 1914 91, 104, 114
Sartori, Paul 25
Schieppati, Augusto 263, 265
Schmid, Ernest 255
Schmidt, Albert 258
Schmidt, Charles 40
Schnaitmann, Karl 161, 164
Schroeder, Edward J. 22, 42, 79, 91, 132, 161–162

Schroeder, Eric 155, 192
Sebring-Duesenberg 1915 118
Secuws, Achille 141–142, 255
Segrave, Henry 212, 221, 224–227, 230, 246
Sennett, Mack 114
Shambaugh 1914 176
Shanley, Bernard 19–20, 22
Sheepshead Bay Track 187, 190
Shepard, Elliott Fitch 29
Simplex 1904 41
Sioux City 1914 115, 137, 146
Sivocci, Ugo 218, 228
Sizaire, Maurice 67
Slaby, Rudolf 164
Smith & Mabley 41
SRO 255
Stafford 1914 176
Stead, Edmund T. 60
Sterlich, Diego de 263–265
Stutz, Harry Clayton 97–99, 104, 137, 178, 183, 193
Stutz 1912 98
Stutz 1913 101
Stutz 1914 104
Stutz 300 c.i. 1915 178–179
Sunbeam 2-liter 1922 211–212
Sunbeam 2-liter 1923 224
Sunbeam 2-liter 1924 225
Sunbeam 4.5-liter 1914 140
Sunbeam 4.9-liter 1916 210
Sunbeam-Talbot-Darracq 1921 211
Szisz, Ferenc 64

Tacoma 1912 98–99
Tacoma 1913 102
Tacoma 1914 104
Taine, Émile 67
Talbot 1.5-liter 1926 226
Tangeman, Cornelius 42
Targa Florio 1919 202, 215
Tart, Henry 20–21, 60
Teste, Georges 20–21, 60
Tetzlaff, Teddy 85, 98–99, 175
Théry, Léon 12
Thomas, Edward R. 15, 20–22, 24, 29, 41
Thomas, Harold E. 22
Thomas, Orlando F. 21
Thomas, René 60, 136, 138, 143–147, 197, 199, 200–202, 204, 210–211, 254, 256
Thorn, William K. 15
Tire Pressures 1914 145
Toft, Omar 138, 184
Torchy, Paul 256, 258
Toutée, Henri 252
Tower, Jack 111–112
Tracy, Joe 22–23, 165

Troubetzkoy, Paul 192
Tulsa 1913 102, 106, 108

Vadier, Fernand 202, 210
Vail, Ira 191, 194
Vanderbilt, Alfred G. 20, 25, 39
Vanderbilt, William K., Jr. 14–20, 26, 30
Vanderbilt Cup 20
Vanderbilt Cup 1904 20–21
Vanderbilt Cup 1905 23
Vanderbilt Cup 1906 27
Vanderbilt Cup 1910 73
Vanderbilt Cup 1911 79
Vanderbilt Cup 1912 85
Vanderbilt Cup 1914 91, 114
Vanderbilt Cup 1915 149
Van Ranst, Cornelius 205
Velghe, Alfred "Levegh" 9–10
Venice 1915 177
Villemain, Louis 62
Vincent, Jesse 167, 169, 171
Vizcaya, Fernand de 244
Vizcaya, Pierre de 221, 237, 239, 241, 244, 247–248
Voigt, Émile 8–9
Vulpès 65

Wagner, Fred 52, 89, 187
Wagner, Louis 27, 29, 60–62, 199, 201, 218, 227, 229–230, 244, 255
Walker, Fritz 106, 165–166
Weightman, William 120, 194
Weisweiller, Edmond de 67–68
White "Whistling Billy" 39
Wilcox, Howdy 72, 80–81, 118, 132, 143, 149, 156–157, 160, 178–179, 191, 201, 205
Williams, Grover-Williams 227
Winton, Alexander 8, 35, 37–38
Winton Bullet 37
Wisconsin engine 97, 101, 106–107, 178
Wishart, Spencer 78, 86, 88–90, 93–94, 105, 109, 115–116, 131–132

Zborowski, Louis 213, 230, 237–238, 242
Zborowski, William Elliott 17–18
Zengle, Len 76, 80, 98
Zerbi, Tranquillo 222
Ziegler, William 105, 142, 177
Zuccarelli, Paolo 122–123, 125–132